Dennis Doyle's revised edition of *The C* *II-Inspired Approach* updates and enhances what has long been a understanding Catholicism today. Marked by clear writing, a balanced approach, and attention to real-life questions, this book explores a variety of contemporary issues including authority, ecumenism, justice, ecology, and economics. Anyone seeking an introduction to the Catholic Church will find this book informative, accessible, and a source of rich discussion. Doyle's volume demonstrates, once again, that the best books are often written by the best teachers who have refined their presentation after years in the classroom and pastoral settings. As someone who has long benefitted from using Doyle's work with students, I am excited to make regular use of this new volume.

—Kristin Colberg
Saint John's School of Theology and Seminary

This book encapsulates decades of Dennis Doyle's devoted teaching and perceptive scholarship. *The Catholic Church in a Changing World* brings the Second Vatican Council to life for a new generation of college students, and under Doyle's expert guidance, the council emerges as the ecclesial foundation for Catholics in the twenty-first century. The author weaves the council's constitutions together with helpful summaries and interpretations of magisterial documents from Pope John Paul II and Pope Francis. Doyle's classroom experiences enable him to articulate the questions today's students have about the Catholic Church, and this book does not shy away from highlighting the difficulties and disagreements within the Church on various theological issues. Packed with helpful discussion questions and bibliographies, *The Catholic Church in a Changing World* exemplifies one of the best introductions to Catholicism available to students today.

—Christopher Denny
St. John's University

A superb overview of the Catholic faith, presented with clarity, nuance, depth, and breadth. Highly readable and thoroughly engaging, this book is a must read for anyone who wants to better understand the Catholic tradition!

—Mary Doak
University of San Diego

This new edition of Dennis Doyle's *The Catholic Church in a Changing World*, the fruit of long classroom experience, reflects on every page his deep conviction that to be an informed Catholic today one must not only live the fruits of the council but connect, in some deep way, with the entire witness to the church in space and time. That conviction is set forth with clear writing, wide learning, and a great spirit of Christian generosity.

—Lawrence A. Cunningham
University of Notre Dame

At more than fifty years since Vatican II, ecclesiology is still the key issue to understand Catholicism in the global world of today. I highly recommend Dennis Doyle's book on the ecclesiology of Vatican II—especially for those who want to connect the conciliar teaching, Pope Francis, and the issues facing the Church.

—Massimo Faggioli
Villanova University

Winsomely written, *The Catholic Church in a Changing World* analyzes contemporary Catholic teachings and practices in light of their historical roots. Accessible, accurate, and balanced, the book concentrates on what unites Catholics. Dennis Doyle presents the various positions on contemporary disputed questions clearly and fairly. Never presuming to resolve divisive issues, he shows what is at stake and leaves readers to reflect on their own responses. This book makes an excellent textbook for undergraduate courses in religion and for study groups.

—Terrence W. Tilley
Fordham University

Dennis Doyle's third edition of *The Catholic Church in a Changing World: A Vatican II-Inspired Approach* is a reflective study of Catholicism explained and Catholicism lived! The engaging anecdotal stories that begin each chapter connect the reader with the ever-evolving understanding and experience of Catholicism. Doyle taps into the rich heritage of the Church through the lens of the Second Vatican Council. Two indispensable documents of Vatican II, *Lumen gentium* and *Gaudium et spes*, provide the framework for examining the essential elements of the Tradition and the incredible impact the Council continues to have on the Church. Raised before the Council and then schooled as a theologian in light of Vatican II, Doyle brings a unique perspective to his reading of the Tradition. It is at once apparent that Doyle views his task as not only an academic examination of the Church, but a walk in faith that connects belief with life. This book includes a "live look" at the issues of today and demonstrates how the Spirit continues to move in the life of the Church.

—Sr. Shannon Schrein
General Councilor, Sisters of St. Francis

I welcome Dennis Doyle's update of his excellent text on the nature and mission of the Catholic Church today. He is right, a lot has happened during the pontificates of Benedict and Francis. Hence, the update of the second edition of his book. I have used his books in some of my classes at the University of Southern California, and students consistently find Doyle's explanations clear and engaging.

—Fr. James L. Heft, S.M.
President, Institute for Advanced Catholic Studies at USC

For years I used, with great success, the two earlier editions of this textbook with undergraduates, who appreciate its focus on their own experience and their desire to understand the Catholic faith. Doyle uses the documents of Vatican II in such a creative and intelligent way that, as a teacher, I have always felt confident that the book is the best introduction to the Church in contemporary society. I am grateful for this splendid updated edition, which integrates the papacy of Pope Francis and the continuing tensions within our pilgrim community.

—David Hammond
Saint Joseph's College

The
Catholic Church
in a
Changing World

A VATICAN II-INSPIRED APPROACH

DENNIS M. DOYLE

ANSELM
ACADEMIC

Created by the publishing team of Anselm Academic.

Cover image: © John August Swanson, artist (www.johnaugustswanson.com)

PENTECOST, 2013, is based on a small etching from 1983. The scene is of the Holy Spirit descending upon the people, as mighty winds and tongues of fire, enabling them to speak of all the wonders of God.

In my image of PENTECOST, I see the Spirit of God, re-energizing all people and bringing us together to work for peace, to heal the Earth, and to honor the diversity of our life's journey.

May God bless all of us in this search—
no matter which road we take,
no matter which path we need to follow.
No matter which way the Spirit leads us.
But let us journey it together.
"You must be born from above. The wind blows wherever it pleases; you hear its sound,
but you cannot tell where it comes from or where it is going.
That is how it is with all born of the Spirit.
Amen"

—*Fr. Aelred Niespolo, OSB,*
St Andrew's Abbey

Dedication

For my grandchildren, Maggie Jane, Annie, and Liam

Author Acknowledgments

I wish to thank first my wife, Pat, who read and critiqued much of the manuscript. Her willingness to work with me on my projects over the years has contributed in no small way to whatever reputation I have as a writer. I thank also the Bavarian government, which provided me with funding to study and teach at the University of Regensburg for the summer of 2017, and especially Thomas Schärtl, who secured my grant and shepherded my stay. Thanks to Hans Hafner of the University of Potsdam for providing me office space near the end of my time in Germany. Thanks to Dan Thompson and also to more people than I can name at the University of Dayton for continually supporting and encouraging me in my research and writing. My gratitude goes also to my graduate assistants, Michael Romero and Scott Howland, for all of their help. I am grateful to the editorial staff at Anselm Academic for their interest in and support for this book. Finally, I sincerely thank my students at the University of Dayton, who continue to inspire me after several decades of teaching.

Publisher Acknowledgments

Thank you to the following individuals who reviewed this work in progress:

Brian Flanagan, *Marymount University, Arlington, Virginia*
Paul Lakeland, *Fairfield University, Fairfield, Connecticut*

Contents

PART 3

GAUDIUM ET SPES:

THE CHURCH ENGAGING THE WORLD / 255

SECTION 10 / Church and World

SECTION 11 / Principles, Family, Culture

SECTION 12 / Economics, Politics, Peace, Ecology

Church Documents

Listed below are Catholic Church documents with Latin titles cited in this book. The Latin title is listed first, followed by the English translation in parentheses. In the book, such document titles will also appear in Latin followed by the English translation in parentheses at first mention in a chapter; any subsequent mention of the same title within that chapter will be the Latin title only.

An exception is made to this style for the documents *Lumen gentium* (*Dogmatic Constitution on the Church*) and *Gaudium et spes* (*Pastoral Constitution on the Church in the Modern World*). As these two documents receive multiple mentions throughout the book, the Latin with English convention will be observed at first mention in each three-chapter section, with any subsequent mentions in that section using the Latin version only.

All titles are listed here for ease of cross-referencing, as the Latin will be unfamiliar to most readers.

Ad gentes (*Decree on the Missionary Activity of the Church*), Second Vatican Council, 1965

Amoris laetitia (*On Love in the Family*), Pope Francis, 2016

Apostolicam actuositatem (*Decree on the Apostolate of the Laity*), Second Vatican Council, 1965

Centesimus annus (*On the Hundredth Anniversary [of Rerum novarum]*), Pope St. John Paul II, 1991

Christifideles laici (*The Vocation and the Mission of the Lay Faithful in the Church and in the World*), Pope St. John Paul II, 1988

Christus dominus (*Decree on the Pastoral Office of Bishops in the Church*), Second Vatican Council, 1965

Dei verbum (*Dogmatic Constitution on Divine Revelation*), Second Vatican Council, 1965

Dignitatis humanae (*Declaration on Religious Freedom*), Second Vatican Council, 1965

Donum veritatis (*Instruction on the Ecclesial Vocation of the Theologian*), Sacred Congregation for the Doctrine of the Faith, 1990

Ecclesia in Africa (*On the Church in Africa and its Evangelizing Mission Towards the Year 2000*), Pope St. John Paul II, 1995

Evangelii gaudium (*The Joy of the Gospel*), Pope Francis, 2013

Familiaris consortio (*On the Role of the Christian Family in the Modern World*), Pope St. John Paul II, 1981

Gaudet Mater Ecclesia (*Opening Speech to the Council*), Pope St. John XXIII, 1962

Gaudium et spes (*Pastoral Constitution on the Church in the Modern World*), Second Vatican Council, 1965

Gravissimun educationis (*Declaration on Christian Education*), Second Vatican Council, 1965

Inter insigniores (*Declaration on the Question of Admission of Women to the Ministerial Priesthood*), Sacred Congregation for the Doctrine of the Faith, 1976

Inter mirifica (*Decree on the Mass Media*), Second Vatican Council, 1963

Laborem exercens (*On Human Work*), Pope St. John Paul II, 1981

Laudato si': On Care for Our Common Home, Pope Francis, 2015

Libertatis conscientia (*Instruction on Christian Freedom and Liberation*), Sacred Congregation for the Doctrine of the Faith, 1986

Libertatis nuntius (*Instruction on Certain Aspects of the "Theology of Liberation"*), Sacred Congregation for the Doctrine of the Faith, 1984

Lumen gentium (*Dogmatic Constitution on the Church*), Second Vatican Council, 1964

Mulieris dignitatem (*On the Dignity and Vocation of Women*), Pope St. John Paul II, 1988

Mystici corporis Christi (*On the Mystical Body of Christ*), Pope Pius XII, 1943

Nostra aetate (*Declaration on the Relation of the Church to Non-Christian Religions*), Second Vatican Council, 1965

Octogesima adveniens (*A Call to Action*), Pope Paul VI, 1971

Optatam totius (*Decree on Priestly Training*), Second Vatican Council, 1965

Ordinatio sacerdotalis (*Priestly Ordination*), Pope St. John Paul II, 1994

Orientalium ecclesiarium (*Decress on the Catholic Eastern Churches*), Second Vatican Council, 1964

Pastores dabo vobis (*I Will Give You Shepherds*), Pope St. John Paul II, 1992

Perfectae caritatis (*Decree on the Adaptation and Renewal of Religious Life*), Second Vatican Council, 1965

Populorum progressio (*On the Development of Peoples*), Pope Paul VI, 1967

Presbyterorum ordinis (*Decree on the Ministry and Life of Priests*), Second Vatican Council, 1965

Rerum novarum (*On the Condition of Labor*), Pope Leo XIII, 1891

Sacrosanctum concilium (*Constitution on the Sacred Liturgy*), Second Vatican Council, 1963

Sollicitudo rei socialis (*On Social Concerns*), Pope St. John Paul II, 1987

Unitatis redintegratio (*Decree on Ecumenism*), Second Vatican Council, 1964

Ut unum sint (*That They May Be One*), Pope St. John Paul II, 1995

Preface

This is the third edition of a book first published in 1992, then titled *The Church Emerging from Vatican II: A Popular Approach to Contemporary Catholicism*. Many important developments have happened since then, including the papacies of Benedict XVI and Francis. The purpose of this new edition is to update the content for a new generation of readers. The new title, *The Catholic Church in a Changing World: A Vatican II–Inspired Approach*, acknowledges both the further distance in time and the continuing relevance of the Second Vatican Council.

This book can be used as an introduction to Catholicism. Since it focuses on the topic of church from a Catholic perspective, it can also be used as a text in ecclesiology, understood in a broad sense. I recommend that it be used in conjunction with two Vatican II documents, *Lumen gentium* (*Dogmatic Constitution on the Church*) and *Gaudium et spes* (*Pastoral Constitution on the Church in the Modern World*).[1] The organization of these documents provides the basic framework for this book.

The church is an interpersonal reality, as are faith and religion more generally. For this reason, I intend this book to be also about you and about me, about our fears and hopes, our sorrows and our joys, our needs and our satisfactions. The church, faith, and religion exist within the context of our life stories, and these cannot be adequately understood apart from them. For this reason, I include throughout references to my own life and to the lives of others. When I use this material in a classroom, I begin by having my students write an auto-biographical statement about their own faith and value development and where the church (or something analogous) does or does not fit for them.

I have found that many of my non-Catholic students feel by the end of the course that they have learned not only about Catholicism but also about their own denomination, religion, or worldview. I try to facilitate this in several ways. First, I stress the ecumenical nature of contemporary Catholicism and the open attitude toward other Christian traditions, religions, and worldviews. Today one cannot be a faithful Catholic without being ecumenically minded. Second, I spend significant time near the beginning of the course covering ecumenism. We discuss various ecumenical issues in the New Testament, the Reformation, and

---

1. All quotations in this text from *Lumen gentium* and *Gaudium et spes* are taken from *http://www.vatican.va/archive/hist_councils/ii_vatican_council/index.htm*.

current interfaith dialogues. Throughout the course, I treat the divisions among Christians as stemming from complex causes with many rights and wrongs on both sides. Third, I encourage non-Catholic students to do their term projects on topics related to their own denomination, religion, or worldview. Fourth, I try to encourage ecumenical sensitivity in the classroom. I know from early on the religious or nonreligious background of each student, and I respectfully make this part of the ongoing conversation. There may be some teachers who feel that a student's personal background is irrelevant in an academic course. I am not one of them.

"Church" as Understood in this Book

As used in this text, "Catholic Church" is intended to include those churches led by Catholic bishops who are in communion with the pope in Rome. It is customary in the ecumenical movement to specify "Roman Catholic Church," but those in Eastern Catholic Churches with distinct liturgical rites feel excluded by such terminology. In public documents and formal agreements, the church as led by the pope is called the "Catholic Church."

The word *church* has many legitimate meanings that can be viewed from different theological and historical standpoints. Resulting ambiguities can make editorial decisions about capitalization difficult, no less so in this book. The basic option in this text is to use a lowercase "church" whenever the term stands alone and to use "Catholic Church" in those instances when the worldwide Catholic Church is intended. In addition, because repeated use of "Catholic Church" can become cumbersome, a lowercase shorthand "church" may also sometimes refer to the Catholic Church, if the context makes the intention sufficiently clear.

Still, complications arise. Did Jesus found the "Church" or the "church"? The Second Vatican Council (1962–1965) taught that various Christian churches and communities share in a partial (though not yet full) communion with the Catholic Church. Virtually all Christians today in some way claim their origins lie in Jesus and the apostles. Catholics retain the theological position, however, that the primacy of Peter and the leadership of the bishops as successors of the apostles reflect the witness of Scripture and Tradition, and that the Catholic Church is not to be regarded as simply one "denomination" among others. For ecumenical purposes, "church" will be the default when ambiguities arise, though without intending to deny such complexities.

For all of my ecumenical openness, my belonging to the Catholic Church leaves more than a slight trace throughout this book. It is only fair to tell you that I write from a Catholic perspective. That said, I believe that my commitment makes me neither uncritical nor disinterested in the pure search for truth.

It is my hope that whoever reads this book may find it useful in their own faith- and life-journey.

$$1$$

INTRODUCTION

The Catholic Church Today

I t was a mild but breezy September afternoon when Pope Francis emerged from his plane in Washington, DC, to begin a weeklong tour of the United States. This 2015 visit, the first time ever in the United States for this pope, who hails from Argentina, took place fifty years after the Second Vatican Council[1] had ushered in a new era in the history of the Catholic Church.

Pope Francis received a warm welcome throughout his journey not only from Catholics but also from many people from various faiths and backgrounds. This wide-ranging acceptance may have something to do with the unconditional acceptance that he has extended to others. Inclusion has been a major

Pope Francis, reaching out to the crowds, sets an example for a more inclusive, welcoming attitude in the Catholic Church. Is such a change possible without changing fundamental beliefs and practices?

---

1. The Second Vatican Council (often called "Vatican II") took place between 1962 and 1965. It was the twenty-first ecumenical council in the two-thousand-year history of the Catholic Church. Over two thousand bishops as well as many theologians and observers met to address major challenges facing the church in the twentieth century. This council will be the main topic of the next chapter.

theme throughout Francis's papacy. For example, in an early papal interview, when asked about gay priests, Francis responded, "Who am I to judge?" Another time, when washing feet during a Holy Thursday ceremony that traditionally had included only men, Francis washed the feet of two young women, one of whom was a Muslim. About two years later, he issued a papal order that Holy Thursday foot washings should include men and women, old and young, in accordance with the meaning of the ritual. During his tour of cities in the eastern United States, Francis continued his practice of reaching out to people in the crowds, especially the afflicted, the disabled, and the young.

There are many such examples of Francis speaking and acting inclusively. He appears to be signaling at least a change in tone and atmosphere in Catholic attitude, if not changes in basic Catholic teaching. Most Catholics have welcomed his words and deeds as a breath of fresh air. Some traditional and conservative Catholics, however, view him suspiciously. Will this pope be able to change attitudes and outlooks without eventually changing basic Catholic Church teachings?

Overview

This chapter introduces the Catholic Church of today by considering the views and actions of Pope Francis against the background of the Second Vatican Council. This entire book takes its outline and structure from two of the council's documents, *Lumen gentium* (*Dogmatic Constitution on the Church*) and *Gaudium et spes* (*Pastoral Constitution on the Church in the Modern World*).

Inclusion Rooted in the Second Vatican Council

Pope Francis's emphasis on inclusion embodies and extends one of the key themes of Vatican II. The word *inclusion* has many distinct but overlapping meanings. To avoid confusion, it is helpful to consider some of those meanings:

- Getting people already within a group more involved and valued, such as by emphasizing equality in spiritual dignity among all the members of a parish and increasing participation in carrying out the Catholic Church's mission

- Reaching out to those on the margins of one's group, such as by being more accepting toward those who have been divorced and remarried, are single parents, or are gay, lesbian, or transgender

- Consulting and taking seriously a wide range of voices and opinions when making important judgments and decisions

- Developing positive connections with other groups, such as by recognizing and cooperating with members of various Christian traditions and other religions, and also other worldviews

- Reaching out to the socially marginalized, such as by attending to the needs of ethnic and racial minorities, the sick and the elderly, the disabled and the mentally ill
- Respecting the "Other" (those markedly different from YOU), not simply as they can be assimilated into one's viewpoint, but precisely as "Other," with their own culture, faith, history, distinctive characteristics, and viewpoints

A notably inclusive teaching of Vatican II, the universal call to holiness, is expressed in chapter 5 of *Lumen gentium*. When I was growing up in Philadelphia in the 1950s, there was a tendency among Catholics to interpret a young person's inclination toward holiness as a sign that that person was most probably called either to priesthood (if a male) or to religious life as a sister or a brother. The very word *church*[2] at that time was most often used to refer collectively to the ordained and religious as distinct from laypeople.

Lumen gentium declared that the call to holiness includes all members of the church (*LG* 40). In its most basic sense, "the church" includes the entire People of God prior to any distinction among clergy, religious, and laypeople (*LG* 9–17). Distinctions among these states in life were still retained, and the ordained and the religious remain important in the Catholic Church of today. In *Lumen gentium*, however, these distinctions were contextualized within a larger framework acknowledging that there is no distinction when it comes to being called to holiness. All Catholics are fully included in that call.

Moreover, the efforts at inclusion in *Lumen gentium* did not stop with the Catholic Church's own members. Chapter 2 of the document begins with a paraphrase of something Peter says in Acts 10:35: "At all times and in every race God has given welcome to whosoever fears Him and does what is right" (*LG* 9). In what at the time was a striking move, the chapter goes on to recognize in a positive way the relationships between the Catholic Church and various other Christian traditions. Moreover, the chapter then expresses an open, welcoming manner toward people of various faiths. Although the chapter clearly retains the Catholic belief that the Catholic Church represents in the fullest way the church as planned, founded, and sustained by God, the move toward a radically more inclusive approach to others, especially when compared with earlier official statements, is unmistakable. *Lumen gentium*'s inclusiveness helped set the stage for the argument in *Gaudium et spes* that "since Christ died for all men, and since the ultimate vocation of man is in fact one, and divine, we ought to believe that the Holy Spirit in a manner known only to God offers to every man the possibility of being associated with this paschal mystery" (*GS* 22).

---

2. For a relatively full discussion of when and how the terms *church* and *Catholic Church* are used in this book, please see the preface.

Balance Achieved through *Aggiornamento* and *Ressourcement*

Recognizing that inclusion was an important and central theme of Vatican II should not be done one-sidedly, disregarding how the council's teachings represented a delicate balance between the old and the new. *Aggiornamento*, or "updating," is the Italian word used by Pope St. John XXIII in naming the goal of opening up the windows of the Catholic Church, letting in fresh air, and engaging in dialogue with the modern world.

John XXIII, however, had no intention of throwing away anything truly basic to Catholic tradition in exchange for more modern ideas. As he stated in his opening address to the council, "The substance of the ancient doctrine of the deposit of faith is one thing, and the formulation in which it is clothed is another."[3] John XXIII's goal was to preserve the basic teachings of the faith without simply repeating formulas from famous popes and theologians of the past. He wanted instead for the bishops and their theological experts to express the meaning of the gospel and the teaching of the Catholic Church in a way that would engage the people of that time. A term often used to describe the way to accomplish *aggiornamento* is *ressourcement*, a French term meaning "return to the sources." In other words, the way to bring the church "up to date" is by drawing, in a fresh way, upon its richest traditions. It is important neither to exaggerate nor underappreciate the type and degree of changes brought about by Vatican II. Many voices contributed to the documents, often with strong disagreements underlying compromises in wording. At the council's end, the consensus was that through and, at times, in spite of the sometimes all-too-human contributions, the teaching of the council was ultimately the work of the Holy Spirit.

Pope Francis has an interesting connection with Vatican II. His five immediate predecessors attended the council.[4] All of them were involved in the excitement of this Spirit-filled event as well as in the political wrangling that often took place behind the scenes. Francis, in his priestly education and formation, has been deeply formed by the teaching of the council without having been present for the struggles and maneuvering. He has come to the office of the papacy with fresh eyes and renewed hope. Each pope brings with him not only his own style but his own priorities. Like his predecessors, and like Vatican II itself, Francis maintains a strong concern for handing on the Catholic Tradition while engaging the issues of his time—for the issues that people face today are also issues that Catholics face.

---

3. *Gaudet Mater Ecclesia*, "Pope John's Opening Speech to the Council," trans. Joseph A. Komonchak, *https://jakomonchak.files.wordpress.com.*

4. John XXIII was the pope who called for the council. Paul VI became pope during the time of the council. John Paul I and John Paul II were bishops at the council. Pope Benedict XVI attended the council as a theological expert.

The Challenges and Opportunities of Today

The world of today is different from the world of the early 1960s when Vatican II took place. The continuing process of globalization has brought with it many difficulties and many opportunities. Communications technology has shrunk the world, making it more and more apparent that ultimately one human community underlies the great variety of human groupings. There is also a developing sense of pluralism within and beyond nations.

As more and more people interact across the globe, however, there is a growing awareness that when it comes to wealth, education, and social opportunity, people are not equal at all. Although evidence shows that many people each year are being lifted out of abject poverty, other evidence indicates that both within countries and between nations the gap between the rich and the poor continues to widen. In addition, global awareness and concern is growing about the seriousness of the ecological crisis of climate change and its notable impact on the poor, as Pope Francis indicates in his 2015 encyclical, *Laudato si': On Care for Our Common Home* (*LS* 13, 20, 25).[5] For example, climate change caused, at least in part, by overconsumption in relatively affluent countries contributes to the loss of farmland and famine in Africa (*LS* 51).[6] There is also much global unrest, and terrorist threats and attacks have brought to contemporary life an everyday angst that is truly terrifying.

For more than a century, the percentage of Catholics in the US population had remained stable (between 24 and 26 percent). In recent decades, the large number of Catholic immigrants from Latin America had helped to maintain this percentage. Current studies, however, suggest that the percentage of Catholics in the United States has begun to drop significantly, to about 20.8 percent, whereas the percentage of nonreligious persons (nones) has increased rapidly—from about 16 to 23 percent in seven years.[7] Most of those who now claim to be nonreligious are former Catholics.

The causes of this drop in the percentage of Catholics are many and varied. Catholicism in the United States has long been linked with immigrants, ethnic neighborhoods, and close-knit urban communities. High levels of education, affluence, and mobility among Catholics may have contributed to a breakdown

---

5. Quotes from *Laudato si'* are from *http://w2.vatican.va/content/francesco/en/encyclicals/documents/papa-francesco_20150524_enciclica-laudato-si.html*.

6. Jeffrey Gettleman, "Loss of Fertile Land Fuels 'Looming Crisis' across Africa," *New York Times*, July 30, 2017, *https://www.nytimes.com/2017/07/29/world/africa/africa-climate-change-kenya-land-disputes.html*.

7. "America's Changing Religious Landscape," Pew Research Center, Washington, DC, May 12, 2015, *http://www.pewforum.org/2015/05/12/americas-changing-religious-landscape*; also "US Public Becoming Less Religious," Pew Research Center, Washington, DC, November 3, 2015, *http://www.pewforum.org/2015/11/03/u-s-public-becoming-less-religious*.

of older patterns and values.[8] Secularization, the process in which religions lose their influence in a society, is also a likely factor in the drop in numbers.

As the percentage of Catholics in Europe and in the United States has declined, the overall number of Catholics in Latin America and Africa has grown, causing some commentators to say that the center of gravity of the Catholic Church has shifted to the Southern Hemisphere.[9] It seems no accident that the Catholic Church now has its first Latin American pope. Evangelical Protestants and Pentecostals have also experienced dramatic rates of growth throughout the global South.

I get the impression from students in my classes that many young Christians today are interested in whatever will unite people rather than divide them. My students tend to be suspicious of religion as an agent of division within a pluralistic world. What may look like "relativism" (a lack of concern for truth) to their elders often reflects the high value that young Christians place upon respecting the Other as "Other." What many young people seem to be saying is not so much that all viewpoints are equal but rather that all people should be equal and that their viewpoints must be respected.

When Pope Francis responded to the aforementioned question about gay priests by saying, "Who am I to judge?" some Catholics worried. For many more Catholics, however, the humble and open-minded tone of his response seemed a breath of fresh air, and especially for those who place a priority on the Vatican II theme of inclusion as extended and applied to a pressing concern for the world today.[10]

Summary

This chapter has shown the shared commitment of Vatican II and Pope Francis to values of inclusion and balance. The next chapter explores some of the challenges faced by the Catholic Church that led to the calling of the council.

---

8. Among the many possible causes for the drop in numbers is a sex abuse scandal that rocked the United States, with its high point coming in 2002. Not only had priests abused children, but, in a number of cases, bishops were proven to have covered up the problem by transferring abusive priests from parish to parish and keeping silent about the problem. A new wave of media attention was directed towards such scandals after the release of a Pennsylvania Grand Jury Report covering the past seventy years was released on August 14, 2018.

9. Philip Jenkins, *The Next Christendom: The Coming of Global Christianity* (New York: Oxford University Press, 2007).

10. Radically different assessments of Pope Francis's approach to controversial issues can be found in two books with an interesting overlap in their titles. For a traditional view, see Ross Douthat, *To Change the Church: Pope Francis and the Future of Catholicism* (New York: Simon and Schuster, 2018); for progressive views, see Gerard Mannion, ed., *Pope Francis and the Future of Catholicism:* Evangelii Gaudium *and the Papal Agenda* (New York: Cambridge University Press, 2017). Pope Francis gives an explanation of his "who am I to judge?" comment in his book, *The Name of God Is Mercy: A Conversation with Andrea Tornielli*, trans. Oonagh Stransky (New York: Random House, 2016), 61–62.

For Further Reflection

1. Where do you stand, in terms of your life experience, in regard to matters of faith, religion, Christianity, and Catholicism? How do you think that your social location (family, community, friends, etc.) might affect how you relate to this book?
2. What is your response to Pope Francis's reference to gay priests when he said, "Who am I to judge?"
3. What do you think are the major causes of the recent drop in the number of Catholics in the United States?
4. Do you think that a strong acceptance of various viewpoints represents an indiscriminate, anything-goes "relativism" or an important respect for the Other as "Other"?
5. What might Catholics and other Christians hope to gain from a study of the Catholic Church? What might people of other faiths and worldviews hope to gain?

Suggested Readings

Gehring, John. *The Francis Effect: A Radical Pope's Challenge to the American Catholic Church*. Lanham, MD: Rowman and Littlefield, 2015.

Going, Going, Gone: The Dynamics of Disaffiliation in Young Catholics. A study by St. Mary's Press of Minnesota, Inc., in collaboration with the Center for Applied Research in the Apostate (CARA). Winona, MN: Saint Mary's Press, 2017.

Jenkins, Philip. *The Next Christendom: The Coming of Global Christianity*. New York: Oxford University Press, 2007.

2

CHAPTER

Challenges for the Church

Imagine you are a powerful ruler living in a large castle, isolated from the modern world. One day, at your doorstep, there appears a note telling you that your worldview is inadequate. The next day, another note appears, this one saying that you are thoroughly corrupt. The following day you find yet another message, this one telling you you are no longer important. In succeeding days, you find notes saying that you don't know anything, that you are a ruthless dictator deaf to reason, and that you are a degenerate ruler who sides with the establishment against the poor. Under these circumstances, you might become suspicious of the outside world and somewhat defensive about its accusations.

The ruler in this story can represent the Catholic Church. The notes represent the many challenges posed to the church through various developments in Western civilization. The ruler's suspicion and defensiveness represent the posture of the church in the period immediately preceding Vatican II.

How did the Catholic Church come to be somewhat like this ruler? The following paragraphs are broad and general in scope, yet are intended to represent how a church that often thinks more in terms of centuries than days could see the threats piling up on its doorstep one by one.

Christianity began as an underground, sometimes persecuted religion. For much of the first three centuries after the birth of Jesus, it was illegal not to worship the Roman gods. Then in 313 CE, Constantine issued the Edict of Milan, which declared freedom of religion. By 380 CE, Christianity had become the official religion of the Roman Empire.

In the years following Constantine's edict, the Catholic Church adopted many of the structures and trappings of the Roman Empire and the feudal society of the Middle Ages. By the thirteenth century, not only was most of the Western world Christian, but the Catholic Church was by far the single most important influence on Western civilization. Western culture had itself become Christian and offered a completely integrated view of the cosmos, nature, faith, and everyday life. Although theological debates raged hot and heavy throughout the Middle Ages, they took place within a Christian worldview with rock-certain premises: that the world had been saved through the Incarnation of Christ; that Christ founded the church; that the church and the sacraments provided people with access to the saving grace of Christ. The unquestionable nature of this worldview was rarely challenged.

As the Middle Ages came to a close, however, this medieval synthesis of the Catholic Church faced many challenges and began to unravel. In the fourteenth century, the bubonic plague, or the Black Death, devastated much of the world, wiping out about one-third of the European population and raising many questions about God, suffering, and the purpose of life. In the fifteenth century, widespread corruption in the Catholic Church gave rise to serious calls for reform. In the sixteenth century, some of these reform movements took institutional form as Protestant denominations. Their growth was aided by a simultaneous rise of nationalism, the formation of new economic arrangements, and the growth of literacy and education brought about by the printing press. These developments also paralleled the emergence of a "secular," or nonreligious, world that had no direct need for a Catholic Church. This constituted quite a change from the medieval world that depended wholly on the church and in which a secular world simply did not exist.

In more recent centuries, the development of the natural and social sciences has posed additional challenges to the Catholic Church. In the seventeenth century, astronomers such as Galileo challenged the cosmic view of a world as depicted in the book of Genesis and taught by the church. The eighteenth century brought an even deeper emphasis on human reason, fostering new experiments in revolutionary politics that sought to put democratic authority in the hands of common people liberated from traditional tyrannies—think American and French revolutions. In the nineteenth century, a new industrial society emerged, bringing with it new forms of human exploitation. During each of these periods, many social analysts and reformers interpreted the Catholic Church's role in negative terms, seeing it as a traditional reinforcer of the structures of oppression.

Somewhat like the ruler in this chapter's opening story, the Catholic Church saw the accusations piling up on what seemed to be a daily basis. By the period immediately preceding Vatican II, the church had developed what some have called a "fortress mentality," defensively isolated from developments in the modern world.

Overview

The purpose of this chapter is to explore, within a historical context, some of the many challenges the Catholic Church had to address at Vatican II. After placing Vatican II in the context of the history of earlier councils, we will discuss the challenges posed to the church by the modern world and explore, briefly, some of the ways Vatican II responded to these challenges; such responses will be investigated in more detail in later chapters.

Twenty-One Councils Accepted by Catholics

Vatican II is one of twenty-one ecumenical councils affirmed by Catholics as authentic. Of these councils, only the first seven are affirmed by Eastern Orthodox Christians, who have since added councils of their own.[1] Protestant denominations differ in how many councils they accept.

The first seven ecumenical councils passed judgments on Scriptures, creeds, and calendars but were mainly occupied with clarifying what it is that Christians believe about Jesus. The Council of Nicaea in 325 CE condemned the Arian heresy that Jesus, though greater than human beings, is somewhat less than God. The council declared that Jesus is "one in being with the Father." The Council of Chalcedon in 451 argued against those who would reduce Jesus either to only a human being or to only God. It declared that Jesus is one person with two natures, fully human and fully divine.

The next eight councils affirmed as ecumenical by Catholics (councils eight to fifteen) often concerned relations between the Eastern Orthodox and the Roman Catholic churches. Constantinople IV (869–70), for example, deposed a patriarch of Constantinople and played a role in the coming schism between Greek and Roman churches. Lyons II (1274) established a short-lived reunion between the two churches.

One council during that time period, Lateran III (1179), condemned the pre-Reformation movements known as the Waldensians, which focused on radical poverty and lay preaching, and the Albigensians, which disparaged the material world and called for church reform. The condemnation of various attempts at church reform became a major thrust of councils sixteen through nineteen. The Council of Constance (1414–18), most famous for settling a controversy about who of three claimants was to be pope, issued decrees against the early reformers John Hus and John Wyclif, both of whom favored Scripture versus church authority. Lateran V (1512–17) tried to correct scandalous behavior by church officials in the face of many calls for reform, but lacked the decisive action to stem the tide of the coming Reformation. The Council of Trent (1545–63) condemned the positions of the Protestant Reformers while taking strict measures to improve the quality of pastoral care in the Catholic Church. In its sharp reaction against anything Protestant, this council brought about an emphasis on rules and regulations that would remain with the church until the 1960s and the Second Vatican Council.

The First Vatican Council (Vatican I) (1869–70) had a document on the church on its agenda, but the document was not passed before the council ended prematurely because of the Franco-Prussian War. The council did manage, however, to pass two very important documents: a document on faith and reason that

---

1. Yves Congar, *Diversity and Communion* (Mystic, CT: Twenty-Third Publications, 1985 [1982]), 92–93.

expressed how, for Catholics, faith and reason are ultimately compatible, and a document (originally a segment of the document on the church) defining the primacy and infallibility of the pope.

The Second Vatican Council (Vatican II) took place between 1962 and 1965. The council did not meet continuously, but rather, convened for about two months in each of the four years. Vatican II was the twenty-first council. Except for the unfinished Vatican I, an ecumenical council had not met for four hundred years.

Modern Challenges

The Catholic Church faced many challenges in the period immediately preceding Vatican II. It is possible to think of the entire four hundred years between the Council of Trent and Vatican II as characterized by an overemphasis on rules and regulations stemming from Trent. To move beyond these excesses, the Catholic Church needed to reverse its extreme anti-Protestantism and balance its top-heavy hierarchical authority structure. It needed to redress its mutual grievances with the Eastern Orthodox churches and come to terms with its relations with the Jews and with other world religions in the emerging global community.

Challenges at least as serious, however, came from outside the religious realm. The Catholic Church had established an ambivalent relationship with science: on the one hand, it had acknowledged, in theory, the basic validity of human reason; on the other hand, it had hesitated over, and even rejected, some scientific breakthroughs in the name of defending the faith. By the 1960s, what many perceived as a war between science and religion seemed to have been won handily by science. Technological developments had brought disease cures, space exploration, mass transportation, skyscrapers, and increased food production. It was an age of unparalleled optimism in human progress in which the authority of the Catholic Church was beginning to lack credibility for many.

The most intense challenges were posed by respected voices that were quite vocally atheist. Karl Marx, the nineteenth-century philosopher who had predicted and encouraged worldwide communist revolution, interpreted religion as false promises about an afterlife that hold people back from doing something about their oppressive situations here and now.[2] Sigmund Freud, the founder of psychoanalysis, believed that notions of God and religion should be abandoned by the mature individual and culture. Science, Freud declared, is the only way one can know things.[3] The French existentialist philosopher Albert Camus

2. A collection of Marx's writings on religion can be found in K. Marx and F. Engels, *On Religion* (Moscow: Foreign Languages Publishing House, 1955).

3. Freud's most concise critique of religion can be found in *The Future of an Illusion* (Garden City, NY: Doubleday, 1957 [1927]).

argued that religion is powerless to address the basic questions that face human-kind.[4] The sufferings and evil that people endure seem to reveal not an all-good and all-powerful loving God but rather an absurd universe in which the human heart cries out for meaning but finds no response.

Even for those not attracted to the various forms of atheism, these critiques of religion struck a chord, because they articulated the doubts and questions of ordinary people. Many in the modern world had become agnostic, secularist, and humanistic. To be agnostic is to take the position that one does not know if there is a God or not; to be secularist is to live in a world in which the church is experienced as irrelevant; to be humanistic is to hold a fundamental belief in the goodness of human endeavors without necessarily connecting them to supernatural purposes. It appeared to some that the Catholic Church was trying to stand its ground on a down escalator while the rest of the world was moving onward and upward.

Vatican II as a Pastoral Council

Like the first twenty ecumenical councils, Vatican II needed to address many challenges both internal and external. Unlike the previous councils, however, Vatican II was not intended to condemn heretics through dogmatic pronouncements. Rather, it was to proceed in a more positive vein by formulating a new self-definition and engaging the modern world in dialogue.

For this reason, Pope John XXIII said that the main purpose of Vatican II was *aggiornamento*, that is, bringing the Catholic Church up to date. He called for the council to be "pastoral" in that it would define no new dogmas but rather explore how Catholic teaching might be communicated more fully and put to use more effectively. In other words, this council was called so that the Catholic Church might renew itself to carry out more effectively its mission in the world.

It would be misleading, however, to ignore the challenge-response dimension of the council altogether. Although Freud and Marx and Camus are not mentioned in the documents by name, there are clear attempts to address the issues they and other critics had raised. Moreover, Vatican II established a direction and momentum through which the Catholic Church has continued to explore such issues.

Vatican II did not simply refute such challenges and then dismiss them, however. Although it did ultimately reject the atheism of Freud, Marx, and Camus, it allowed their critiques to have a positive impact on the Catholic

---

4. A good introduction to Albert Camus's philosophical writings on religion is "The Myth of Sisyphus," in *The Myth of Sisyphus and Other Essays*, trans. Justin O'Brien (New York: Random House, 1955 [1942]). A novel that captures some of his even more mature thought is *The Plague*, trans. Stuart Gilbert (New York: Alfred A. Knopf, 1948).

Church's self-understanding. That is, in Vatican II there is much evidence that the church did not simply defend itself but grew from the challenges.

This point is important because the critiques of Freud, Marx, Camus, and others represent not just historical arguments but the doubts and concerns that any person, believer or unbeliever, might face in society today. Many people wonder, at some point in their lives, if religion might not be a psychological crutch, a controlling tool of social leaders, or a set of too-easy answers to difficult questions.

By respectfully addressing these matters, the Catholic Church emerged from Vatican II with more explicit concern for individual dignity and maturity of faith, for human progress and transformation of social structures, for the unfathomable mystery of life, and a sense of the need for the church to engage in self-criticism. The Catholic Church thereby became better equipped to deal with the critics of religion, to take seriously their legitimate concerns, and to grow from the encounter.

Summary

This chapter addressed how the Catholic Church developed its "fortress mentality" prior to Vatican II. It examined Vatican II against the background of previous ecumenical councils and the challenges of modern times. Finally, it discussed Vatican II as a pastoral council that needed to address various challenges in its attempt to bring the church up to date. The next chapter introduces the sixteen documents of Vatican II, with particular attention to *Lumen gentium* and *Gaudium et spes*, the two documents that provide the organizational plan for the remaining chapters of this book.

For Further Reflection

1. What images and ideas, if any, do you most associate with the Catholic Church of the nineteenth and early twentieth centuries? Do they tend to be more positive or more negative?

2. Which of the modern challenges posed to the Catholic Church do you find to be the most serious?

3. Which of the modern challenges posed to the Catholic Church most represent your own questions, doubts, and concerns?

4. Would some people be better off if they did not know about the modern challenges posed to the Catholic Church?

5. How is it that the Catholic Church can benefit by taking seriously the criticisms posed by atheists?

Suggested Readings

Camus, Albert. *The Myth of Sisyphus.* Translated by Justin O'Brien. New York: Vintage Books, 1991 (1942).

De Lubac, Henri. *The Drama of Atheistic Humanism.* Translated by Mark Sebanc. San Francisco: Ignatius, 1995 (1944).

Freud, Sigmund. *The Future of an Illusion.* Translated by James Strachey. New York: Norton, 1989 (1927).

Küng, Hans. *Does God Exist? An Answer for Today.* Translated by Edward Quinn. Garden City, NY: Doubleday, 1980 (1978).

Marx, Karl, and Friedrich Engels. *On Religion.* Mineola, NY: Dover, 2008.

Tanner, Norman P., SJ, ed. *Decrees of the Ecumenical Councils.* 2 vols. London: Sheed and Ward; Washington, DC: Georgetown University Press, 1990.

3

CHAPTER

The Documents of Vatican II

n 1995, I participated on an academic panel along with a former professor of mine. Many of my comments referenced the Second Vatican Council. Afterward, my former teacher asked, "Why are you still talking about Vatican II? That was thirty years ago." Although I am not sure what I said, I do remember that I respectfully refrained from saying that in the previous year, 1994, Pope St. John Paul II had issued a document in which he declared, "The Second Vatican Council was a providential event, whereby the Church began the more immediate preparation for the Jubilee of the Second Millennium."[1] Nor did I bring up how the pope went on to say, "The best preparation for the new millennium, therefore, can only be expressed in a renewed commitment to apply, as faithfully as possible, the teachings of Vatican II to the life of every individual and of the whole Church" (*TMA* 20). My teacher would not have been impressed anyway by my quoting an answer from someone else, no matter who it was.

Now, more than fifty years since the end of Vatican II, the importance of the council remains. In the past few years, there has been a virtual deluge of colloquia, books, and articles addressing the council's legacy. There are discussions about the historical context of the council as well as the interpretation of the documents and their ongoing impact. Vatican II now functions somewhat like a conceptual battlefield upon which struggles about the meaning of the Catholic Church today are being fought. For Catholics, the council is perhaps one of the best examples of what William Faulkner meant when he famously wrote, "The past is never dead. It's not even past."[2]

---

1. Pope John Paul II, *Tertio millennio adveniente* (*On the Coming of the Third Millennium*), 18, *http://w2.vatican.va/content/john-paul-ii/en/apost_letters/1994/documents/hf_jp-ii_apl_10111994_tertio-millennio-adveniente.html.*

2. William Faulkner, *Requiem for a Nun* (New York: Random House, 1951), act 1, scene 3.

31

Overview

This chapter offers an overview of the sixteen documents of Vatican II. First, the documents are listed, along with a brief description of each. Then the relative importance of the documents is discussed. Finally, special attention is paid to *Lumen gentium* and *Gaudium et spes*, the two main documents on the topic of church that provide the underlying structure for the remainder of this book.

Documents of Vatican II

Many of the sixteen documents of Vatican II are related to the topic of church. Drafts of each document were prepared by commissions of bishops and theologians and put forth for vote by the bishops at the council. The original preparatory commissions were highly traditional; during the very first session of the council, however, a vote was taken to reject a prepared list of commission members in favor of electing new ones. This vote was significant, for it launched the council from its beginning on the path of change and renewal. Most of the documents went through several drafts, and the final results were quite different from the originals. The following list is intended to be only a most general overview of the documents.

© Album / Oronoz / Newscom

Although Vatican II, shown here, ended in 1965, knowledge of the documents it produced is essential for understanding today's Catholic Church. *Lumen gentium* and *Gaudium et spes* are among the most important of these documents.

Documents from 1963

- *Constitution on the Sacred Liturgy (Sacrosanctum concilium)* expresses principles for liturgical renewal that laid the groundwork for many liturgical reforms that followed the council.

- *Decree on the Mass Media (Inter mirifica)* discusses the importance of communications for continuing human progress and the contribution that Catholics in particular might make.

Documents from 1964

- *Dogmatic Constitution on the Church (Lumen gentium)* promotes an understanding of the Catholic Church that highlights mystery, ecumenism, collegial authority, the laity, the universal call to holiness, and the need for reform and renewal.
- *Decree on the Catholic Eastern Churches (Orientalium ecclesiarum)* praises the theological and liturgical heritage of those churches in the East that have remained united with Rome.
- *Decree on Ecumenism (Unitatis redintegratio)* acknowledges blame on both Catholics and Protestants for the controversies underlying divisions among Christians; seeks dialogue and unity with "our separated brethren."

Documents from 1965

- *Decree on the Pastoral Office of Bishops in the Church (Christus dominus)* defines the authority and duties of bishops in their own dioceses, in regional gatherings, and in the Catholic Church as a whole.
- *Decree on the Adaptation and Renewal of Religious Life (Perfectae caritatis)* calls for reforms in institutional structures and regulations, but sees the key to renewal as the practice of the vows of poverty, chastity, and obedience.
- *Decree on Priestly Training (Optatam totius)* calls for sound formation of priests, including particular attention to high standards in academic, spiritual, and pastoral training.
- *Declaration on Christian Education (Gravissimum educationis)* affirms the importance of Christian education in home, school, and church and calls for an updating of methods in line with the social sciences.
- *Declaration on the Relation of the Church to Non-Christian Religions (Nostra aetate)* calls for openness toward and cooperation with the major religions of the world.
- *Dogmatic Constitution on Divine Revelation (Dei verbum)* defines how Scripture and Tradition function as the primary expressions of Christian revelation; notable for its acceptance of up-to-date methods in Scripture study and theology.
- *Decree on the Apostolate of Laity (Apostolicam actuositatem)* encourages the laity to live a spiritual life and proclaim the gospel through family, work, and social action.
- *Declaration on Religious Liberty (Dignitatis humanae)* argues that the basic dignity of human beings demands freedom from coercion in matters of religion. All people should be free to worship according to their conscience.

- *Decree on the Church's Missionary Activity* (*Ad gentes*) stresses the importance of the missionary outreach of the Catholic Church, particularly through the formation of community in local churches.
- *Decree on the Ministry and Life of Priests* (*Presbyterorum ordinis*) clarifies the duties of priests and their relations with bishops and laypeople.
- *Pastoral Constitution on the Church in the Modern World* (*Gaudium et spes*) portrays the Catholic Church as being in service to the world; it presents, in particular, the church's positions concerning family, culture, economics, politics, and peace.

The Relative Importance of the Documents

The preceding list of Vatican II documents is arranged in the order in which the documents were released. The question of which documents are the most important is debatable.

Many theologians see *Lumen gentium* as the centerpiece of the council. It is in this document that the Catholic Church articulated its identity for the twentieth century and beyond. Many of the most important changes of the council can be found in it. Several of the other documents, such as the ones on ecumenism, non-Christian religions, bishops, religious life, priests, priestly formation, and laity, can be read as extensions of points made in *Lumen gentium*.

Other theologians like to point out that one cannot have a full understanding of what Vatican II said about the Catholic Church without studying *Gaudium et spes*. This is the great social justice document of the council and represents what many consider the most profound change—from being a church in conflict with the world to being a church making a contribution to the world.

Yet other theologians argue that the document on revelation represents the council's most profound statement. This document has implications for the most basic ways that Catholics think about the Christian message as it is communicated through Scripture and Tradition. It acknowledges how the expression of the church's teaching changes within the changing contexts of history, and affirms the Catholic openness to modern tools of biblical study and contemporary methods in theology.

Although few would claim that the document on religious liberty is the council's most important, it stands for many as the clearest symbol of change at Vatican II. In it, the Catholic Church reverses an earlier stand that encouraged Catholic countries to restrict the religious practices of others. The acknowledgment that people must follow their consciences in religious matters represents a profound growth, with possibilities for further development. For example, when discussing matters of divorce and remarriage, Pope

Francis has stated that pastors need to "make more room for the consciences of the faithful."[3]

The document on missionary activity may be the one most relevant to contemporary developments in the Catholic Church. In recent decades, the most important areas of renewal have centered on evangelization and the development of local faith communities.

The document on the liturgy stands out for being the first released. The changes in our understanding of sacraments set the pattern for changes to come later. The most obvious effects of the council in the early years had to do with changes in the liturgy, such as having the priest face the people and the use of local languages rather than Latin.

Lumen gentium

One of the reasons that a council needed to be called was to complete the unfinished agenda of Vatican I (1869–70). Vatican I had, on the table, a proposed document on the Catholic Church that defined the duties of the pope and bishops. This document reflected many juridical concerns about the distribution of power in the church. Segments of the document regarding the primacy and infallibility of the pope were passed. Before Vatican I could finalize the parts of the document dealing with bishops, however, the council was interrupted and then adjourned because of the Franco-Prussian War. As a result, the church tended to emphasize the power of the pope to the neglect of the bishops, since the bishops' powers remained relatively undefined.

In retrospect, it is cause for some relief that the full document on the church did not pass at Vatican I. If it had, official Catholic teaching about the church today would remain extremely traditional and conservative. The Vatican I document put forth a vision of the church much less open than the vision of Vatican II. The language and concepts of the document reflect the defensive institutional focus of the Catholic Church struggling to fight against Protestantism and secularism.

Evidence of the evolution of Vatican II's *Lumen gentium* is found in the progress of its three major drafts. The first draft of the document on the church proposed at Vatican II was written by a rather traditional preparatory commission. It contained significant advances, but in some ways had more in common theologically with the unpassed Vatican I document than with the final version of *Lumen gentium*. Even from its chapter titles, one can gain a sense of the archaic language and stark tone of the early document:

---

3. Pope Francis, *Amoris laetitia* (*Joy of Love*), 37, *https://w2.vatican.va/content/francesco/en/apost _exhortations/documents/papa-francesco_esortazione-ap_20160319_amoris-laetitia.html.*

FIRST DRAFT, 1962

1. The Nature of the Church Militant
2. The Members of the Church and the Necessity of the Church for Salvation
3. The Episcopate as the Highest Grade of the Sacrament of Orders; the Priesthood
4. Residential Bishops
5. The States of Evangelical Perfection
6. The Laity
7. The Teaching Office (Magisterium) of the Church
8. Authority and Obedience in the Church
9. Relationship between Church and State and Religious Tolerance
10. The Necessity of Proclaiming the Gospel to All Peoples and in the Whole World
11. Ecumenism

Appendix: "Virgin Mary, Mother of God and Mother of Men"[4]

In a famous address at the council, Bishop Emile De Smedt of Brugge denounced this first draft for its clericalism, juridicism, and triumphalism.[5] Clericalism is an attitude that overly emphasizes priests, bishops, and other clergy; juridicism focuses too much on the legal and organizational; triumphalism focuses uncritically on one's achievements and potentials to the neglect of one's problems and need for growth. A new draft was called for that stressed more the call to holiness throughout the people of the church, the mystery of the church in the plan of salvation, and the need for the church to tread the path of reform and renewal.

A second draft, written by a new commission set up by Pope John to represent both traditional and progressive views, was put forward in 1963.[6] It contained many of the sweeping changes that would characterize the third and final draft. The topics of chapters 9, 10, and 11 in the first draft were seen as so important as to call for separate documents on each (religious liberty, missionary activity, and ecumenism). The strictly institutional concerns of chapters 3, 4, 7, and 8 in the first draft were collapsed into one segment and, therefore, received

---

4. Gérard Philips, "History of the Constitution," in *Commentary on the Documents of Vatican II,* ed. Herbert Vorgrimler, 5 vols. (New York: Herder and Herder, 1967–69), 1:106.

5. For a discussion of De Smedt's talk, see Avery Dulles, *Models of the Church* (Garden City, NY: Doubleday, 1987), 39. An English translation of the text can be found in Vincent A. Yzermans, *A New Pentecost: Vatican Council II: Session 1* (Westminster, MD: Newman, 1963), 204–7.

6. Giuseppe Alberigo and Joseph A. Komonchak, eds., *History of Vatican II,* 2 vols. (Maryknoll, NY: Orbis, 1995), 1:264–66.

relatively less emphasis in the second draft. The term "People of God" emerged as the title of one segment addressing the laity. The call to holiness in the church received its own section. The second draft was organized as follows:

SECOND DRAFT, 1963

Section 1:

I. The Mystery of the Church

II. The Hierarchical Constitution of the Church and the Episcopate in Particular

Section 2:

III. The People of God and the Laity in Particular

IV. The Call to Holiness in the Church[7]

The second draft was accompanied by a supplement that suggested that "The People of God" should become its own chapter. Accepted at once, almost unanimously, this change was extremely significant insofar as it marked a shift away from an exclusive emphasis on the hierarchical nature of the church to a new emphasis on the church as made up, in a primary sense, of its members. In the final version of *Lumen gentium*, the chapter on the People of God appeared second, right after the opening chapter that stressed the mysterious (more than the juridical) nature of the church. Triumphalism was replaced by a sense of a more humble church on a journey:

FINAL VERSION, 1964

1. The Mystery of the Church

2. The People of God

3. The Hierarchical Structure of the Church, with Special Reference to the Episcopate

4. The Laity

5. The Call of the Whole Church to Holiness

6. Religious

7. The Eschatological Nature of the Pilgrim Church and Her Union with the Heavenly Church

8. The Role of the Blessed Virgin Mary, Mother of God, in the Mystery of Christ and the Church

---

7. Philips, "History of the Constitution," 110.

This final version of *Lumen gentium* continues to set the course of the Catholic Church as it journeys through the twenty-first century. The document's eight chapters provide the basic structure for the following twenty-four chapters of this book. For each chapter of *Lumen gentium*, there are three chapters in this book that discuss the document and explore related contemporary themes.

Gaudium et spes

On December 4, 1962, Cardinal Léon-Joseph Suenens urged that the council find a central vision to articulate how the Catholic Church conceived of its relation to the world of today. His remarks were echoed the next day by Giovanni Battista Montini, who within the year, would become Pope Paul VI.[8] Paul VI promoted the theme of human progress throughout his pontificate.

Much of the impetus for *Gaudium et spes*, however, can be traced to Pope John XXIII. The central vision for which Suenens called had already been expressed in an initial way in John XXIII's opening address to the council. The actual text of *Gaudium et spes* draws heavily upon John XXIII's social encyclicals, *Mater et magistra* (*Mother and Teacher*), 1961, and *Pacem in terris* (*Peace on Earth*), 1963. *Gaudium et spes* maintains the basic posture associated with these encyclicals. Instead of simply proclaiming to the world how it should be run, *Gaudium et spes* offers to the world the services of the Catholic Church for contributing to dialogue and ongoing human progress.

In one sense, *Gaudium et spes* is a summation of the growing tradition of papal social teaching that finds its beginnings in Leo XIII's *Rerum novarum* (*On the Condition of Labor*), 1891. This tradition has been continued in recent years by Paul VI in *Populorum progressio* (*On the Development of Peoples*), 1967, and by John Paul II in *Laborem exercens* (*On Human Work*), 1981, *Sollicitudo rei socialis* (*On Social Concerns*), 1987, and *Centesimus annus* (*On the Hundredth Anniversary* [*of* Rerum novarum]), 1991.

Gaudium et spes begins with a brief introduction, followed by two major sections. Part 1 consists of four chapters that examine the question of what it means to be human as well as basic principles underlying the relationship between the church and human progress. Part 2 consists of five chapters that address particular cultural and social issues.

---

8. Donald R. Campion, "The Church Today," in *The Documents of Vatican II*, ed. Walter M. Abbott, SJ (New York: America Press, 1966), 184.

PREFACE

Introductory Statement

Part 1: The Church and Humankind's Calling

1. The Dignity of the Human Person
2. The Community of Humankind
3. Humankind's Activity throughout the World
4. The Role of the Church in the Modern World

Part 2: Some Problems of Special Urgency

1. Fostering the Nobility of Marriage and the Family
2. The Proper Development of Culture
3. Economic and Social Life
4. The Life of the Political Community
5. The Fostering of Peace and the Promotion of a Community of Nations

---

Gaudium et spes, by far the longest of the council's documents, attests to the importance of the tradition of Catholic social teaching and stamps that teaching with a direction of openness and dialogue. The document's structure provides the inspiration for the final nine chapters of this book. Part 1 gives rise to chapters 28–31, and part 2 to chapters 32–36.

Summary

This chapter provided an overview of the documents of Vatican II, focusing especially on the two major documents on the church, *Lumen gentium* and *Gaudium et spes*. A discussion was initiated concerning how Vatican II brought about many changes as it struggled to express, faithfully, the Catholic tradition. The next three chapters will take chapter 1 of *Lumen gentium* as their point of departure in exploring contemporary issues facing the Catholic Church.

For Further Reflection

1. Had you heard about Vatican II prior to reading this book? What images, if any, did you have of the council?
2. If you could read only one of the sixteen documents of Vatican II, which would you choose and why?

3. Why was it important for *Lumen gentium* to focus on the church as a "mystery" and as the "People of God" rather than simply as a structured organization?

4. Why would a council that ended more than fifty years ago still be relevant for many people today?

5. Is it time for Vatican III? Why or why not?

Suggested Readings

Alberigo, Giuseppe. *A Brief History of Vatican II.* Maryknoll, NY: Orbis, 2006.

Alberigo, Giuseppe, and Joseph A. Komonchak, eds. *History of Vatican II.* 5 volumes. Maryknoll, NY: Orbis, 1995–2006.

Faggioli, Massimo. *Vatican II: The Battle for Meaning.* Mahwah, NJ. Paulist Press, 2012.

Gaillardetz, Richard R. *An Unfinished Council: Vatican II, Pope Francis, and the Renewal of Catholicism.* Collegeville, MN: Liturgical Press, 2015.

Gaillardetz, Richard R., and Catherine Clifford. *Keys to the Council: Unlocking the Teaching of Vatican II.* Collegeville, MN: Liturgical Press, 2012.

Hahnenberg, Edward P. *A Concise Guide to the Documents of Vatican II.* Cincinnati, OH: St. Anthony Messenger Press, 2007.

Melloni, Alberto. *Vatican II: The Complete History.* Mahwah, NJ: Paulist Press, 2015.

O'Malley, John W. *What Happened at Vatican II.* Cambridge, MA: Harvard University Press, 2010.

Wilde, Melissa J. *Vatican II: A Sociological Analysis of Religious Change.* Princeton, NJ: Princeton University Press, 2007.

LUMEN GENTIUM: A NEW SELF-DEFINITION FOR THE CHURCH

The Nature and Mission of the Church

During my college years, I went through a period when I was apart from the Catholic Church. For a time, I was agnostic; for a time, atheist; for a time, I was interested in the philosophies of the East as well as American transcendentalism. When I first came back to the Catholic Church, I was somewhat embarrassed and more than a little defensive. For a while, I could hardly get into a conversation without trying to turn it into a debate about the primacy of the Catholic Church. My understanding of my own faith lacked depth, yet I felt compelled to justify my return by arguing against anything that was not distinctly Catholic.

Today, after many years of study and trying to live my faith, I am much less defensive. My faith remains the single most important thing in my life. I am more inclined, however, to be open to other viewpoints and not perceive them as necessarily threatening my worldview. I am not only a member of the Catholic Church, but I am also a participating citizen of a global society, and I look toward other viewpoints to enrich my own. This *doesn't* mean I accept everything without hesitation or there is no opinion I would not patently reject. It is just that my basic attitude has changed from one of being suspiciously disposed toward rejection of other beliefs to being appreciatively open toward them.

Overview

This change in my life is a microcosmic reflection of the growth in the Catholic Church that had its high point at Vatican II. *Lumen gentium* (*Dogmatic Constitution on the Church*) signaled a shift in Catholic understanding of the church. This chapter offers an example of how the Catholic Church was understood prior to Vatican II, and then examines several post–Vatican II, contemporary models of the church. This chapter relates to *Lumen gentium* in two ways. First, it explores the nature and mission of the church as mentioned in *Lumen gentium*'s opening paragraph. Second, it discusses the models of the church present in various ways throughout *Lumen gentium*.

The Baltimore Catechism

Many Catholics in the United States were instructed from the *Baltimore Catechism*, a religious education text first published in 1884 and used extensively from 1910 through 1965. The catechism explained the basics of the Christian faith in question-and-answer form. "Who made us?" asks the *Baltimore Catechism*, then answers itself, "God made us." "Who is God?" asks the next question. "God is the Supreme Being, infinitely perfect, who made all things and keeps them in existence," the catechism responds. The *Baltimore Catechism* has major sections on beliefs, commandments, and sacraments.

Martin Luther (1483–1546), the Protestant Reformer, published the first catechism, in Germany, in 1529 to help put the faith into the hands of the common people. Many Catholic catechisms followed in response, such as the one by Peter Canisius (1521–97) in 1555, the Catechism of the Council of Trent (known as the Roman Catechism) in 1566, and the catechism of Robert Bellarmine (1542–1621), issued in 1599.

The period in which these first Catholic catechisms appeared is known as the Counter-Reformation. This period and the texts it spawned reflect a diametrical opposition to anything Protestant. Many of the early Catholic catechisms told one as much about how not to be a Protestant as how to be a Catholic. The same is true in reverse of the Protestant versions.

The *Baltimore Catechism* is a direct descendant of these Counter-Reformation texts. One of its main purposes was the preservation of the Catholic faith in the United States, a predominantly Protestant country with a secular school system. Although one can still find, without much difficulty, a reasonable account of the truth of the Christian faith in the *Baltimore Catechism*, it is marred by an air of defensiveness and a disproportionate treatment of issues. For example, several pages of questions and answers concern which church is the one, true church within which one could be assured of eternal salvation. There is little, however, on the life and teaching of Jesus. The Resurrection, which St. Paul calls the foundation of our faith, receives but one short question and answer. This is because the Resurrection was not an issue of major debate during the Counter-Reformation, whereas the questions of how one is saved and to which church one must belong were hotly disputed.

The defensive stance of the *Baltimore Catechism* reflects something of the theological and pastoral climate of the Catholic Church in the pre–Vatican II period. It was a church concerned with maintaining internal unity and sacramental integrity, while casting suspicious and sometimes hostile glances toward outsiders who did not accept the Catholic faith.

Models of the Church

An air of openness in inquiry characterizes the documents of Vatican II. *Lumen gentium* states its own purpose as unfolding the "inner nature and universal mission" of the Catholic Church (*LG* 1). The document does not simply present the church as a monolithic institution established by God for the salvation of its members; several models and images of the church are put forward. In his now classic work, *Models of the Church*, Avery Cardinal Dulles (1918–2008) explores several of the underlying, guiding concepts of "church" in contemporary Catholic theology.[1] Each of these models finds significant support in the Vatican II documents. Dulles discusses the following five overlapping models, each with its own distinct nature and mission. They are: institution, mystical communion, sacrament, herald, and servant.

DULLES'S MODELS OF THE CHURCH	
Nature	**Mission**
Institution	Offer salvation to members
Mystical communion	Provide spiritual support
Sacrament	Make Christ present
Herald	Preach the gospel
Servant	Transform society

The Institution Model

The *institution* model, as Dulles characterizes it in the original version of his book, makes primary the institutional elements of the church, such as offices, doctrines, laws, and ritual forms. The people, their relationship with God, the Scriptures, and justice issues become subordinate. This model, then, unlike the other four, is by definition a limited starting point. Dulles states that any of the models could be a good starting basis for one's view of church, except this one. He does add, though, that whatever one's model of church, one needs to incorporate and appreciate the institutional elements.

In a chapter added to a later edition of his book, Dulles admits that he was somewhat too severe in his portrayal of the institution model. He still holds that institutional structures should not be taken as primary, but he adds

---

1. Avery Dulles, *Models of the Church* (Garden City, NY: Doubleday Image Books, 1987 [1974]).

that some of the problems with the institution model could be overcome if one thinks not simply in sociological terms but in terms of "what God 'instituted' in Christ."[2] In other words, there are ways of thinking of the church as basically an institution without pitting the structural elements over and against the people and their spirituality. This clarification is important because the institution model is the one most directly associated with pre–Vatican II views of the Catholic Church.

The Mystical Communion Model

The *mystical communion* model emphasizes the people who make up the church and their interconnectedness—with each other and God. This model, while not necessarily rejecting institutional elements, stresses spirituality, community, and fellowship. The church in this view is something of a spiritual support group that aids people in their quest to live holy lives.

Dulles associates two images with this model, the Body of Christ and the People of God. These images, although they can be harmonized, stand in conflict with each other in contemporary theological debates. Both functioned prominently at Vatican II as images for church renewal. The Body of Christ image is often used today to support a strong role for the hierarchy as the particular "member" that functions in the place of Christ as the "head" of the body. The People of God image tends to be favored by those who push for continuing reform in the church by granting larger roles in ministry and decision-making to women and laypeople.

The Sacrament Model

Focusing on the church as the continuing presence of Christ in the world is at the heart of the *sacrament* model. Sacrament in this use is understood as a way of making a sacred reality present and active. As Christ can be thought of as the sacrament of God, so the church can be thought of as the sacrament of Christ.

Dulles saw the sacrament model as especially useful in that it reconciles elements that were in tension in the previous models. The institution model stresses the visible organization to the neglect of the spiritual; the mystical communion model can leave one wondering why a visible organization is necessary at all. The sacrament model explains how visible realities mediate invisible realities. An object or word or gesture that is present can make available something that is otherwise not present.

---

2. Dulles, *Models of the Church*, 196.

The sacrament model also allows the believer to maintain a critical distance from the symbols themselves. The church is the sacrament of Christ, but the church must also be clearly distinguished from Christ. The sacraments make real the saving action of Christ, but the forms and words are not the reality. The sacrament model is the most theoretical of the models. As Dulles pointed out, it is the most useful model for theologians, but, due to its abstract nature, probably the most difficult one for others to understand.

The Herald Model

The *herald* model emphasizes the primacy of the Bible. The church consists of those who hear the Word and are converted. The mission of the church is to preach the Word to the ends of the earth.

Evangelical Christians accept the primacy of Scripture over all other forms of tradition and authority. Many evangelical Christians are also fundamentalists who interpret the Scriptures as historical fact that is inerrant in every way. There are some Protestants, however, who insist on the primacy of Scripture while accepting basic historical-critical approaches to it. Rudolf Bultmann (1884–1976), for example, is a famous liberal Protestant whose existential methods of interpreting the Scriptures fit with the Protestant herald model yet are not fundamentalist.[3]

The herald model, more than any of the other models, can be directly associated with Protestantism. Karl Barth (1886–1968), the great twentieth-century evangelical theologian, exemplified the herald model when, drawing upon the thought of Martin Luther, he distinguished between a theology of glory and a theology of the cross.[4] A church that proclaims its own glory is working counter to the gospel; the task of the church is to point humbly away from itself toward its Lord and Redeemer. Hans Küng (b. 1928), a Catholic theologian censured by the Vatican for his controversial theological stances, took a similar position when he emphasized that the church is not the kingdom of God but, rather, its proclaimer or herald.[5] The official Catholic position, in contrast, holds that the church is the seed of the kingdom but not the fullness of the kingdom.

---

3. Rudolf Bultmann's first impact was through his *History of the Synoptic Tradition*, trans. John Marsh (San Francisco: Harper and Row, 1976 [1921]).

4. See Karl Barth, *The Epistle to the Romans*, trans. from the 6th ed. by Edwyn C. Hoskyns (London: Oxford University Press, 1933 [1918]).

5. See Hans Küng, *The Church*, trans. Ray and Rosaleen Ockenden (New York: Sheed and Ward, 1967).

The Servant Model

The *servant* model emphasizes the need for the church to engage in social transformation. If, traditionally, the church had been presented as a refuge from a
world of vice and temptation, this model presents a church that should be at
the service of a world that is basically good. Members of the church are seen as
part of the larger human family. God is known not simply through the church
but also through human experience and the things of this world. Culture and
science are recognized as having their own legitimate autonomy apart from the
dominance of the church.

Evangelicals and Politics

When Dulles wrote *Models of the Church* in 1974, he was able to comment accurately that those who subscribe to some form of the herald
model tend not to be politically engaged.[6] This situation changed dramatically in the United States in the 1980s, when evangelicals in great
numbers turned their efforts toward political reform. In 1989, evangelical
leader Jerry Falwell (1933–2007) disbanded his political group, the Moral
Majority, proclaiming that the organization had accomplished its objective
of making evangelical Christians politically involved. Evangelical Christians were prominently involved in the social and political movements that
supported the Reagan and Bush presidencies (1980–1992), and they continue to support conservative candidates in present times. Though most
evangelical Christians have been strongly conservative, not all are. The
magazine *Sojourners* has for decades represented the voice of evangelical Christians who are committed to more radical social change.

Dulles linked this last model both with Vatican II's *Gaudium et spes* (*Pastoral Constitution on the Church in the Modern World*) and with the pioneering work
of Pierre Teilhard de Chardin (1881–1955).[7] Teilhard, a Jesuit priest as well as a
paleontologist, is best known for his attempt to reconcile evolutionary theory with
Christianity. He envisioned the church as a progressive society intended to function as the spearhead of evolution. *Gaudium et spes* incorporated some of Teilhard's
basic themes by affirming the importance of Catholics working together with people of various backgrounds for the betterment of the human community.

The most striking contemporary example of a servant model can be found
in the liberation theology developed in Latin America. The original edition of

---

6. Dulles, *Models of the Church*, 79–80.

7. Dulles, *Models of the Church*, 79–80.

Models of the Church had but one scant allusion to this then young phenomenon; the added chapter in the expanded edition has a more substantial reference. In the thirteen years between editions, liberation theology exploded onto the world scene. Gustavo Gutiérrez's (b. 1928) *A Theology of Liberation* (1971) is now a classic text.[8] Liberation theology begins with the experience of political, social, and economic oppression of the people of Latin America. It exemplifies a version of the servant model in that it emphasizes strongly the need for the church to be involved in social change. It differs from other forms of the servant model, however, in that it does not begin with an optimistic view of the basic goodness of human beings and of human progress. Instead, it focuses on the structures of sin that seem to dominate human affairs.

A Tool for Sorting Out Perspectives

These five models—institution, mystical communion, sacrament, herald, and servant—formed the basis of Dulles's original text. *Models of the Church* was an important book in that it made clear that Catholics have several legitimate starting points for thinking about the church. In the first decade after Vatican II, most Catholics not only still operated out of some form of institution model, but also did not know that other visions that reflected the council were available. These models were also useful for labeling some of the issues that might otherwise have polarized Catholics. Instead of arguing back and forth about conceptions of the church, with no resolution in sight, many Catholics were relieved to find that there may be many acceptable views. Today, more than forty years after the book's initial appearance, Dulles's famous models remain an important tool for helping Catholics who wish to examine where they themselves stand, as well as for helping the general public have insight into some key Catholic self-understandings.

Community of Disciples

In the expanded edition of *Models of the Church*, Dulles adds a new category, the *community of disciples* model. He took the phrase from a passing comment made by John Paul II in his first encyclical, *Redemptor hominis* (*The Redeemer of Man*), 1979.[9] The community of disciples is not just another model to be added to the

---

8. Gustavo Gutiérrez, *A Theology of Liberation: History, Politics, Salvation*, trans. Sister Caridad Inda and John Eagleson, in Spanish and English (Maryknoll, NY: Orbis Books, 1988 [1971]).

9. The quote reads, "The Second Vatican Council devoted very special attention to showing how this 'ontological' community of disciples and confessors must increasingly become, even from the 'human' point of view, a community aware of its own life and activity." Pope John Paul II, *Redemptor hominis*, 21, w2.vatican.va/content/john-paul-ii/en/encyclicals/documents/hf_jp-ii_enc_04031979 _redemptor-hominis.html.

others, but a more inclusive model intended to integrate what is best in the other five. Dulles says that it is, in a sense, a version of the mystical communion model but without the tendency to be satisfied with internal, mutual support. Rather, this model focuses on discipleship. What does it mean to follow the Lord and to seriously carry out the implications of this in one's life? This model is intended to illuminate the purposes of the institutional structures and the sacramental aspects of the church, and to ground the missionary thrust toward evangelization and social transformation.

Dulles called the community of disciples a "contrast community" in that it socializes people into choosing higher values in the face of a secularized society that promotes pleasure, wealth, and power. The community of disciples model emphasizes the formation of Christians in communities small enough to foster networks of close, interpersonal relationships that will shape the attitudes and feelings of the members. Christian formation, it argues, should take place within communities that can invoke the memory of Jesus together with the twelve apostles. Such communities will be filled not with alienated or merely communal Catholics but with those who are truly committed to evangelization and service.

Critical questions can be raised about this model. Are the only good Christians the ones who center their lives around the church? Do people go through different stages in their life, some of which often legitimately entail alienation from the church? Are Catholics to turn their backs on the good dimensions of the secular world just a few decades after Vatican II recognized them?

Dulles himself argued that some tension between the church and the world seems inevitable. Although he was a pioneer in offering Catholics various options that have emerged from Vatican II, Dulles later took a somewhat stronger stand that, although there may be a legitimate pluralism of starting points and styles, not just anything goes if one is to talk in a comprehensive sense about the nature and mission of the church. The community of disciples model is therefore not just another option but an attempt at a higher synthesis of the best elements of the earlier models.

Summary

This chapter considered how the Catholic Church appeared in the pre–Vatican II *Baltimore Catechism*, and then examined several models of the church that serve as optional starting points for constructing a more contemporary view. On the whole, the Catholic Church has grown less defensive and more open throughout the years. The challenge today is to find ways to appreciate and maintain a distinctive Catholic identity in a world that takes pluralism for granted and that seems inclined to reduce everything to a common denominator.

The next chapter discusses ways in which the church is linked with, and yet quite distinct from, God.

For Further Reflection

1. Have you ever met anyone who seemed defensive about his or her religion?
2. Did you receive a specifically religious education in your childhood? If so, what types of textbooks or other resources were used? What images of church or religious community did these resources reflect?
3. Which of the models of the church discussed in this chapter holds the most appeal for you? Which holds the least appeal?
4. How would you construct your own model of the church (or synagogue, mosque, or other faith community)?
5. Should the Catholic Church raise its standards for membership, or should it include people at various levels of participation and even nonparticipation?

Suggested Readings

Dulles, Avery. *Models of the Church*. Garden City, NY: Doubleday Image Books, 1987 (1974).

Baltimore Catechism. New York: Benziger Brothers. 1884, with various revisions and editions throughout the years.

5

CHAPTER

God and the Church

When I was a child in Philadelphia in the 1950s, I grew up in "Holy Mother Church." That was not the name of my parish; it was the way I was socialized into thinking of the Catholic Church. The church was not just a building, nor was it the congregation, any combination of congregations, or even the hierarchy. The "church" was the whole array of everything associated with my religion. The church was the Bible, the creed, the sacraments, the commandments, salvation, and, above all, God. To be in church was to be in the House of God. To disagree with the Catholic Church was to disagree with God. To leave the church was to abandon God.

Catholics today, young and old, tend to be more differentiated in their ways of distinguishing among various elements of their faith and also to have critical opinions about the Catholic Church. Various cultural shifts, from the 1960s on, have encouraged skepticism toward all institutions. By the time the sex abuse crisis in the United States reached its apex around 2002, it had already long been the case that few Catholics held a naively romantic view of the church.[1] Many Catholics today are fond of pointing out that the church is not God. They are correct. The church is *not* God, and to think otherwise is a mistake.

Yet I cannot help but wonder if some contemporary Catholics might emphasize this crucial point with just a bit too much zeal. Just as many Catholics before Vatican II failed to distinguish adequately between the church and God, some Catholics today seem hard pressed to see a connection.

---

1. The sex abuse crisis in the United States found not only an estimated 4 percent to 6 percent of priests had abused children but also numerous bishops had simply transferred abusers to new locations rather than remove them from ministry; many had also covered up these cases to avoid financial responsibility. For an in-depth account of the crisis in Boston, see David France, *Our Fathers: The Secret Life of the Catholic Church in an Age of Scandals* (New York: Broadway, 2004).

Overview

This chapter examines the link between the church and God, then the relationship between the church and the kingdom in the teaching of Jesus, and finally the importance of both distinguishing and connecting God and the church. In chapter 1 of *Lumen gentium*, sections 2, 3, and 4 address the links among God, church, and kingdom. Section 8 speaks of the intermingling of human and divine elements in the church. These passages help the reader make positive connections between God and the church without forgetting the distance between them.

Making the Connection

The title *Lumen gentium*, literally "Light of the People," applies directly to Christ. A close reading of section 1 of the document reveals this. The church is *lumen gentium* to the extent that the light of Christ "is brightly visible on the countenance of the church." That is, the light that the church has to offer is not, strictly speaking, of itself, but is rather a reflection of Christ shining upon it. So, right from the beginning, *Lumen gentium* lays a solid foundation for distinguishing between the church and Christ, and thus between the church and God.

This important distinction, however, should not obscure the main thrust of *Lumen gentium*'s opening sections, which highlight the connections between God and the church. Section 1 emphasizes that since the light of Christ is brightly visible on the countenance of the church, the church itself is like a sacrament, "a sign and instrument both of a very closely knit union with God and of the unity of the whole human race." To call the church itself a sacrament is to link it with God. A sacrament, as Avery Dulles pointed out, "is more than just a sign. It betokens the actual presence, in a hidden way, of that to which it points."[2]

Sections 2, 3, and 4 address respectively the connections between the church and the Father, the Son, and the Holy Spirit. These sections place the church within the context of the Christian story. The church is part of the mysterious plan of the Father; the church is the kingdom of God present in mystery that was inaugurated by the Son; the church is kept continually fresh and sanctified by the Holy Spirit. There is no attempt in these sections, nor should there be, to distinguish between the literal and the symbolic, between images and realities. The point is to situate the church within the cosmic and historical dimensions of the Christian story in a simple manner that allows people of various levels of sophistication to enter into the story on their own terms.

---

2. Avery Dulles, *Models of the Church* (Garden City, NY: Doubleday Image Books, 1987), 114.

GOD AND THE CHURCH	
Person of the Trinity	**Role**
Father	Establishes church in plan of salvation
Son	Inaugurates kingdom and church
Holy Spirit	Keeps church fresh and holy

These points are of tremendous significance, because one of the great Catholic insights has been the importance of the connection between the church and God. The French philosopher Albert Camus (1913–60) has said that the world is absurd, because the human heart cries out for meaning but the universe gives no response.[3] Catholics have claimed throughout their history that God has given a response through Christ, and that Christ can be encountered through the church, which is informed by the Holy Spirit.

Preaching the Kingdom, Founding the Church

Lumen gentium draws out the relationship between the church and the kingdom of God to further highlight the church's connection with God. Prior to Vatican II, such church documents as Pius XII's 1943 encyclical *Mystici corporis Christi* (*On the Mystical Body of Christ*), as well as the writings of many theologians, identified the church with the kingdom of God. There was no distinction whatsoever between the kingdom of God, which was the central focus of the teaching of Jesus, and the church that Jesus founded. As sophisticated a scholar as Yves Congar, a French theologian whose work helped lead to Vatican II, could quote Jesus talking about the kingdom and go on to explain the point Jesus was making about the church. When Catholics were taught that Jesus founded the church, the implication was that Jesus intentionally envisioned the institution of the Catholic Church, with its offices and its seven sacraments.

Such beliefs about Jesus' explicit intentions are difficult to justify today in the light of scriptural scholarship. What Jesus meant by the kingdom of God seems broader and more inclusive than any concept of an organized church. Also, while it is defensible to claim that the church that emerged is continuous with the community Jesus founded, Catholics acknowledge that much of what developed as Catholicism over the centuries, though guided by the Spirit, cannot in its complete structure be literally traced back to an explicit intention of Jesus.

---

3. Albert Camus, *The Myth of Sisyphus and Other Essays*, trans. Justin O'Brien (New York: Alfred Knopf, 1955 [1942]), 16.

Lumen gentium itself clearly operates with a distinction between the church and the kingdom. The church is not the "completed kingdom" but rather "the initial budding forth of the kingdom" (*LG* 5). The kingdom is not finally established, but it has been "inaugurated." Some scholars, such as Hans Küng, focus emphatically on this distinction between the church and the kingdom. Küng goes so far

as to portray the church not as embodying the kingdom but rather as simply being its proclaimer or herald. The intention of *Lumen gentium*, however, is not only to highlight the connection between the church and the kingdom but also to acknowledge the distinction between the two. The church is not the fullness of the kingdom, pure and simple, but the church is the seed of the kingdom, which is now present in mystery.

Some Christians are anti-institutional in their approach to church. They see the church as counter to the kingdom and think that each individual must relate to God on his or her own through prayer and Scripture

© Album / Oronoz / Newscom

Worshippers join hands to say the Lord's Prayer: "Thy kingdom come." *Lumen gentium* explores the relationship between the church and the kingdom of God.

reading. In this view, church may be important for Christian fellowship, but it does not mediate the power and presence of God to believers. Such a position is completely foreign to the Catholic mind-set, which stresses the social and communal context that makes the fruitful lives of holy individuals possible. For the Catholic, there is no such thing as Christianity without the church.

Importance of the Distinction

Before exploring why the connection between church and God is so important, it is equally important to distinguish the two. Making this distinction helps believers emphasize God's presence in their daily lives, appreciate people of other faiths, and retain the ability to be critically minded.

First, when God is exclusively connected with the church, there may be a tendency to underemphasize or ignore the experience of God that is available in the everyday lives of people. Christ is present not only in the church but also can be encountered in peak moments in our lives, in deep relationships, in the midst of suffering, and in the faces of poor people and those in need.

Second, identifying God exclusively with the church can hamper one's ability to appreciate the richness of other religious traditions and their ability to mediate that which is ultimate to their participants. Is the Holy Spirit at work within the devout Hindu, Buddhist, Jew, Muslim? Most Catholic theologians today would say enthusiastically, yes!

Third, there is a danger that one might come to worship the church as equivalent to God. It is important to be aware the church is on a journey that is not yet finished. The church is not perfect. It can make mistakes. God is greater than the church, and so it is important one develop a critical ability to assess whether the church is truly representing the will of God in a particular case.

Importance of the Connection

Although it is important to recognize that the church is, in one respect, the imperfect human receiver of what God has revealed to Christians, in another respect, the church is part of that revelation. In other words, Catholics believe the church is not simply an organization that human beings decided to make up; rather, they believe the church is part of the divine plan instituted by Christ and sustained by the Holy Spirit.

Lumen gentium emphasizes that the church is made up of a human element and a divine element:

> The society structured with hierarchical organs and the Mystical Body of Christ, are not to be considered as two realities, nor are the visible assembly and the spiritual community, nor the earthly Church and the Church enriched with heavenly things; rather they form one complex reality which coalesces from a divine and a human element. For this reason, by no weak analogy, it is compared to the mystery of the incarnate Word. (*LG* 8)

Lumen gentium thus powerfully emphasizes the deep and complex connections between the church and God.

Why is this simultaneous humanity and divinity of the church a difficult teaching for some Catholics today? Even now, fifty years after the council, many Catholics are still in a transitional period from a time when the Catholic Church could hardly be questioned to a time when the church is more open to criticism. To some, it seems the church is being suspiciously questioned about everything. Catholics have yet to achieve a balance.

Among some Catholics, alienation from the Catholic Church is intensified today—not only because of the sex abuse crisis but also because of the range of issues on which devout people disagree: from birth control to legalized abortion to premarital sex to priestly celibacy to women's ordination to participation in decision-making to the question of dissent itself. In recent years, LGBTQ+ issues have become especially prominent. For many Catholics, the official Catholic positions on these sex, gender, and autonomy issues place the Catholic Church's very credibility in question.

Dulles's *Models of the Church* can help us see that recognizing the divine dimension of the church need not lead one to a narrow institutional view. The church is the mystical Body of Christ made available for our sanctification; the church is the sacrament that makes Christ explicitly present in our world; the church is the proclamation of the divine word that leads to conversion; the church is the beginning of the kingdom that is experienced whenever oppression is overcome and human relationship is set right. The church has to do with God, and one who would call oneself Catholic must come to grips with that claim.

After the exciting yet tumultuous decades since Vatican II, many Catholics have come to realize that neither trust in nor loyalty to the Catholic Church is incompatible with being critically minded and working for positive change. The church is to be treasured as a gift from God that makes possible growth in holiness, both individually and socially. God is not limited to the church, and some things put forth in connection with the church may have little or nothing to do with God. For Catholics, however, it is through the church that God comes to us most explicitly and thus helps us attune to the presence of the divine in the midst of our everyday lives.

Historically, the tendency to associate the church too closely with God has been labeled idolatrous. Idolatry is putting something less than God in the place of God. Catholics have, at times, been guilty of making the church into an idol. However, what is the opposite of idolatry? Catholics can also be praised for their emphasis on the need to recognize the sacramental presence of God not only in the church but also in everyday life. Yet cautions about idolatry must still be taken seriously. The church's sometimes all-too-human side must not be ignored.

The community-oriented, sacramental, Word-inspired, servant church is supported by certain institutional structures that Catholics regard as essential. I will speak for myself here. As a Catholic, I experience God, and trust that, in the long run, the Holy Spirit will help the leadership of the Catholic Church be competent and responsible. In my opinion, disagreement over a few issues or even over a whole range of important issues should not, in itself, alienate a person from the church. Catholics still have many issues to resolve in the coming years; it will be important to have a charitable, forgiving, and persevering attitude reigning among us as we do, and to believe that God will remain present in our midst as we address our differences. Pope Francis has recently inspired Christians in this regard with his blend of traditional faith and inclusive outreach to all.

Church and Eucharist

The connection of the church with God is often felt at communion. At Mass, I am aware of being gathered with my fellow Christians to worship God. We bring the elements of our daily lives, large and small, to offer at the altar. We celebrate the depth of meaning encountered in the everyday. We are in the presence of Christ, reflecting on our triumphs and failures, on the love we give and receive and on the sins we commit. As I make my way to the altar, I know Christ is there for me and that as I accept him into my body, Christ has accepted me.

The church, in this context, is most basically the people assembled at the Eucharist for the praise and glory of God. We are the Body of Christ, with Christ present as our head. We are the Communion of Saints, sharing the same love of God that sustains the People of God throughout the world and including those who have gone before us in death and are now with God. We are the hearers of the Word, who place the will of God above all things. We are the doers of the Word, who carry away with us a sense of mission for bringing about a better world.

Summary

This chapter discussed the importance of seeing the connection between God and the church, as well as the importance of distinguishing the two. To do one without the other is to miss something essential to Catholic tradition. Catholics still need to find the balance between the "Holy Mother Church" of the 1950s and the contemporary tendency to overlook the divine element in the church.

The next chapter will explore the value of myth and symbol as tools for coming to appreciate the reality of the church.

For Further Reflection

1. Have you ever known anyone who seemed to treat their church or their religious tradition as if it were God?
2. Has the sex abuse crisis affected your views of the Catholic Church? If yes, how?
3. Why is it important to distinguish between the church and God?
4. In what ways do you experience your church, synagogue, mosque, or other faith-based community as being linked with God?
5. What does it mean to say that Jesus founded the church? What doesn't it mean?

Suggested Readings

Bartunek, Jean M., Mary Ann Hinsdale, and James F. Keenan, SJ, eds. *Church Ethics and Its Organizational Context: Learning from the Sex Abuse Scandal in the Catholic Church.* Lanham, MD: Rowman and Littlefield, 2005.

Francis, Pope. *Evangelii gaudium (The Joy of the Gospel).* 2013. *http://w2.vatican.va/content/francesco/en/apost_exhortations/documents/papa-francesco_esortazione-ap_20131124_evangelii-gaudium.html.*

Küng, Hans. *The Church.* Translated by Ray and Rosaleen Ockenden. New York: Sheed and Ward, 1967. Part B, 41–104.

Lohfink, Gerhard. *Does God Need the Church? Toward a Theology of the People of God.* Translated by Linda M. Maloney. Collegeville, MN: Liturgical Press, 1999 (1998).

Reiser, William, SJ. *Jesus in Solidarity with His People: A Theologian Looks at Mark.* Collegeville, MN: Liturgical Press, 2000.

6

CHAPTER

The Symbolic Character of the Church

A student of mine was having trouble selecting a topic for her term project. In a discussion, I discovered that although she had been raised a Catholic and until recently had been involved in her faith, she now could muster little interest in religion. She explained that in her religion course of the previous semester her teacher had pointed out that most things she had believed were merely myths. In fact, the student was very upset that she had been lied to about these things throughout grade school and high school.

In addition to suggesting to her that perhaps she did not hear all that the teacher had been trying to say on the subject, I recommended she investigate the topic of the meaning and truth of myths. She agreed readily to this, and we worked out a reading list of several articles.

The results were dramatic. The student not only did a good job of reporting back on the readings and relating them to each other, but she had integrated the material into her own view of things. She talked about the value of myth in structuring a meaningful view of the world and the new appreciation she had of her own religion when she could interpret it in mythic terms. She had a sense of attraction to her church community because of her new mythic awareness. She recognized that Christianity has historical roots and that these roots are important. She concluded that she still has a good deal of sorting out to do concerning where history ends and where myth begins.

Overview

This chapter explores the symbolic and mythic dimensions of religion, religious language, the sacraments, and the church. This chapter draws upon sections 6 and 7 of chapter 1 of *Lumen gentium*, which offer various images and symbols drawn from Scripture to express the mystery of the church.

Religion as Symbol System

Anthropologists have given us a point of view from which to appreciate religions as systems of symbols. Famous in scholarly circles is Clifford Geertz's definition of *religion* as "a system of symbols which act to establish powerful, pervasive, and long-lasting moods and motivations in men, by formulating conceptions of a general order of existence and clothing these conceptions with such an aura of factuality that the moods and motivations seem uniquely realistic."[1] This valuable definition reflects the point of view not of a believing theologian but of a social scientist seeking the objectivity of an outside observer. Most believers think their beliefs are true rather than "the effect of the symbols is so powerful as to clothe them with an aura of factuality."

But the perspective of the social scientist is valuable not just for other scientists but for believers. On one level of analysis, a religion is a system of symbols and needs to be understood as such. Believers who deny the symbolic content of their religion risk being one-dimensional, literalist, or rejecting of other faiths. Moreover, religious symbols do have powerful and long-lasting effects upon believers. Although religious persons want to be careful not to ignore the claims to truth made within their religion, they also want to appreciate how the symbolic nature of their religion allows them to bear deep and forceful meanings with the potential to transform their lives in positive ways.

Joseph Campbell became famous in the 1980s for his television program and book *The Power of Myth*. Although Campbell admits truth claims are important, he is not personally interested in maintaining the systematic truth claims associated with any particular religion. In fact, he tends to see truth claims as often getting in the way of allowing symbols and myths to do their job. Campbell describes myths as "clues to the spiritual potentialities of the human life." He advises, "Read myths. They teach you that you can turn inward, and you begin to get the message of the symbols. Read other people's myths, not those of your own religion, because you tend to interpret your own religion in terms of facts—but if you read the other ones, you begin to get the message. Myth helps you to put your mind in touch with the experience of being alive."[2]

Campbell's advice is controversial to say the least. He can be challenged on several points. First, doesn't the usefulness of a particular faith (not to mention its truth) depend upon factors other than simply whether the religion is one's own? And isn't a person's own religion usually a most suitable context for genuine religious experience? Second, isn't the purpose of religion at least as much

---

1. Clifford Geertz, "Religion as a Cultural System," *The Religious Situation*, ed. D. C. Cutler (Boston: Beacon, 1968), 643.

2. Joseph Campbell, *The Power of Myth* (Garden City, NY: Doubleday, 1988), 6.

to draw one outside of oneself as to turn oneself inward? That is, shouldn't one's faith lead one to develop deeper human relationships and work for a more just society, and not simply to enjoy the inner experience of being alive? Third, isn't it possible to think of fact and myth in ways that are not so dichotomous? That is, Campbell speaks as though the two are mutually exclusive, yet in Christianity as well as in some other religions, the interrelationship between fact and myth is much more complex.

Campbell's advice is more provocative than precise or accurate. Yet his basic message—that myth puts one's mind in touch with the experience of being alive—is worth savoring. What good is a religion if it doesn't on some level turn you on? If this were Campbell's only true point, he would be worth listening to, the point is that important. However, the wealth of Campbell's work goes far beyond this message.

Symbols

What Campbell says about myth can give us a starting point for explaining the meaning of *symbol*. A symbol is something that puts one in touch with a

© Dan Costa / Shutterstock.com

reality that would be otherwise out of reach. Money is a good example of a symbol. It is more than a coin or a piece of paper or an account balance. Money is symbolic in that it functions as and represents stored and measured bits of economic power. We can distinguish between the economic power and the pieces of paper, yet few of us would nonchalantly tear up $20 bills because they are merely paper. Money takes on the reality of what it represents. A primitive society cut off from the larger world may have no value for money, but for one who participates in that larger world, the real power of national currencies is beyond question.

In Christian iconography, the dove represents the Holy Spirit. The use of such a symbol is more evocative than definitive, inviting reflection on possible meanings of the symbol.

Like other religions, Christianity abounds in symbols. The cross, the Madonna, the baptismal water—all are symbolic of various aspects of the Christian faith. Such symbols do not have one direct referent, but many layers of meaning. The cross represents first and foremost the cross on which Christ died. But it also represents the suffering of all people, our own personal suffering, the things in our lives that are difficult to bear, the expectancy that each of us will die someday, and the call to strive for justice and charity no matter where the path leads. The particular meanings that the cross has for people are as varied and personal as the difficulties people experience in their lives.

The dove is another such symbol. On one level, it represents the Holy Spirit, who descended on Jesus at his baptism. On other levels, the dove represents the inner peace or serenity of one who is filled with the Spirit, the innocence of one who is newly baptized, and the freedom of the Christian's spirit to soar through the heavens.

Most Christians do not thoroughly analyze or even consciously reflect upon the various levels of meaning of most symbols they encounter, yet by living within the tradition in which these symbols have meaning, Christians become deeply familiar with their richness.

The Symbolic Nature of Sacraments

The seven Catholic sacraments are symbolic in nature. Catholics have traditionally believed that sacraments are *effective signs*. To say they are "effective" is to say they make something happen. To say they are "signs" is to say they represent things beyond themselves that are already happening. Baptism is effective in that it makes someone fully part of the Christian community. Yet baptism is a sign of something that is already happening; it would make no sense to baptize a person who was not in a real way being socialized into the community.

The same pattern is true of the sacrament of reconciliation. The sacrament is effective in that through it one receives the forgiveness of one's sins. Yet reconciliation is also a sign in that it celebrates the forgiveness that one is already experiencing from God and the community.

Catholics strive to achieve a balance between the "effective" and the "sign" nature of sacraments. To overemphasize the "effective" nature entails the danger of understanding sacraments as presto-chango magic tricks that simply make things happen without reference to real-life events (for example, "Of course we have a good marriage—the ceremony was performed properly and legally."). To overemphasize the "sign" nature of sacraments risks one's seeing the sacraments as superfluous, because they are simply representations of things that are happening well enough anyway ("Why should we bother to get married? What difference does a piece of paper make if we really love each other?"). The Catholic tradition tries to emphasize both dimensions simultaneously. Getting married makes a world of difference. The quality of a marriage must be understood as involving much more than a ceremony or a piece of paper.

Symbolism and the Renewal of the Liturgy

The first document approved at Vatican II, and the one that has had the most immediate impact on Catholics, was *Sacrosanctum concilium* (*Constitution on the Sacred Liturgy*).[3] In the years following the council, the following changes were made:

- The altar was pulled out from the wall.
- The priest began facing the people.
- Latin gave way to the vernacular.
- The rites, including the Mass, were revised for clarity and to encourage more response and participation.
- Scripture received more prominence in worship.
- Art and ornamentation were simplified.
- Permanent deacons appeared.
- Lay ministers took over many functions.
- The Eucharist was received in the hand.
- The cup of wine was given with the host.
- Local customs were incorporated more freely.
- The liturgical calendar was revised in collaboration with other Christian denominations.
- The litanies of saints were revised for historical credibility.

Sacrosanctum concilium did not enact most of these changes directly. Rather, it articulated principles according to which these changes were made later. One of the thrusts of the document was to move Catholics to "a full, conscious, and active part in liturgical celebration" (*SC* 14).

A strong liturgical reform movement prior to the council had prepared the ground theologically for many of these changes. Most Catholics found the changes enriching and life-giving. Other Catholics, however, experienced them as sudden and shocking. Any change was enough to disturb some worshippers who had experienced liturgy in the same way throughout their entire lives. Added, however, were some rare but 1960s-style experimental extremes such as "marijuana Masses, Mass with crackers and whiskey used as the elements of consecration, teenage Masses with Coca-Cola and hotdog buns."[4] Liturgical issues hit Catholics in their most basic relationship with their church, and they embody some of the overall conservative-liberal polarizations that have emerged since Vatican II.

---

3. *Sacrosanctum concilium*, 1963, *http://www.vatican.va/archive/hist_councils/ii_vatican_council /documents/vat-ii_const_19631204_sacrosanctum-concilium_en.html*.

4. Andrew Greeley, "Religious Symbolism, Liturgy, and Community," in *Encounter with God: Concilium 2*, no. 7 (February 1971): 66.

Today, at the beginning of a new millennium, most of the wide swings of the liturgy pendulum have settled down. Yet the liturgy still functions as a focal point those who want more change as well as for those who want to retrieve missing elements of traditional practice. Some see in liturgy an appropriate place to fight for more involvement of women, incorporation of local customs, and expression of the need to work for social justice. Others lament what they experience as diminishments—in the sense of the sacred in worship, the quality of liturgical music, the beauty of churches once ornate but now reduced to plainness in the name of simplicity.

Nonetheless, many Catholics today simultaneously affirm aspects of both of these agendas. In liturgy, these Catholics encounter the most basic symbols expressing the core elements of their faith.

The Symbolic Nature of Religious Language

Not only are religious traditions filled with symbols, but the nature of religious language is also symbolic. In a way, all language is symbolic, for words are themselves symbols representing realities beyond themselves. The word *table* is not a table, it simply represents a table. Yet when we speak of "symbolic language," we mean something more. We refer to language that goes beyond a simple one-to-one literal correspondence between word and referent.

The language of fiction and poetry is symbolic in this way. Stories and poems can hold many levels of meaning simultaneously. On one level, Albert Camus's *The Plague* is a story about what happens when bubonic plague hits a city in northern Africa. On another level, it is a metaphoric story about World War II and Western civilization. On yet another level, it is a metaphoric tale about the universal plight of human beings in the face of terrible and seemingly senseless suffering.

In the same way, religious language tries to express dimensions of reality that cannot be expressed in a clear, concrete fashion; it tries to express what can be called "the ultimate." Religious language deals with the meaning of life, the point of it all, the highest values, God, human relationships, basic life orientations, human growth and development, the deepest levels of self-awareness and self-acceptance.

A true story told to me by a pastoral minister illustrates this point. As a pastoral minister, this woman often had to deal with people in crisis situations, sometimes involving matters of life and death. She told me about how fifteen years earlier, her four-year-old daughter had suddenly taken ill and died. For years she struggled with the question, "Why did God permit this to happen? All things happen for a reason. What meaning did God intend for this to have in my life?" Yet over time, the woman had come to see that her experience of suffering had enabled her to enter into the pain of those with whom she ministered. Without the tragic event of her daughter's death, she said she would not have become familiar with the depths of meaning that her life's work routinely required.

When this woman told this story from her life, she used symbolic, religious language. It was not as though she literally believed that God directly intended for her child to die to make her a better minister; "God's intention" functioned symbolically for her. She knew well that the mysterious ways of God are beyond human comprehension. But she was able to tell a story that grapples with the ultimate meaning of things and why they happen. She was able, through the use of language that was not to be understood in an overly literal fashion, to come to terms with significant life events by relating them to matters of ultimate meaning and purpose. Understood properly, her story is a "true" one in that it expresses, in a real way, her personal integration of her life experiences in terms of her relationship with God and her fruitful life's work.

The Church as Symbol within the Context of the Christian Story

In the *Baltimore Catechism*, in a definition that hearkened back to the catechisms of the sixteenth century, the Catholic Church was said to be "the congregation of all baptized persons, united in the same true faith, the same sacrifice, and the same sacraments, under the authority of the Sovereign Pontiff and the bishops in communion with him." This particular definition was aimed more at emphasizing that Protestants and others are not members than it was at clarifying what is the nature of the church. The defensively institutional nature of the definition is perhaps understandable, because it stems from a time when the institution's very existence was seen as gravely threatened. The definition, however, explains little about what the church is. If I were not already Catholic, it would say little to inspire me to join the Catholic Church.

Rather than offering a clear definition of the church, the first chapter of *Lumen gentium* speaks of the church symbolically within the context of the Christian story. The first part of the chapter tells the story of how the church is part of the eternal plan of the Father, was inaugurated by the Son, and is sustained by the Spirit. When the document focuses on the church itself, it relies upon images drawn from the Scriptures. As *Lumen gentium* says, "In the Old Testament the revelation of the kingdom is often conveyed by means of metaphors. In the same way the inner nature of the church is now made known to us in different images taken either from tending sheep or cultivating the land, from building or even from family life and betrothals" (*LG* 6).

Some Christians might find the selection of images to be overly passive in what they imply about the role of the members. The church is God's sheepfold, God's tillage, God's building, God's fishing net, Christ's bride. Church members are thereby sheep, earth, stones, fish, traditional brides. It should be kept in mind, however, that when speaking of the church in a mystical sense, it is appropriate to emphasize that it is, above all, a work of God. The church is a glorious gift from God. Later chapters in *Lumen gentium* highlight more dynamic, community-oriented images, such as the People of God, the pilgrim church, and the Communion of Saints.

The final image explored in *Lumen gentium* chapter 1 is that of the Body of Christ. The Body of Christ is an active and community-oriented image. It is used in several places in the New Testament, from Jesus' "This is my body" to the famous passages in 1 Corinthians, Ephesians, and Colossians. The Body of Christ has been one of the most important images of the church in the twentieth century. It was used by Pius XII in his 1943 encyclical *Mystici corporis Christi* (*On the Mystical Body of Christ*) as a way of getting beyond more legalistic, bureaucratic, and mundane concepts of the church to a concept that connects the church with Christ and makes clear the spiritual character of its nature and mission.

Thinking of the church as the Body of Christ, I consider myself a member of that Body related to other members. Each member has an important role. We share an equality in spiritual dignity. We are interconnected. The joy of others is my joy; their sorrow is my sorrow. We celebrate with one another, and our sharing in the same sacraments symbolizes our partaking in the same love of God. Christ is our head, which means that as human beings we seek first the will of God and the coming of the kingdom in a way that complements our individual gifts.

In contrast to the definition of *church* in the *Baltimore Catechism*, the Body of Christ is an image that captures my imagination and spirit. What does this image imply, however, for how I relate with other people who are not explicitly members of the Body of Christ? There are many solutions proposed by contemporary theologians to the problem of religious pluralism. Personally, I interpret the Body of Christ image in a way that does not contradict but, rather, is in harmony with my belief in the interconnectedness and solidarity of all people. In other words, rather than setting me apart from other human beings, my membership in the Body of Christ functions symbolically to represent my relationship with them.

The Church as Story

Christians believe that God has come to us in the person of Jesus Christ. Catholics as well as many other Christians believe in Christ's ongoing presence in the church. On a fundamental level, the story of the church is a story about the meaning of life. The world of meaning in which each of us lives is shaped and, to some degree, even constituted by stories. As a religious story, the church tells about the ultimate dimensions of life and thus provides a framework within which other levels of the stories of our lives take place.

Of course, the church is more than just a story. The story of the church refers to things that have happened in the past and that continue to happen. The church is the story of those who have lived their lives in a world whose meaning takes its structure from the story of Jesus. Jesus is a person who really lived, who died on a cross, who rose from the dead, and who was experienced by his followers as God-incarnate on earth. It is difficult, if not impossible, to draw a sharp line between where "facts" end and where "story" begins. Story functions to interpret the deeper dimensions of the true meaning of things that have really happened.

Summary

This chapter considered the symbolic nature of religious language, as well as the story dimension of the church. It then examined how *Lumen gentium* preferred scriptural images and symbols to precise definitions when it came to talking about the church.

Recall from the beginning of this chapter, the story of the student who, at first, had a difficult time adjusting to the idea that her religion had mythological dimensions. What she realizes today is that *mythological* does not mean "false," and that a life lived without such dimensions would be short on ultimate meaning.

The next chapter will examine a basic shift in outlook at Vatican II concerning the relative status of Catholics, both among themselves and with other Christians.

For Further Reflection

1. What do you think that Joseph Campbell means when he says that "myth helps you to put your mind in touch with the experience of being alive"?
2. Have you ever known anyone whom you thought overly literal-minded about religion? How would you describe that person?
3. What, in your own life, did you once understand only literally but now also appreciate symbolically?
4. Is it possible to be too symbolic in one's interpretation of faith, without giving enough attention to the literal?
5. In what ways is "symbol" a liberating category for religious persons?

Suggested Readings

Avis, Paul. *God and the Creative Imagination: Metaphor, Symbol and Myth in Religion and Theology*. London and New York: Routledge, 1999.

Campbell, Joseph, with Bill Moyers. *The Power of Myth*. Garden City, NY: Doubleday, 1988.

Greeley, Andrew. *The Catholic Myth: The Behavior and Beliefs of American Catholics.* New York: Scribner, 1990.

McDannell, Colleen. *Material Christianity: Religion and Popular Culture in America.* New Haven, CT: Yale University Press, 1995.

McNamara, Denis R. *How to Read Churches: A Crash Course in Ecclesiastical Architecture.* New York: Rizzoli International Publications, 2011.

Parys, Johan Van. *Symbols That Surround Us: Faithful Reflections.* Ligouri, MO: Liguori, 2012.

Schloeder, Steven J. *Architecture in Communion: Implementing the Second Vatican Council through Liturgy and Architecture.* San Francisco: Ignatius, 1990.

Shea, John. *Stories of God.* Chicago: Thomas More, 1978.

Tilley, Terrence. *Story Theology.* Wilmington, DE: Michael Glazier, 1985.

Ratzinger, Joseph Cardinal. *A New Song for the Lord: Faith in Christ and Liturgy Today.* Translated by Martha M. Matesich. New York: Crossroad, 1996.

7

CHAPTER

An Ecumenical Outlook

A student of mine, raised Catholic, is now alienated from the Catholic Church. He has approached me a couple of times, seemingly to get into an argument. Inevitably, he raises the point that Catholics hold the ugly belief that anyone who is not Catholic cannot be saved. Apparently this is the impression he received as a child and, because he is deeply angry with the Catholic Church, he has a hard time giving it up. I point out to him that Catholics throughout history have held a wide range of positions on this issue. I show him clear statements in current church documents that contradict his belief. I point out that in the early 1950s, Father Feeney of Boston was excommunicated for obstinately continuing to preach that no one outside the Catholic Church can be saved.

So far, however, all of this has been to no avail. He was taught a certain way as a child, and every once in a while, an unfortunate incident of Catholic narrow-mindedness reinforces his position. For example, he was working on a food-relief project when he encountered a fellow Catholic who preferred to donate food to a Catholic—rather than a Protestant—institution. The student took this as yet another instance of Catholic exclusivity. He claims that history books and official church documents do not reveal the intolerance actually put forth in childhood religious education. Although I hope this young man will soon let go of his position and realize that the overwhelming majority of Catholics today are not taught such exclusivity, I do have to admit to him that what he says sometimes reminds me of what I was taught in my own religious education in the 1950s.

Overview

It might be difficult for people today to grasp that just over half a century ago many Christians were quite unsure about the possibility of salvation of other Christians outside of their own particular tradition. Today, such a view still exists but only as a minority position. Understanding *Lumen gentium* in its historical context is important for appreciating both how radically new its teachings on relations with other Christians sounded in its own time and yet how underdeveloped they might sound to people today.

This chapter examines how *Lumen gentium* changed Catholic attitudes and outlooks concerning the salvation of non-Catholic Christians.[1] It focuses especially on three points from *Lumen gentium* (*Dogmatic Constitution on the Church*): how various churches today relate to the church Christ founded; who can be considered a member of the church; and how Christians are called to share in the ministry of Christ as priest, prophet, and king. The first point is drawn from section 8 of chapter 1 of *Lumen gentium*; the next two points are drawn from throughout chapter 2.

Salvation Outside the Church?

When I was a child, a question in the *Baltimore Catechism* read, "Are all obliged to belong to the Catholic Church in order to be saved?" The ominous answer followed: "All are obliged to belong to the Catholic Church in order to be saved."[2] This was followed by another question and answer that explained that "those who through their own grave fault do not know that the Catholic Church is the true church or, knowing it, refuse to join it, cannot be saved." Yet another question and answer assured us that those who do not know that the Catholic Church is the true church can be saved by making use of the graces God gives them. In more advanced seminary manuals written to train priests, this state of not knowing was called "invincible ignorance." In popular practice, it was assumed that those raised as Protestant from birth were in little danger, but those who themselves chose to leave the Catholic Church had much for which to answer.

The traditional Christian adage, "No salvation outside the church," is first attributed to Cyprian, Bishop of Carthage, in the third century, during a period of great persecution. He addressed his message to those who were already Christian, advising them that followers of Christ should choose martyrdom over the public denial of their faith. Cyprian himself was martyred for refusing to offer sacrifice to pagan gods.[3]

As hard as Cyprian's words might be, they are a far cry from a sweeping statement that would send to hell people from all over the world who are not members in good standing of the Catholic Church. Harsher statements followed in subsequent centuries, however. In 1215, at the Fifth Lateran Council,

---

1. Relationships between Christians and members of other world religions are addressed in chapter 29.

2. *The New Baltimore Catechism and Mass*, no. 2, official revised edition (New York: Benziger Brothers, 1941), 73. A 1964 edition adds a qualification: "All are obliged to belong to the Catholic Church, *in some way*, to be saved."

3. Cyprian of Carthage, "To Jubaianus, Concerning the Baptism of Heretics," *New Advent, www.newadvent.org/fathers/050672.htm*.

Pope Innocent III declared, "There is but one universal church of the faithful, outside of which no one at all can be saved." In a Bull of 1441, Pope Eugene IV stated even more strongly that the church "firmly believes, professes, and teaches that none of those who are not within the Catholic Church, not only Pagans, but Jews, heretics, and schismatics, can ever be partakers of eternal life, but are to go into the eternal fire 'prepared for the devil and his angels' (Mt 25:41), unless before the close of their lives they shall have entered into that church." It is clear that some medieval popes took "no salvation outside the church" quite literally. A tension can be found throughout the Catholic tradition between positions of openness to people of other faiths and positions that unequivocally condemn all those who are not explicitly Catholic. The position in the *Baltimore Catechism*, which clearly allows for the salvation of non-Catholics, appears rather mild when compared with the Bull of 1441.

Vatican II made great strides in ecumenical openness. For the first time in official church writings, Protestant congregations were referred to as "churches" or "ecclesial communities," rather than merely "sects." Protestants themselves are called our "separated brethren." It is said, "In some real way they are joined with us in the Holy Spirit, for to them too he gives his gifts and graces whereby he is operative among them with his sanctifying power" (*LG* 15). To say that the Holy Spirit is at work with sanctifying power is to grant a good deal more than salvation through the loophole of invincible ignorance. It is to say that God is at work among Protestant believers.

The overall stance taken by the Catholic Church toward Protestantism in *Lumen gentium* can be explored by examining three points mentioned earlier: the relationship between various churches and the church founded by Christ, the membership of the church, and the sharing of Christians in the threefold ministry of Christ as priest, prophet, and king. Each of these points represents grounds for a new openness in Catholic-Protestant relationships.

Where Can the Church That Christ Founded Be Found?

In the first draft of what would become *Lumen gentium*, after a discussion of the church that Christ founded, it states, "This Church of Christ . . . is the Catholic Church." For explicitly ecumenical purposes, the final draft was changed to read, "This Church of Christ . . . subsists in the Catholic Church . . . although many elements of sanctification and of truth are found outside of its visible structure. These elements, as gifts belonging to the Church of Christ, are forces impelling toward catholic unity" (*LG* 8).

The shift from "is" in the first draft to "subsists in" in the final draft signals a change from presenting the Catholic Church as the only true church to a new openness to other churches. That is, in the first draft, the church that Christ founded is identified as the Catholic Church, pure and simple. In the final draft, the "Church of Christ" is said to "subsist in" or "dwell within" the Catholic Church, but not exclusively so. In other words, although this Church of Christ is basically and fundamentally found dwelling in the Catholic Church, elements of this church can also be found in Christian churches that are not Catholic. These authentic elements are positive signs of ecumenical progress.

Lumen gentium still gives a clear priority to the Catholic Church insofar as there is a certain fullness or completeness in the way that the Church of Christ can be found within it. By implication, Protestant churches are necessarily incomplete to the extent that they disagree with the Catholic tradition on key issues. Some Catholics involved in the ecumenical movement today find this an unsatisfactory position. They would like to see a position more open to the admission of mistakes and even incompleteness on both sides. The following two points may help make a more sympathetic reading of the document possible.

First, one should appreciate how radical and progressive the position of *Lumen gentium* seemed in 1964. For Catholics who in their youth were taught to question the very salvation of Protestants, the acknowledgment that the Holy Spirit is at work in Protestant churches represented a revolutionary change in attitude.

Second, the position of *Lumen gentium* is stated against the background of a Catholic tradition that presupposes a distinction between abstract essentials and concrete practice. That is, while *Lumen gentium* says that in essential beliefs and structures the Catholic Church enjoys a certain priority, it does not deny that many Protestant congregations may be doing a better job in practice. In other words, the position in *Lumen gentium* is simply that the Catholic Church is the church that has a "complete set of tools," that is, the correct teachings, number of sacraments, and apostolic leadership. It is presupposed that some Catholic congregations may not be doing a very good job with their tools or are even keeping them "locked up in the woodshed"; some Protestant congregations may be doing an excellent job with the tools that they have.

The Catholic Church has continued to grow in its outlook toward other denominations. In the pre–Vatican II period, ecumenical progress from a Catholic perspective seemed to mean the other side showed signs of collapsing or surrendering and was going to rejoin the Catholic Church to ensure its salvation. Today, ecumenical progress is more often envisioned as members of the various Christian traditions being encouraged to recognize the authentic Christianity of each other.

Recognizing Salvation beyond the Church?

English composition textbooks teach that one way to emphasize a particular sentence is to place it at the beginning or end of a paragraph. If you wish to say something, but at the same time, deemphasize it, stick it somewhere in the middle.

In the middle of chapter two of *Lumen gentium* the reader is told,

> Basing itself upon Sacred Scripture and Tradition, [the council] teaches that the church, now sojourning on earth as an exile, is necessary for salvation. Christ, present to us in his Body, is the one Mediator and the unique way of salvation. In explicit terms he himself affirmed the necessity of faith and baptism, and thereby affirmed also the necessity of the church, for through baptism as through a door men enter the church. Whosoever, therefore, knowing that the Catholic Church was made necessary by Christ, would refuse to enter it or to remain in it, could not be saved. (*LG* 14)

And so *Lumen gentium* thereby affirms the traditional teaching about no salvation outside the church and the allowance for invincible ignorance. However, the placement of the passage in the chapter undercuts the traditional force of this position and demands that it be read in the most open way possible. It does this in two ways.

First, in a chapter that includes Catholics, Protestants, people of various faiths, and even secularists, this statement is placed in a section that deals directly with the Catholic faithful. In addressing itself primarily to Catholics, the text hearkens back more to the warning to the faithful made by Cyprian in the third century than it does to the sweeping condemnation made by Pope Eugene IV in his Bull of 1441. In other words, more stress is placed on the idea that those who already accept the Catholic Church should not turn away from it than on the idea that unless nonmembers are invincibly ignorant they will not be saved.

Second, the statement on salvation outside the church appears in the middle of a chapter that otherwise lays the groundwork for a broadscale ecumenical understanding. The very first sentence of chapter 2 reads, "At all times and in every race God has given welcome to whosoever fears him and does what is right" (*LG* 9). Given that this statement comes first and is used to introduce the structure of the chapter, it is appropriate to read the necessity of the church for salvation in the light of it rather than vice versa. In other words, we are to interpret the necessity of the church for salvation in such a way that we keep in mind the prior position that God welcomes, at all times and in every race, those who fear him and do what is right. The necessity of the church for salvation appears in the chapter because conservative forces rightfully insisted that it is part of the Catholic tradition. Its placement in the document, however, gives it more the status of a qualification than of a basic, grounding position. There is indeed salvation outside the church, although many traditional theologians take, instead, the route of defining "church" in such a general way that it includes all people of goodwill and actions.

This is not to say that the document minimizes the role of the church in God's plan of salvation. We are told God does not simply save people as individuals, but gathers them together as a people. The People of God have historical and continuing roots in the Jews as God's chosen people. Through Christ was formed a new People of God that calls together all people in catholic unity. Catholics are full members, catechumens are joined through their intention, Protestants are linked through the Holy Spirit, and people of various faiths and backgrounds are in some way related. The document explicitly states that salvation is possible for all of these people, although the church retains its mission to preach the gospel to all nations.

Meeting Martin Luther Halfway

Another way *Lumen gentium* reveals a positive ecumenical outlook is by affirming, from a Catholic standpoint, several key ideas associated with the most famous of Protestant Reformers, Martin Luther. A joint commission of Lutheran and Roman Catholic scholars has issued a document, "Martin Luther's Legacy," which includes a discussion of Luther's influence on Vatican II.[4] Some commentators have even joked that Vatican II represents the Catholics finally catching up with the Protestants after four hundred years. A more serious analysis reveals a Catholic Church trying to maintain its essential identity as it attempts to formulate mutually acceptable positions on important matters. In the second chapter of *Lumen gentium*, two ideas historically associated with Luther stand out: that the church essentially is to be considered a community of people and that all Christians participate in the ministry of Christ, the one Mediator. Luther expert John Dillenberger describes the Reformer's position:

> As the community of believers, Christians bear each other's burdens and the burdens of the world, as Christ did before them. . . . [Thus] the ministry was no longer understood as a position of *necessary* mediatorship. . . . Rather, in the community of the church, all men were priests to each other, that is, occasions for and messengers of grace and support. This was expressed in the notion of the priesthood of all believers.[5]

Lumen gentium clearly differs from Luther in its strong reaffirmation of the crucial importance of the structural elements of the church and the essential distinction between the ordained ministries and the common priesthood of the faithful. The document moves unmistakably in the direction of Luther, however, concerning the church as community and the universal call to share in Christ's ministry.

---

4. Lutheran-Roman Catholic Statement, "Martin Luther's Legacy," *Origins* 13 (June 9, 1983): 65–69.

5. John Dillenberger, ed., *Martin Luther: Selections from His Writings* (Garden City, NY: Doubleday, 1961), xxxiii.

The existence and placement of chapter 2 of *Lumen gentium*, on the People of God, reveals a strong emphasis on the church as a community. The first draft of the document contained no chapter on this matter. In the second draft, the concept of the People of God was connected with the laity and included as the next-to-last section in the document. In the final draft, this chapter was placed ahead of the chapter on the hierarchical nature of the church and became second only to the chapter on the mystery of the church and its connection with God. This move can be interpreted as signaling a shift in emphasis from a pyramidal structure of the church with the pope at the top, followed by the bishops, followed by the priests, followed by the religious, with the laity at the bottom, to a more circular, inclusive structure of the church formed by all the People of God and served by a hierarchy.

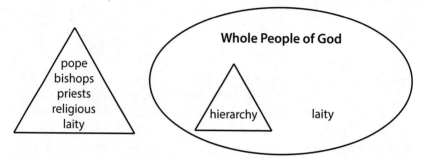

Prior to Vatican II, the Catholic Church was commonly equated with its pyramidal hierarchy. Vatican II, however, placed the pyramidal image of the church within the entire People of God.

Chapter 2 of *Lumen gentium* emphasizes that all members of the People of God share in the threefold ministry of Christ as priest, prophet, and king. This notion becomes a major structuring element throughout the rest of the document. For example, chapter 3 of *Lumen gentium* tells how the hierarchy shares in this threefold ministry, chapter 4 discusses the ways in which the laity shares in it, and chapter 6 discusses the share of those who have taken religious vows. This concept has roots in the New Testament notion, so important to Luther, that Christ is now the one Mediator who replaces the Old Testament priesthood by forming a priestly people. This priestly people can pray and offer sacrifice to the Father without the need of any mediator other than Christ. This concept also has roots in the writings of several of the Church Fathers who expressed that Christ is the fulfillment of the messianic prophecies in that he has taken over the functions of the priestly books, the prophetic books, and the kingly books (a traditional way of categorizing all of the books of the Old Testament).[6]

---

6. See Thomas Halton, *Church: Message of the Fathers of the Church*, no. 4 (Wilmington, DE: Michael Glazier, 1985), 70–73.

Each Christian is called, in accordance with one's state in life, to be the presence of Christ (priest), to bear witness to Christ in one's life (prophet), and to serve in the coming of the kingdom of God (king).

Summary

This chapter investigated how the Catholic Church has shifted from a position of casting doubts about the possibility of the salvation of "outsiders" to a position of ecumenical openness. The Catholic Church today recognizes the Spirit in Protestant communities, the broad membership of the People of God, and the sharing of Christians in the threefold ministry of Christ as priest, prophet, and king.

It is my hope that the student discussed in the beginning of this chapter, and others like him, will come to appreciate the ecumenical openness of the positions taken at Vatican II. Nevertheless, it is also true that Christian churches, both Catholic and Protestant, still have a long way to go on these matters.

The next chapter examines the historical background of some of the divisions within Christianity.

For Further Reflection

1. What might prompt a narrow interpretation of "no salvation outside the church"?
2. Have you ever personally experienced discrimination among Christian denominations?
3. How did the concept of "the People of God" function ecumenically at Vatican II?
4. Do you think the concept of the "common priesthood of the faithful" should be taken to mean that, in a way, every Christian is a priest?
5. What types of experiences might make people grow in their ecumenical awareness?

Suggested Readings

Clifford, Catherine E. *Decoding Vatican II: Ecclesial Self-Identity, Dialogue, and Reform*. Mahwah, NJ: Paulist Press, 2014.

Congar, Yves. *True and False Reform in the Church*. Translated by Paul Philibert. Collegeville, MN: Liturgical Press, 2011.

Gros, Jeffrey, et al. *Introduction to Ecumenism*. Mahwah, NJ: Paulist Press, 1998.

Kinnamon, Michael. *The Ecumenical Movement: An Anthology of Key Texts and Voices.* Geneva: World Council of Churches, 2016.

Sullivan, Francis. *Salvation Outside the Church? Tracing the History of the Catholic Response.* Mahwah, NJ: Paulist Press, 1992; Eugene, OR: Wipf and Stock, 2002.

Diversity and Divisions within Christianity

I n the Gospel of John, Jesus prays to the Father: "I ask not only on behalf of these, but also on behalf of those who will believe in me through their word, that they may all be one. As you, Father, are in me and I am in you, may they also be in us, so that the world may believe that you have sent me" (Jn 17:20–21). Jesus is not only asking that his followers be one, but he is explicitly linking their unity with their credibility. Why should the world believe that Jesus was sent by the Father if his followers are divided among themselves?

Overview

A good way to begin understanding the current state of divisions among Christians is to examine the history of how diverse communities have emerged within Christianity. It would take, of course, many volumes to do justice to this issue. This chapter presents a quick overview of diversity in the New Testament, the schism between Greek Orthodox and Roman Catholics, and the Protestant Reformation. This material is most related to chapter 2 of *Lumen gentium* and to *Unitatis redintegratio* (*Decree on Ecumenism*) from Vatican II.

Diverse Communities in the New Testament

In *The Churches the Apostles Left Behind*, noted biblical scholar Raymond Brown investigates various communities to whom different books of the New Testament were addressed.[1] Brown argues that each community had a particular identity associated with the apostle or apostolic guide who founded it. As he investigates these communities, Brown seeks to understand how each was able to survive after the apostolic guide had departed the scene. In other words, if the

_____
1. Raymond Brown, *The Churches the Apostles Left Behind* (New York: Paulist Press, 1984).

founding authority is the original link between the community and Jesus, then what structures or authoritative ideas serve to maintain the community once the founder has left?

Brown finds significant variety in community structure and identity in the seven churches he investigates. The first three communities discussed have characteristics often associated with Catholicism. In the Pastoral Epistles (1 Timothy, 2 Timothy, and Titus), for example, the element of survival is the appointment of a bishop in every town. In Colossians and Ephesians, it is the ideal concept of the church as the mystical Body of Christ. In Luke and Acts of the Apostles, the continuous element is the Holy Spirit that guides the leaders.

The next three communities Brown discusses are more closely associated with Protestantism. In 1 Peter, the guiding factor is the understanding of the church as the new People of God against the background of Israel as God's chosen people. In the Gospel of John, the enduring element is the relationship of the individual to Jesus grasped through the image of the vine and the branches. In the epistles of John, it is the Holy Spirit ("advocate") in the individual that gives authority (though, as Brown shows, this concept tends ultimately to cause great divisions).

Brown ends by discussing a community of ecumenical balance. In the Gospel of Matthew, the element that allows for survival is a stress on authoritative structure balanced by an even greater stress on the compassionate and nonlegalistic attitude of Jesus. Brown explains in detail not only how each of these elements provides continuity, but also the strengths and weaknesses of each type of community.

WHAT STRUCTURING ELEMENT REPLACED THE APOSTOLIC GUIDE?	
Biblical Books	**New Structuring Element**
Pastoral Epistles	bishop in each town
Colossians/Ephesians	mystical Body of Christ
Luke/Acts	Holy Spirit guides leaders
1 Peter	new People of God
John	individual connected with Jesus
Epistles of John	Holy Spirit within each individual
Matthew	authority with great compassion

Brown's work is radically ecumenical for several reasons. First, the variety of communities discussed shows that many denominations can find solid grounding for their own church structure within the text of the New Testament. Catholics, mainline Protestants, and evangelicals can all point to passages that justify their approach.

Second, Brown's investigation suggests that no one denomination is currently hearing all of the biblical witness. Each denomination must let itself be challenged by the whole range of biblical testimony. Catholics may tend to underemphasize the importance of the Spirit's presence in each individual; mainline Protestants may undervalue the need for church unity; evangelical Christians may be ignoring the scriptural support for the leadership of bishops.

Third, Brown's analysis of the distortions that arise from argumentative presentations of the faith, whether in New Testament times, the Reformation, or today, nudges all parties in the direction of listening sympathetically and working toward reconciliation. Brown shows how the emergence of two opposing sides causes disputed issues to take center stage and the more important basics of the faith to be pushed aside. For example, Christians in the community addressed by the epistles of John were so intent on defending the divinity and preexistence of Jesus that they had trouble affirming that Jesus was human. Catholics, at the time of the Reformation, were so intent on discrediting the Reformers that they looked upon Bible reading as suspect. Brown sees a similar thing happening in post–Vatican II rejection of pre–Vatican II Catholicism:

> I, . . . while enthusiastic for what was introduced into Catholicism by Vatican II, see no need for the concomitant losses, e.g., of inner-Catholic loyalty, obedience, and commitment to the church; of dignity in liturgy; of Gregorian chant; of a knowledge of the Latin tradition reaching from Augustine through Thomas to the Middle Ages. To try now to recoup some of those losses while still advancing the gains of Vatican II would be an act of eminent good sense.[2]

Brown's approach represents a peaceful spirit that seeks unity, not by avoiding differences but by avoiding the bitter arguments that so often result in defensive attitudes and the accompanying temptation to hold others and their ideas in contempt.

Brown does not leave his reader with the impression that contemporary churches are equally incomplete. He has a distinct preference for churches that follow the model of Matthew's Gospel, in which authoritative structures are essential, yet come in a noticeable second to pastoral sensitivity and loving human relationships. Matthew has traditionally been known as "the church's

---

2. Brown, *The Churches the Apostles Left Behind*, 118.

gospel." Brown does leave his reader, though, with a clear picture of legitimate diversity in the New Testament and of the need for Christians of all stripes to listen closely to each other and value each other's insights.

The types of diversity manifested in the New Testament have existed in various forms throughout the history of Christianity. At various times, organized movements have arisen that have been labeled heretical, such as Marcionism, Arianism, and Waldensianism.[3] For world Christianity, though, three major divisions stand out from the rest: the schism between the Greek Orthodox and the Roman Catholics of the eleventh century, the Protestant Reformation of the sixteenth, and the Pentecostal movement that has spread globally over the past one hundred years.

Eastern Orthodox and Roman Catholic

The Greek-Roman schism was prior to and in a sense deeper than the Protestant Reformation. The former represented a split between the East and West, whereas the latter was simply a split within Western Christianity. The Greek-Roman schism began in the break between the Latin-speaking church, centered in Rome, and the Greek-speaking church, centered in Constantinople (modern-day Istanbul, in Turkey). Although the split took place gradually over a period of centuries, the event to which scholars point most often is the excommunication, by a personal representative of the pope, of Michael Cerularius, patriarch (head) of the Greek Orthodox Church, during a Mass in the patriarch's own cathedral in Constantinople in 1054 CE. Cerularius returned the favor by excommunicating the papal representative.

This event was preceded by several hundred years of mutual rivalry and dislike between the two churches. Although the Greeks somewhat acknowledged Rome's claim to priority, the nature and extent of this priority was disputed. For example, Roman Catholics held that ecumenical councils had authority because the pope accepted them. Greek Orthodox Catholics claimed that ecumenical councils had their own authority and that papal acceptance simply represented a final confirmation of that authority.

A related theological dispute concerned the Roman addition to the Nicene Creed of a term, *filioque* ("and the Son"), indicating that the Holy Spirit proceeded both from the Father and the Son. The Greek original had said only that the Holy Spirit proceeded from the Father. This debate had its own connection with papal authority, for in the Greek version, divine authority is mediated more directly by the Spirit through tradition, whereas in the Roman version, the mediation is through Christ and the church, and thus through structures of authority.

---

3. Marcion (c. 85 CE–c. 160 CE) rejected the Old Testament; Arius (c. 250 CE–366 CE) denied the full divinity of Christ; Peter Waldo (c. 1150 CE–c. 1205 CE) endorsed radical poverty and lay preaching while opposing church authority.

Most scholars agree, though, that the real disputes between Constantinople and Rome were more cultural and political than theological. Greek priests were married, bearded, and used leavened bread in the Mass; Roman priests were celibate, clean-shaven, and used unleavened bread. Deeper than these differences, though, was the attitude toward each other. As colorfully expressed by one commentator: "To the Byzantines [Greeks], the Latins, people from dark-age countries, were wild and uncultured savages with huge appetites. To the Latins, the Greeks were degenerate, effeminate hair-splitters."[4]

After the mutual excommunications in 1054 CE, there was still some openness toward reconciliation, but it did not materialize. In 1204 CE, Venetian merchants with commercial interests duped Crusaders from the West into sacking the city of Constantinople. These Crusaders established the Latin empire of Constantinople, and imposed Latin liturgy and practices upon unwilling Greek Christians, until the Crusaders were finally ousted in 1261 CE. From an Orthodox perspective, the Latin occupation of Constantinople contributed more to the continuation of the still-existing schism than did the mutual excommunications of 1054 CE. Hopes of reconciliation were buried further when Constantinople fell to the Turks in 1453 CE.

What today is known as Eastern Orthodoxy encompasses five major patriarchates, residences for a patriarch: Constantinople, Alexandria, Antioch, Jerusalem, and Moscow. There are several other Orthodox churches, such as the Greek, that have their own patriarch as well. The Orthodox Church in America, though now independent, began as a Russian Orthodox mission. In the United States, most Orthodox attend, when possible, a church connected with their own ethnic or national background, although the various Orthodox churches are in communion with each other.

Throughout the Eastern world, there are also many different Eastern Catholic Churches. These churches share much in cultural and liturgical tradition with the Orthodox, but they have remained in communion with Rome. Some tensions still exist between Orthodox and Eastern Catholic Catholics.

Martin Luther and the Protestant Reformation

Scholars can identify many complex causes of the Reformation. Most noticeable were the widespread corruption in the Catholic Church, marked by such abuses as the sale of sacraments and absentee bishops who made their living through collections, as well as rampant superstition and an undereducated clergy. Yet deeper factors were broad cultural changes, such as the shift from a feudal to a capitalistic social system, bringing with it a rise in nationalism, literacy (because of the printing press), and a new middle class. A church that seemed entrenched

---

4. Jean Comby, *How to Read Church History* (London: SCM, 1985), 1:132.

in the thought-forms of the Middle Ages came to be disrespected by many people who had new sets of expectations prompted by these cultural shifts.

Although many organized protest movements in Christianity preceded and came after Martin Luther, Luther himself symbolizes the heart of the Protestant Reformation. An Augustinian monk who originally intended only internal church reform, and who preferred that his followers be called "Christians," not "Lutherans," Luther did not set out to be excommunicated for refusing to back down on the charges he laid at the doorstep of the Catholic Church and of the papacy. "Here stand I; I can do no other," he told his accusers.

Initially, Luther became upset over the fund-raising by the sale of indulgences to raise money for building St. Peter's Basilica in Rome. His famous *Ninety-Five Theses* of 1517 concern entirely this issue.[5] Indulgences are remissions of punishment due for sins, usually granted in recognition of good works, pilgrimage, or prayer. Luther objected to indulgences being sold for money, being applied to punishment in purgatory, and being "plenary," meaning that all punishment whatsoever would be remitted. Luther held that the authority of the pope to bind or loose (release) from specific penalties was limited to canonical penalties in this life. The *Ninety-Five Theses* were widely distributed throughout Europe. The next few years were filled with various threats, engagements, disputes, and debates between Luther and representatives of Rome.

In 1520, Luther wrote three works now known as the "Three Treatises" or "Reformation Treatises" that contain his full-blown theology of reform.[6] His attacks on the papacy and the current state of the church escalated enormously. Luther saw the Catholic Church and the papacy as human inventions that were falsely claiming divine power. In this, they represented not God but the Devil. Luther called for recognition that Christians possess the spiritual power to baptize, forgive sins, and consecrate the Eucharist, even though it remains appropriate that certain people be officially ordained as ministers to do these things. In contrast with traditional Catholic teaching, Luther argued that ordained ministers differ only in function, not in essence, from other Christians. He condemned the worldly, ostentatious style of the pope. He called for the abolition of forced celibacy among clerics, endowed Masses for the dead, chapels intended as places of pilgrimage for the raising of money, church licenses, papal bulls, and begging, as well as indulgences. He argued that Christians are saved by faith alone, not by their works; that Scripture alone is the Word of God, not the decisions of human beings; that the church should humbly pick up its cross, not proclaim its own glory.

---

5. The *Ninety-Five Theses* can be found on the website of Project Wittenberg, *http://www.iclnet .org/pub/resources/text/wittenberg/luther/web/ninetyfive.html*.

6. The *Three Treatises* are *An Open Letter to the Christian Nobility, http://www.iclnet.org/pub /resources/text/wittenberg/luther/web/nblty-01.html; The Babylonian Captivity of the Church, http:// www.lutherdansk.dk/Web-babylonian%20Captivitate/Martin%20Luther.htm; and Concerning Christian Liberty, http://www.iclnet.org/pub/resources/text/wittenberg/luther/web/cclib-1.html*.

That same year, 1520, a papal bull was issued that condemned Luther's writings and gave him sixty days to recant. At the imperial Diet of Worms in 1521, Luther stated unequivocally that he would not withdraw his positions, because he found nothing in reason or Scripture to convince him to do so. At that, the Reformation was fully underway. Luther spent his remaining years working for church reform. Among other things, he tried to make the basics of the Christian faith available to all the people by translating the Scriptures into German and writing the first catechism in history.

Until recent years, it was difficult to find a balanced treatment of the Reformation. Protestants and Catholics have both been grossly one-sided in their portrayals of the characters and events of the time. However, each side can point proudly to instances of true outreach and attempts at compromise. Each side can also find plenty of examples of its own pride, arrogance, stubbornness, and narrow-mindedness.

During the last five hundred years, hundreds of Protestant denominations have emerged. All share in having some distance from the papacy. Some, such as Episcopalians, maintain an apostolic succession of bishops. Others, such as Methodists and Presbyterians, place democratic authority in the people who form the congregations. Yet others, such as Baptists, grant final authority to the individual who interprets Scripture by the Holy Spirit within.

The Worldwide Pentecostal Movement

In the early twentieth century, groups of Christians experienced spiritual phenomena that they interpreted as representing gifts (or charisms) of the Holy Spirit, such as speaking in tongues, prophesying, and healing. The movement that sprang up among these Christians is known as Pentecostalism. Pentecostals see a strong link between their movement and the story of Pentecost found in Acts of the Apostles:

> When the day of Pentecost had come, they were all together in one place. And suddenly from heaven there came a sound like the rush of a violent wind, and it filled the entire house where they were sitting. Divided tongues, as of fire, appeared among them, and a tongue rested on each of them. All of them were filled with the Holy Spirit and began to speak in other languages, as the Spirit gave them ability. (Acts 2:1–4)

Some Pentecostals still identify as Protestants, but others think of themselves as having moved beyond the constraints of the old Protestant-Catholic divides to have a more immediate link to God through the Holy Spirit present and active among them in spontaneous and even playful ways.

Starting in the 1960s, many Catholics, while remaining within the Catholic Church, joined what is called the charismatic renewal, which itself shares many features of Pentecostalism. Today, more than 200 million Catholics are included among those who make up the charismatic renewal. When this number is added to the more than 400 million Pentecostals in the world today, one arrives at the staggering figure of 600 million, which accounts for more than one-quarter of the 2.18 billion Christians in the world.[7] Much, though by no means all, of this growth has been in what statisticians call the Global South. Christians overall represent close to one-third of the current world population.

Summary

To gain perspective on the divisions that exist within Christianity today, this chapter reviewed the diversity in the New Testament, the Greek-Roman schism, the Protestant Reformation, and the Pentecostal movement.

Many Christians, looking to what Jesus says in the Gospel of John about his desire for unity among his followers, consider Christian division a scandal. There are no easy answers for people, whether Protestant or Catholic, about these issues. An ecumenical perspective acknowledges there are two sides of the story as Christians try to work out a reconciliation that respects their diversity while bringing about real unity.

The next chapter examines some of the progress being made in the ecumenical movement today.

For Further Reflection

1. Which of the many issues that have divided Christians strike you as most significant?
2. Which of the many issues that have divided Christians strike you as least significant?
3. How might Raymond Brown's study of diversity in the New Testament be useful for ecumenical dialogue today?
4. For both the Greek-Roman schism and the Protestant Reformation, can you distinguish between issues that are "religious" and issues that are more "cultural"?
5. Are you surprised to learn about the number of Pentecostals and charismatic Catholics in the world today? What do you think might account for the rapid growth of these styles of worship?

---

7. Pew Research Center, "The Global Religious Landscape," Washington, DC, December 2012, http://www.pewforum.org/2012/12/18/global-religious-landscape-exec.

Suggested Readings

Brown, Raymond. *The Churches the Apostles Left Behind.* New York: Paulist Press, 1984.

Cleenewerck, Laurent. *His Broken Body: Understanding and Healing the Schism between the Roman Catholic and Eastern Orthodox Churches.* Washington, DC: Euclid University Consortium Press, 2008.

Lull, Timothy F., and William R. Russell. *Martin Luther's Basic Theological Writings.* Minneapolis: Fortress, 2012.

MacCulloch, Diarmaid. *All Things Made New: The Reformation and Its Legacy.* New York: Oxford University Press, 2016.

VanDoodewaard, Rebecca. *Reformation Women: Sixteenth-Century Figures Who Shaped Christianity's Rebirth.* Grand Rapids: Reformation Heritage, 2017.

Vondey, Wolfgang. *Pentecostalism: A Guide for the Perplexed.* New York: Bloomsbury, 2013.

Ware, Kallistos. *The Orthodox Way.* Crestwood, NY: St. Vladimir's Seminary Press, 1995.

9

Ecumenical Progress

Martin Luther taught that justification—the removal of the guilt of sin and restoration to communion with God—comes through faith and not works. When I was in Catholic grade school in the early sixties, however, I was taught that I needed to work out my salvation through a combination of faith and works. It was even suggested that if I was approaching a Protestant church while walking down the street, I should cross the street and pass it from the other side. Not everyone said such things, but the overall atmosphere was anything but Protestant-friendly.

Years later, as Catholic parents, my wife and I would use a joke to explain why we sent one of our four sons to a Lutheran university. We said we had to find a school that would accept him on faith without works. The actual reason was that he wanted to play football there. The true feeling that my wife and I had was we were glad he chose a Lutheran university that embraced faith as an explicit part of its mission. We did not have anything against public or state universities—quite the contrary. It occurred to us, however, that, after all, it was a Christian school. We lived in a world that had made enough ecumenical progress since the time I was a child that we didn't really have to explain our decision—we just thought the joke was funny.

Overview

This chapter will examine progress toward the goal of the ecumenical movement, expressed as "full, visible unity." Some clear advances have been made concerning former divisions over the topic of justification and the role of good works in relation to salvation. More progress is needed concerning matters of church structure, such as the role of the papacy. This chapter will also address the debate concerning how much more progress is needed before full communion can be achieved. Finally, despite the many frustrations experienced within the ecumenical movement, a great cultural shift has been taking place whereby more and more Christians accept each other on an everyday basis. That fact is not ignored.

Full, Visible Unity

The World Council of Churches (WCC), founded in 1948 and centered in Geneva, does not consider itself to be a "church," but rather, a worldwide fellowship of churches seeking full, visible unity. Visible unity is not a vague belief that, ultimately, Christians are one despite their differences. It is, rather, a reality expressed in common worship and shared Christian service.

The Catholic Church is not formally a member of the WCC. This was decided prior to Vatican II, a decision based on the Catholic Church's historical understanding of itself as not simply one church or denomination among others, but rather as the church founded by Christ with authority passed down from the apostles, and also as the church from which other Christians have broken away. The Catholic Church's expectations regarding ecumenism prior to Vatican II are often labeled a "theology of return." In this view, ecumenism is accomplished when other Christians surrender and return to the true church.

Despite its lack of formal membership in the WCC, however, the Catholic Church is a highly active participant in many of the dialogues and projects the council sponsors. Since Vatican II, the Catholic Church has considered other Christian churches and ecclesial communities to be in partial, but not full, communion with itself. Through ecumenical dialogue and other shared endeavors, the Catholic Church hopes to move toward full, visible communion. The Catholic Church leaders of today do not envision full, visible communion as an institutional merger that would halt the continued existence of various Christian traditions. There would still be Methodists, Presbyterians, Anglicans, Orthodox, Baptists, Pentecostals, Catholics, and others. Instead, full, visible communion will be accomplished when Christians can recognize and affirm sufficiently the authentic Christianity of each other and are able to justify sharing sacraments and exchanging ministers.

The Ecclesial Gift Exchange

Today, ecumenical progress is envisioned as an "ecclesial gift exchange." Each Christian tradition has its own distinctive history, beliefs, and practices that can be offered to other Christian traditions and received as gifts.[1] Can the pacifist witness of Mennonites, Quakers, and other Christian peace traditions be recognized and valued by Christians in traditions that allow for talk about just war? Can Christians appreciate the role of the papacy in creating cohesion and fostering unity in other traditions that insist upon the radical autonomy of local congregations?

---

1. Margaret O'Gara, *The Ecumenical Gift Exchange* (Collegeville, MN: Liturgical Press, 1998).

The ability for Christians to recognize and affirm each other requires two movements. The first involves particular churches making changes. How far can Christians go in finding ways of moving toward each other? The second movement, often achieved through dialogue and fellowship, involves learning and appreciating. How far can Christians go in stepping back and reconsidering the possibility of valuing differences that have historically divided churches from each other as acceptable options along a broad spectrum of legitimate options? Both movements are important for ecumenical progress.

First Movement Examples: Churches Making Changes

Several examples of churches making changes can be found in the documents of Vatican II. A strong affirmation of the role of bishops in local churches (here understood as dioceses) brought Catholics more into alignment with the Eastern Orthodox Churches (*LG* 26). The elevation of Scripture from being part of Tradition to being, along with Tradition, one of the two expressions of the one revelation in Jesus Christ, brought Catholics closer to Protestants.[2] The recognition of the importance of religious freedom and the separation of church and state opened a significant point of agreement between Catholics and Christians in Free Church traditions.[3]

Another example of churches making changes can be found in a 2004 document of the United Methodist Church, *This Holy Mystery*.[4] Much of the document is devoted to explaining the meaning and role of Holy Communion, specific to Methodist history and practice. At the same time, though, the document intends to enrich the sacramental life of Methodists by moving their beliefs and practices toward alignment with those of other Christian sacramental traditions. For example, United Methodist congregations are encouraged to hold, weekly, at least one service in which Holy Communion is offered. Also, United Methodist ministers are encouraged not to dispose of remaining bread and wine from the service but, rather, to consume whatever is left over. United Methodists are making these changes to facilitate recognition of the authenticity of their Christian beliefs and practices among Anglicans, Lutherans, Catholics, and Orthodox. Although these developments might temporarily move United Methodists further from the beliefs and practices of free churches, such as Baptists, Mennonites, Disciples of Christ, and Pentecostals, many voices in

2. *Dei verbum* (*Constitution on Divine Revelation*), 9–10, *http://www.vatican.va/archive /hist_councils/ii_vatican_council/documents/vat-ii_const_19651118_dei-verbum_en.html.*

3. The themes of religious freedom and separation of church and state run throughout *Dignitatis humanae* (*Declaration on Religious Liberty*), *http://www.vatican.va/archive/hist_councils /ii_vatican_council/documents/vat-ii_decl_19651207_dignitatis-humanae_en.html.*

4. Gayle Carlton Felton, *This Holy Mystery: A United Methodist Understanding of Holy Communion* (Nashville: Discipleship Resources, 2005).

the ecumenical movement hope for richer sacramentality to be developed, eventually, across the entire spectrum of Christian witness.

Second Movement Examples: Listening and Appreciating

A good example of the second movement, listening and appreciating, is found in the 1999 consensus document of the Lutheran World Federation and the Catholic Church, the *Joint Declaration on the Doctrine of Justification* (JDDJ).[5] Luther held that Christians are justified (saved) by faith alone and merit nothing through works that contribute to this free gift from God. Traditionally, Catholics held that although the first grace of justification is a free gift, the Christian is still responsible for working out one's salvation through works. Lutherans and Catholics retained different understandings of the importance and meaning of the doctrine of justification, but each side was willing to phrase its positions in such a way that those of the other tradition could recognize, in what was said, an authentic expression of Christian doctrine. For example, the JDDJ states Catholics believe

> good works, made possible by grace and the working of the Holy Spirit, contribute to growth in grace, so that the righteousness that comes from God is preserved and communion with Christ is deepened. When Catholics affirm the "meritorious" character of good works, they wish to say that, according to the biblical witness, a reward in heaven is promised to these works. Their intention is to emphasize the responsibility of persons for their actions, not to contest the character of those works as gifts, or far less to deny that justification always remains the unmerited gift of grace. (JDDJ 38)

Lutherans, on the other hand, believe in

> the concept of a preservation of grace and a growth in grace and faith. They do emphasize that righteousness as acceptance by God and sharing in the righteousness of Christ is always complete. At the same time, they state that there can be growth in its effects in Christian living. When they view the good works of Christians as the fruits and signs of justification and not as one's own "merits," they nevertheless also understand eternal life in accord with the New Testament as unmerited "reward" in the sense of the fulfillment of God's promise to the believer. (JDDJ 39)

---

5. Lutheran World Federation and the Catholic Church, *Joint Declaration on the Doctrine of Justification*, *http://www.vatican.va/roman_curia/pontifical_councils/chrstuni/documents/rc_pc_chrstuni _doc_31101999_cath-luth-joint-declaration_en.html*.

The JDDJ is labeled a "consensus," not because the two sides agree on exactly the same position, but rather, because they agree that their different understandings and expressions of the doctrine of justification no longer represent a church-dividing issue. Each is able to recognize, in the doctrinal understanding of the other, when phrased in a particular way, an authentic understanding of Christian faith, even though that understanding is not identical with their own understanding.

Ready or Not?

Reaching consensus on the doctrine of justification represents a significant step toward full, visible communion between Lutherans and Catholics. During the past few decades, Lutherans and Catholics have reached consensus on a number of specific questions. Still, a number of problems persist. Some Catholics think that justification is a relatively small issue when compared with the remaining church-dividing differences over the nature of church authority, ordained ministry, and sacraments. Some Lutherans do not belong to the Lutheran World Federation. Even among those who do belong, there was dissent concerning the JDDJ document. Some believe the Catholic Church today is every bit as corrupt and self-glorifying as it was during the Reformation.

In recent decades, a number of Protestant communities, often groups of Lutherans and Reformed Christians and some Anglicans, have reached full visible communion. Such breakthroughs, though, have their limits: they represent a very small percentage of world Christians, and there remain many different types of Lutherans (e.g., Evangelical Lutheran Church of America or Missouri Synod Lutherans) who are not in full communion with each other. The same is true among Reformed Christians. Even in those cases where full communion has been achieved, there can be remaining difficulties, such as churches that do not ordain women accepting only male ministers from those who do ordain women, and those who do not ordain active LGBTQ+ individuals as ministers accepting only heterosexual ministers from those who do. The ordination of LGBTQ+ persons has also led to disagreements and even splits among groups of Christians who had been formerly united.

Is the cup of ecumenical progress half full or half empty? On the one hand, the number and quality of ecumenical study documents, convergence texts, and consensus agreements is impressive. If full communion requires mutual understanding and affirmation, then the long, hard work of the formal ecumenical dialogues is justified and necessary. The late Jeffrey Gros, a Catholic leader in ecumenical matters, once told a dialogue group that full visible communion, when it comes, will not be like the result of a clear logical equation by which A leads to B, which leads to C, which finally yields the conclusion D. Still, at that time, Christians will be able to say the achievement was built upon the difficult, sometimes painful efforts of those now participating in this process.

Some voices in the ecumenical movement are so frustrated with what they perceive to be the lack of sufficient progress in the formal dialogue process that they wish to simply declare unity now. They argue that the time has come to act more urgently in forging bonds of unity and addressing, together, the pressing challenges of poverty, war, and ecological destruction posed by the world today. Even if there is still a long way to go in coming to understand and appreciate one another, much has been achieved and a pattern of reconciliation has been established. For various reasons, it is better to pray and act together now and pursue further understanding and mutual appreciation as time goes by.[6] Those who favor this direction tend to think that remaining differences have more to do with historical contingencies, political developments, and cultural differences than with anything theologically relevant to Christian faith.

Others argue, to the contrary, that many Christians have not yet reached the point at which they can reasonably claim to be in full communion with each other. These individuals worry that if full, visible communion is declared too soon, the changes that all churches need to make as well as the efforts at appreciating others will quickly slow to a halt. To ignore that full, visible communion requires a true sharing of faith would result in a watered-down form of unity. Would it be okay, for example, for a Christian who held many misunderstandings and even deep prejudices about the Catholic Church to receive the Eucharist at a Catholic Mass? Is there value in the Catholic belief that those who receive the Eucharist together should share the same faith?

The Papacy, Change, and Contrasting Ecumenical Goals

Catholics cannot, however, expect other Christians to be the only ones who need to change. Catholics will need to change too. On the one hand, as Avery Dulles said, "No Catholic theologian will deny the desirability of all Christians coming to accept the Petrine office [the papacy, or office of Peter] as exercised by the Bishop of Rome."[7] On the other hand, the exercise of the papacy is a crucial

---

6. See Paul M. Collins, Gerard Mannion, Gareth J. Powell, and Kenneth Wilson, eds., *Christian Community Now: Ecclesiological Investigations* (New York: T&T Clark, 2008); Roger Haight, *Christian Community in History*, vol. 3, *Ecclesial Existence* (New York: Continuum, 2004); Konrad Raiser, "Ecumenism in Search of a New Vision," in *The Ecumenical Movement: An Anthology of Key Texts and Voices*, ed. Michael Kinnamon (Geneva: World Council of Churches Publications, 2016), 49–54.

7. Avery Dulles, "The Church as Communion," in *New Perspectives on Historical Theology: Essays in Memory of John Meyendorf*, ed. Bradley Nassif (Grand Rapids: Eerdmans, 1996), 138. Dulles adds, though, that ecumenism cannot be reduced to this one objective.

point for change if ecumenical progress is to take place. As Archbishop John Quinn said,

> In considering the papal office and the call to Christian unity, we have to confront the challenging truth that it is not permitted to defer unity until there is a pope who can fulfill everyone's expectations or agenda. We cannot hold unity hostage until there is a perfect pope in a perfect church. Christian unity will require sacrifice. But it cannot mean that all the sacrifices must be made by those who want full communion with the Catholic Church while the Catholic Church herself makes no significant sacrifices.[8]

John Paul II expressed his openness to reexamining the role of the papacy in his 1995 encyclical, *Ut unum sint* (*That They May Be One*), in which he asked forgiveness for past failings of the papacy (*UUS* 88) and spoke appreciatively of the fresh look being given to the office by other ecclesial communities (*UUS* 89). He asked that Catholics and other Christians might consider, together, the forms that the Petrine ministry might take:

> This is an immense task, which we cannot refuse and which I cannot carry out by myself. Could not the real but imperfect communion existing between us persuade Church leaders and their theologians to engage with me in a patient and fraternal dialogue in which, leaving useless controversies behind, we could listen to one another, keeping before us only the will of Christ for his church . . . ? (*UUS* 96)[9]

On the one hand, the pope asking for advice from Christians of other traditions concerning the form his Petrine ministry might take represented a surprising and radical move. On the other hand, there are many Christians who hope full visible communion requires only that other Christians be willing to understand and appreciate the role the pope plays in the Roman Catholic tradition and in Eastern Catholic Churches, not that they accept the papacy as directly involved in their own traditions. Such differences in ecumenical goals and expectations can be as difficult to work out as the differences in beliefs and practices themselves.

---

8. John Quinn, "The Exercise of the Primacy and the Costly Call to Unity," in *The Exercise of the Primacy: Continuing the Dialogue*, ed. Phyllis Zagano and Terrence W. Tilley (New York: Crossroad, 1998), 1–28, especially 25. This Oxford Lecture of Quinn is also available here: "The Exercise of the Primacy: Facing the Cost of Christian Unity," *Commonweal* (1996): 11–20, and "Considering the Papacy," *Origins* 26 (1996): 119–28.

9. Pope John Paul II, *Ut unum sint*, http://w2.vatican.va/content/john-paul-ii/en/encyclicals/documents/hf_jp-ii_enc_25051995_ut-unum-sint.html.

Beyond the Official Dialogues

Much ecumenical growth takes place outside of officially sponsored dialogues and institutional agreements. Consider spiritual ecumenism, receptive ecumenism, and the progress being made in everyday Christian life.

Vatican II's *Unitatis redintegratio* (*Decree on Ecumenism*) called for Catholics to practice a "spiritual ecumenism" (*UR* 8–9). Spiritual ecumenism begins with a change of heart. Catholics must acknowledge their own sinfulness. They must be open to forgiving others. They need to pray that they can renew their lives. They must also pray for church unity. Such prayer should occur not only among themselves but also along with their separated brothers and sisters. Further, Catholics need to learn about their separated brothers and sisters and engage in dialogue with them.

Something of this spirit is being lived out in the academic world through a practice called "receptive ecumenism."[10] Receptive ecumenism is an intellectual movement not intended to replace the official ecumenical dialogues but to run parallel to them and support them. Often, the dialogues become bogged down in negotiations in which the participants, ultimately, defend their own turf, even as they are learning from the other and perhaps making concessions. In their rare worst moments, the official ecumenical dialogues can become a showdown, similar to landowners haggling about boundary lines. A degree of this defensiveness is on an unconscious level. Some might, at times, be justified. After all, unity is not to be bought at just any price.

Receptive ecumenism focuses on the process by which Christians of one tradition learn about and come to appreciate what Christians of other traditions have to offer. Baptists engage in appreciative studies of Catholic traditions and practices. Methodists study Anglican perspectives on worship. Catholics study the Pentecostal experience of the Holy Spirit. The point of receptive ecumenism is to shelve our tendencies for defensiveness as we learn to understand and appreciate the perspective of others. This process lays the groundwork for the real growth in communion that needs to precede official declarations.

Beyond these intellectual efforts are shared prayer and practices that have been taking place among Christians from varied traditions. In 1986, John Paul II led a World Day of Prayer in Assisi that involved thirty-two Christian organizations and eleven non-Christian religious organizations. Since then, there have been several similar meetings.[11] Among its many efforts, the World Council of Churches sponsors "The Ecumenical Prayer Cycle" that gathers together

---

10. Paul D. Murray, ed., *Receptive Ecumenism and the Call to Catholic Learning: Exploring a Way for Contemporary Ecumenism* (Oxford: Oxford University Press, 2008).

11. Pope Francis's message given at the 2016 World Day of Prayer in Assisi can be found at *http:// w2.vatican.va/content/francesco/en/speeches/2016/september/documents/papa-francesco_20160920_assisi -preghiera-pace.html*.

Representatives of many faith traditions unite to pray for world peace in a service in Assisi on October 27, 1986. Left to right are the Anglican Archbishop of Canterbury Robert Runcie, the Orthodox Archbishop of Thyateira and Great Britain Methodios, Pope John Paul II, and the Dalai Lama.

Christians of various traditions to direct their prayers toward causes throughout the globe.[12] The WCC also sponsors ecumenical efforts for addressing climate change, disease, hunger, and other social issues. Various forms of ecumenical prayer and action can be found on national, regional, and local levels.

Perhaps the most striking ecumenical development in the past several decades is the deep and widespread change of heart evident among many Christians on an everyday level. One can still find misunderstanding, harsh feelings, and mutual rejection in the Christian world. The momentum, however, appears to be in the direction of open-mindedness and goodwill. Today, I tell my students that to be Catholic is to be ecumenically minded. Anything less would be in contradiction to our clear teachings. I experience a similar new openness in Christians of many faith traditions.

Summary

In the beginning of this chapter, I mentioned the joke my wife and I told about sending our son to a Lutheran university that would take him on faith without works. Those who most appreciated our joke were Lutherans. On the university

---

12. Hugh McCullum and Terry MacArthur, eds., *In God's Hands: Common Prayer for the World* (Geneva: World Council of Churches, 2006); see also the website: *https://www.oikoumene.org/en/resources/prayer-cycle?b_start:int=2.*

website, I once read that they called their teams "Crusaders" because of their Lutheran heritage. In the spirit of ecumenical cooperation, I emailed the provost to explain that, although I had no objection to the name "Crusaders," Luther had condemned religious crusades. The statement tying the name in with their Lutheran heritage was removed within the hour.

This chapter set an ecumenical tone and framework for understanding the Catholic Church that can be presupposed throughout the rest of this book. Chapter 10 will examine the basic structures of the Catholic Church.

For Further Reflection

1. Do you have your own story or a story from your family concerning either ecumenical prejudices or ecumenical growth?

2. Are you more inclined to support those who urge immediate widespread sacramental sharing among Christians of different traditions or those who caution that deeper mutual understanding is still needed? Why?

3. Some Christians think full, visible communion should include a universal, though transformed, role for the papacy. Others think simply understanding and appreciating the role the pope plays in the Catholic Church is enough. Can a bridge be built between these alternative visions?

4. Why is it that attempts at ecumenical progress can be so difficult and frustrating?

5. Do you see hope for full, visible communion to be achieved among large numbers of Christians in the not-so-distant future?

Suggested Readings

Evangelical Lutheran Church of America and the US Conference of Catholic Bishops. "Declaration on the Way: Church, Ministry and Eucharist." 2015. *http://www.usccb.org/beliefs-and-teachings/ecumenical-and-interreligious /ecumenical/lutheran/upload/Declaration_on_the_Way-for-Website.pdf.*

Felton, Gayle Carlton. *This Holy Mystery: A United Methodist Understanding of Holy Communion.* Nashville: Discipleship Resources, 2005. *http:// s3.amazonaws.com/Website_Properties/what-we-believe/documents/this -holy-mystery-communion.PDF.*

Kinnamon, Michael. *The Ecumenical Movement: An Anthology of Key Texts and Voices.* Geneva: World Council of Churches Publications, 2016.

Lutheran World Federation and the Catholic Church. *Joint Declaration on the Doctrine of Justification.* 1999. *http://www.vatican.va/roman_curia/pontifical*

_councils/chrstuni/documents/c_pc_chrstuni_doc_31101999_cath-luth
-joint-declaration_en.html.

Lutheran World Federation and the Pontifical Council for Promoting Christian Unity. *From Conflict to Communion: Lutheran-Catholic Common Commemoration of the Reformation in 2017.* https://www.lutheranworld.org/sites/default/files/From%20Conflict%20to%20Communion.pdf.

O'Gara, Margaret. *The Ecumenical Gift Exchange.* Collegeville, MN: Liturgical Press, 1998.

Peterson, Cheryl M. *Who Is the Church? An Ecclesiology for the Twenty-First Century.* Minneapolis: Fortress, 2013.

Pontifical Council for Promoting Christian Unity. Documents. *http://www.vatican.va/roman_curia/pontifical_councils/chrstuni/index.htm.*

US Conference of Catholic Bishops. Ecumenical and Interreligious Affairs. *http://www.usccb.org/beliefs-and-teachings/ecumenical-and-interreligious/index.cfm.*

World Council of Churches. Documents. *https://www.oikoumene.org/en/resources/documents.*

Bishops and the Pope

Some years ago, I began a class on the episcopacy, the office of bishop, by asking students, "What do you think a bishop is?" After a pause, a student raised her hand and said that a bishop is someone who is higher than a priest. The rest of the students nodded; the explanation had captured their ideas well.

As a teacher, I talk about bishops in various ways. I speak about the historical development of their office, of their place in the structure of the Catholic Church, and of the nature and extent of their powers and authority. Through the course of my theological studies, however, I had forgotten the common sense experience of the ordinary Catholic without specialized training. "A bishop is someone who is higher than a priest." Why didn't I think of that?

It is important for us to remember this perspective as we explore the episcopacy in a more structured and theoretical fashion. For Catholics, bishops function symbolically, as people who are "up the ladder" of power, authority, and prestige. They are the leaders of the Catholic Church. Many people function in various leadership roles, but it is the bishops—together with the pope, the bishop of Rome—who have the official capacity to lead and have the final say in matters affecting the Catholic Church as a whole.

Overview

This chapter will discuss the collegial power of the bishops, their role in the Catholic Church, papal primacy and infallibility, and the current emphasis on humility and service. This material corresponds with chapter 3 of *Lumen gentium* (*Dogmatic Constitution on the Church*). Also relevant is Vatican II's *Decree on the Pastoral Office of Bishops in the Church*. Following the organization of *Lumen gentium*, I have intentionally delayed any in-depth exploration of the structure of the Catholic Church until it could be appreciated within the more general context of the mystery of the church and relations among Christians of various traditions. Now we are ready to address church structure.

Collegiality

Clarifying the role of bishops was a priority on the Vatican II agenda. Vatican I had declared the primacy and infallibility of the pope, but that council had not completed its work on bishops because the Franco-Prussian War forced it to adjourn abruptly. This is one reason why that understanding of papal power tended to be exaggerated among Catholics: there was no complementary appreciation of the authority of the bishops. Vatican II needed to clarify the relationship between papal and episcopal authority.

Although strongly reaffirming the Vatican I teaching about papal primacy and infallibility, *Lumen gentium* introduced the concept of collegiality. The bishops form a stable group or college. This college of bishops is continuous with the twelve apostles whom Jesus sent to preach the gospel. This continuity is known as apostolic succession. Acting as a brother bishop, the pope functions within this college as its head. The papacy finds its heritage in Peter, whom Jesus chose to be the head of the apostles. Current theological debates concern whether the office of the papacy must always be considered in conjunction with the college or whether it can, in some sense, function independently. Interpreters of *Lumen gentium* agree, though, that the document emphasizes both the apostolic authority of the bishops and the primacy of the pope.

"Collegiality" functions today with two meanings. In its strict sense, the term refers to the sharing of authority among bishops and the pope as detailed in *Lumen gentium*. In its broader, unofficial sense, "collegiality" refers to a general movement within the church toward more sharing of authority on all levels.

In the 1980s, during the early years of John Paul II's papacy, the US bishops wrote pastoral letters on peace and economic justice. The process by which they wrote these documents reflected the broader meaning of "collegiality." The bishops formed a writing committee that interviewed experts. Then a first draft was widely distributed in dioceses and universities to solicit the feedback of the Catholic faithful as well as other interested persons. A second draft was written in response to the suggestions and criticisms. This second draft was distributed in the same manner as the first draft. After another revision, the letter was presented for the bishops' final approval.

The bishops presented their teachings to the public with a clear note of humility:

> We believe that the recommendations in our letter are reasonable and balanced. In analyzing the economy, we reject ideological extremes and start from the fact that ours is a "mixed" economy, the product of a long history of reform and adjustment. We know that some of our specific recommendations are controversial. As bishops, we do not claim to make these prudential judgments with the same kind of authority that marks our declarations of principle. But we feel obliged to teach

by example how Christians can undertake concrete analysis and make specific judgments on economic issues. The church's teachings cannot be left at the level of appealing generalities. (no. 20)[1]

Many US Catholics at that time thought the collegial spirit reflected in this process should become a model for how authority might operate throughout the church as a whole.

In more recent years, as the culture wars have gained an ever greater foothold in the United States, the bishops have taken strong stands against what John Paul II had labeled the "culture of death" that offers legalized abortion on demand and that accepts assisted suicide, embryonic stem cell research, and unsubtle encouragements for teenagers to engage in safe sex. Supporters of this cultural critique add to this list narcissism, cynicism, and despair.

In 2012, the US bishops launched a controversial campaign called "Fortnight for Freedom," aimed to defend religious liberty. The Fortnight for Freedom is now a yearly event. In contrast to the documents issued in the 1980s, the bishops' declarations issuing from the Fortnight concerning religious freedom have had an authoritative and even alarmist character. Some bishops openly denounced the Obama administration for provisions within the Patient Protection and Affordable Care Act (popularly known as Obamacare) that require businesses to provide contraceptives as part of their employee health care packages. Some methods of contraception were claimed to be abortive. The Obama administration's attempts to have contraceptive coverage be paid separately by the insurance companies were rejected as conceptual manipulations that do nothing to change the underlying realities. Defenders of the bishops' actions portrayed the Obama administration as an authoritarian secular state that denies rather than protects the religious freedom of its citizens.

US Catholics have been deeply divided about the bishops' strategies and tactics. Many interpreted the government administration as trying to mediate between the legitimate concerns of the Catholic Church and the competing but also legitimate concerns of those who see the availability of contraception as an issue of women's health and women's rights.

Catholics on both sides of this issue felt relief during Pope Francis's 2015 visit to the United States, during which he met with the president and delivered speeches to congress, the United Nations, and the citizens gathered at the Independence Mall in downtown Philadelphia. On the one hand, Pope Francis clearly and unambiguously spoke in defense of life as well as religious liberty. The substance of his message included positions deeply challenging to both the

---

1. US Catholic Bishops, *Economic Justice for All: Pastoral Letter on Catholic Social Teaching and the US Economy*, 1986, *http://www.usccb.org/upload/economic_justice_for_all.pdf*.

left and the right. On the other hand, his engaging, respectful, persuasive, and humble tone seemed to set a standard for how to communicate both within the Catholic Church and with others.[2]

Pope Francis has been a strong supporter of the collegiality associated with Vatican II.[3] Collegiality differs from both monarchy and democracy. An absolute monarch may seek advice but is not bound to take it. In representative democracy, the voice of the people is the final word, and any representative who does not reflect the will of the majority may be voted out of office. In Catholic collegiality, the head of a college or authoritative body must take ultimate responsibility for decisions that are made, but is expected to act in a consultative manner so that what is expressed is not a personal opinion but the faith of the church. When a leader is said not to have acted in a collegial manner, the implication is that other peoples' opinions were not considered seriously.

Bishop as Priest, Prophet, King

Lumen gentium's chapter on the People of God proclaimed that Christians participate in the threefold ministry of Jesus as priest, prophet, and king (PPK). The particular way that bishops participate in this ministry is by sanctifying, teaching, and governing. As Jesus instituted the Eucharist in memory of his life, death, and Resurrection, so the bishop takes the place of Christ in the diocese and is charged with administering the Eucharist and other sacraments. As Jesus taught in parables and preached the coming of the kingdom, so the bishop is charged with teaching and preaching the gospel. As Jesus led the disciples and formed a community that continues even in the present time, so the bishop is charged with the official leadership of the diocese.

THREEFOLD MINISTRY OF THE BISHOP	
Bishop's Ministry	**Tasks**
Priest	Sanctify, give sacraments
Prophet	Teach, preach the gospel
King	Govern, lead

---

2. All of Pope Francis's official speeches given during his journey to the United States in September 2015 can be found at *http://w2.vatican.va/content/francesco/en/speeches/2015/september.index.html#speeches.*

3. Pope Francis, *Evangelii gaudium*, no. 32 and no. 246, *http://w2.vatican.va/content/francesco/en/apost_exhortations/documents/papa-francesco_esortazione-ap_20131124_evangelii-gaudium.html.*

Taken together with the pope as their head, the college of bishops has authority over the whole Catholic Church. When the bishops are referred to specifically in regard to their teaching authority, again taken together with the pope, they are known as the magisterium. The magisterium, then, is the authority exercised by those responsible for the official teaching of the Catholic Church. Its highest forms of expression are papal statements proclaimed *ex cathedra*, that is, in the pope's capacity as the official head of the church, and the formal doctrinal definitions of ecumenical councils. Magisterial teaching is also found when there is fundamental agreement among the bishops, even when not gathered in council; in the teachings of synods that are representative of the bishops; and in documents issued by Vatican offices approved by the pope.

Taken individually, the bishop is the head of a diocese. No individual bishop (other than the pope) has authority over the church as a whole or over any diocese other than his own. The bishop does, though, have complete authority over his own diocese. This authority is proper to his office as a successor of the apostles, and so the bishop is not simply the representative of the pope.

The succession of church leadership from Christ to the apostles to the bishops cannot be traced with pinpoint historical detail. Theologian Jean-Marie Tillard, who specializes in the church of the early centuries, sees a complex history of Church Fathers coming to affirm strong links between the bishops and the apostles.[4] By about the middle of the second century, a structure was in place throughout the Christian world of local communities (now dioceses) headed by a bishop. Each bishop represented the faith and love of the people in his local church, as well as the connection of the local church with the universal, or catholic, church. The bishop's role was linked with the celebration of the Eucharist, itself an expression of unity in Christ. In this ritual sense, the bishop was seen as acting in the place of Christ in his local church.

Francis Sullivan, a theologian who specializes in church authority, compares the affirmation of the church-wide episcopacy to the development of the canon of Scripture, a process that took several centuries.[5] Those who decided which books did and did not belong in the Bible were bishops who decided such matters in councils. Catholics believe the Holy Spirit guided the development of a church-wide episcopacy. So, too, did the Holy Spirit guide the gradual development, throughout many centuries, of the role of the bishop of Rome as the head of the entire Catholic Church.

---

4. Jean-Marie Tillard, *Church of Churches: The Ecclesiology of Communion*, trans. R. C. De Peaux, O. Praem (Collegeville, MN: Liturgical Press, 1992 [1987]).

5. Francis Sullivan, *From Apostles to Bishops: The Development of the Episcopacy in the Early Church* (Mahwah, NJ: Paulist Press, 2001), 229–30.

Power to the Pope

Papal primacy means that the pope, by virtue of his office, is the head of the Catholic Church. Throughout much of the church's history, there has been controversy about whether an ecumenical council representing the bishops might not constitute the highest church authority. In the Catholic Church, this matter has been settled decisively in favor of the pope. The passages in Scripture in which Jesus chooses Peter to be the head of the twelve apostles, as well as the long and complex tradition of the leadership of the bishop of Rome, provide the underpinnings for this position. One of the main purposes of the office of the papacy is to function as a source of unity for all Christians.[6]

Contemporary theologians disagree about the extent of the pope's constitutional obligation to consult other bishops and the faithful as a whole when making decisions, but *Lumen gentium* is clear that the pope is not simply a dictator who has no restraints on his authority. Take, for example, the doctrine of papal infallibility. To say that the pope is infallible does not mean that the pope as an individual can never make a mistake. Infallibility refers only to the pope's official capacity to define a teaching as true such that it is considered as settled beyond question for the Catholic faithful. The French Dominican theologian Yves Congar has referred to the popular tendency to include a growing body of ordinary papal teaching within the category of infallible truth as "creeping infallibility." Some Catholics may quote everyday teachings of a pope concerning a sacrament or a biblical passage as if his words automatically put all further questions to rest. Actually, only a few teachings, such as the Immaculate Conception of Mary and the Bodily Assumption of Mary, have been formally defined as infallible by a pope. Many teachings, such as the doctrine of Christ's Resurrection, could potentially be taught infallibly by the pope, but there has been no need to do so.

The Catholic Church's gift of infallibility functions as a tool to be used rarely, such as in cases when the beliefs of the faithful need special support or when false beliefs are endangering the basic teaching of the church. Who is to decide answers to crucial questions that may threaten the church's very unity? Catholics say it is the pope who has the official authority, grounded in Scripture, to decide such issues. This is what infallibility concerns.

When *Lumen gentium* emphasizes that infallible definitions of the pope are true because the pope says so, and not because of the approval of others, the point is that the office of the papacy constitutes the highest authority in the Catholic Church. If the pope, by church law, needed the approval of others, then those others would constitute a higher authority. This does not mean, though, that the opinion of others is completely disregarded.

---

6. It is unfortunately ironic that for many Protestants the papacy is a great stumbling block to unity, given that church unity is the main reason for having a pope.

Sullivan, the expert on structures of authority mentioned earlier, offered an explanation of this point of tension in his book *Magisterium*.[7] Suppose the pope came out tomorrow with a pronouncement about the faith—one that he claimed to be infallible but which the majority of Catholics around the world rejected. Is *Lumen gentium* claiming the pope must be right and those who disagree should get in line? Sullivan argues that that is one of two possibilities.

The first possibility is the pope is right and the majority of Christians need to change their belief to be in accordance with him. Sullivan gives the example that it took about fifty years for the teaching of Nicaea that Jesus is "one in being with the Father" to gain church-wide acceptance as a way of combating the Arian heresy, which denied the full divinity of Christ. So, if one accepts, today, the authority of Nicaea, one should also accept the possibility that authoritative statements can take some time to be fully received.

The second possibility discussed by Sullivan is that the pope might be wrong, not because he needs the approval of others, but because there may have been some deficiency in the process through which the pope arrived at his decision. There are several conditions that function as limitations on the official ability of the pope to define a matter infallibly. The pope must be speaking *ex cathedra*. He must not be openly in heresy or schism. He must be of sound mind and free of coercion. He must be defining a matter of faith and morals that is necessary for salvation, and so it must either be part of divine revelation or a teaching necessary to explain and defend divine revelation. Sullivan discusses how these conditions require that the pope consult the faith of the church, though they do not specify precisely *how* the pope must do this. It could be possible, then, that if the faithful, on a large scale, rejected a teaching a pope had proclaimed as infallible, the process might be reviewed to see if the pope is not a heretic, insane, being coerced, or inadequately consulting the faith of the church. When a teaching is determined to be true, though, it is technically defined as such by the pope, not needing the rubber stamp of the faithful as if they constituted a higher authority.

Lumen gentium fights against exaggerated notions of papal infallibility not only by stating its limitations but also by placing it within the context of the infallibility of the church as a whole. Infallibility, the capacity to define essential matters as certainly true, belongs, first of all, to the church. It is manifested in different ways in the pope, the bishops, and the faithful. Hence, *Lumen gentium* tells how the bishops teach infallibly when "they are in agreement on one position as to be definitively held" (*LG* 25). This is especially clear when the bishops are gathered in an ecumenical council. The document also says, "The entire body of the faithful, anointed as they are by the Holy One, cannot err in matters of

---

7. Francis A. Sullivan, *Magisterium: Teaching Authority in the Catholic Church* (New York: Paulist Press, 1983). See especially ch. 5.

the faith" (*LG* 12). This property of the People of God is called the *sensus fidei* or "sense of the faith."

Infallibility is an important characteristic of the Catholic Church as well as a useful tool that helps the church maintain the integrity of its most basic teachings. It is also, however, a source of confusion for Catholics and non-Catholics alike. Many Catholic theologians who agree wholeheartedly with the doctrine of infallibility wish that it had been called something different. In the nineteenth century, when the doctrine of papal infallibility was defined, the very concept of faith was under attack by those who claimed that faith was, at best, uncertain and more likely irrational. To people in our culture, however, "infallible" seems to imply arrogance. Nobody is infallible, we are told.

Ironically, the technical doctrine of papal infallibility does not at all mean that the pope is personally infallible; in fact, it functions as much to define the limitations of his office as it does to grant him a special ability. Infallibility is related to the Catholic belief that the church is indefectible insofar as the Holy Spirit will not ultimately mislead it. Indefectibility does not guarantee that the church will never make mistakes. Rather, it assures that the Holy Spirit will not let the church down in the long run on matters that are essential for its very identity.

Humility and Service

Amid the centuries-old arguments about who has how much authority, there has been a distinct movement stemming from Vatican II toward taking the church's connection between leadership and service more seriously than ever. Jesus said the one who would be the greatest should be as the least. He washed the feet of his disciples at the Last Supper. He said he came not to be served but to serve. He gave his life so that others might live. *Lumen gentium* says, "Just as Christ carried out the work of redemption in poverty and persecution, so the church is called to follow the same route that it might communicate the fruits of salvation" (*LG* 8). Specifically of the bishops, the document says that in the use of their power they need to remember "that one who is greater should become as the lesser and one who is the chief become as the servant" (*LG* 27; Lk 22:26–27).

In the early centuries of the Catholic Church, bishops functioned as pastoral ministers who provided spiritual leadership for their particular church. Through the growth of the church as a huge and complex organization, bishops gradually became more administrator than minister. A bishop today can be more easily compared to the CEO of a large corporation than to a priest working directly with the people. For that matter, some priests today complain that they themselves entered the priesthood to work with people and yet now function more as administrators.

In recent years, the pope and bishops have moved in the direction of a simpler lifestyle. The pope is installed rather than crowned; kissing his ring is optional; he is no longer carried into ceremonies by four seat-bearers. Pope Francis is often praised for living in the Vatican guesthouse rather than the papal apartments, for driving an old car, and for carrying his own luggage. After an investigation of a German bishop who had earned the nickname "Bishop of Bling" for his 30 million euro renovation of his residence, Pope Francis permanently removed him from office.

The role of the bishop is fraught with a difficult mixture of raw power and Christian service. In the words of St. Augustine as quoted in *Lumen gentium*, "'What I am for you terrifies me; what I am with you consoles me. For you I am a bishop; but with you I am a Christian. The former is a duty; the latter a grace. The former is a danger; the latter, salvation" (*LG* 32).

Bishops are fellow human beings and fellow Christians. Their office presents the danger that they might become out of touch with the people. Yet through that office, which bishops are called to fill in a spirit of humility, they provide the authoritative and continuous structure that links current Catholic belief and practice with the ministry of Jesus Christ.

Summary

This chapter examined collegiality and the authority of bishops, papal primacy and infallibility, and the new emphasis on humility and service. The experience of the ordinary Catholic is that a bishop is someone "higher than a priest." A more systematic overview shows that bishops are the leaders of the Catholic Church who succeed the apostles and who are responsible for sanctifying, teaching, and governing. The next chapter will focus on the priesthood.

For Further Reflection

1. What are your images of the Catholic hierarchy today?
2. Do you think that church authority should be more traditional, more collegial, or more democratic? Why?
3. How do you think most people understand the concept of papal infallibility? How does the popular understanding relate with the information in this chapter?
4. How do you understand shifts in teaching style among the US bishops? Do they represent reasonable responses to different cultural situations, or is it more complicated than that?
5. Do you find it personally important that the pope as well as many bishops seem to be pursuing simpler lifestyles?

Suggested Readings

Faggioli, Massimo. *Pope Francis: Tradition in Transition*. Mahwah, NJ: Paulist Press, 2015.

Gaillardetz, Richard R. *By What Authority? Primer on Scripture, the Magisterium, and the Sense of the Faithful*. Collegeville, MN: Liturgical Press, 2018.

Sullivan, Francis A. *From Apostles to Bishops: The Development of the Episcopacy in the Early Church*. Mahwah, NJ: Paulist Press, 2001.

Tillard, Jean-Marie. R. *Church of Churches: The Ecclesiology of Communion*. Translated by R. C. De Peaux, O. Praem. Collegeville, MN: Liturgical Press, 1992 (1987).

Ordained Priesthood

remember well a difficulty I had during my first week in graduate school at Catholic University in Washington, DC, in the late 1970s. My professors, many of whom were priests, expected to be called by their first names. At that time, I could hardly call a priest anything but "Father" without choking a bit, but I quickly got past this hesitancy.

The issue of names arose later that week when I addressed a fellow graduate student, a priest from my native Philadelphia, by his first name. He replied testily, "Didn't they teach you in your Catholic education to address a priest as 'Father'?" Embarrassed, I mumbled an apology. Standing with us, though, were two other priests, one of whom took up my cause. Whereas the average Catholic in a parish situation should address a priest formally, he argued, in our situation, as fellow students, we should be peers. The third priest agreed. The priest from Philadelphia was irritably silent. Whenever I saw this priest after that, I greeted him as "Father," but my voice strained awkwardly. We never had conversations after that initial one.

In the years prior to Vatican II, priests were regarded as far superior to laypeople. Although the life of the average priest was never easy, priests were well educated and trained in virtue. More than that, they were responsible for making Christ present in the community through the Eucharist. Their direct connection with the sacred made them men set apart. In my youth, my Catholic family and Catholic school taught me, in no uncertain terms, that the priesthood was the highest vocation to which a young man could be called. Many of the best and the brightest among male Catholic youth aspired to be priests.

Overview

The number of priests in the Catholic community shifted after Vatican II. For instance, in 1965 there was a total of 58,632 priests in the United States. In 2015, the number was 37,578.[1] A close reading of both Vatican II

---

1. Center for Applied Research in the Apostolate (CARA), "Frequently Requested Church Statistics," *http://cara.georgetown.edu/frequently-requested-church-statistics.*

and contemporary Catholic culture reveals a complex situation that reflects a shift in the very meaning of priesthood.

This chapter will discuss first a current problem with the image of the priesthood, then the meaning of the priesthood as put forth by Vatican II, and finally, the current shortage of priests as well as proposed solutions. The material in this chapter draws upon section 28 of chapter 3 of *Lumen gentium*. Two other documents of Vatican II are also relevant: *Optatam totius* (*Decree on Priestly Training*) and *Presbyterorum ordinis* (*Decree on the Ministry and Life of Priests*).[2] A related question, the ministry of women, is addressed in chapter 27 of this book.

Image Problems

Post–Vatican II, the priesthood has suffered an identity crisis. Long before the clergy sex abuse crisis, the meaning of the priesthood shifted relative to the rapid secularization of society that began to question institutional forms of authority as well as restrictions on lifestyle choices. The virtual disappearance of the US Catholic subculture that automatically respected and even revered its priests took away its main source of support.

Perhaps the perspective of the future will classify this image problem as a by-product of a long and rocky transitional period during which one meaning of priesthood was lost and had not yet been replaced by the fuller meaning of priesthood articulated at Vatican II. Vatican II helped unsettle the traditional concept of priesthood in a couple of ways. First, so much emphasis is given to the bishops in *Lumen gentium* that priests are characterized mainly as "bishop's helpers" who have little identity of their own. Although Vatican II issued an entire document that recognized the importance of priests, *Presbyterorum ordinis*, the fullness of this teaching has yet to affect the church.

Second, Vatican II tended to relativize the priesthood by placing it within a context that emphasized the ministry of all Christians through their participation in the priesthood of Christ. *Lumen gentium* insisted that the ordained priesthood is essentially different from the common priesthood of the faithful, but the precise nature of that essential difference still has not been clearly spelled out. What remains is that the role of the ordained priest is considered more analogous to the role of the laity than in the past.

---

2. See *Optatam totius* (*Decree on Priestly Training*), 1965, *http://www.vatican.va/archive/hist _councils/ii_vatican_council/documents/vat–ii_decree_19651028_optatam-totius_en.html*. *See also Presbyterorum ordinis* (*Decree on the Ministry and Life of Priests*), 1965, *http://www.vatican.va/archive /hist_councils/ii_vatican_council/documents/vat–ii_decree_19651207_presbyterorum-ordinis_en.html*.

The Meaning of Priesthood at Vatican II

In an insightful work, theologian Kenan Osborne traces the history of the Catholic priesthood through the teaching put forth at the Second Vatican Council.[3] Osborne finds, in the Vatican II documents, a coherent and profound vision capable of reviving current appreciation of the priesthood and furthering ecumenical progress. He sees the concept of the priest in the Counter-Reformation period (the four hundred years between the Council of Trent and Vatican II) being taken over and transformed within a much broader view. This broader view emerges from Vatican II's integration of new scriptural and historical perspectives available through scholarly studies. Osborne is careful to insist that the new vision does not contradict the old, but rather subsumes it within a fuller understanding.

Within this careful framework, however, Osborne is clear about the limitations of the Counter-Reformation concept of priesthood. Its main limitation is in linking the very definition of "priest" almost exclusively with the power to consecrate the Eucharist. Osborne characterizes this definition as narrow and one-sided. This definition provided the underpinning for a concept of priesthood that was overly separate, personal, and otherworldly. The priest was set apart from other people. He was thought to personally possess the priestly character and power derived from ordination, rather than exercise an office that belongs first to the church community. The role of the priest was to pray the Divine Office and distribute the sacraments, not to become caught up in the transitory, vain things of this world.

Osborne cites several significant developments in the meaning of the priesthood in the documents of Vatican II. Vatican II rooted the ministry of the priest in the ministry of Jesus as prophet, priest, and king, not just in the power to consecrate the Eucharist. Thus there was a new stress placed upon the duty of the priest to preach the gospel. There was a corresponding stress on the service role of the priest as a community leader. The priest's role in presiding at liturgy remains strong but is situated within the context of prophetic and kingly roles. The priesthood is presented in a way that is more related to other ministries in the church and thereby less separate. It is more connected with church structure and less personal or individual, and more connected with community involvement and less otherworldly.

Whereas in the pre–Vatican II church the priest would "say Mass" or even "read Mass" to the congregation, today, the priest leads the congregation in celebrating the Mass. The priest presides over the congregation, each member of which participates in a real way. *Lumen gentium* speaks of how the laity brings with them to the Mass the spiritual sacrifices of their everyday life, which "are most fittingly offered in the celebration of the Eucharist. Thus, as those everywhere

---

3. Kenan Osborne, *Priesthood: A History of the Ordained Ministry in the Roman Catholic Church* (Mahwah, NJ: Paulist Press, 1988).

who adore in holy activity, the laity consecrate the world itself to God" (*LG* 34). The traditional emphasis on the real presence of Christ in the consecrated bread and wine is complemented by a contemporary focus on the presence of Christ throughout the Eucharistic assembly. In the celebration of the Mass, there is new stress on the common priesthood of the faithful, importance of the community, spiritual value of everyday life, preaching of the word, and connection between the Eucharist and social justice. The image of the priest has been shifting accordingly.

This shift in meaning is partly what was symbolized by moving the altar away from the wall and having the priest face the people. The priest today symbolizes not only a mediator between the people and God but also a representative of a priestly people who experience Christ present among them.

A Relational Ontology

Martin Luther taught that Christians belong to the "priesthood of all believers." To become an official minister in the church is to take on a special function. In response, Counter-Reformation Catholic theology strongly emphasized the medieval concept that priesthood did not simply represent a special function within the church. Rather, an essential or "ontological" change took place within a Christian once he was ordained. "Ontology" is a branch of metaphysics that deals with the very nature of being, that is, the essence of a person or thing. "Ontological change" was thus a fancy way to say that the change brought about by the sacrament of ordination was real and integral, not simply one of function. Protestants characterized the Catholic position as "essentialism," claiming it unnecessarily treated what is simply a function as a metaphysical reality for the purpose of emphasizing the power of the priests over people. Catholics characterized the Protestant position as "functionalism," claiming it denied that priestly ordination brought about a real change for the purpose of denying the sacred power entrusted to the church and administered through the sacraments.

In recent years, some Catholic theologians, inspired by the Greek Orthodox metropolitan John Zizioulas, have tried to work out a middle position on this question. Susan Wood suggests one that tries to avoid either functionalism or essentialism.[4] A concept used to undergird this position is "relational ontology."[5] In this view, the change that takes place in the priest consists in *the relationship* he assumes with the people of the church, understood as a liturgical community.

---

4. Susan Wood, "The New Intra-Ecclesial Context for Understanding the Priesthood Today," paper given at the Common Ground Conference, San Antonio, February 28–March 2, 2003, quoted in Christopher Ruddy, *Tested in Every Way: The Catholic Priesthood in Today's Church* (New York: Crossroad, 2006), 46–47.

5. See an explanation of " relational ontology" in Richard R. Gaillardetz, "The Ecclesial Foundations of Ministry within an Ordered Communion," in *Ordering the Baptismal Priesthood: Theologies of Lay and Ordained Ministry*, ed. Susan K. Wood (Collegeville, MN: Liturgical Press, 2003), 26–51.

This new relationship is acted out most fully *within* the context of the Eucharistic assembly. It is a "real" change, but this change in relationship cannot be understood merely as either a function or as something that happens to the priest as an individual without reference to his communal connectedness. This position attempts to acknowledge that a priest is one set apart and, at the same time, a leader who represents a priestly community.

A Different Point of View

Not everyone endorses the shift in the meaning of the priesthood as explained by Osborne and by those who advocate a relational ontology. Pope John Paul II, for example, emphasized the role of the priest as a living representation of the Christian mystery.[6] Along this line, Bishop Robert Barron, a theologian, attempts to recapture the sacred and mysterious dimensions of the priest. He defines the priest as "a mystagogue, one who bears the Mystery and initiates others into it."[7] He writes,

> In the preconciliar period, the official theology of the church spoke of an "ontological change" that occurs at ordination: the priest does not simply receive the commission to perform specific tasks, he becomes someone different. This language, understood as elitist and exclusionary, has fallen into desuetude. Rather than misinterpreting the terminology of ontological change as clericalism, one should embrace the truth enshrined in the formulation. For the mystagogue is not primarily a functionary, nor someone entrusted with tasks to perform. He is a priest, someone who in his very being is the mediator between heaven and earth. Called and formed by God for the service of the community, the mystagogue is separate, unique, set apart, in the language of Scripture, holy. Priesthood affects one in one's very being, else it is a sham. Understood as a job or a ministry, priesthood becomes a shadow of itself and loses its fascination and appeal.[8]

Barron's emphasis clearly differs from Osborne's. Still, the two are not complete opposites. Speaking descriptively, it remains true to say that the Vatican II concept of the priesthood is more connected with the ministry of Jesus, more connected with the people of the church, more connected with a scripturally

---

6. Maryanne Confoy, *Religious Life and Priesthood: Perfectae Caritatis, Optatam Totius, and Presbyterorum Ordinis* (Mahwah, NJ: Paulist Press, 2008), 134–38; see also Pope John Paul II, *Pastores dabo vobis* (*I Will Give You Shepherds*), 1992, *http://w2.vatican.va/content/john-paul-ii/en/apost_exhortations/documents/hf_jp-ii_exh_25031992_pastores-dabo-vobis.html*.

7. Robert Barron, "Priest as Bearer of the Mystery," in *Priesthood in the Modern World: A Reader*, ed. Karen Sue Smith (Franklin, WI: Sheed and Ward, 1999), 94.

8. Barron, "Priest as Bearer of the Mystery," 97.

based spirituality, and more connected with community issues of justice. A relational ontology tries to emphasize simultaneously how the priest is both set apart and a leader within a priestly community. Barron's ardent stress on the priest as one set apart can be read as a rejection of what he perceives to be one-sided, overly practical, and utterly demystified views. He is not necessarily opposed to positions that truly seek a balance.

Diocesan seminaries in the United States in recent decades have earned a reputation for being more traditional than progressive. Young priests often tend to sound more like followers of Barron than of Osborne. Now, more than fifty years after Vatican II, it appears that the current state of affairs represents a transitional period that accompanies any major shift in vision.

Dealing with the Priest Shortage

From 1965–2015, the number of Catholics in the United States increased from about forty-seven million to sixty-eight million (registered in parishes) or 81.6 million (self-identified). As mentioned earlier, the number of priests has dropped from 58,632 to 37,578.

Where there used to be an average of two priests per parish, there is now one. Many parishes have merged into pastoral regions that share one priest among them. About 3,500 parishes are without a regular priest pastor. Many priests now serving in US parishes come from other countries.

In addition, there are now more than eighteen thousand permanent deacons serving in parishes. Before Vatican II, the diaconate was a temporary stage along the way to priesthood. The diaconate has now been revised to restore a concept of ministry from the early Christian centuries. It is open to married men. Deacons perform many tasks in a parish, some previously reserved to priests, such as reading the Gospel at Mass and giving the homily. Deacons perform baptisms and serve as the witness at weddings. Furthermore, in 2016 Pope Francis created a commission to study the possibility of ordaining women as deacons. There is strong historical evidence that women did serve as deacons in the early years of the church.

The biggest development so far in addressing the priest shortage has been the emergence of lay ecclesial ministers, of whom nearly forty thousand now serve in parishes. Lay ecclesial ministers will be addressed in a later chapter. Perhaps the most immediate way to increase the number of priests would be to drop the requirement for celibacy.

The Celibacy Requirement

There are many arguments in favor of retaining celibacy as a requirement for priesthood. Many Catholics view priestly celibacy as an invaluable sign of transcendence. Although it is usually admitted that celibacy is a Catholic

Church rule that can change, some argue it is a good rule that should remain in effect.

Defenders of the celibacy requirement reason along lines similar to the following: since Catholic tradition holds that Jesus himself was celibate and since the priesthood is a special way of following Jesus, such a sacrifice is appropriate. Some passages in Scripture can be interpreted as supporting this position. Further, defenders argue, celibacy functions as a sign of total dedication to bringing about the kingdom of God. It enables the priest to operate free of the obligations that come with a family. For the parish priest, one's first love is God and one's family is one's parish. Celibacy functions further as a witness that sexual activity, though beautiful and important, is not the absolute necessity it is held to be in our culture. Many of the defenders of the celibacy requirement believe that eliminating it would be simply giving in to a culture that needs to be challenged by this witness.

There are also many arguments in favor of dropping celibacy as a requirement. Here are some of the more common ones:

- There are already about two hundred married Catholic priests who had been ordained in other Christian traditions but later became Catholic.
- Some cultural changes concerning the value of sex have been good; it is no longer necessary to cut a priest off from sexual intercourse in order to see him as "pure."
- Although celibacy can function as a sign of the kingdom and a witness to sexual responsibility, that is no reason against making it optional rather than required of all.
- Although it might be true that Jesus never married, many apostles were married. To follow Jesus, should one need to have a beard or be an experienced carpenter?
- Married priests might be more pastorally sensitive to the needs of married couples and families. Moreover, is it not possible to have a total love commitment to God *and* to one's spouse at the same time? What is the conflict between loving God and loving one's spouse?
- Finally, the obligation of the Catholic Church to provide ministers for people in this time of shortage may outweigh its preference for required celibacy.

The issue of priest celibacy is a difficult one, with strong arguments on both sides. Of late some who want to drop the celibacy requirement claim a link with the sex abuse crisis; others point to sex abuse in education, the Boy Scouts, and other values-based organizations and social institutions and argue that celibacy has nothing to do with it. Inevitably, a debate about an issue such as this leads people to examine their deeper presuppositions about God, Tradition, culture, and the church.

Why Become a Priest?

Why would a Catholic man of today become a priest? Catholic priest and author Donald B. Cozzens speaks movingly of his own vocation:

> I cannot think of a more meaningful life than the life of a priest. . . .
> Here meaning and mystery embrace. The priest, as minister of God's word, is a messenger of meaning. It is his primary task to proclaim the paradox of the gospel: that life is to be found in dying to oneself; that freedom rests in our surrender to God's loving plan for us; that happiness follows upon selfless care and concern for our neighbor; that the first shall be last and the last first; that the least among us shall be the greatest! The priest knows in his heart, from his attempts to minister faithfully as a disciple of Christ and from his humbling witness to the grace of God reconciling broken spirits, that a life rich in meaning and grace flows inevitably from the gospel he is privileged to preach. In our confusion and heartache we cry, "Is there any word from the Lord?" The priest answers with a resounding *Yes!*[9] (emphasis original)

In introducing this passage, Cozzens says he does not intend any implied comparisons that would appear to diminish the worth of other paths. His exuberance for his own path, nonetheless, is inspiring.

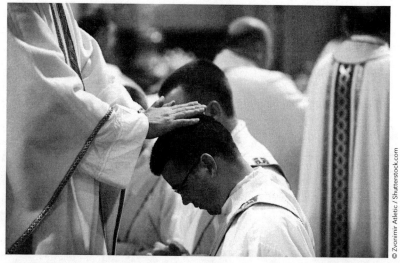

© Zvonimir Atletic / Shutterstock.com

The Catholic Church has traditionally stressed that ordination to the priesthood produced an ontological change in the ordained individual. Many theologians today argue that the change is not just to the individual but to the individual's relationship within the church community.

---

9. Lawrence Boadt and Michael J. Hunt, eds., *Why I Am a Priest: Thirty Success Stories* (Mahwah, NJ: Paulist Press, 1999), 110–11.

Summary

This chapter has examined current concern over the shortage of priests against the background of shifting images and understandings of the priesthood. It seems as though the priesthood is in a difficult transitional period when one vision is fading while another has not yet taken its place. In this way, what is happening to the priesthood symbolizes what is happening to the Catholic Church itself.

The next chapter will examine the relationship between the official teaching of the Catholic Church and the beliefs of Catholics.

For Further Reflection

1. What did Vatican II teach about the meaning of the priesthood?
2. How does a "relational ontology" help in understanding the priesthood?
3. Do you tend to read the approaches of Osborne or of Barron in understanding the meaning of priesthood as more complementary or as more in opposition to each other? Why?
4. Do you think the celibacy requirement should be changed?
5. In today's world, what might attract a young Catholic man to the priesthood?

Suggested Readings

Boadt, Lawrence, and Michael J. Hunt, eds. *Why I Am a Priest: Thirty Success Stories.* Mahwah, NJ: Paulist Press, 1999.

Confoy, Maryanne. *Religious Life and Priesthood:* Perfectae Caritatis, Optatam Totius, *and* Presbyterorum Ordinis. Mahwah, NJ: Paulist Press, 2008.

Osborne, Kenan. *Priesthood: A History of Ordained Ministry in the Roman Catholic Church.* Mahwah, NJ: Paulist Press, 1988.

Ruddy, Christopher. *Tested in Every Way: The Catholic Priesthood in Today's Church.* New York: Crossroad, 2006.

Smith, Karen Sue, ed. *Priesthood in the Modern World: A Reader.* Franklin, WI: Sheed and Ward, 1999.

Wood, Susan K., ed. *Ordering the Baptismal Priesthood: Theologies of Lay and Ordained Ministry.* Collegeville, MN: Liturgical Press, 2003.

Levels of Teaching, Levels of Assent

I n Catholic circles, one sometimes hears a phrase I find unfortunate: "cafeteria-style Catholicism." This describes a practice by which individual Catholics "pick and choose" what they will believe. I once had a conversation with an author who had written a book about disagreement in the church. He said, as soon as you admit you can disagree, you have bought into the "cafeteria-style" model.

But I find a huge intellectual mistake at the heart of the "cafeteria-style" model of Catholicism. It assumes Catholics start off with an empty tray, and then move around to select what beliefs suit them. Nothing could be further from the truth. To be a Catholic is to start out with a full tray. Catholicism is a package deal. You buy the whole thing. Once you have a full tray, though, you might find you want to rearrange a few things, or put a couple of things back, or maybe you don't feel up to finishing everything on your plate. But you definitely do not start out with an empty tray.

Overview

This chapter considers the importance of beliefs, the relative ranking of beliefs, and matters of assent and disagreement in the Catholic Church. In *Lumen gentium*, most relevant to these matters are section 25 in chapter 3 and section 37 in chapter 4. Also relevant is Vatican II's *Dignitatis humanae* (*Declaration on Religious Liberty*).

Beliefs Are Crucial

A pluralistic society such as in the United States has a tendency to downplay the importance of religious beliefs. The rights and dignity of every person regardless of religious affiliation is affirmed and protected under law. One has the same constitutional rights as everyone else, regardless of belief.

In the United States, the tendency to minimize the importance of belief has spread to religions themselves. Sometimes it is done out of deference to other world religions. Sometimes it is done in reaction against past tendencies to over-emphasize the role of belief to the neglect of other religious elements such as prayer, religious experience, or social transformation. Orthopraxy (right doing), we are told, is more basic than orthodoxy (right belief).

It is possible, however, to combine an affirmation of human rights, other faiths, and religious experience with the recognition of the crucial role that beliefs play in the life of the individual and the community. As the theologian Bernard Lonergan (1904–84) points out, beliefs shape the very world in which a person lives.[1] Social institutions and human cultures have sets of meanings at their core. These meanings can be detected as presuppositions and formulated as beliefs. For example, the judicial system of the United States rests upon a set of beliefs about the meaning and importance of justice. The institutions of marriage and the family rest upon a set of beliefs about how spouses should relate with each other in regard to sex and children.

Religious beliefs shape one's understanding of the meaning and purpose of life. They are part of the world in which we live. When you wake in the morning, into what kind of world do you awaken? What do you perceive? Is it a world created by an all-powerful and all-loving God who has a good purpose in mind? Or do you awaken into an absurd world that yields no ultimate meaning no matter how much you long for answers? Do you awaken into a world that, though fallen in sin, has been redeemed by Christ? Or is it a world in which the false, nasty belief in sin has covered the true innocence of human beings? Do you awaken into a world in which the Spirit is guiding us to relate with each other more fully and deeply as human beings? Or is it a world in which each of us needs to look out for number one, because if we don't nobody else will? What do we believe about the ultimate nature of reality and the purpose of our lives?

The dichotomies offered in the preceding paragraph are not the only choices available. My religion is not the only one in the world. Even secular worldviews can offer alternative meanings without preaching despair. I do not wish to suggest that people's civil rights, dignity, or freedom should be determined according to religious beliefs. I only want to emphasize that what you believe is crucial to who you are as a person and to what sense your life will make.

---

1. See Bernard Lonergan, *Method in Theology*, vol. 14 of *Collected Works of Bernard Lonergan*, ed. Robert M. Doran and John D. Dadosky (Toronto: University of Toronto Press, 2017 [1972]). See especially the chapters "Meaning," 55–95, and "Doctrines," 275–309.

Some Beliefs Are More Central than Others

Vatican II's *Unitatis redintegratio* (*Decree on Ecumenism*) called for partners in interfaith dialogue to "remember that in Catholic doctrine there exists an order or 'hierarchy' of truths, since they vary in their relation to the foundation of the Christian faith" (*UR* 12). In other words, Catholics recognize that some beliefs are more central to Christian faith than others. When engaging in ecumenical dialogue, it is often appropriate to put disagreements on less central matters to the side in order to affirm agreements on more basic points. For example, when Catholics dialogue with Lutherans, it may be desirable to dwell first on areas of agreement, such as salvation through Christ being a free gift, without always concentrating on such disputed points as whether good works can merit some reward.

At present, there is no sure way to determine a ranking of beliefs in a hierarchy of truths. Perhaps some guidance can be drawn from Lonergan, who speaks about the "original message" of Christianity. All other teachings are "doctrines about this doctrine."[2] For a reference to this original message, he cites 1 Corinthians 15:3–11, in which Paul says, "For I handed on to you as of first importance what I in turn had received: that Christ died for our sins in accordance with the scriptures, and that he was buried, and that he was raised on the third day." Paul then lists many witnesses to the Resurrected Christ, and concludes, "so we proclaim and so you have come to believe." The core of the Christian message is the good news that, through the Risen Christ, who fulfills the expectations of the Old Testament, we find salvation from sin.

The hierarchy of truths would then be determined by assessing how close to this basic core any particular belief is. That in itself is far from easy. One of the arguments in favor of strong authoritative leadership in the church is the almost endless variety of interpretations one might give to the original message and its implications. Who is to say which interpretations fall within an acceptable range? Who is to say which beliefs are crucial and which are less central?

The official Catholic position is that the magisterium of the Catholic Church has the power to define the meaning and importance of matters of faith and morals. The position articulated at Vatican II in the *Dei verbum* (*Dogmatic Constitution on Divine Revelation*) is that the gospel message is expressed through Scripture and Tradition. The magisterium of the church does not have authority over Scripture or Tradition, but it does have authority over human interpretations of Scripture and Tradition. At present, though, there exists no systematic presentation of the hierarchy of truths.

In my opinion, the belief that Christ rose from the dead is central; the belief that Christ walked on water is not as central. The belief that adultery is wrong is central; the belief that artificial birth control is always immoral is not as central. It is unfortunate when a not-so-central issue receives attention disproportionate

---

2. Lonergan, *Method in Theology*, 276.

to its worth and thereby takes attention away from more central matters. This is not to suggest that beliefs that are not central are necessarily less true; it is to suggest, rather, that such issues do not have to be made pressing concerns in ecumenical dialogue.

What Must Catholics Believe?

The basics of the Christian story are found in the Apostles' Creed and in the more technical Nicene Creed. Catholics are expected to accept the faith witness of the Bible, the three persons in one God, decisions of the ecumenical councils, teachings of the pope and bishops, and the sacraments as instruments of grace.

Some theologians have attempted (amid controversy) to apply the idea of a "hierarchy of truths" beyond ecumenical dialogue to internal matters of Catholic belief. What beliefs must be accepted if one is to consider oneself a Catholic?

Theologian Monika Hellwig (1925–2005), drawing upon the work of theologian Yves Congar, distinguishes between capital "T" Tradition and small "t" tradition.[3] On the one hand, "Tradition" refers to those things that are an essential part of the Catholic faith; if Tradition changed, faith would be altered. On the other hand, "tradition" refers to those things that may be important but are not essential. For example, the Catholic belief in Christ's presence in the Eucharist is part of "Tradition"; the rule that the priest giving communion must place the host directly on the tongue was a "tradition" that could and has been changed.

This distinction between "Tradition" and "tradition" is helpful, but it does not by itself settle all matters. Catholics still can disagree about whether a particular issue is "Tradition" or "tradition." The Catholic Church's official position that it does not have the authority to ordain women is based on the judgment that an all-male priesthood is a "Tradition" established by Christ himself. Catholics who favor the ordination of women argue that the all-male priesthood is a "tradition" related to an ancient, patriarchal culture and not something essential to the gospel.

Also, when asking questions about which beliefs are crucial, we should not forget that many believers have different understandings of the same beliefs. What one Catholic accepts when believing in the doctrine of the Assumption may be very different from what another Catholic accepts. One Catholic may recite the Creed and believe everything quite literally; another might recite the Nicene Creed and understand just about everything symbolically; yet another might have a nuanced understanding of how myth and history interrelate, and understand the creed accordingly. Though it is not necessary for all Catholics to understand every belief in exactly the same way, Catholics can only share the

---

3. Monika Hellwig, "Tradition in the Catholic Church—Why It's Still Important," in *Catholic Update* (Cincinnati, OH: St. Anthony Messenger Press, 1981).

same faith when there is some recognizable degree of unity. The question of doctrinal pluralism, like that of the hierarchy of truths, is one that is not currently clarified, and one that should receive more attention in the future.

Responsible and Irresponsible Disagreement

In the Catholic Church today, disagreement is a reality that is unlikely to go away. Some theologians argue that disagreement is part of a healthy process by which the church changes. Not all disagreement, though, is legitimate. There is a need to distinguish between responsible and irresponsible disagreement.

Theologian Francis Sullivan explains that Catholics are expected to give basic assent to church teaching. One cannot disagree with those teachings that are held infallible if one wishes to remain Catholic. But if a Catholic approaches a non-infallible teaching with an attitude of openness, tries to conform one's mind and will, and still, after a period of struggle, cannot wholeheartedly assent to the teaching, the result is a disagreement that is probably both responsible and legitimate.

Sullivan points out that, in the original draft of Vatican II's *Dignitatis humanae*, a sentence read, "In the formation of their consciences, the Christian faithful ought carefully to attend to the sacred and certain doctrine of the church." During council debate of the document, it was proposed that the wording be changed from "ought carefully to attend to" to "ought to form their consciences according to." The committee in charge of the document rejected the proposed change on the grounds that it was excessively restrictive.[4] The original statement stands as is in the final document (*DH* 14). This example illustrates that although the council calls Catholics to be predisposed to assent to church teachings, it also recognizes that Catholics have personal responsibility in the formation of their consciences. Catholics are not robots programmed by the Vatican. As I interpret it, both Sullivan and John Paul II stress, from different angles, the complex interrelationship between two fundamental Catholic principles: first, you must follow your conscience, and second, you are obligated to have a well-formed conscience.

Years ago, after much reading and classroom discussion, I formulated ground rules for disagreement with church teaching that conform to official outlooks. From that point of view, responsible and legitimate disagreement requires the Catholic to do the following:

1. have an open attitude, including a predisposition to give religious submission of mind and will to official church teaching
2. not challenge the very ability of the church to teach authoritatively

---

4. Francis A. Sullivan, *Magisterium* (New York: Paulist Press, 1983), 169–70.

3. investigate the matter in question to a reasonable degree, including the reasoning behind the church's teaching
4. continue to be open-minded and willing to be challenged periodically by the church's position
5. not scandalize others by encouraging them to disagree

These ground rules can be useful for thinking, in general, about the topic of responsible disagreement. They are not sufficiently precise, however, for judging whether a particular disagreement is itself responsible. Most disagreements among US Catholics would not strictly measure up to these ground rules, and yet, personally, I would be hesitant to label them irresponsible. For example, some Catholics disagree with church teaching about artificial birth control and they would meet these criteria. Others, who have closed-minded attitudes on the subject, might be labeled irresponsible. The majority of US Catholics who disagree with church teaching about artificial birth control, however, probably neither meet the criteria listed above nor could be facilely dismissed as irresponsible.

Some Catholics have found Natural Family Planning methods have more to offer than artificial means of birth control; a large majority of Catholics, however, do not share this point of view. The historical impact of this issue in US Catholicism makes disagreement too complex a matter to be judged by any preset criteria. Birth control was the first issue subject to massive disagreement by the laity. It stands today as a symbol that much remains to be worked out concerning the manner in which the church should teach and the manner in which believers are to respond. Most Catholics who disagree do so because a teaching both interferes with their lifestyles and does not make any sense to them. It is simplistic to label their disagreement irresponsible. On a deep level, there is a communication problem, with each side needing to listen more attentively and speak more sensitively to the other.

Pope John Paul II Attacks "Dissent"

John Paul II spoke out against dissent in the Catholic Church when he visited the United States in the fall of 1987. Noting that many Catholics had not accepted certain church teachings, "notably sexual and conjugal morality, divorce and remarriage, and abortion," the pope said, "It is sometimes claimed that dissent from the magisterium is totally compatible with being a good Catholic and poses no obstacle to the reception of the sacraments. This is a grave error." Later, when talking with a group of bishops about theological freedom, the pope said that the bishops "should seek to show the inacceptability of dissent and confrontation as a policy method in the area of church teaching." In the same talk, he said, "Dissent remains what it is: dissent. As such it may not be proposed or received on an equal footing with the church's teaching."

A document from the Congregation for the Doctrine of the Faith (CDF), *Donum veritatis* (*Instruction on the Ecclesial Vocation of the Theologian*), distinguishes between dissent and disagreement. The former implies an organized revolt. The latter is something that the CDF recognizes that theologians can respectfully engage in.[5] Guidelines for legitimate disagreement among theologians existed long before Vatican II. Since Vatican II, Catholic theologians and Catholic textbooks have clarified conditions when an ordinary believer's disagreement from official teaching is legitimate. Even bishops' conferences and individual bishops have issued documents that discuss when disagreement is legitimate and when it is irresponsible.

Pope John Paul II and the CDF did not endorse disagreement by ordinary believers. They were more concerned with buttressing the weight of ordinary church teaching, which they perceived to have slipped in recent decades. In his 1993 encyclical *Veritatis splendor* (*The Splendor of Truth*), the pope addresses the freedom of conscience of every believer. In matters of morality, he teaches, it is a mistake to think that a believer should choose the very principles by which to make moral judgments. The freedom of the believer comes first of all in entering into a relationship with God through Jesus. This freedom is also carried out in the practice of applying basic principles to particular situations. John Paul II did not think freedom comes from making up one's own rules.

It appears John Paul II was launching a full-scale attack against an attitude that promotes dissent as normal and that places disagreement on the same level as the acceptance of fundamental beliefs. The pope stomped on what, in the beginning of this chapter, we called "cafeteria-style Catholicism": the attitude that Catholics are free to select some beliefs and reject others without giving serious attention to church teaching. He is saying that behaviors such as sex outside of marriage, remarriage without annulment, and abortion are grave matters that are not just questions of personal conscience. He is saying these things are sinful and Catholics are not free simply to pick and choose what they personally consider to be right and wrong.

Pope Francis and Mercy

Whereas John Paul II was clearly trying to stem the tide of liberal changes and the loosening of rules within the Catholic Church, Pope Francis has concentrated on embracing people where they are and then accompanying them on their journey. Francis stresses that each of us is the subject of God's mercy. The church itself is imperfect and on a journey. God's justice is shaped by God's mercy.

---

5. Congregation for the Doctrine of the Faith, *Donum veritatis* (*Instruction on the Ecclesial Vocation of the Theologian*), *Origins* 20 (1990): 117–26.

In *Amoris laetitia* (*The Joy of Love*), Francis addresses the problem of those who live in irregular situations in relation to the church's teachings.[6] He teaches that individual conscience needs to be better incorporated into the church's praxis in certain situations that do not objectively embody our understanding of marriage. It is reductive, he argues, simply to consider whether an individual's actions correspond to a general rule or law, because that is not enough to discern and ensure full fidelity to God in the concrete life of a human being. In some cases, such as that of a previously married couple who have not obtained annulments but who have been raising children together for years, it may be more sinful for the couple to abandon their relationship than to maintain it. It is important for pastors to discern, on a case-by-case basis, the best way to accompany people in their present life situations.

Pope Francis differs from Pope John Paul II in style, emphasis, and direction. Both popes embrace the basic substance of traditional Catholic Church teachings. Some commentators claim that John Paul II was exactly what the church needed in 1978, and that Pope Francis is the leader that the church needs for the present time.

Summary

This chapter has explored the importance of belief, the hierarchy of truths, the relation between assent and disagreement, and some ground rules for responsible disagreement.

At the beginning of this chapter, I mentioned an author who endorsed the notion of "cafeteria-style Catholicism." He and I never did agree about this term. As for me, not only does the "cafeteria-style" concept miss the reality that a Catholic starts out with a full tray, but it also overly emphasizes disagreement and underemphasizes belief. Basic belief is a thousand times more important than one's disagreement on a few points. Basic belief awakens one to a world that has been created and redeemed by God. It opens one to the sacramental life of grace. Our ability to disagree on a few points might enable us to negotiate practical concerns as we live our faith in the world. This can be very important, but it does not compare with the importance of the faith that transforms our lives to begin with—and that puts us in touch with the saving love of God.

Still, that author and I do agree that some disagreement can be legitimate. Yet the range of beliefs, attitudes, and behaviors that many of my students may seek to justify through rationalization is worrisome. However, I would be equally concerned if they did not take seriously their responsibility to think for themselves.

6. Pope Francis, *Amoris laetitia*, 2016, *https://w2.vatican.va/content/dam/francesco/pdf/apost_exhortations/documents/papa-francesco_esortazione-ap_20160319_amoris-laetitia_en.pdf*.

The next chapter investigates the changing status of laypeople in the Catholic Church.

Further Reflection

1. Do you think that problems over controversial issues can get in the way of a person's basic beliefs?
2. Do you think that most issues in dispute in the Catholic Church today are "Tradition," or "tradition"?
3. How would you distinguish between "responsible disagreement" and "cafeteria-style Catholicism"?
4. Do you think that Catholics tend to be more responsible or irresponsible in their disagreements?
5. How would you characterize the differences in emphases between Pope John Paul II and Pope Francis?

Suggested Readings

Congregation for the Doctrine of the Faith. *Donum veritatis* (*Instruction on the Ecclesial Vocation of the Theologian*), 1990. *http://www.vatican.va/roman _curia/congregations/cfaith/documents/rc_con_cfaith_doc_19900524 _theologian-vocation_en.html.*

Gaillardetz, Richard R. *By What Authority? A Primer on Scripture, the Magisterium, and the Sense of the Faithful.* Collegeville, MN: Liturgical Press, 2003.

Marthaler, Berard. *The Creed: The Apostolic Faith in Contemporary Theology.* Mystic, CT: Twenty-Third Publications, 2007.

Pope Francis. *Amoris laetitia* (*The Joy of Love*), 2016, *https://w2.vatican.va /content/dam/francesco/pdf/apost_exhortations/documents/papa-francesco _esortazione-ap_20160319_amoris-laetitia_en.pdf.*

Sullivan, Francis. *Magisterium.* New York: Paulist Press, 1983.

13

CHAPTER

Laypeople

Alcoholics Anonymous (AA) consists of an extensive network of various-sized groups spread throughout the world. If you want to contact AA, you can call the number listed on their web page. There is, however, another way to contact the organization: talk to any member. Any and every member of AA is a representative of the group. Members think of themselves as the hand of AA. Whenever and wherever someone needs help, AA members take responsibility to be of service. If you are talking with a member, you are talking with AA.

This has generally not been the case with laypeople in the Catholic Church.[1] If you want to talk with someone who represents the Catholic Church, you will probably be told to make an appointment with a priest. A bishop represents a higher level, and of course, the pope represents the highest level. Catholic laypeople do not usually regard themselves as representing "the church."

Like the Catholic Church, AA does have its own centralized organization. However, the point of comparison is that members of AA think they represent the group, such that they themselves can share with newcomers the basics of staying sober one day at a time. Most Catholics have not traditionally thought of themselves as being able to share the basics of Christian living with newcomers or those interested in the faith.

Overview

The need for, and the willingness of, the laity to take personal responsibility for the Catholic Church is changing. This chapter discusses four interconnected issues: the laity's relation to church, their spiritual dignity, their sharing in the ministry of Christ, and the particular ways in which they are called to live a Christian life. These issues are drawn from chapter 4 of *Lumen gentium* (*Dogmatic Constitution on the Church*).

---

1. In *Lumen gentium*, a "layperson" is anyone who has neither been ordained nor taken religious vows of poverty, chastity, and obedience. In practice, however, this definition is complicated, because in canon law anyone who is not ordained is treated as laity.

127

We Are the Church

Daniel Pilarczyk, retired Archbishop of Cincinnati, once wrote that the church is basically an organization of laypeople who are served by a hierarchy. This revolutionary definition reverses the centuries-old Catholic tendency to think of the church most basically as a hierarchical institution in which bishops, priests, and religious were the real members of the club and the laity were the sheep to be led and tended. To this day, when most Catholics think of "the church," they imagine the pope and the bishops in Rome making up rules and regulations for the preservation of Catholic teaching. It is the rare Catholic who has appropriated the spirit of Vatican II that leads one to say, "We are the church!"

The late Bishop James Malone of Youngstown once said to me that his main disappointment in the implementation of Vatican II has been that the members of the laity have not yet begun to think of themselves as the church. "You are the church!" was his message. The church is not just located in Rome. The church is the People of God. The church is composed of each individual member.

Thinking of the church as a lay organization carries forward the thrust of Vatican II, which stressed the equality in spiritual dignity of all who are baptized, the common priesthood of the faithful, and the importance of Christian involvement in the everyday world of human affairs. At the same time, such thinking does not, in any way, have to be anti-institutional or antihierarchical; a confident lay-centered church can arrive at a renewed appreciation of the hierarchy that serves it.

Equality in Spiritual Dignity

Clericalism is the practice of granting too much influence and power to the clergy. To say that pre–Vatican II Catholicism tended to be clericalistic is utterly and obviously true; it should not be forgotten, however, that many pre–Vatican II priests as well as laypeople fought hard against these tendencies. It should also be remembered that the current overreaction against the clericalism of the past might be a contributing factor in the shortage of priests.

As a practical issue in the Catholic Church, clericalism has most often been thought of as placing priests and religious so high on pedestals that one forgets that they are just as human as the rest of us. There is, however, another way to think of the problem: clericalism can result from not recognizing the importance and dignity of laypeople. In other words, instead of thinking of priests as "too high" and "needing to be dragged down," it may be better to think of laypeople as being considered too low and needing more recognition.

Lumen gentium takes this approach when it says, "The chosen People of God is one: 'one Lord, one faith, one baptism'; sharing a common dignity as members from their regeneration in Christ; having the same filial grace and the same vocation to perfection; possessing in common one salvation, one hope and one undivided charity" (*LG* 32). The document is emphasizing that, in a most fundamental spiritual sense, the members of the church are equal. By virtue of one's baptism, one is a full member of the church with a full share in God's grace insofar as one perseveres in love. When it comes to faith, spiritual dignity, grace, salvation, hope, and love, each member is invited to share fully. There are no second-class Catholics. There is no hierarchy when it comes to being called to holiness.

Becoming a priest, brother, or sister may play a crucial role in the life of an individual and in the life of the church as a whole. It changes one's status in relation to the hierarchical structures of the church. But it does not change one's status in relation to one's basic membership in the church or one's most fundamental relationship with God. Every member of the church is called to a life of holiness:

> All are called to sanctity and have received an equal privilege of faith through the justice of God. And if by the will of Christ some are made teachers, pastors and dispensers of mysteries on behalf of others, yet all share a true equality with regard to the dignity and to the activity common to all the faithful for the building up of the Body of Christ. (*LG* 32)

Laypeople, vowed religious, and ordained clergy are called to collaborate in carrying out the mission of the church. They are not to get hung up in worrying about who is holier.

This strong assertion of the equality in spiritual dignity among members of the church raises some critical questions for Catholics today. If we are all equal, why cannot laypeople preside at the Eucharistic celebration? Why are laypeople not permitted to preach without special permission? Why does it seem that in many places laypeople do not experience great respect from the hierarchy? It seems as though, à la George Orwell's *Animal Farm*, some people are more equal than others.

One way of responding to these issues is to point out that saying people are equal in spiritual dignity is not the same as saying they are equal in everything. It is true that no one can claim entitlement or privilege for themselves over others in regard to the grace of God. But this does not mean that everyone is equal in talents and abilities, intelligence and wit, social status and rank, or compassion and understanding. The church has hierarchical structures that specify offices and functions, but this does not detract from its assertion of the spiritual equality of its members.

An alternative response to the charge of real inequalities still existing in the Catholic Church is to point out that Vatican II took place so recently in the history of the church that its full implications are still being worked out. Many changes loom on the horizon. Both of these responses can be taken seriously. Not everyone is equal in everything. Many new things are yet to come.

Another challenge to the claim of the spiritual equality of members is the question of the relative status of nonmembers. Is the Catholic Church implying that non-Catholics and non-Christians are spiritually second class? This is a difficult issue that arises in other places in this book. In this context, I wish to say only that the matter of spiritual equality was dealt with at Vatican II as an internal question, and that there was no intention of implying anything derogatory about people of other faiths.

Laypeople as Priests, Prophets, and Kings

We have seen how *Lumen gentium* declares that all members of the church participate in the threefold ministry of Christ as priest, prophet, and king (PPK). We have seen further how the document specifies that the particular way the bishops and priests participate is through sanctifying, teaching, and leading. *Lumen gentium* also spells out the specific ways in which the laity are called to participate in Christ's threefold ministry.

MINISTRY OF THE LAYPERSON	
Layperson as PPK	**Tasks**
Priest	Bring holiness to the world
Prophet	Let the gospel shine through daily life
King	Work toward the kingdom

Laypeople carry out Christ's *priestly* function through their sacrifice and holiness as they live their lives in the world:

> For all their works, prayers, and apostolic endeavors, their ordinary married and family life, their daily occupations, their physical and mental relaxation, if carried out in the Spirit, and even the hardships of life, if patiently borne—all these become "spiritual sacrifices acceptable to God through Jesus Christ." Together with the offering of the Lord's body, they are most fittingly offered in the celebration of the Eucharist. Thus, as those everywhere who adore in holy activity, the laity consecrate the world itself to God. (*LG* 34)

In other words, laypersons act as priests insofar as they offer their very lives to God. In practical terms, this can mean the layperson makes God present in the world by striving to live a holy life.

Lumen gentium depicts the prophetic function of the laity as the promise that "the power of the Gospel might shine forth in their daily social and family life" (*LG* 35). Members of the laity are to give witness to their faith by the way they live. The kingly function of the laity is expressed in *Lumen gentium* as the call to spread the kingdom of God throughout the world. The laity must work to bring the world in the direction of "truth and life . . . holiness and grace . . . justice, peace, and love" (*LG* 36). Again, it is through the manner in which the layperson lives life that the mission of Christ is carried to the world.

Spheres of Lay Activity

Lumen gentium does not shut laypeople out from ministry within the church. The laity "carry out for their own part the mission of the whole Christian people in the church and in the world" (*LG* 31). Indeed, the document says, "The laity can also be called in various ways to a more direct form of cooperation in the apostolate of the Hierarchy. . . . Further, they have the capacity to assume from the Hierarchy certain ecclesiastical functions, which are to be performed for a spiritual purpose" (*LG* 33). And so, since Vatican II, there has been a virtual explosion of lay ministries within the church.

The main thrust of *Lumen gentium*, however, emphasizes that the special function of the laity is precisely their role in the world. The document states, "What specifically characterizes the laity is their secular nature. . . . The laity, by their very vocation, seek the kingdom of God by engaging in temporal affairs and by ordering them according to the plan of God" (*LG* 31). Three worldly spheres of lay activity are stressed in *Lumen gentium*: family, work, and social transformation. It is through family life, work, and striving for a better world that laypeople find their most basic call to live as followers of Christ.

SPHERES OF LAY CHRISTIAN ACTIVITY			
Lay ecclesial ministry	Special vocation of laity in the world		
Church	Family	Work	Society

One upshot of this delineation of lay spheres of activity was Pope John Paul II's insistence that priests and religious not hold political office. As he saw it, such worldly activity is properly the role of laypeople. Those who officially represent the church should preach high ideals, but should not become overly identified with particular nations, political parties, or ideological platforms. This division of labor is intended to allow laypeople, motivated by their Christian consciences, to become deeply and passionately involved in the ambiguities of human affairs, without being perceived as acting as representatives of official Catholic policies.

John Paul II reinforced this division of labor in a 1989 document on the laity. He warned laypeople against "the temptation of being so strongly interested in church services and tasks that some fail to become engaged in their responsibilities in the professional, social, cultural, and political world."[2] As the pope saw it, it is the general calling of laypeople to work for the transformation of the world and the coming of the kingdom through their family and work life and their political involvements. Otherwise, laypeople might fall prey to a second temptation, that of "legitimizing the unwarranted separation of the Gospel's acceptance from the actual living of the Gospel in various situations in the world."[3] Laypeople are not to use the church as a place to hide from the world but as a source of faith and holiness for tackling life's challenges.

In 2005, the US Conference of Catholic Bishops issued a document, *Co-Workers in the Vineyard*, which offered a more serene and balanced approach to the tensions between ordained ministers and lay ecclesial ministers. On the one hand, the bishops reiterated that the proper vocation of laypeople is in the world. On the other hand, they affirmed lay ecclesial ministers not simply as temporary helpers in an emergency situation but, rather, as sharing in the mission of the church and being empowered by their baptism.[4] They were able to cite passages from John Paul II that showed that, by the final years of his papacy, he had softened on this issue.[5]

Theologian Richard Gaillardetz explained that too exclusive an emphasis on the distinction between laity and clergy does not capture the full thrust of the documents of Vatican II. *Lumen gentium* does attest to an essential distinction between the ordained priesthood and the common priesthood of the faithful. It does so, however, within a context that stresses, at least as deeply, that both clergy and lay share a membership in the church as the People of God, a mutual empowerment through baptism, an equality in spiritual dignity, a call to holiness, and a participation in the threefold ministry of Christ as priest, prophet, and king.[6]

Lumen gentium went far in trying to erase the clericalism that plagued the Catholic Church throughout long segments of its history. Current attempts to reemphasize the lay–clergy distinction need to be complemented by parallel efforts to affirm the role of the laity in the church and the world. To say the least, it is difficult to find the right balance when trying to emphasize, simultaneously, the distinctiveness of priests and religious and the spiritual dignity of all.

---

2. Pope John Paul II, *Christifideles laici* (*The Vocation and the Mission of the Lay Faithful in the Church and in the World*), 1988, 2, *http://w2.vatican.va/content/john-paul-ii/en/apost_exhortations/documents /hf_jp-ii_exh_30121988_christifideles-laici.html.*

3. Pope John Paul II, *Christifideles*, 2.

4. US Conference of Catholic Bishops, *Co-Workers in the Vineyard of the Lord*, 2005, 8–9, *http:// www.usccb.org/upload/co-workers-vineyard-lay-ecclesial-ministry-2005.pdf.*

5. US Conference of Catholic Bishops, *Co-Workers in the Vineyard of the Lord*, 10, 18, 28.

6. Richard R. Gaillardetz, "Shifting Meanings in the Lay–Clergy Distinction," *Irish Thological Quarterly* 64 (1999): 115–39.

Summary

The chapter examined the shift in the role of the laity signaled by the documents of Vatican II. In particular, it focused on laypeople sharing in the threefold ministry of Christ, being equal in spiritual dignity, and being called to action in the spheres of family, work, and social justice.

This new focus on the laity is part of a broadened understanding of the mission of the church in the world. One cannot understand "church" just by concentrating on matters of internal structure and authority. What it means to live as a Christian in the world is as much a part of the church as what it means to be a bishop.

"We are the church!" is the new cry of the laity. It is the joyful cry of a new birth. It is the cry of pain that accompanies the demands of a new responsibility. It is hard for me to envision the ordinary lay Catholic assuming the kind of personal ownership for the church that a recovering alcoholic assumes for AA. But if I stretch my imagination, then perhaps it is possible.

The next chapter will study various ways that Catholics are revitalizing lay participation in the life of the church.

For Further Reflection

1. Have you had any experience of lay Catholics displaying a sense of "ownership" in the church?
2. Do you tend, on an everyday basis, to regard laypeople as equal in spiritual dignity with ordained ministers?
3. Should "equality in spiritual dignity" mean that all roles in the church should be open to everyone, or do you agree that different people can play different roles and still share a fundamental equality?
4. What value might there be in emphasizing that the laity's primary mission is in the world, not in ministries within the church?
5. Do you think it is common for people to make a mental division between their religious life in church and their everyday life in the world? If so, how might such a split be healed?

Suggested Readings

Congar, Yves. *Lay People in the Church: A Study for a Theology of Laity.* Translated by Donald Attwater. Westminster, MD: Newman, 1957.

Doyle, Dennis M. "Extraordinary Love in the Lives of Laypeople." In *God Has Begun a Great Work in Us*, College Theology Society Annual Publication 60, edited by Jason King and Shannon Schrein, 149–63. Maryknoll, NY: Orbis Books, 2014.

Fletcher, Christine. M. *24/7: The Secular Vocation of the Laity.* Collegeville, MN: Liturgical Press, 2015.

Gaillardetz, Richard R. "Shifting Meanings in the Lay–Clergy Distinction." *Irish Theological Quarterly* 64 (1999): 115–39.

Hagstrom, Aurelia A. *The Emerging Laity: Vocation, Mission, and Spirituality.* Mahwah, NJ: Paulist Press, 2010.

John Paul II. *Christifideles laici (The Vocation and the Mission of the Lay Faithful in the Church and in the World).* Washington, DC: US Catholic Conference, 1988.

Muldoon, Tim. ed. *Catholic Identity and the Laity.* College Theology Society Annual Publication 54. Maryknoll, NY: Orbis Books, 2009.

US Conference of Catholic Bishops. *Co-Workers in the Vineyard of the Lord.* 2005. *http://www.usccb.org/upload/co-workers-vineyard-lay-ecclesial-ministry-2005.pdf.*

Tools for Church Renewal

A thirteen-year-old girl used to deliver the newspaper to my door. She was tall, slender, and tended to stand a bit hunched over, looking down at the ground. She mumbled when she spoke, and I often had to ask her to repeat what she said. She babysat my children a couple of times, and so we got to know a little about each other. She knew that I was a Catholic teacher of religion. I knew that she had been brought up Catholic but was now a non-churchgoer from a family of alienated Catholics.

There came a point when she became more talkative. She started asking many questions about the Bible. She began to share with me about her home life and her father's drinking problem.

What had brought about this openness in her was the experience of going to a new church. A friend of hers in junior high had invited her to the services at a Pentecostal church. She had gotten into the habit of going regularly, and then her mother started to attend. She and her mother went to three-hour services twice a week and also volunteered several hours cleaning the church.

The people in her new church interpreted the Bible literally, word for word. They told the young woman that she should not cut her hair, because the Bible says that a woman's hair is her glory. They told her not to swim at public pools, because the Bible says that she should dress modestly. They told her that people who weren't born again could not be saved, because the Bible says that unless a man be born again of water and the Spirit he will not enter God's kingdom. She still continued to cut her hair, swim, and believe in the salvation of non-Christians. Her pastor said that was all right for now. He told her that when she was ready, she would accept these teachings by the conviction of the Holy Spirit within her, not because anyone told her to do it.

The girl looked to me for the reassurance that she did not have to interpret the Bible that way at all. She told me she still believed the Catholic way, but there was something about this church that she knew was right for her.

And there was. She had found a group of people who were willing to reach out and love her until she could love herself. They told her she was a creature of God, and God didn't make junk. They welcomed her, got to know her, got her talking about her life, and helped her to turn her life around. The transformation

135

they generated in her was nearly miraculous. She was visibly changed. She stood up straighter. She dressed better. She had more confidence. She spoke up so that she could be understood the first time. She talked about the real issues in her life and expressed her deepest feelings and beliefs. She stood up to her father and confronted him about his drinking and his need to get help.

My overwhelming reaction to her experience is positive. I thank God for the people in that Pentecostal church and for the grace that worked through them. I maintain some sharply different beliefs about interpreting the Bible, but I am also left with a twinge of jealously for their church's spirit. Sometimes I wonder: Why isn't my church more like that? Why isn't my church more of a welcoming community?

Overview

In recent years, the Catholic Church has been consciously moving toward building dynamic faith communities. There already exists a growing sense of participation whereby the laity assume more personal ownership for the parish. This chapter will discuss three developments that are functioning as tools for the renewal of the Catholic Church: the Rite of Christian Initiation for Adults, lay ministries, and Renew—a program for community formation in the parish.

This chapter reflects on developments relevant to the laity's shift in status, discussed in chapter 4 of *Lumen gentium*. It is also related to the discussion of the development of local faith communities in Vatican II's *Ad gentes* (*Decree on the Mission Activity of the Church*).

TOOLS FOR CHURCH RENEWAL	
Tools	Goals
Adult initiation process	Initiate into community
Lay ministries	Empower people to serve
New Ecclesial Movements	Build faith communities

Rite of Christian Initiation for Adults

The Rite of Christian Initiation for Adults (RCIA) is the preparation process for adults considering joining the Catholic Church. Participants are introduced to various aspects of Catholic faith and life, then received into the church at the Easter Vigil Mass, where they receive the sacraments of baptism, confirmation, and Eucharist.

The RCIA functions as a tool for renewal in the Catholic Church. For more than a thousand years prior to Vatican II, Catholic theology concerning baptism focused on infants, who constituted the great majority of people being baptized. Numerically, this remains true, but, since the council, the theological focus of baptism has been on adults. In other words, when those in the Catholic Church think of what baptism means, they should think first of what it means to initiate an adult into a faith community. Baptism involves more than pouring water on a head and saying words; it involves a complex process of socialization through which a person truly becomes part of a community that is struggling to live the life of grace.

Preparation for adult baptism prior to Vatican II centered around "convert classes" in which those who wished to become Catholic would learn the basic beliefs taught by the church. Often, the text was the same catechism used by children. The focus was on information: what Catholics believe about God, grace, church, sacraments, and commandments. If the prospective convert could demonstrate an understanding of the faith commensurate with personal ability, he or she was deemed ready to be baptized. The brief baptismal ceremony most often took place in a room separate from the main church and with only a few friends or relatives present.

Promulgated in 1972, the RCIA restores the basic sacramental process used by the church in the third through the fifth centuries. This process can last anywhere from one to three years. The focus is on formation rather than information; that is, the main concern is one's growth as a member of the church community more than one's understanding of Catholic beliefs. This is not to say that beliefs are not important, even crucial; it is only to say that beliefs do not take priority over the even more important element of experiencing life as a committed Christian within the context of a spirited faith community.

The RCIA centers on meetings of small groups that include catechumens (those who wish to be baptized), candidates (those already baptized who wish to be received into full communion with the Catholic Church), sponsors, and an adult initiation team. Typically, these groups meet twice a week: one evening, and then again on Sunday after the liturgy of the Word. Catechumens, or those being initiated, participate in the liturgy of the Word, but then are dismissed after the homily to attend their meeting. The prebaptismal period is, in a sense, a time of anticipation for the full Eucharist. This period highlights for the catechumens, as well as for full-fledged Catholics, the distinct privilege of participating in and receiving the Eucharist.

The meetings are times to not only learn about Catholic beliefs but also pray, read Scriptures, share experiences, socialize, establish relationships, and grow in faith. The process is a time for becoming Catholic together. One of the beautiful dimensions of adult initiation is the underlying philosophy that what it takes to *become* a Christian and what it takes to *remain* a Christian both involve basically the same process of growth in faith. The newcomer can offer as much to the old hand as vice versa. It is not as though Catholics are saying, "We've got it," and are going to let the catechumens and candidates "get it" also. It is more that these Catholics are growing in faith and are asking the catechumens and candidates to join them in the journey. Catholics do not assume they are light years ahead of the initiates when it comes to the most basic issues of relationship with God and spiritual maturity. Many sponsors claim their own encounter with the RCIA gave them an experience of the Catholic faith on a level they had never known existed.

Catechumens who are preparing for baptism at Easter are enrolled in the book of election during a Mass on the first Sunday of Lent. Lent begins a more intense period of preparation. The catechumens will be baptized during the Easter Vigil on Holy Saturday night. They will also receive the sacraments of confirmation and communion. These three sacraments are known as the sacraments of initiation; in the early centuries of the church, they were administered together. At the Easter Vigil, those who had been baptized previously receive confirmation and communion only. During the next few weeks following the vigil, the newly initiated group continues to meet to reflect more deeply on the meaning of receiving the sacraments and becoming full-fledged Catholics.

What makes adult initiation a tool for church renewal is the way that it thrusts the parish in the direction of community formation. Once a parish begins celebrating the rites for initiating adults, that parish feels more than a little pressure to become a dynamic faith community. The initiation group itself—inquirers, catechumens, candidates, the elect, the newly baptized, sponsors, catechists—functions as a model that draws the whole parish to participate in some way. Sponsors and other parishioners represent the presence of the parish within the group itself. Parishioners and catechumens get to know each other through events in the normal course of parish life. Parishioners witness the catechumens leaving Mass after the homily, building community awareness of the RCIA process. Parishioners participate in the liturgies when the catechumens are elected and when they receive the sacraments of initiation. The process of initiation calls upon all Catholics to reflect more deeply upon what it means to be a Christian. The congregation's renewal of baptismal vows at Easter takes on a new depth. The RCIA can generate a contagious spirit that catches fire throughout the parish.

Lay Ministries

Today, many Catholic parishes employ lay ecclesial ministers. Pastoral associates, directors of religious education, youth ministers, and others work alongside priests in running entire parishes, performing virtually every service short of celebrating the Eucharist and hearing confessions. In priestless parishes, the pastoral administrator runs the parish. Directors of religious education are responsible for adult education programming and classes for youth who do not attend Catholic schools. Youth ministers run comprehensive programs for adolescents.

The laypeople who fill these positions often have either an academic degree in theology or pastoral ministry or have completed an extensive program for lay ministry training in their diocese. The need for such people is still growing, both within and beyond the parish. Lay Catholics today serve as ministers in Catholic high schools, colleges, hospitals, dioceses, and social service organizations.

Even exceeding the growth of lay ecclesial ministers in the Catholic Church is the expansion of services performed by nonprofessional lay ministers. Since Vatican II, virtually every parish has developed a council of members that evaluates the state of the parish and advises the pastor on major decisions. Various parish committees or commissions are responsible for particular ministries. For example, most parishes have a worship commission, an education commission, and a finance commission. In my parish, we have a visitation committee that visits the sick; a bereavement committee that ministers to families when a loved one has died; a welcoming committee that smooths the entry of newcomers into the parish; a peace and justice committee that addresses social issues and holds letter-writing campaigns; an evangelization team that tries to spread the gospel within the parish and to reach out to the unchurched; a parish outreach that runs programs that provide shelter, food, and literacy training to those in need; and many other forms of volunteer involvement of laypersons in ministry.

© iStock.com / KatieDobies

Lumen gentium (33) declares, "The Laity . . . have the capacity to assume from the Hierarchy certain ecclesiastical functions." The growing ranks of lay ecclesial ministers, like the one shown here, implement this principle.

The committees of parishioners that participate in the various ministries function as small faith communities. Many who join these committees had an initial experience in a small faith community through the RCIA, either as a catechumen or a sponsor. Many other small faith communities are based simply on shared prayer or Scripture study.

I recently attended a Mass in my parish in which the pastor asked all who served in parish ministries to come to the front of the church. More than 80 percent of those attending came forward. During the fifty years since Vatican II, lay ministries and related small faith communities have functioned as a tool for church renewal, because they get the people to claim ownership of the spiritual life of the parish. The main role of the priest, the pastoral associate, and the director of religious education is to train, facilitate, coordinate, and empower the people of the parish to form a vibrant faith community. The paid staff cannot simply do it for them. Members of the Catholic laity today are treated as adults who need to take responsibility for their own spiritual growth.

New Ecclesial Movements

Beyond parishes, new ecclesial movements have exploded onto the scene throughout the past century, though they have been an especially important development since Vatican II. The Pontifical Council for the Laity recognizes more than 120 associations in its online directory.[1] There is a great deal of diversity among the new ecclesial movements. Communion and Liberation, Focolare, the Neocatechumenal Way, the Catholic Worker Movement, *Regnum Christi*, *Opus Dei*, *Sant'Egidio*, the Legion of Mary, and the Community of St. John are all very different from one another. Some of these groups are lay only; others contain lay, religious, and priests. Many of these groups are notably conservative and traditional; a few are quite progressive. Many, though not all, are somewhat like religious orders in that they have founders with a special charism and follow strict rules. A few of these groups consist of laypeople who are attached to a religious order. Virtually all of these groups focus, in some way, on the role of the laity—either in forming tightly knit faith communities or in transforming the world.

The Catholic charismatic renewal, though it does not consider itself to be a movement, has affected more people and had more impact by far than all the new ecclesial movements put together. The Renewal finds some of its roots in Pentecostalism and is characterized by a focus on baptism in the Holy Spirit, along with signs like speaking in tongues, prophesying, and healing. By some estimates, there are now more than 600 million Pentecostals in the world, which equates to about one in every twelve or thirteen people worldwide and almost one-fourth of all Christians. That number includes 200 million Catholic charismatics, which is about one in six of all Catholics.[2]

The new ecclesial movements have brought some problems as well, a point most members acknowledge. Among those problems can be a degree of spiritual

1. See the Pontifical Council of the Laity's directory, International Associations of the Faithful, at *http://www.vatican.va/roman_curia/pontifical_councils/laity/documents/rc_pc_laity_doc_20051114 _associazioni_en.html.*

2. See the Pentecostal Resource Page on the Pew Research Center website: *http://www.pew forum.org/2006/10/05/pentecostal-resource-page/.* I also received some figures in private conversation with Pentecostal theologian, Amos Yong.

elitism, manifested as a holier-than-thou attitude toward outsiders. Perhaps this can be expected in groups that offer members a spiritual awakening that makes their former lives seem dark by comparison. A related problem can be a strong traditionalism that motivates many of these groups to think and act like culture warriors against the outside world, from which they tend to withdraw.

Both Pope Francis and the Congregation for the Doctrine of the Faith have, in recent years, expressed a mixture of appreciation and caution toward these new ecclesial movements.[3] On the one hand, they recognize the presence and activity of the Holy Spirit within these groups. On the other hand, they urge members to accept that the Holy Spirit ultimately moves groups of Christians toward communion with others.

Summary

This chapter examined several means that the Catholic Church is using to build community: adult initiation, lay ministries, and new ecclesial movements.

Catholic parishes, in general, still have a long way to go in becoming lively communities of people who empower members to live as disciples of Christ. Much more is needed toward becoming attractive communities that draw people in and make them feel welcome. At the same time, though, the Catholic Church has come a long way in these areas, is setting its goals clearly, and has in place many effective tools. Has the day finally arrived when I can say to the young woman who used to deliver my newspaper that the Catholic Church is not only offering a wide array of true beliefs but also has something that is right for her?

The next chapter will examine the spiritual dimensions of one of the main spheres of lay activity: the world of work.

For Further Reflection

1. Do you know any stories of people who have been changed through their experience within a church community?

2. Can you think of an example to illustrate the difference between treating laypeople as children and treating them as adults who have responsibility for their own spiritual life?

3. See, for example, "Address of His Holiness Pope Francis to Participants in the Third World Congress of Ecclesial Movements and New Communities," November 22, 2014, *http://w2.vatican .va/content/francesco/en/speeches/2014/november/documents/papa-francesco_20141122_convegno -movimenti-ecclesiali.html*; also Congregation for the Doctrine of the Faith, "Letter '*Iuvenescit Eccle-sia*' to the Bishops of the Catholic Church Regarding the Relationship between Hierarchical and Charismatic Gifts in the Life and the Mission of the Church," May 15, 2016, *http://www.vatican.va /roman_curia/congregations/cfaith/documents/rc_con_cfaith_doc_20160516_iuvenescit-ecclesia_en.html*.

3. Do you personally feel as comfortable being ministered to by laypeople as you do by ordained priests or ministers?
4. Have you ever experienced a "dead" Catholic parish or other church community? What might make such a community come to life?
5. Do you believe rites of initiation and vigorous lay ministries will revitalize Catholic parishes, or is more or something other needed?

Suggested Readings

Dunning, James B. *New Wine, New Wineskins: Exploring the RCIA.* Chicago: W. H. Sadlier, 1981.

Faggioli, Massimo. *The Rising Laity: Ecclesial Movements since Vatican II.* Mahwah, NJ: Paulist Press, 2016.

Ganim, Carole. *Shaping Catholic Parishes: Pastoral Leaders in the 21st Century.* Chicago: Loyola Press, 2008.

Hater, Robert J. *The Catholic Parish: Hope for a Changing World.* Mahwah, NJ: Paulist Press, 2004.

Leahy, Brendan. *Ecclesial Movements and Communities: Origins, Significance, and Issues.* Hyde Park, NY: New City Press, 2011.

Lee, Bernard J., and Michael A. Cowan. *Gathered and Sent: The Mission of Small Church Communities Today.* Mahwah, NJ: Paulist, 2003.

Macalintal, Diana. *Your Parish Is the Curriculum: RCIA in the Midst of Community.* Collegeville, MN: Liturgical Press, 2018.

Nordenbrock, William A. *Beyond Accompaniment: Guiding a Fractured Community to Wholeness.* Collegeville, MN: Liturgical Press, 2011.

Porteous, Julian. *New Wine and Fresh Skins: Ecclesial Movements in the Church* Leominster, UK: Gracewing, 2010.

United States Conference of Catholic Bishops. *Co-Workers in the Vineyard of the Lord.* Washington, DC: US Conference of Catholic Bishops, 2005.

A Spirituality of Work

A first-year student in an introductory course I teach came to see me. About nineteen years old, she told me she had decided to major in ecological science. What had made her decide that? I asked. She replied that her brother had told her there were good jobs open at the Environmental Protection Agency (EPA) and that they paid a decent salary. Given present trends, she thought there would be a secure future in such work.

"Are there any other reasons for your choice?" I asked. She thought for a second and said, "Yes, there are." She had always wanted to be a police officer. Law enforcement attracted her. When she watched cop shows on television, she felt that was what she wanted to be. The type of work she would go into at the EPA would allow her to combine law enforcement with a technical skill. She could have a well-paying job and still do something that would allow her to be herself.

"Are there any other reasons for your choice?" I persisted. None that came right to mind, she said. "Do you have any personal concern for the environment or for the impact of environmental deterioration on human society?" I asked. Although she had never thought of that, she was not against considering it.

Some people might feel tempted to interpret this young woman's response as a depressing sign of an age when students are interested in making money and doing what they like without any broader social commitment. If this student had been a graduating senior, her response would represent a real problem; for an entering student, however, she had many positive things to say. In fact, measured against the four main purposes of work talked about by Pope John Paul II—to make a living, to practice self-expression and find fulfillment, to contribute to society, and, through the first three purposes, to connect with life's deepest spiritual meanings—her response exhibits the first two and shows openness to the third. Perhaps the fourth will come in time.

Overview

As discussed in an earlier chapter, the main spheres of lay Christian activity outlined in *Lumen gentium* are work, family, and social transformation. This chapter considers the place of a person's work in living a Christian life, that is, a spirituality of work. In doing so, this chapter draws heavily upon themes from Pope John Paul II's 1981 encyclical on work, *Laborem exercens* (*On Human Work*).[1]

Four Purposes of Work

I attended college in the early 1970s, an era that was still part of the 1960s—think Vietnam, rock music, sexual freedom, and cultural revolution. At that time I held a snobbish belief. I thought that to be a real human being, a person had to major in a subject like English, philosophy, or social work. I tended to look down on students who majored in business or technical areas, considering them copouts who had joined the corrupt military-industrial establishment. I divided the world into two kinds of people: those who cared about life and love and peace and brotherhood, and those who wanted to make a living.

I have learned a lot since those days. I no longer divide the world as I did then. Nor do I pit making a living against social commitment. What I have come to realize is that the world is crying out for socially committed people to go into business and technical areas. We do not need a world populated solely by English teachers and social workers. What we need, rather, are business people, English teachers, technicians, and social workers who care about the world beyond themselves and are committed to a vision of a more just society.

John Paul II's thinking about the four purposes of work is helpful in this regard. First, he does not say it is sinful to want to make a decent living; rather he recognizes people work not only to sustain themselves but also to better their material condition. Second, he does not say it is selfish to be concerned about self-fulfillment; rather, he values self-expression and personal fulfillment as an important dimension of one's work life. Third, he offers a vision in which the first two purposes are integrally connected with a person's contribution to the larger society. Fourth, he offers a vision in which the first three purposes are set within the context of the person's relationship with God.

The first purpose of work is to earn enough money to support oneself and one's family. This should not be an exclusive or overriding concern, but it holds an important place. The second purpose is to find self-expression and fulfillment. Work is what most of us do for a large percentage of our waking life. What we do is an expression of who we are. The third purpose is to contribute

---

1. Pope John Paul II, *Laborem exercens* (*On Human Work*), 1981, *http://w2.vatican.va/content/john-paul-ii/en/encyclicals/documents/hf_jp-ii_enc_14091981_laborem-exercens.html*.

to the larger society. We work not simply for ourselves but for the good of others. We draw upon our talents and strengths to provide services for those who need them. The fourth purpose is to connect work with the deepest spiritual meanings in life.

What is important about these four purposes is that they are not pitted against each other. They can coexist in harmony. John Paul II suggests that all four are important, and that the absence of one or more of these purposes can indicate a problem in the meaning of work for that person.

These purposes may seem idealistic when applied to the real world. Some people hate their jobs. For many, work is nothing more than a way to make a living. Some people are embarrassed by the work they do because of its low social status. Others do not think about the service they provide, but rather, resent their customers and try to get by with doing as little as possible. For many people, work is anything but fun. Instead of being a means of self-fulfillment and an avenue of social contribution, it is a prison from which they seek to escape during off-hours.

John Paul II was not unaware of the ambiguity of work. In *Laborem exercens*, he says, "Human life is built up every day from work, from work it derives its specific dignity, but at the same time work contains the unceasing measure of human toil and suffering and also the harm and injustice which penetrate deeply into social life" (*LE* 1).

In the face of this ambiguity, it is important to examine other dimensions of what the pope offers for considering work's meaning.

The Dignity of Work

What gives work its dignity? In addressing this question, John Paul II distinguishes between the subjective and objective dimensions of work. Work in the objective sense refers to the various technologies by which human beings manipulate the world for the fulfillment of human needs. The pope mentions agriculture, industry, service industries, and research as examples of fields of economic activity in the objective sense. That is, work in the objective sense refers to the type of work that is done.

Work in the subjective sense refers to the activity of the worker in a way that is independent from the particular type of work being done. That is, whenever work is being accomplished, it involves a human being, made in the image of God, called to self-realization, performing certain tasks and activities. This is true no matter what the tasks and activities are. Work in the subjective sense thus recognizes that no matter what the particular task, the one doing the work is a human being.

John Paul II draws two points from this distinction that are important in discussing a spirituality of work. First, he declares that, by his definition, virtually all people are workers. Whether one is a housewife, student, bricklayer, artist, manager, investment broker, owner, or professor, one is a worker. One performs tasks that are both expressive of self and in the service of others. John Paul II devotes a subsection to explaining how people with disabilities are also workers and have opportunities to contribute.

In my neighborhood, there is a tension between mothers who work and mothers who stay home to raise their children. Each group has a way of resenting and looking down at the other. Each group also seems to be somewhat aware of the ridiculousness of this and tries to overcome it. By John Paul II's definition, both groups are made up of workers. Getting paid a salary is not what differentiates a worker from a nonworker. At least on that point, the mothers should be united.

The idea that all people are workers also has implications in the economic and social spheres. Although there may be different classes economically and socially, in the subjective sense, we are all workers. Capital investment is only an instrument; work has to do with people. Work must be recognized as being in the service of human beings, because people are more important than things. Labor takes priority over capital. In saying this, though, John Paul II does not elevate laborers over capitalists; rather he calls for the realization that all stand, ultimately, on the same side as workers. John Paul II thus subverts the notion of classes when it comes to the value of the human person. Rich people are not better than poor people or working-class people; everyone is a worker called to self-expression and social contribution.

A second point John Paul II draws from his distinction between the objective and subjective dimensions of work is that work takes its dignity primarily from the subjective dimension. That is, what gives work its dignity is not the type of work being done but that the one doing it is a person. By this measure, there is nothing less dignified about being a migrant farmer, a sanitation worker, or a car wash attendant than about being a doctor, an engineer, or a manager. In *Laborem exercens*, John Paul II is clear about this point and its connection with the notion of class:

> The basis for determining the value of human work is not primarily the kind of work being done, but the fact that the one who is doing it is a person. The sources of the dignity of work are to be sought in the subjective dimension, not in the objective one.
>
> Such a concept practically does away with the very basis of the ancient differentiation of people into classes according to the kind of work done. This does not mean that from the objective point of view human work cannot and must not be rated and qualified in any way. It only means that the primary basis of the value of human work is human beings themselves, who are its subject. (*LE* 6)

John Paul II is not saying all workers should receive exactly the same salary; he is not saying that objectively speaking there should be no classes. Rather, he is saying that the basic human dignity connected with work does not derive from its social status.

His positions have many practical implications. Everyone is a worker. All workers should keep in mind that work is in the service of human beings. All workers have a basic dignity that does not derive from the type of work being done. All workers have rights, including the right to just wages and benefits and the right to form unions for defending vital interests. Ultimately, workers should share as much as possible in the decision-making and ownership of the firms for which they work. These practical points have been emphasized in recent Catholic social teaching.

In *Laborem exercens*, Pope John Paul II insists that the dignity of work derives not from the type of work performed, but from "the fact that the one who is doing it is a person" (*LE* 6).

The real world seems a long way from the vision offered by Pope John Paul II. Could it really be true that we can experience each other as equal in spiritual dignity in a way that is independent of our social status? The British Catholic author G. K. Chesterton describes this ability as one of the distinguishing characteristics of St. Francis of Assisi:

> St. Francis . . . honoured all men; that is, he not only loved but respected them all. What gave him this extraordinary personal power was this; that from the Pope to the beggar, from the sultan of Syria in his pavilion to the ragged robbers crawling out of the woods, there was never a man who looked into those brown burning eyes without being certain that Francis Bernadone was really interested in *him*; in his own inner individual life from the cradle to the grave; that he himself was being valued and taken seriously . . . he treated the whole mob of men as a mob of kings.[2]

For most of us, such an ability is a long way off.

---

2. G. K. Chesterton, *St. Francis of Assisi* (New York: George H. Doran, 1924), 141–42.

The Cross and the Resurrection

Yet, the ambiguity of work remains. John Paul II returns to this issue in the final section of *Laborem exercens* in order to explore the fourth purpose of work. He expresses his points on this purpose with an explicitly Christian focus. On the one hand, work is a sharing in the creative activity of God. God is still actively at work in the world, and when people work, they participate in a limited way in this creativity. Jesus himself was a working man, a carpenter, who was familiar with the world of work and who frequently referred to workers in his parables and other teachings.

On the other hand, though, work is toil and suffering, pain and sweat. What meaning does this have?

John Paul II refers us to the cross of Christ. Jesus' work of redemption involved a great deal of pain and suffering. Through work, human beings share in the cross of Christ and in his work of redemption: "One shows oneself a true disciple of Christ by carrying the cross in one's turn every day in the activity one is called upon to perform" (*LE* 27).

John Paul II reminds us that the cross leads to the Resurrection. The work we do contributes to bringing about a new earth that awaits its final redemption through the coming of the kingdom of God. The positive results of work should reinforce one's ultimate hopes by revealing a "glimmer of new life."

In other words, in this final section, the pope uses explicitly Christian concepts and language to remind us that work is one of the main ways Christians participate in the mystery of Christ. The suffering involved in work is not explained away, but rather is placed in the context of this mystery. We do not know the answer to the why of the pain, but we can look at the cross and believe that, through the suffering Christ, this too will ultimately make some sense.

Work and Leisure

In *Laborem exercens*, John Paul II mentions that both work and rest involve a sharing in the creativity of God. When Genesis says God rested on the seventh day, this is interpreted as a comment on the appropriateness and even holiness of rest.

This is an important point to consider in a society that has witnessed a rise in workaholism. A workaholic is a person who compulsively seeks escape through work. Usually what the workaholic is seeking to escape is low self-esteem, inadequate human relationships, and a truncated spiritual life. Workaholism can build social status and bank accounts as it destroys the lives of individuals and families.

Jesus was not a workaholic. Jesus did not ask for the sick and possessed to be lined up so he could labor from dawn to dusk healing and casting out demons. Jesus is portrayed in the Scriptures as often seeking out time for prayer and rest.

Rest and leisure are as important as work. The development and enjoyment of human relationships is as much a part of an individual's purpose on earth as any external social contribution. John Paul II says the rhythm of work and leisure "must leave room for human beings to prepare themselves, by becoming more and more what in the will of God they ought to be, for the 'rest' that the Lord reserves for his servants and friends" (LE 25).

Summary

This chapter discussed various dimensions of a spirituality of work: the purposes of work, the source of its dignity, the meaning of toil and accomplishment, and the need to balance labor and leisure.

I still think the young woman who told me of her decision to major in ecological science is off to a good start. She sees a way to make a living. She is attracted to an occupation that will allow her to express herself. She is not closed to the idea that her work will enable her to make a needed social contribution. Eventually, she may come to identify her work with the cross and Resurrection of Christ. How will she see herself in relation to other workers? From what source will she derive a sense of her own dignity in work? How will she interpret the pain and toil that inevitably go along with work? Will she become lost in her work, or will she maintain a strong sense of human relationships and personal spirituality?

The next chapter will discuss Christian spirituality in connection with the universal call to holiness.

For Further Reflection

1. Have your own experiences of work been more positive or negative in regard to fostering good human relationships?
2. Are students these days too focused on making money?
3. Do you think that it is common for young people to take social contribution into account in career decisions?
4. Is workaholism truly a major problem, or is it just a trendy way of talking about people who simply work too much?
5. Does it sound far-fetched to suggest that everyday people relate their work with Christ's death and Resurrection?

Suggested Readings

Baum, Gregory. *The Priority of Labor: A Commentary on* Laborem exercens. New York: Paulist Press, 1982.

John Paul II. *Laborem exercens (On Human Work)*, 1981, *http://w2.vatican.va/content/john-paul-ii/en/encyclicals/documents/hf_jp-ii_enc_14091981_laborem-exercens.html.*

Oates, Wayne E. *Confessions of a Workaholic: The Facts about Work Addiction.* Nashville: Abingdon, 1971.

Palmer, Parker J. *The Active Life: A Spirituality of Work, Creativity, and Caring.* San Francisco: Harper and Row, 1990.

Placher, William, ed. *Callings: Twenty Centuries of Christian Wisdom on Vocation.* Grand Rapids: Eerdmans, 2005.

Vest, Norvene. *Friend of the Soul: A Benedictine Spirituality of Work.* Cambridge, MA: Cowley Publications, 1997.

Volf, Miroslav. *Work in the Spirit: Toward a Theology of Work.* Eugene, OR: Wipf and Stock, 2001 (1991).

Spirituality as a Journey in Faith

When I was in Catholic grade school in the early 1960s, I was deathly afraid of God. I lived by what I now think of as "musical chairs spirituality." In musical chairs spirituality, the focus is on what happens to you when you die. That is, when the music of life stops, is there a place open for you in heaven? The fear of hell, the belief that it would not be difficult to go to hell, the trap of mortal sin—these specters haunted me.

I also learned many wonderful things about religion in that school. I learned about the importance of loving God and neighbor. I learned about receiving Jesus in the Eucharist and the other sacraments. I learned how to tell basic right from wrong. I learned the value of sacrifice and discipline.

Nonetheless, the fear of God and of hell that pervaded my youth went hand in hand with my understanding of what it meant to live a Christian life. Being a Christian involved more than just loving God and neighbor. It involved getting ready for the Day of Judgment. In fact, it was as though a whole system was set up according to which God would judge your eternal state of being.

Basically, it went like this:

If you die in a state of grace, you go to heaven. If you die out of a state of grace, you go to hell. If you die with a lot of venial sins but still in the state of grace, you spend time in purgatory, but that is all right because you end up making it into heaven.

What determines whether you are in a state of grace?

First of all, whether you are baptized. Unbaptized people such as infants or those from cultures foreign to Christianity go to limbo rather than hell. For Catholic students, however, baptism is a must. Once baptism puts you in a state of grace, you need to maintain it by keeping the Commandments and not committing mortal (very serious) sins. Venial (less serious) sins put a mark on your soul, but they would not put you totally out of a state of grace. You know a sin is mortal if it is (1) a seriously wrong thought, word, or deed; (2) you have given sufficient reflection before committing it; and (3) you chose to do it with no one forcing you. If you commit a mortal sin, you are no longer in a state of grace and are thereby a candidate for hell if you should die.

And if you are in a state of mortal sin?

Then you need to have your mortal sins forgiven. The best way to have mortal sins forgiven is by telling them to the priest in confession and receiving absolution. If you cannot make it to confession immediately, then say an act of contrition (a prayer asking God to forgive you) and strive to have true sorrow for your sins. Perfect contrition, which is sorrow out of love of God and revulsion at having offended God, wipes out mortal sin immediately with or without confession, though one is still obliged to go to confession when able. Imperfect contrition, or sorrow out of a fear of punishment, is sufficient for the forgiveness of mortal sin in the context of the sacrament of confession. Once your mortal sins are forgiven, you are back in a state of grace.

This system provided the underlying philosophy for our religion textbook, the *Baltimore Catechism*, throughout grade school. This textbook contained beautiful teachings about the meaning of life, such as God creating us because of love, the commandment to love God and neighbor, the virtues, the gifts and fruits of the Holy Spirit, the spiritual and corporal works of mercy, the Beatitudes, and other treasures that genuinely inspired me and continue to enrich my life. I still also believe that some notion of hell and the possibility of throwing one's gift of life away for all eternity remain meaningful and in some sense true. To this day, I believe that if you take away the overly systematic and impersonal nature of the system, it can function as a way of opening up truth about the meaning of life. As I remember it, though, the quality of these teachings was hampered by the strong focus on hell and the overly mechanical ways one could use to judge where one stood in relation to God and eternity.

A distorting element of my early spirituality was thus a near obsession with staying in a state of grace. This was accompanied by the belief that it was easy to commit a mortal sin and not even be aware of it. I also believed that probably many people went to hell. I thought of God as one who, as a punishment for original sin, had made the world a place from which only the lucky few would be saved. God was a stingy and angry God who needed to be appeased.

Is this an accurate picture of how I thought about God in those days? Probably not. The stingy, angry God and the loving, generous God were mixed in my mind. Did the grade school really teach me these fearful images of God? Yes and no. These ideas were in the air, but I am sure I latched onto them in relation to my own already established fears and insecurities. No matter where the ideas came from, much of my spirituality as a child was based on a mechanical system implemented by an angry God who struck fear into the very depths of my soul.

Overview

The fifth chapter of *Lumen gentium* (*Dogmatic Constitution on the Church*) speaks of the universal call to holiness in the church. When I was a child, holiness was something for priests and sisters and brothers and saints to worry about, not for regular people. Vatican II called for more than that by stressing that all Christians are called to live a holy life. This shift is one of the most important developments of the entire council.

The topic of this chapter is Christian spirituality. It addresses the issue of what it means to live a holy life. This topic is at the heart of understanding the church. Prior to Vatican II, official Catholic theology dealt with the topic of church too impersonally and without reference to love and holiness. It was as though "church" had to do only with things like organizational structures and appropriate procedures. Love and holiness were important topics, but they were dealt with in separate treatises on grace and sacraments. Vatican II changed that segmented approach to theology by making the chapter on holiness the centerpiece of one of the two main documents on the church. The church is holy, marked with a holiness that comes from Christ himself. Anyone who is a member of the church is called to follow Christ by striving to lead a holy life.

The rest of this chapter explores some contrasts between the spirituality I lived as a child and some things I have learned since.

Personal and Ongoing

Spirituality deals with our faith-journey through rich, multilayered territories. There are no foolproof systems that guarantee growth. Systems can function as useful maps, but it should be remembered that the map is not the territory. The territory has too much depth and too many dimensions to be captured by any one map. There is always more to the mystery of God and the mystery of life than can be realized in any one system.

The God of Christians is personal, not mechanical. God does not operate with a big scoreboard in the sky to decide, by numbers, who will go to heaven or to hell. Holiness is more about acknowledging our vulnerabilities and weaknesses and being open to the embrace of a merciful God. Christian doctrines about sin put us in touch with the reality of the negative side of our shared human situation, individual inclinations, and the tremendous and terrible choice we face: will we ultimately embrace God and life, or will we reject them? Sin is a reality; the reality, however, has to do most basically with our relationship with God and with other human beings. When the level of personal relationships remains primary, institutional expressions of these relationships are put in their place as useful but partial tools that aid in understanding.

For example, what do I take as evidence that offers me hope for my salvation? Today my first inclination is not to think hard about whether I have committed mortal sins. Rather, I am inclined to think first about my ongoing commitment to God and others. This includes my prayer life, commitment to family, involvement in deep human relationships, disposition toward honesty, concern for social and environmental improvements, and faith in a loving God who accepts me despite my deep and many faults. In other words, when I think about salvation, I think first about personal relationships. Thinking in terms of a system of sin and grace can help me assess such relationships, but should not become more important than the relationships themselves.

My understanding of the sacraments, like my understanding of God, has become less mechanical and more personal. Sacraments are not just rituals that dispense grace; rather, sacraments give grace in a way that keys into and celebrates the religious dimensions we experience in the context of our lives. Baptism celebrates entry into the faith community. Confirmation celebrates conscious embracing of the faith. Eucharist celebrates ongoing personal unity with Christ, with other Christians, and with the entire human family. Reconciliation celebrates forgiveness received from God and others. Anointing of the Sick celebrates the healing love of God and community. Marriage celebrates the ongoing covenant of married love. Holy orders celebrates the reality of sacramental leadership. Sacraments give grace, but they do so in conjunction with the meaning that we experience at the depth of our lives as we relate with God and others.

Spirituality, then, has to do with an ongoing process in the midst of our lives. Preparing for the Day of Judgment retains a certain power, but it should not provide the main focal point of spiritual life. Laypeople live their spirituality not only in church but also in the context of their family, work, and efforts toward social transformation.

Love and Fear

I am not of the trendy school of thought that says all fear is bad. The Scriptures in several places tell us, "Fear of the Lord is the beginning of wisdom." Yet it says in 1 John 4:18 that "perfect love casts out fear." I think that fear has its place in this world, where we do not, as yet, know perfect love. Thomas Aquinas taught there are different types of fear. The fear of punishment will not remain with the blessed in heaven. But the fear of offending God and others, which is a healthy fear, will remain.[1]

Just as fear of physical harm can keep us alert to possible dangers, so fear of offending God can aid in our spiritual journey. The Protestant theologian

---

1. Thomas Aquinas, *Summa theologiae*, II, Q. 19, A. 11.

Rudolf Otto described the fundamental religious experience as being that of the "holy," an overpowering mystery that elicits dread, awe, majesty, urgency, and fascination.[2] God is not a familiar pal whose back we feel free to smack. God is one who holds our attention, one whose enormity and otherness can make us quake in our boots. Watch out for God. God will change you. If you encounter God, your life will never be the same.

My teachers in grade school did me a favor by introducing me to this God. And I must say that if I knew I was going to meet God in the next five minutes, I would be more than a little awestruck. A problem arises not when someone is taught a basic, healthy fear of God, but when fear becomes ingrained as the primary means of relating to God.

It is possible for fear to become the ruling emotion in a person's life. There are people who live by what they fear others will think. Such is the case with the speaker in T. S. Eliot's poem, *The Love Song of J. Alfred Prufrock*, whose introverted life is ruled by his insecurities:

Shall I part my hair behind? Do I dare to eat a peach?

I shall wear white flannel trousers, and walk along the beach.

I can hear the mermaids singing each to each.

I do not think that they will sing to me.

There are other ways to live a life ruled by fear. Some people fear that they are worthless and, therefore, will not really try to communicate who they are to others. Some fear loneliness or abandonment, and so they remain in relationships in which they are abused. Some fear they will not be successful, and so they lie and cheat and deceive others for money. Alcoholics and compulsive gamblers live in such fear they often cannot admit to themselves that they have a problem. Some people live with a deep-seated fear of God.

Fear has many companions. Anger, resentment, self-pity, jealousy, self-righteousness, and ingratitude can often be found associating with fear. A life of fear is a terrible way to go.

The Christian God, the Father about whom Jesus taught, is a God who can inspire fear in the hearts of the wicked. Ultimately, though, the God about whom Jesus taught is a God who loves and accepts. This is not a God who wants to make sure that a large enough quota of people goes to hell. God numbers and treasures the very hair on our heads. God is like the father of the prodigal son; he hurries out to forgive his son before his son even reaches his home (Lk 15:11–32). God so loved the world that he gave his only begotten Son that the world might be saved through him (Jn 3:16–17).

---

2. Rudolf Otto, *The Idea of the Holy* (London: Oxford University Press, 1923).

And yet, this God challenges us to grow. Jesus never said to his disciples, "Don't change a thing. I love you just the way you are." God is not a rubber stamp; God is one who calls us to stretch and at times to groan. I think of a saying I saw on a poster: "Just because I love you unconditionally does not mean that I have given up all hope for your improvement."

Faith, hope, and love are the Christian remedies against fear and its companions. Faith gives us the trust that opens us to a worldview based on the goodness of God. Hope enables us to take the risks of honesty and humility in reaching out to others for help and support. Love opens us up to care for others in a way that takes us out of our problems and heals us. Paul says, "And now faith, hope, and love abide, these three; and the greatest of these is love." (1 Cor 13:13).

In the Catholic Church today, the need to grow in one's individual and communal faith journey is balanced by the need to work for peace, justice, and ecological wholeness. In these issues, too, we are called to be motivated out of love rather than fear.

Summary

In this chapter, I described something of my personal journey from a spirituality based in fear to one more grounded in faith, hope, love, and social commitment. The more I think about what I said in the beginning of this chapter about my own education, however, the more I wonder whether I was really being accurate. Few things are harder to interpret than one's own life story. In the midst of the negativities from grade school, I retain clear memories of how much was taught to me about the love of God.

As expressed in chapter 5 of *Lumen gentium*, at the core of Christian spirituality is the following of Christ. Holiness belongs first to Christ and is a gift given by Christ to the church. Christians are holy through participation in the church as it participates in Christ's holiness.

Following Christ requires seeking and doing the will of the Father. One comes to know the will of the Father by listening to the Holy Spirit. Christian spirituality is thus Trinitarian. This chapter focused on Christian spirituality as the universal call to holiness. The next two chapters will consider, respectively, Jesus Christ and the Holy Spirit.

For Further Reflection

1. Have you ever been taught to fear God?
2. Do you believe some people go to hell?
3. What is it that can move a person from fear to love?

4. In what ways has your religious education focused on your life-journey and on the quality of your relationships?
5. How do you think Christian religious education today most differs from that of the early 1960s?

Suggested Readings

Bernardin, Joseph Cardinal. *The Gift of Peace: Personal Reflections.* Chicago: Loyola Press, 1997.

Elizondo, Virgilio. *Charity.* Maryknoll, NY: Orbis Books, 2009.

Francis, Pope. *Gaudete et exsultate. (Apostolic Exhortation on the Call to Holiness in Today's World). http://w2.vatican.va/content/francesco/en/apost_exhortations /documents/papa-francesco esortazione-ap 20180319 gaudete-et-exsultate .html.*

Gonzalez, Adele J. *The Spirituality of Community.* Maryknoll, NY: Orbis Books, 2009.

LaCugna, Catherine Mowry. *God for Us: The Trinity and Christian Life.* San Francisco: Harper, 1991.

Merton, Thomas. *New Seeds of Contemplation.* New York: New Directions, 1961.

Merton, Thomas. *Seeds of Contemplation.* Norfolk, CT: New Directions, 1949.

Nouwen, Henri. *Making All Things New: An Invitation to the Spiritual Life.* San Francisco: Harper and Row, 1981.

O'Malley, William J. *Holiness.* Maryknoll, NY: Orbis Books, 2008.

Breaking the Cycle

My wife and I have four grown children, all boys. When they were young, there were times they seemed locked in conflict. They would play together fine one minute, but the next minute, things would degenerate into "he took my seat," "stop making that noise," "yes I did," "no you didn't," "I don't want to play with you," "you're the biggest creep I ever met," "why do I have to have you for a brother?"

One day, when the two older boys were playing a basketball game called HORSE, the eight-year-old made his shot, and then, just for fun, tossed up a quick practice shot that he missed. The six-year-old did not see the first shot but did see the missed practice shot, which he thought should count. The younger one called the older one a name. The older one hit him with the ball. The younger one ran into the house screaming.

It took me a while to get the two of them to speak calmly enough to help us figure out what had happened. Even when they both understood that there was just a big mix-up, each defended his own position vehemently and said nasty things about the other.

Clearly, the argument between these two went far beyond the precipitating incident. There are extremely deep and complex issues that underlie this type of sibling rivalry. As Jacob was born with his hand on Esau's foot, so any two siblings close in age find themselves engaged in an ardent contest. Does an eighteen-month-old baby really have room in his heart for a competitor? Will a newborn grow to love the idea that someone comes before him or her in rank, privilege, and opportunity?

I separated the two boys and briefly comforted the six-year-old. Then I went to have a talk with the eight-year-old. Without his brother around, he was like a different kid. He got over his anger and was willing to talk. We talked in general about what kind of family we want to have: a family where everybody gets along, where no one has to be afraid of another, where we love and forgive one another. He agreed. Then we talked about his relationship with the six-year-old. I invoked a phrase that has been a useful catchword in our ongoing discussions: I asked, "Who is going to *break* the cycle?"

My son understood what I meant. He and his brother were locked in a conflict with such complex roots in the distant past that it never was either of their faults. They were born into rivalry. It was a no-win situation as long as each simply defended himself. One of them had to break the cycle of conflict by dropping his defenses and reaching out to the other. Somebody had to be willing to start a new cycle of forgiveness and love.

The six-year-old went over to a friend's house to play. The eight-year-old read a book, practiced piano, and watched part of a ball game. Later that evening, we all went swimming as a family, and the boys got along fine. All was well—until the next conflict.

Overview

This chapter considers the mission of Jesus against the background of human conflict. After discussing the meaning of original sin, it will examine Jesus' teachings about the kingdom of God. This material is related to chapter 5 of *Lumen gentium*.

A Global Cycle

Human society on a global scale can be compared to the relationship between my boys. There are so many conflicts of class, sex, race, nation, and creed, with such complex roots so deep in the past, that no one could ever dream of sorting them all out. We are born into this world of continual conflict for which we are not ourselves initially responsible, but that we inherit and that conditions the fabric of our lives. Many people benefit from institutions and social systems that have unfairness built into them. Many who are disadvantaged are socialized into having traits that work against them. As we live our lives, we inevitably become collaborators in structures that help cause human misery.

This profound truth is part of what Catholic doctrine is trying to get at in its teaching about original sin. The effects of sins of the past are structured into the world in which we are born. As we grow, we internalize these structures. They become part of us. Eventually, they help to lead us to make our own sinful choices.

An obvious example is racial prejudice. If one is born into a family and a neighborhood that manifests deep racial prejudice, at what point does one become responsible for being prejudiced oneself? This is a difficult issue to sort out. What makes this even more difficult is that there are many sinful structures we do not recognize as such because we buy into them so deeply. Some socially "successful" people do not recognize any problems whatsoever in our social and economic structures and just think that if everyone would be like them the world would be a perfect place. Some disadvantaged people think it is perfectly all right to "beat the system" (cheat), because they never had a fair chance.

The world is basically good, and human society represents a tremendous achievement. But the world is also plagued by hunger, poverty, lack of medical care, war, and wide ecological destruction. The first world points its finger at the second and third worlds. The second and third worlds point their fingers at the first world. Nuclear armaments remain poised as international terrorism grows. Who is going to break the cycle?

I do not wish to propose any vague idealistic or utopian solutions to the complex problems of the world. My Catholic faith calls me not to be a silly dreamer, but rather, to have a realistic hope that collaboration with our loving God can move us in the right direction. But who is going to break the cycle?

There are many profound ways of interpreting Jesus. One useful way to see Jesus is as one who came to break the cycle.[1] He lit up the path and showed us the way. The path is the journey toward the kingdom of God. The way to follow the path is through self-sacrificing love. In this chapter, we will concentrate on Jesus' teaching about the kingdom.

A Kingdom of Love

When I shared, with my eldest son, a vision of what our family might be like, I was doing on a very small scale what Jesus was doing when he taught about the kingdom of God and what the human family might be like. Jesus' teaching, of course, was much more powerful and mysterious. As he is depicted in the Gospels, Jesus does not matter-of-factly offer a clear vision with a few well-defined values; rather, he teaches through proclamation, parable, confrontation, healing, and example.[2]

The coming of the kingdom of God is the central focus of the teaching of Jesus. In the Gospel of Mark, which most scholars think is the earliest of the Gospels, the first thing Jesus says is, "The time is fulfilled, and the kingdom of God has come near; repent, and believe in the good news" (Mk 1:15). The kingdom of God is breaking in; it is right within our grasp; it is inside us. What opens us up to the kingdom is our willingness and effort to change our lives.

---

1. I first learned this point from David M. Hammond, whose insights into this topic can now be found in *Lonergan and the Theology of the Future: An Invitation* (Eugene, OR: Pickwick, 2017), 104 and 151.

2. Today, many scholars raise legitimate questions about exactly what Jesus taught and how accurately the Gospels communicate his teaching. In this chapter, I subscribe to the basic belief that the Gospels, although not literal news reports, give us a fairly good picture of how Jesus was remembered by the early Christian communities. On that basis, I will talk about "what Jesus taught," but it should be understood that I am more directly talking about how the teaching of Jesus is portrayed in the Gospels.

Jesus stressed that we must remain ready for the coming of the kingdom. He told stories about servants who were unprepared for the return of the master, and about virgins who were unprepared to keep their lights burning when the bridegroom arrived. He said, "Beware, keep alert; for you do not know when the time will come" (Mk 13:33).

The Lord's Prayer is itself a prayer about the coming of the kingdom:

Thy kingdom come
Thy will be done
On earth as it is in heaven.

One might paraphrase this by saying that the kingdom of God exists wherever and whenever the will of God is being done. Jesus exemplifies this by his prayer in the Garden of Gethsemane, as he contemplates his impending death: "Abba, Father, for you all things are possible; remove this cup from me; yet, not what I want, but what you want" (Mk 14:36). Just as Jesus brings about the entry of the kingdom by his obedience to the will of his Father, he calls us to the kingdom through our own seeking and doing of the will of God.

The will of God is, above all, that we love one another. When queried as to which commandment was the greatest, Jesus replied,

"You shall love the Lord your God
with all your heart,
and with all your soul,
and with all your mind."
This is the greatest and first commandment.
And a second is like it:
"You shall love your neighbor as yourself." (Mt 22:37–39)

When Jesus gave his farewell discourse to his disciples at the Last Supper, he said,

As the Father has loved me,
so I have loved you;
abide in my love.
If you keep my commandments,
you will abide in my love,
just as I have kept my Father's commandments
and abide in his love.
I have said these things to you
so that my joy may be in you,

and that your joy may be complete.

This is my commandment,

that you love one another

as I have loved you. (Jn 15:9–12)

There is an irony in the commandment to love one another. People tend to think of commandments as stern obligations. To be ordered to love one another is the best commandment a person could hope for; it is what people really want for themselves.

Blest Are the Poor

Loving one another entails a special concern for the poor and the socially disenfranchised. Jesus reached out to those whom others found unacceptable. He had dinner at the house of Zacchaeus, a much-disliked tax collector (Lk 19:1–10). He told stories about how the beggars, cripples, and lame were the ones invited to the banquet (Lk 14:12–24). He broke custom by socializing with the Samaritan woman at the well (Jn 4:4–42), and even made one of the hated Samaritans the hero of the parable about the man who helps a Jew in trouble after many respectable Jews pass him by (Lk 10:25–36). Jesus includes, in his family, those who share his love and vision, not necessarily just those related to him by blood or nationality. When told that his mother and brothers were outside, he replied, "'Who are my mother and my brothers?' And looking at those who sat around him, he said, 'Here are my mother and my brothers! Whoever does the will of God is my brother and sister and mother'" (Mk 3:33–35).

Jesus teaches that we should not be selective or exclusive in whom we love. In the radical Sermon on the Mount, Jesus says,

But I say to you, love your enemies and pray for those who persecute you, so that you may be children of your Father in heaven; for he makes his sun rise on the evil and on the good, and sends rain on the righteous and on the unrighteous. For if you love those who love you, what reward do you have? Do not even the tax collectors do the same? (Mt 5:44–46)

The Sermon on the Mount is filled with provocative, challenging teachings that show that no one can perfectly live up to the law. We should thereby relate with others humbly out of a sense of our own weaknesses and failings. We are not to sit in judgment; otherwise, we ourselves might be liable to judgment.

The New Testament records Jesus as emphasizing the danger that material riches pose to entry into the kingdom. He says, "Truly I tell you, it will be hard for a rich person to enter the kingdom of heaven. Again I tell you, it is easier for a camel to go through the eye of a needle than for someone who is rich to enter the kingdom of God" (Mt 19:23–24). Yet Jesus adds that although such would be impossible for human beings, for God all things are possible. In the Beatitudes, Jesus proclaims, "Blessed are the poor in spirit, for theirs is the kingdom of heaven" (Mt 5:3). In Luke he says even more bluntly, "Blessed are you who are poor," without the additional "in spirit" (Lk 6:20).

More than the other Gospel writers, Luke portrays Jesus as admonishing the rich, which has led scholars to speculate that issues of wealth and poverty were of pressing concern to the community Luke was addressing. Luke's Jesus tells of a foolish rich man who wanted to store more and more of his earthly harvest, not realizing that he was to die that very night and that he could not take it with him (Lk 12:16–21). It is in Luke that Jesus says that the poor and crippled are invited to the banquet; that no servant can serve two masters, God and money; that the rich man who disdained Lazarus in his poverty will have a parched tongue in hell; that the higher choice for the rich young man is to leave his wealth behind to follow Christ; that the poor widow with her mite gives more than the rich, because she has given out of her need; and that the one who would be the greatest should be as a servant.

Other Gospel stories seem to soften or at least contextualize Jesus' warnings to the rich. In John's Gospel, for example, when Judas complains that the expensive oil for anointing Jesus should have been sold and the money given to the poor, Jesus responds, "You always have the poor with you, but you do not always have me" (Jn 12:8). No matter how we might interpret or contextualize them, however, Jesus' warnings are too well recorded to simply ignore.

Stories of the Kingdom

Jesus taught mainly through parables, evidence in the New Testament suggests. Parables are compressed stories bursting with meaning. By now you will not be surprised to learn that the parables of Jesus are stories about the kingdom of God.

The parables share similar characteristics. Most draw their materials from ordinary, everyday events. They thereby create a set of expectations as to how things should go. Then they pull the rug out from under these expectations, thus reorienting the hearer on a new level of understanding.

The parables of Jesus usually can be interpreted as having meanings on many levels. They are not intended to communicate some clear piece of information about the kingdom of God; rather, they are meant to have an impact upon the consciousness of the hearer. They give one a feel for what the kingdom of God is like that would be difficult to express without simply repeating the story!

Take the following parable told by Jesus as an example:

For the kingdom of heaven is like a landowner who went out early in the morning to hire laborers for his vineyard. After agreeing with the laborers for the usual daily wage, he sent them into his vineyard. When he went out about nine o'clock, he saw others standing idle in the marketplace; and he said to them, "You also go into the vineyard, and I will pay you whatever is right." So they went. When he went out again about noon and about three o'clock, he did the same. And about five o'clock he went out and found others standing around; and he said to them, "Why are you standing here idle all day?" They said to him, 'Because no one has hired us." He said to them, "You also go into the vineyard." When evening came, the owner of the vineyard said to his manager, "Call the laborers and give them their pay, beginning with the last and then going to the first." When those hired about five o'clock came, each of them received the usual daily wage. Now when the first came, they thought they would receive more; but each of them also received the usual daily wage. And when they received it, they grumbled against the landowner, saying, "These last worked only one hour, and you have made them equal to us who have borne the burden of the day and the scorching heat."
But he replied to one of them,

The Metropolitan Museum of Art, Gift of Mrs. Henry Goldman, 1944

The Parable of the Vineyard, illustrated in this stained glass panel by Jan Rombouts (c. 1525–30), can be interpreted a number of different ways. Each interpretation can teach an important truth about the kingdom of God.

"Friend, I am doing you no wrong; did you not agree with me for the usual daily wage? Take what belongs to you and go; I choose to give to this last the same as I give to you. Am I not allowed to do what I choose with what belongs to me? Or are you envious because I am generous?" So the last will be first, and the first will be last. (Mt 20:1–16)

We know that this parable is *about the kingdom of God* because, like so many others, it says as much in the opening verse. It *draws its materials from the ordinary* event of hiring laborers to work in a vineyard. We have *a certain expectation*: people who work longer should receive more pay. That *expectation is thwarted* by the owner who claims that his generosity toward some does not make him unjust toward others. What does this have to do with the kingdom of God?

Instead of trying to offer one single interpretation, I will share a few of the *many interpretations* that students have related to me in class. First is the traditional "death-bed conversion" interpretation that stresses that even though one has lived a bad life one can still be saved if one repents. Another interpretation is that God's justice is not our justice, and that we simply cannot understand why things in this life often do not seem fair. Yet another interpretation focuses on the theme that in the kingdom the first shall be last and the last first, applying this maxim to the upending of contemporary social judgments about so-called winners and losers. Still another interpretation is that those who have just begun to live their life on a spiritual basis can be just as close to God as those who have been trying for years; seniority does not count for much when it comes to holiness.

The most important thing about a parable is not how you interpret it but how it strikes you (*reorients the hearer*). The multiple meanings are like tiny bombs that go off in a series of synchronized explosions. When you have been hit, you know that you are that much closer to being open to the coming of the kingdom.

Following Jesus

Jesus' teaching of the kingdom offers an inkling of what things could be like if human beings would drop their defenses, reach out to each other in love, and together seek out the will of a loving God. *Lumen gentium* speaks of "a kingdom of truth and life, a kingdom of holiness and grace, a kingdom of justice, love, and peace" (*LG* 36). The church itself is not fully the kingdom, but is the seed of the kingdom (*LG* 5). The church is not without imperfections, but strives to be a model community in which love is truly the first and final word. The church also works as a leaven in the world, pointing the world in the direction of the kingdom (*GS* 40).

Christians believe that Jesus, through his life, death, and Resurrection, broke the cycle of sin and hate and rationalization that holds us back from being prepared for the kingdom to come. He dropped his defenses, taught the truth, acted out of self-sacrificing love, and was put to death as an innocent man. Christians have traditionally interpreted the Resurrection as God's final seal of approval of the path that Jesus walked. Jesus' life and death were vindicated by his rising from the dead.

One way of understanding the fifth chapter of *Lumen gentium*'s universal call to holiness is to see it as a mandate for all Christians to follow Christ in breaking the cycle of sin. Jesus taught to love even our enemies and to do good to those who hate us. He broke the cycle of sin by living a life based on love. *Lumen gentium* says that for love to grow, "each of the faithful must willingly hear the Word of God and accept his will, and must complete what God has begun by their own actions with the help of God's grace" (*LG* 42). To follow Jesus is to break the cycle of sin by making love the basis of one's life: "It is the love of God and the love of one's neighbor which points out the true disciple of Christ" (*LG* 42).

Summary

This chapter examined the teaching of Jesus, concentrating on Jesus' proclamation of the kingdom, his special concern for the poor, and his parables. Through his words and deeds, Jesus taught people how to break the cycle of sin.

The cycle of sin has deep and unrecoverable origins. Its roots are personal, but it has branched out in social, economic, and political spheres. As noted earlier, I try not to be wildly utopian or idealistic in my expectations of what we can make this world to be. And yet I also do not wish to underestimate the tremendous and far-reaching impact of even one human being truly repenting, forgiving others, and seeking to bring about the kingdom of God. I see one sign of hope in that my four adult children no longer fight with each other; in fact, they get along amazingly well.

Having considered Christian spirituality in relation to the Father and Jesus, the next chapter will turn to the Holy Spirit.

For Further Reflection

1. How can a person come to know the will of God?
2. What is your understanding of original sin?
3. How might Jesus' warnings to the rich apply today?
4. Saying Jesus "broke the cycle" of sin through his life based on love is one interpretation of his mission. How does this interpretation compare with other interpretations with which you are familiar?
5. What images come to mind when you think about the kingdom of God?

Suggested Readings

Chilton, Bruce, ed. *The Kingdom of God in the Teaching of Jesus*. Philadelphia: Fortress, 1984.

Crossan, John Dominic. *In Parables: The Challenge of the Historical Jesus.* New York: Harper and Row, 1973.

Dunn, James D. G. *Christology in the Making: A New Testament Inquiry into the Origins of the Doctrine of the Incarnation.* Philadelphia: Westminster, 1996 (1980).

Johnson, Luke Timothy. *The Real Jesus: The Misguided Quest for the Historical Jesus and the Truth of the Traditional Gospels.* San Francisco: Harper, 1996.

Loewe, William P. *The College Student's Introduction to Christology.* Collegeville, MN: Liturgical Press, 1996.

Rausch, Thomas P. *Who Is Jesus? An Introduction: An Introduction to Christology.* Collegeville, MN: Liturgical Press, 2003.

Schrein, Shannon: *Quilting and Braiding: The Feminist Christologies of Sallie McFague and Elizabeth A. Johnson in Conversation.* Collegeville, MN: Liturgical Press, 1998.

Tilley, Terrence W. *The Disciples' Jesus: Christology as Reconciling Practice.* Maryknoll, NY: Orbis Books, 2008.

18

CHAPTER

A Job Description for the Holy Spirit

ome Catholics who do not like Vatican II tell this joke about Pope John XXIII, who convened the council. After the pope died and went to heaven, Peter brought him through the gates and began introducing him to various personages. When the pope was introduced to the Holy Spirit, the Spirit appeared momentarily puzzled and then, after a flash of recognition, looked slightly embarrassed. "Oh, yes, yes, that's right," the Spirit said. "You know, I did receive the invitation you sent me to that council, but I'm sorry, I just couldn't make it."

This joke illustrates more than just the type of humor that Catholics can revert to when they feel their faith has been threatened or diminished. It also illustrates more than the deep feelings of resentment some Catholics harbor toward the council. What this story most reveals is the Catholic belief that it is the abiding presence of the Holy Spirit that guides the church on the proper path. If someone thinks the church is straying from the path, the absence of the Spirit can be cited as the reason.

Like other Christians, Catholics believe in the Trinity, three persons in one God. The church is not based solely on a belief in God the Father or solely on the teachings of Jesus. The church also finds its origins in the encounter with the Resurrected Christ and in the experience of being filled with the Holy Spirit on Pentecost. It is the Spirit who transforms the lives of individuals, who inspires people in praise of God, who guides leaders in making intelligent decisions, and who accompanies the church in its journey toward truth and holiness. The Spirit is also the presence of God to be encountered through the people and events of the world.

Catholics today experience the Resurrected Christ and reception of the Spirit in a way that is, perhaps, not unlike the experience of the original apostles. The encounter is mediated; that is, Christ is not encountered directly through personal appearances, but through people and events. For Catholics, the encounter with Christ is represented above all through Christ's real presence in the Eucharist. The Eucharist points also to the places that Christ is met in the everyday: in prayer, loving relationships, experiences of growth, and especially the faces of the poor, suffering, and anyone who is in need. The transformation experienced through encounters with Christ fills one with the Holy Spirit.

Such language is, of course, highly symbolic. Religious language must be symbolic because it "packages" things that one otherwise would not be able to understand. To say religious language is symbolic is not to say it is not true; it is to say the truth of the language can only be grasped by those for whom the language is meaningful. In the case of religious language, this usually means those who structure the meaning of their lives according to that particular religion. In an academic setting, however, those who understand religious language can include anyone willing to try thinking analogously in terms of that religion.

For example, a student who takes a course on the church might not believe in Christianity or the Holy Spirit; that student, however, can relate to this language as a way of talking about human openness and transformation. Most Christians believe this language is more than just labeling; it is, rather, a key to entering into a tradition that communicates the very revelation of the three-personed God. Both believer and nonbeliever, however, can recognize the symbolic nature of the language as it tries to put one in touch with the meaning of life.

Overview

In my classroom experience, I have found many students, both Christian and non-Christian, to be thoroughly confused by the concept of the Holy Spirit. To address this confusion, I have formulated a job description for this least familiar person of the Trinity.

Some job descriptions let employees know what is expected of them; that is not my purpose here. Another common function of a job description is to communicate to others what a person does. This can happen in parishes. Parish council members sometimes wonder what it is that particular employees do—such as a pastoral associate or a director of religious education. Job descriptions provide this information. In this chapter, I furnish a job description that attempts to reflect the various functions, attributed by Catholics, of the Holy Spirit. This material relates to chapter 5 of *Lumen gentium*.

Summary Job Description—Holy Spirit: Be the Presence of God Working through People

Former Work Experience

- Participated in the creation of the world (God's breath, sometimes symbolically identified as the Holy Spirit, is involved in the creation of the universe and particularly in the creation of human beings, when "the LORD God

formed man from the dust of the ground, and breathed into his nostrils the breath of life" [Gen 2:7].)
- Spoke through the prophets (as recited in the Creed)
- Inspired the entire Bible
- Was the one through whom Mary conceived Jesus (Mt 1:18; Lk 1:35)
- Descended upon Jesus at his baptism (Mk 1:9–11)
- Was the one Jesus promised to send to his disciples (Jn 15:15–16:15)
- Participated in the Resurrection of Jesus (Rom 1:4)
- Empowered the disciples on Pentecost to spread the gospel in continuance of the saving mission of Christ (Acts 2:1–4)
- Worked to bring forth the fruits of holiness in the lives of Christians (Gal 5:22)
- Guided major decisions made by church councils. Even such a crucial decision as which books to include in the Bible was made at an early council. According to Catholic belief at the time, the Holy Spirit guided not only major decisions but also the evolution of the tools and authoritative structures by which decisions are to be made. These include the councils as well as Scriptures, Tradition, threefold office of bishop, priest, and deacon, and the papacy.
- Functioned as the source of holiness and renewed life throughout the history of the church (*LG* 4)

Current Task: Transform the Lives of Individuals

The Holy Spirit has the job of transforming the lives of those who open themselves to God. Many theologians today speak of such life transformation in terms of "conversion." Conversion refers not just to deciding to become religious or to changing denominations, but to a lifelong process of growth in faith. Theologian Bernard Lonergan distinguished three types of conversion: religious, moral, and intellectual.[1] In his perspective, each type of conversion is rooted in the work of the Holy Spirit, for religious conversion is the most basic type from which the others flow.

Religious conversion is an otherworldly falling-in-love with God. It involves getting in touch with the love of the Holy Spirit, which floods our hearts even prior to our being aware of it (Rom 5:5). In other words, every human being is filled at the core with the love of God through the Holy Spirit, believes Lonergan. To be religiously converted is to open ourselves to this love. Lonergan also draws

---

1. See Bernard Lonergan, *Method in Theology*, vol. 14 of *Collected Works of Bernard Lonergan*, ed. Robert M. Doran and John D. Dadosky (Toronto: University of Toronto Press, 2017 [1972]), 223–29.

upon Ezekiel 36:26 to describe religious conversion: it is what happens when God rips out one's heart of stone and replaces it with a heart of flesh. Many people can point to select moments in their lives when religious conversion took place; many cannot. All who are religiously converted, however, are engaged in a lifelong journey of growth.

Moral conversion refers to the process by which a person stops making decisions solely according to self-interest and seeks instead to do what is truly good. We grow through various stages of motivation for being good, from compulsion to social acceptance, principles, and the need to be an authentic person who acts out of love for God and others.

In Lonergan's analysis, intellectual conversion is technical. It involves getting in touch with the process by which one knows things, thereby becoming adept at sorting out various levels of consciousness and various dimensions of reality. For our purposes, intellectual conversion can refer to the gradual process by which one grows in an appreciation of the complexity and multidimensionality of reality, including its transcendent dimensions. That is, the intellectually converted person is one who neither confuses religious language with scientific description nor reduces everything religious to the level of the material. The intellectually converted person has a grasp of how symbolic language can function to put one in touch with the deeper dimensions of human existence.

That the Holy Spirit will transform the lives of individuals who follow Christ is central to the teaching of Paul in the New Testament. The way that Paul spoke of such transformation has been codified in Catholic Tradition as the gifts and fruits of the Holy Spirit. Instead of a life based on fear, resentment, and self-pity, the follower of Christ displays "love, joy, peace, patience, kindness, generosity, faithfulness, gentleness, and self-control" (Gal 5:22–23). Other traditional gifts and fruits of the Spirit found in Paul include wisdom, counsel (ability to make good decisions), piety, moral courage, and fear of the Lord. These characteristics are not so much things sought for themselves; they are the qualities people find themselves possessing as they struggle to follow Christ.

Current Task: Inspire Groups in Prayer and Decisions

In Alcoholics Anonymous, there is a belief in a "group conscience." Individuals are free to express whatever opinions they want at meetings, no matter how profound or ridiculous. The recovering alcoholics trust that the group will be guided by a higher power such that the overall message of the meeting will express the will of a loving God (though not all alcoholics use the term *God*). What an individual says is simply a personal opinion; what comes through the group is a power greater than any one individual, which draws upon the experience, strength, and hope of all present.

In this Gothic Fresco in Fjelie church, Sweden, the Holy Spirit descends upon the apostles (Acts 2). In Catholic Church teaching, the Holy Spirit is active in individuals, in groups, in the church as a whole, and in the world.

Catholics have traditionally believed one of the jobs of the Holy Spirit is to act as a kind of "group conscience" when Christians are gathered in prayer or engaged in decision-making. This belief is reflected in the following traditional prayer:

Come, Holy Spirit
Fill the hearts of your faithful
And kindle in them the fire of your love.
Send forth your Spirit
And they will be created
And you shall renew the face of the earth.[2]

Many Catholics today believe the Holy Spirit is currently engaged in a broadscale renewal of the Catholic Church through small groups. Liberation theologians in Latin America point to the workings of the Spirit through base Christian communities that engage in both the reading of Scripture and political activity. Those involved in the charismatic renewal point to signs of the Spirit in healing, prophecy, and speaking in tongues. Groups of women activists, the Cursillo movement, various prayer groups, Renew groups, parish councils, and other parish committees all point to the activity of the Spirit in their midst.

---

2. Version found at Catholic Online, *https://www.catholic.org/prayers/prayer.php?p=331*.

Current Task: Guide the Church as a Whole

Catholics have traditionally believed that the church is *indefectible*; that is, that the Holy Spirit will protect the church from straying from the true path. Indefectibility is based in part on the Catholic interpretation of Matthew 16:18, when Jesus says, "And I tell you, you are Peter, and on this rock I will build my church, and the gates of Hades will not prevail against it." "Peter" comes from the Greek word for "rock," and so Jesus is portrayed as using a pun in communicating his guarantee of the church's steadfastness through time. This line is often read in conjunction with John 16:13: "When the Spirit of truth comes, he will guide you into all the truth."

Indefectibility should not be read as a guarantee that the Catholic Church will never make a mistake or have to reverse itself on a teaching. History offers too many examples to the contrary. It means, rather, that the church is to be relied upon as the continuation of Christ's saving presence and work on earth. The church might make some mistakes (as in the rejection of Galileo's theories) or its members might engage in horrendous activities (the mass slaughter of Jews and Muslims during some of the Crusades), but in its most important teachings and in its sacramental ministry, it continues to be guided by the Holy Spirit. In a basic sense, the Catholic can trust the church and its teachings.

On an institutional level, the Holy Spirit is believed to have some influence in the election of popes, the selection of bishops, the decrees of councils, and, in general, all teaching, leadership, and sacramental ministry. If Jesus promised that the Spirit would be with us, Catholic belief is that we can expect to experience that presence in these areas. Current disputes about how bishops are selected involve debates about where the voice of the Spirit can most clearly be heard.

From a Catholic perspective, the most profound thing that could be said of any church community is that the Holy Spirit can be found working among its members. This is precisely what the Catholic Church said in *Lumen gentium* about Protestant churches: "We can say that in some real way they are joined with us in the Holy Spirit, for to them too he gives his gifts and graces whereby he is operative among them with his sanctifying power" (*LG* 15).

Often movements in the church are attributed to the work of the Spirit. Many people today point to the explosion of lay ministries, the developing body of Catholic social teaching, the ecumenical movement, and the tendency toward more sharing of authority as evidence of the Spirit's work. Some theologians are fond of claiming that in these days the Spirit prefers to work from the bottom up, moving the church through its people.

Some have even said that the Holy Spirit is behind the current shortage of priests. People who reason this way foresee the resulting changes in Catholic Church structure, such as the need to rely more and more on the laity, as ultimately good things in harmony with God's plan. Personally, I stay away from interpretations such as these. Maybe the Holy Spirit is behind the priest shortage and maybe the Holy Spirit is not. It is at least as likely that the shortage of priests is the result of people not listening to the Spirit as vice versa.

This brings us to an important point: Not everything attributed to the Holy Spirit is from the Holy Spirit. The Catholic tradition has had to fight unbridled enthusiasm that sees the Spirit in everything, just as it has had to fight complacency that is inattentive to the Spirit's workings. An old Buddhist saying illustrates the need to be cautious about claims to religious authority: "If you meet the Buddha on the road, kill him." Why? Because the person claiming to be Buddha has got to be an imposter. I would not suggest killing everyone who claims that the Spirit is working through them or that they are the one most capable of interpreting the Spirit; I will simply encourage the dictum that all spirits are to be tested (1 Thess 5:21).

There is no single, clear formula for the testing of spirits. For starters, ask the following: Does a particular claim align with the best of my religious tradition? Does it square with empirical facts? Does it find harmony with my own religious, moral, and intellectual conversion? Does it seem to continue to make sense as I live with it? Does it draw me outside of myself toward a new appreciation of others? A list of such questions could go on and on.

Current Task: Be the Potential for God's Love in All Human Beings

Many Catholic theologians, Lonergan and Karl Rahner among them, have spoken of the basic orientation of human beings toward the transcendent mystery whom Christians know as God.[3] All people are drawn in self-transcendent motion in the direction of goodness, truth, and love. No matter one's religion, even if one has no religion, everyone is capable of growing in the direction of God when one moves beyond selfishness to embrace higher values, openness, honesty, and loving human relationships. This argument further inclines to attribute this orientation to the presence of the Holy Spirit in all human beings, whether people call it that or not.

For this reason, many Christians who engage in interreligious dialogue draw upon the concept of the Holy Spirit to talk about what is authentic in all religions of the world.[4] Only Christianity sees God in Christ. Some religions do not expressly believe in a God. It is the Holy Spirit, understood as the presence of the divine within us, that often seems to provide the best starting point for a dialogue (though, of course, most religions do not call this divine presence the "Holy Spirit").

---

3. For Lonergan on this topic, see *Method in Theology*, 101–7. For Rahner, see *Foundations of Christian Faith*, trans. William V. Dych (New York: Crossroad, 1982 [1976]), 51–71.

4. See, for example, Raimon Panikkar, *The Intra-Religious Dialogue* (New York: Paulist Press, 1978), and William Johnston, *The Mirror Mind: Spirituality and Transformation* (New York: Harper and Row, 1981).

Summary

This chapter reviewed the workings of the Holy Spirit in individuals, groups, the church, and the world. It appears that the Holy Spirit has a lot of work to do! Yet the Catholic tradition expresses full confidence in the power of God. What one needs to worry about more is our own willingness to listen to the promptings of the Spirit and make them a reality in our lives.

One part of Catholic understanding of the Spirit's job that I failed to mention is the element of surprise: The Spirit blows freely in astonishing ways. The Second Vatican Council is an example of this. I disagree with the minority of Catholics who thought the Spirit was absent from the unanticipated wonder of Vatican II, which happens to be one of the main places I look for the entry of the Spirit into today's world.

The next chapter will examine the life of religious brothers and sisters who take vows and form communities.

For Further Reflection

1. Do you find the concept of the Holy Spirit to be more helpful or confusing?
2. Do you believe the Holy Spirit functions in your life, such as in your prayer life, if you have one?
3. Does the concept of "conversion" apply to your own life-journey?
4. Have you ever experienced a "group conscience" that seemed greater than the sum of the individuals present?
5. How is the concept of the Holy Spirit important for the Catholic Church?

Suggested Readings

Castelo, Daniel. *Pneumatology: A Guide for the Perplexed*. New York: T&T Clark–Bloomsbury, 2015.

Congar, Yves. *I Believe in the Holy Spirit*. 3 vols. New York: Seabury, 1983 (1979, 1980).

Conn, Walter E. *Christian Conversion: A Developmental Interpretation of Autonomy and Surrender*. New York: Paulist Press, 1986.

Thiselton, Anthony C. *A Shorter Guide to the Holy Spirit: Bible, Doctrine, Experience*. Grand Rapids: Eerdmans, 2016.

Yong, Amos. *Who Is the Holy Spirit? A Walk with the Apostles*. Brewster, MA: Paraclete, 2011.

19

CHAPTER

Religious Communities

I n the Catholic Church, an ordained priest is formally addressed as "Father." There are, in addition, those who take religious vows of poverty, chastity, and obedience. The men who do so are called "brothers" and the women, "sisters." The brothers and sisters who take the vows are called "religious." To be "religious" in this sense is to belong to a religious order that follows the rule of a founding figure.

A student recently asked me why any man would choose to be a religious brother when he could be a priest instead. Immediately, I remembered asking the same question of a religious brother who taught me science in high school. I vaguely remembered his response as having something to do with different people having different callings.

In the same split second, I blurted out my own personal response to the student's question: it could be great to live in community with a group of people who share similar interests and goals. During a few periods in my life, particularly in high school and graduate school, I said, I had been part of a highly supportive circle of friends. It was wonderful to have a lifestyle that allowed close, family-like intimacy with a good number of people. One could feel drawn to a community that bases itself on a religious lifestyle without experiencing a call to be a priest.

Once I had made this response, however, I felt how personal, relevant, and yet insufficient and partial it was. I had struck upon something: religious communities can be attractive environments within which to live for many reasons. This attraction can be part of an authentic call to live such a life. My response, however, focused too much on the attractiveness of community life to the neglect of the distinctively religious reasons why a person would choose such a life. Yes, community life can be attractive; why not, then, simply live in a commune? Why live in a community founded by a follower of Jesus Christ?

Overview

Chapter 6 of *Lumen gentium* (*Dogmatic Constitution on the Church*) (together with section 42 of chapter 5) offers different reasons why men and women would experience a call to live in a religious community as "brothers" and "sisters." These reasons do not detract from the attractiveness of community life but provide a deeper foundation. Religious life includes mutual support, broad-based intimacy, and inspiring lifestyles. This chapter, however, explores even deeper motivations against the background of scriptural, historical, and contemporary reflections.

An Exceptional Form of Love

In the Catholic tradition, since there are different ways of following Jesus, it is appropriate to distinguish between different states of life in the church. Each path of discipleship—lay, clerical, or religious—is designed for people who are seriously focused on following Jesus. Although reality is rarely as clear-cut as the ideal vision, the laity represent the many people committed to Christ who do not leave behind their everyday lives; the clergy represent the inner circle of the twelve apostles who carry on the authority of Jesus; religious brothers and sisters represent those who have abandoned the things of this world out of their desire to follow the Lord.[1]

Lumen gentium, section 42, which concludes chapter 5 but provides the lead-in to chapter 6, speaks of the love that is expected from Christians, who are called to accept the will of God. The mark of the true disciple is the love of God and neighbor.

All forms of Christian love are amazing and wonderful. The passage goes on to speak, however, of "exceptional" forms of love. What makes a type of love exceptional is that only certain Christians are called to it. Martyrdom, for example, is described as an "exceptional gift and as the fullest proof of love." It is a means of being transformed into the image of Jesus, who readily accepted death for the salvation of the world. All Christians are to be prepared for this possibility, but only some will actually be asked to embrace it.

Following the paragraph on martyrdom are two paragraphs that discuss the evangelical counsels of chastity, poverty, and obedience. Their connection with martyrdom has long roots in the Catholic tradition: death for one's faith has been called "red martyrdom," and life according to the evangelical counsels has been called "white martyrdom." Following the evangelical counsels represents a form of martyrdom in that it entails a renunciation of or a "dying to" certain worldly values.

The Evangelical Counsels

All Christians are called to reject materialism and consumerism and to have a special concern for the poor; all are called to be chaste insofar as sexual activity

---

1. Many male members of religious communities are also priests; diocesan priests, in contrast, are sometimes called "secular" priests.

is reserved for the most appropriate of contexts; all are called to be obedient to the will of God. What distinguishes those who join religious communities and take vows is their exceptional form of adherence to these principles. Although religious communities differ in their interpretations, basically the call to chastity is for them a call to celibacy; the call to poverty is a call to own nothing themselves but to give all to the community; the call to obedience is a call to renounce one's will in deference to the will of one's religious superior. These principles are adhered to not for their own sake, but because they can function as liberating helps to living a life based on love.

Leave Everything Behind

Lumen gentium combined a new emphasis on the universal call to holiness given to Christians in all states of life with a traditional reaffirmation of the exceptional nature of the evangelical counsels. There exists a tension between, on the one hand, the notion that a person who lives a lay life is called to pursue and experience holiness as devotedly and intensely as any other Christian, and, on the other hand, the notion that life in religious community is somehow exceptional, special, or heroic. Biblical scholarship sheds interesting light on this tension.

Several stories in the New Testament present a contrast between an ordinary, good way of life and a more radical lifestyle based on an intense following of Jesus. Scripture scholar John Meier argues that such stories were originally intended to distinguish between what it meant to be a good Jewish person who follows the law and what it meant to be a follower of Christ.[2] Read in this light, these stories can be seen to apply, in some sense, to every Christian.

Take, for example, the story of the rich young man in Matthew 19:16–22. The man asks Jesus what he must do to inherit eternal life. Jesus, at first, responds that he should keep the Commandments. The man replies that he has kept the Commandments from his youth; what more should he do? Jesus then tells him that he should sell all he has, give the money to the poor, and follow him. At that, the young man becomes sad and walks away. In Mark 10:29–30, following Mark's own version of the story of the rich young man, Jesus is portrayed as saying, "Truly I tell you, there is no one who has left house or brothers or sisters or mother or father or children or fields, for my sake and for the sake of the good news, who will not receive a hundredfold now in this age."

As Meier interprets this story, the rich young man represents, for the Gospel writer, any Jewish person of the first century who is confronted by the challenge to follow Jesus. To follow the law is good; to become a disciple of Jesus represents the fulfillment of what the law is about. Becoming a disciple, however,

2. John P. Meier, *The Vision of Matthew: Christ, Church, and Morality in the First Gospel* (New York: Paulist Press, 1979), 136–41.

may involve being rejected by one's own family and the loss of one's inheritance. The passage thus interpreted is about Christian discipleship and can apply to any Christian in any state of life.

As different states of life developed within the early church, however, the story of the rich young man came to be interpreted as distinguishing between the ordinary lay way of living a good life and the exceptional religious way of following Jesus by renouncing the things of this world. Thus interpreted, the passage is read as referring explicitly to those who take religious vows and implies that their path is a special or more heroic one.

I would not reject either interpretation of this story, but I would place the "religious" interpretation that arose within the Tradition against the background of the earlier and deeper "discipleship" interpretation. That is, I think the most important call to holiness is the one given to all Christians regardless of state of life. This call reflects a fundamental equality in spiritual dignity among all who are baptized; within that context, the call to a vowed religious life represents, in some sense, a more radical renunciation of certain worldly values.

A similar issue arises in the Gospel of Matthew where Jesus seems to advocate the renunciation of sex and marriage: "Not everyone can accept this teaching, but only those to whom it is given. For there are eunuchs who have been so from birth, and there are eunuchs who have been made eunuchs by others, and there are eunuchs who have made themselves eunuchs for the sake of the kingdom of heaven. Let anyone accept this who can." (Mt 19:11–12). In the Catholic Tradition, this passage has, at times, been interpreted as seeing in celibacy a "higher" calling. Meier points out, however, that this passage is linked in the Gospel with Jesus' prohibition against divorce and his affirmation of marriage as part of the Father's plan of creation (19:3–6). Meier says, "Marriage without divorce or celibacy chosen for the Kingdom: these are the signs of a community which lives by the powers of the age to come."[3] It is thus possible to read the passage as endorsing chaste marriage and celibacy as two extremely good paths to holiness. As with the issue of poverty, I experience a tension here. I do not wish to suggest that celibacy is higher than marriage (although Thomas Aquinas as well as the majority of Church Fathers were convinced that it was); at the same time, I want to recognize that celibacy can represent a heroic sacrifice for a particular individual who decides to give up marriage for the sake of the kingdom.

Obedience is the third of the evangelical counsels. Jesus is portrayed throughout the Gospels as one who renounces even his own will in deference to the will of his Father, although ultimately this path leads to his death. Mark depicts Jesus in the garden of Gethsemane, praying, "Abba, Father, for you all things are possible; remove this cup from me; yet, not what I want, but what you want" (Mk 14:36). Jesus challenged his own disciples to do the same: "Are you

---

3. Meier, *The Vision of Matthew: Christ, Church, and Morality in the First Gospel*, 138.

able to drink the cup that I drink, or be baptized by the baptism that I am baptized with?" (Mk 10:38). He counseled them: "No one has greater love than this, to lay down one's life for one's friends" (Jn 15:13). Members of religious orders are expected to accept, in obedience, the directives of their religious superiors.

Many other references could be made to passages in the New Testament that connect the call of some Christians with an explicit renunciation of the world. The areas cited above deal specifically with riches, sex, and personal choice. They form the backdrop of the vows of poverty, chastity, and obedience taken by members of religious communities. Yet they also form the backdrop of the call of Christians to reject materialism, dehumanizing sex, and a life obsessed with personal gratification. They are ultimately connected with a total giving of oneself, even to the point of death.

Why Join?

Most of the time, the majority of human beings act with mixed motives. In the same moment, we might operate out of high principles, concern for others, a desire to serve God, a drive to contribute to society, love, honesty, self-concern, fear, boredom, greed, and the need for security. Some events in life offer a clear choice between sets of motives; most do not.

People who join religious communities usually do not leave their personal needs and reasons behind. A religious sister once remarked to me that a problem facing her community was that many new inquirers seemed to be seeking refuge from broken or dysfunctional families. Such people can be good candidates, but they need to overcome any tendencies to find, in religious life, simply an escape from a world they cannot handle. Personal refuge is acceptable as one level of motivation for joining a religious community, but only if it is ultimately combined with a desire to serve God and others out of a sense of self-sacrificing love.

Section 44 of *Lumen gentium* speaks of the ideal level of motivation in one who professes religious vows:

> Indeed through baptism a person dies to sin and is consecrated to God. However, in order that one may be capable of deriving more abundant fruit from this baptismal grace, one intends, by the profession of the evangelical counsels in the church, to free oneself from those obstacles, which might draw one away from the fervor of charity and the perfection of divine worship. By one's profession of the evangelical counsels, then, one is more intimately consecrated to divine service.

In other words, a person joins a religious community because that person perceives such life as a better way for himself or herself to be dedicated to the love and service of God. Other reasons can and will be present, but this is the highest reason. The document speaks approvingly also of religious communities as "religious families [that] give their members the support of a more firm stability in their way of life" (*LG* 43). That is, the many attractions of a life lived in intimate community can be an authentic reason for joining a religious order.

Origins of Religious Community

Religious communities find the beginnings of their way of life in Jesus' ministry and death. They also find support in the example and advice of St. Paul. The martyrs of the first few Christian centuries, as well as those throughout history until the present day, provide further example of lives of exceptional sacrifice.

During the fourth century, however, Christianity shifted from being an underground, often persecuted religion, to being the official religion of the Roman Empire. Martyrdom was left to the missionaries who preached in foreign cultures. Christians no longer needed to live in small, secret communities. Professing Christianity even came to be an advantage in public life.

The impulse to purer, more countercultural forms of Christianity found an outlet in ascetics who fled the life of the city to dwell in the desert.[4] Some Christians, such as St. Anthony (c. 251– 355 CE), began to live in the desert long before the persecutions were finished. However, the rise of the first desert monasteries in the fourth century roughly parallels the emergence of Christianity as a publicly acceptable religion. Those who discerned in Christianity a personal call to flee from the world could no longer do so just by living their faith in the city.

Monastic life flourished throughout the Middle Ages. Monasteries functioned not only as desert or rural refuges but also as centers of learning. The Benedictines were founded by St. Benedict at Monte Cassino near Naples in the period between 525 and 529 CE. The famous "Rule of St. Benedict," noted for its sensible balance of work, leisure, and prayer, stood in contrast to the more severe rules of other monasteries at the time. To this day, Benedictines are known for their balanced approach to spirituality and their excellent liturgies.

Literally thousands of religious orders have existed in the history of the Catholic Church. Each has a founder whose special gifts and ideas form the vision and goals of the society. Following are a few of these orders:

The Dominicans, founded by St. Dominic, are known for their preaching and teaching.

The Franciscans, founded by St. Francis to bring the ideals of the monastery into life in the city, are today recognized for their social concerns and activity among the poor.

The Jesuits, founded by St. Ignatius of Loyola to further the cause of the Catholic Counter-Reformation, are today famous for their scholarship and high standards in education.

---

4. For a discussion of martyrs and ascetics, see Lawrence Cunningham, *The Catholic Heritage* (New York: Crossroad, 1983), chapters 1 and 2.

The Maryknolls, founded by Thomas Frederick Rice, a priest, and James Edward Walsh, a bishop, as the official missionary society of the United States, are known for their support of social and spiritual activity throughout the world.

The Marianists, founded by William Joseph Chaminade to respond to the needs of postrevolutionary Europe, are known today for their educational efforts, spirit of collaboration, artistic achievements, family-like community, commitment to service, and the special character of their devotion to each member of the Holy Family.

The Sisters of the Blessed Sacrament, founded by Katharine Mary Drexel to minister to Native Americans and African Americans, are known for their various missions and schools throughout the United States, their love for the Eucharist, and their initiatives in addressing social inequalities suffered by minorities.

The Second Vatican Council called for each religious order to rekindle the special charism of their founder. These characteristic tendencies are associated with each order, but do not dictate the exact contribution of every member. Not all Franciscans work with the poor; not all Jesuits labor as scholars; not all Marianists teach or produce works of art. It might be claimed that today each order has its own *esprit*, but that its individual members might engage in a wide variety of activities. What most characterizes the work of members of religious communities is that the great majority are engaged in lives of prayer and of service to others.

© jorisvo / Shutterstock.com

Despite her short life, Saint Thérèse of Lisieux (1873–97), a Discalced Carmelite nun, has provided tremendous inspiration for Catholic religious and laypeople in modern times.

Women Religious

It can be argued that the most influential work done by any group of Catholics in history has been done by religious women. Yet this group has been relatively ignored. If any group of women other than Catholic nuns had achieved even a small percentage of what these women have achieved, the bookstores would be full of accounts of their legendary accomplishments.

Historically, women have found religious communities to be places in which their distinctive gifts have flourished. Women appear in significant numbers among the early

Sister Simone Campbell of "Nuns on the Bus," a Catholic advocacy group, speaks to a gathering in lower Manhattan. Since 2012 the nuns have traveled around the country garnering support for various efforts to help the poor and disenfranchised.

martyrs, the desert ascetics, the monastics of the Middle Ages, the various orders of mendicants, and the religious communities of the modern age. Leaders such as Brigit of Kildare (sixth-century Ireland), Irmengard of Chiemsee (ninth-century Bavaria), and Elizabeth Ann Seton (nineteenth-century United States) exercised far-reaching power in both church and society. Many of the famous mystics, such as Hildegard of Bingen, Teresa of Ávila, and Thérèse of Lisieux, have been women. Through their participation in religious communities, many women have been able to transcend the social limitations of their time and place to make abundant contributions in education, social work, medicine, contemplative prayer, and pastoral care. Up through the twentieth century, religious women have served as notable role models for young girls called to leadership and service in the public sphere.

Whether it be women or men ministering in a parish, hospital, or nursing home; teaching in a grade school, university, or prison; working among the poor in hostels, soup kitchens, or employment training; working in a rural area, an urban area, or a foreign culture, those who take religious vows are most often found engaged in activities that blend prayer with help to others. They do this with the aid of a community lifestyle of renunciation that finds its multifaceted roots in the history of the Catholic tradition. Recently, a political advocacy group known as the "Nuns on the Bus," led by Sister Simone Campbell, helped to put social justice issues, especially immigration reform, in the spotlight during the 2016 US political campaigns.[5]

---

5. The "Nuns on the Bus" homepage is *https://networklobby.org/nunsonthebus/*.

Current Issues

Religious communities today are beset with many challenges and difficulties. On a practical level, there has been the problem of decreasing membership with a corresponding rise in the median age of those who belong. Health care costs, retirement, and management of properties often crowd the agenda of community meetings.

Members of religious communities also struggle to define their identities in a rapidly changing world. In our age, which stresses the autonomy of the individual, the meaning of the traditional vow of "obedience" has been placed in question.[6] Is self-direction in response to one's conscience and calling as important as obedience to one's religious superior? Can responsible obedience be distinguished from blind obedience?

These issues are especially important today in communities of religious women. Catholic men have the possibility of requesting to be a priest, but Catholic women who feel called to roles of leadership do not have such a choice. Many persons today are challenging a church system that calls on communities of women to answer to structures of authority made up of men alone.

Any challenge has its positive and negative sides. Many who belong to religious communities today find that they live in interesting and exciting times. Many also believe that they could hardly find a better path for their struggle to follow the Lord.

Summary

This chapter has explored the evangelical counsels, motivations for joining a religious community, history of religious life, and issues of current concern to religious life. The next time a student asks me why a man would choose to be a brother rather than a priest, I will try not to leap to conclusions. Instead, I will mention the attraction of a communal lifestyle, as well as the notion that different people have different callings. My main emphasis, though, will be on what it can mean to belong to a community founded by someone with a special charism directed toward the following of Christ.

The next chapter will examine liberation theology as an approach to faith that especially emphasizes community.

---

6. Joan Chittister, *Winds of Change: Women Challenge the Church* (Kansas City: Sheed and Ward, 1986), 116–18, 132–34.

For Further Reflection

1. What do you think would most attract someone to life in a religious community?
2. What have been your experiences with people who are members of religious orders?
3. What does it mean to have a "call"? Does everyone have some type of calling in life?
4. Do you find it surprising that some people may be drawn to religious life for other than religious motivations?
5. Are the evangelical counsels "weird" in today's world?

Suggested Readings

Confoy, Maryann. *Religious Life and Priesthood:* Perfectae Caritatis, Optatam Totius, *and* Presbyterorum Ordinis. Mahwah, NJ: Paulist Press, 2008.

Fialka, John J. *Sisters: Catholic Nuns and the Making of America.* New York: St. Martin's Press, 2003.

Grant, Zachary, OFM. *Paths to Renewal: The Spirituality of Six Religious Founders.* New York: Alba House, 1998.

McNamara, Jo Ann Kay. *Sisters in Arms: Catholic Nuns through Two Millennia.* Cambridge: Harvard University Press, 1996.

Merton, Thomas. *The Silent Life.* New York: Farrar, Straus and Cudahy, 1957.

O'Murchu, Diarmuid. *Religious Life in the 21st Century: The Prospect of Refounding.* Maryknoll, NY: Orbis Books, 2016.

Schmitt, Miriam, and Linda Kulzer, eds. *Medieval Women Monastics: Wisdom's Wellsprings.* Collegeville, MN: Liturgical Press, 1996.

Schneiders, Sandra M. *Buying the Field: Catholic Religious Life in Mission to the World.* Mahwah, NJ: Paulist Press, 2013.

Liberation Theologies and Church Community

O nce, I was talking with a student on a crowded elevator in our university library. The student remarked that when he was in high school he had expressed, in class, a political opinion about needing to be concerned about poor people; his teacher responded by calling him a Marxist.

When we got off the elevator, a man who had ridden with us approached the student. The man was about half my student's height. He pointed his finger way up toward my student's face, and said emphatically, in a heavily Latin American accent, "You did not say those things because you are a Marxist; you said them because you are a Christian."

The man started to walk away, but I could not let it end there. I walked along with him and asked who he was. He was a professor of languages from Colombia. He went into a short speech about how there are no real Christians around: "Do I love you? Do you love me? This is not a Christian society. This is a society where people look out for themselves. Tell me, who really lives the Christian life?"

My student's remark had triggered quite a reaction. The professor was not just being philosophical; he was angry and indignant that a student who expressed concern for the poor would be labeled a Marxist. That sounded too close to what often happened in his own country in response to liberation theologians, those who emphasize the integral link between the gospel and social justice.

Overview

This chapter on liberation theology is linked with the theme of religious community in *Lumen gentium* because of its strong focus on a communal form of Christian life. Liberation theology, which began in various countries throughout Latin America in the 1960s, is a movement by which Christians organized into base ecclesial communities. It can also be related to the emphasis on social justice that pervaded the Second Vatican Council.

In the decades since liberation theology began, many kinds of liberation theology have emerged: African liberation theology, Asian liberation theology, feminist liberation theology, black liberation theology, and others. These have undergone many developments, and today are most often found in forms that are blended with other theological methods. For this chapter, I will concentrate on the Latin American variety, relying most on a controversial work written in the 1980s by Brazilian theologian Leonardo Boff, *Church: Charism and Power*.[1]

Intolerable Conditions

Liberation theology advocates political action ultimately in the name of Christian love. It has its beginnings, however, in outrage over the condition of the poor in the countries of Latin America. Boff speaks of his own country of Brazil:

> For example, in Brazil, 75 percent of the people live in relative economic marginalization; 43 percent are condemned to a minimum salary in order to survive. A worker from São Paulo, Manuel Paulo, says it best: "What I earn is so little it only proves that I am alive. . . ." 40 percent of all Brazilians live, work, and sleep with chronic hunger; there are 10 million who are mentally retarded due to malnutrition; 6 million suffer from malaria; 650,000 have tuberculosis and 25,000 suffer from leprosy.[2]

Liberation theologians believe that the gospel must have something to say about such miserable conditions. Could it be the will of a loving God that so many millions live in abject poverty? Or is there a call in the Christian faith to work to alleviate this misery?

Base Ecclesial Communities

Boff claims that liberation theology has its roots not in the speculations of theologians but in the experience of Christians who come together in prayer to read and reflect on the meaning of the Scriptures. These groups usually consist of about fifteen to twenty families. Boff offers the following description of what are called *communidades ecclesiales de base*, or base ecclesial communities:

> Initially, such a community serves to deepen the faith of its members, to prepare the liturgy, the sacraments, and the life of prayer. At a

---

1. Leonardo Boff, *Church: Charism and Power*, trans. John Diercksmeier (New York: Crossroad, 1985 [1981].)

2. Boff, *Church: Charism and Power*, 22.

more advanced stage these members begin to help each other. As they become better organized and reflect more deeply, they come to the realization that the problems they encounter have a structural character. Their marginalization is seen as a consequence of elitist organization, private ownership, that is, of the very socioeconomic structure of the capitalist system. Thus, the question of politics arises and the desire for liberation is set in a concrete and historical context. The community sees this not only as liberation from sin (from which we must always liberate ourselves) but also a liberation that has economic, political, and cultural dimensions.[3]

Even in their heyday, base ecclesial communities comprised only a small minority of Latin Americans. Boff focused on their methods and meanings more than on their numbers. These communities combine a reading of the Scriptures with analysis of the economic and social causes of their difficulties to inspire them into organized political action. Although some liberation theologians have condoned violence, most strongly favor nonviolent revolutionary activities.

According to Boff, the base ecclesial communities have worldwide implications for the nature of the Catholic Church. He criticizes church operations for being top-heavy and bureaucratic, drawing inspiration more from Roman and feudal structures than from the gospel. He sees the Catholic Church in his own country as one that has historically sided with the rich against the interests of the poor. The base ecclesial communities, on the other hand, represent an ideal, classless society in which all members can participate fully. These communities care for the dispossessed and celebrate the true meaning of Christian liberation.

In Boff's vision, base ecclesial communities provide the starting point for the rebirth of the Catholic Church from the bottom up. That is, Boff envisioned a worldwide networking of base ecclesial communities that would infuse a new spirit of egalitarian love throughout the entire church.

Liberating Scriptures

Liberation theologians look to the Old Testament as the source of their faith. They give special attention to the story in Exodus of how God took the side of the oppressed Hebrew slaves versus that of their oppressor, the Egyptian pharaoh. God heard their groaning, raised up a leader, and visited plagues upon the oppressor until God's people were finally released from bondage.

Liberation theologians cry out along with Moses, "Set my people free." They compare the situation of the poor in Latin America with the situation of the Hebrew slaves. They interpret the salvation that comes from God not simply

---

3. Boff, *Church: Charism and Power*, 8.

as a spiritual matter concerning a final judgment for an individual but also as a political, economic, and social matter that has implications here and now.

The story of Jesus has also been of special interest to liberation theologians, who have focused on Jesus' liberating function as one who sets people free. They highlight Jesus' warnings to the rich, his concern for the poor and the socially disenfranchised, his clashes with established religious and political authorities, and the power of his Resurrection as the ultimate liberation from death. Jesus sets us free not only from personal sin but from the institutionalized structures of sin that mar human relationships by keeping people in horrible conditions of poverty and hopelessness.

Preferential Option for the Poor

Liberation theologians draw upon the Scriptures to speak of what they call the "preferential option for the poor," a phrase that has become important also for official Catholic social teaching (CST). The phrase takes its inspiration from the portrayal of God—in the Jewish law and in the teachings of the prophets, as well as in the person and teachings of Jesus—as having a special concern for the poor. The phrase has been interpreted in many ways. Some say that "poor" can refer to many types of poverty, including not only material poverty, but loneliness, alienation, and depression. In this way, one can say God has a special concern for all people in response to their deepest needs.

I once offered this interpretation to a liberation theologian who was visiting the university at which I teach. He practically spat out his answer in contempt, "Phooey! You want to know what poverty is? Come to my country and I will show you what poverty is." He believed I was watering down the meaning of "poverty" to stop it from challenging my way of thinking. Real poverty, he would argue, is the horror of material deprivation that his people experience. If I redefine poverty to include the loneliness of people who are materially well off, I take away from the urgency to do something about the problems of his people.

A common question my students raise at this point is, "Doesn't God have a special concern for all human beings?" The answer that I have heard a liberation theologian give to this is that the option for the poor includes a special concern for all human beings. This is because no one is ultimately served well by oppressive situations. The oppressor is as bound and limited by the situation as the oppressed. The slave-owner is made a small human being by the very fact of owning slaves. When the slaves are set free, the former slave-owner is set free from the bondage of being an oppressor and is now open to new possibilities of entering into more authentic human relationships with those who used to be slaves.

In this interpretation, the "option for the poor" requires that one view reality through the eyes of the poor. To be unaware of what reality looks like through the eyes of the poor is to be out of touch with reality. Decisions taking the perspective of the poor into consideration must, therefore, be made. In this way, liberation theologians advocate the transformation not only of the church but also of society itself, from the bottom up.

Another question commonly raised about the option for the poor is, "Does it represent a glorification of poverty?" Anyone who reads more than a page written by any liberation theologian would stop asking this question. Liberation theologians despise material deprivation. What they advocate is not poverty but justice. They love the poor not because of their poverty, but because they represent the face of Christ who appears in all who are needy. Liberation theologians call for working to reverse injustices that contribute to human degradation. They do not glorify poverty in any way.

Social Analysis

For people to be set free, the church must work toward structural changes in society. Boff writes,

> How the production of wealth functions, how wealth is distributed, the place of individuals in relation to capital, employment, and participation. The community that is awakened to this reality is already conscious of the violation of human rights, of structural poverty, of the social injustices that are the fruits of the organization of an entire system that is often presented as good, Christian, democratic, and so forth. Christian faith awakens one to social justice, to the true meaning of the global liberation of Jesus Christ that demands the transformation, the conversion, not only of the individual but also of the structures.[4]

Members of base ecclesial communities are, therefore, called upon to organize politically to work against the forces of oppression. They balance social analysis and action with a spirituality of "faith, hope, love, trust, and patience."[5] Boff points out that this path often leads to persecution and martyrdom.

The Marxist Label

The term *Marxism* refers to many different things. Pope Paul VI, in *Octogesima adveniens* (*A Call to Action*, 1971), an apostolic letter written on the eightieth anniversary of Pope Leo XIII's encyclical *Rerum novarum* (*On the Condition of Labor*) spoke of four meanings:

---

4. Boff, *Church: Charism and Power*, 135.

5. Boff, *Church: Charism and Power*, 136.

1. The active practice of class struggle
2. The collective exercise of political and economic power under the direction of a single party
3. A socialist ideology based on historical materialism and the denial of everything transcendent
4. A rigorous method of examining social and political reality that links theoretical knowledge with the practice of revolutionary transformation (*OA* 33)

Most liberation theologians are not Marxist by the first definition. Few if any liberation theologians are Marxist by definitions two and three. If by *Marxism*, however, one means definition four, then most liberation theologians have taken some inspiration from a method of social analysis and transformative praxis that is historically linked with Marxism. Liberation theologians have often made sweeping generalizations about capitalism that have a Marxist ring to them. Capitalism and the exploitation of the third world by the first world are sometimes named as the causes of Latin America's economic woes. Social structures are often analyzed in terms of class struggle. These links to Marxism have been a central focus of critics of liberation theology.

Even on these points, however, the connection of liberation theology with Marxism must be highly qualified. The connection is modified especially by liberation theologians' strong affirmation of belief in God, human transcendence, and the Scriptures. Apart from some of the earliest liberation theologians, simply labeling them as "Marxist" is misleading and unhelpful in coming to a clear picture of what they are saying. Yes, liberation theologians draw upon Marxism for vocabulary, concepts, tools of analysis, and sometimes even political prejudices. A few even call themselves "Marxist." Upon examination, however, liberation theologians are far from Marxists in their belief in God, Scripture, transcendence, and the way they use the concepts and tools that they borrow from Marxism.

Utopian?

A well-established critique of Marxism is that it is utopian, because it offers an unrealistic view of a perfect future while sacrificing what good exists in the present. The classic formulation of the anti-utopian position is paraphrased from Voltaire's *Dictionnaire Philosophique*: "Don't make the best the enemy of the good." In other words, do not trade an imperfect but tolerable situation for an intolerable situation by insisting upon unattainable perfection.

Liberation theologians have tried to distinguish their use of "utopia" from the kind of idealistic usage criticized by Voltaire. They draw upon the work of sociologist Karl Mannheim, who distinguishes "ideological" thinking that supports the existing order from "utopian" thinking that criticizes the existing order.[6] In line with this tradition, theologian Gustavo Gutiérrez contrasts his own usage of "utopia" with idealistic interpretations. For him, "utopia" is not an impractical, unrealistic dream. It is a dynamic way of thinking that draws upon the social sciences to create more humane living conditions; it receives its verification in praxis.

Within this framework of concepts, therefore, "utopian" does not mean being wildly idealistic; rather, it means being open to needed changes. It does not try to impose a preset picture of a perfect reality onto the present system, but instead works to change the system one step at a time. Liberation theologians do not think they are trading an imperfect but tolerable situation for a worse one; they believe the situation in which they live is absolutely intolerable and that whatever emerges has got to be better.

Official Catholic Responses

Early official responses to liberation theology were highly negative. In 1973, Father Jorge Bergoglio, who later became Pope Francis, was named the head of the Jesuits in Argentina with the task of cracking down on liberation theology. At that time, much of liberation theology in Argentina was a strongly leftist version. Bergoglio favored a theological approach that focused on the poor without connections to a political ideology. Over the years, however, he gradually modified his views.

In the 1980s, there were two significant responses to liberation theology issued from the Congregation for the Doctrine of the Faith (CDF), under the leadership of Cardinal Joseph Ratzinger, who later became Pope Benedict XVI. In 1984, the CDF published *Libertatis nuntius* (*Instruction on Certain Aspects of the "Theology of Liberation."*)[7] This document expressed a stern warning about the connection of liberation theology with Marxism, especially the danger of distorting traditional Christian doctrines in a way that limits their meaning to worldly political matters. A related document, *Libertatis conscientia* (*Instruction on Christian Freedom and Liberation*), was published in 1986.[8] This second document was more moderate. Although it made but scant mention of liberation theology, it affirmed, in general, many of the basic themes concerning human

---

6. Karl Mannheim, *Ideology and Utopia: An Introduction to the Sociology of Knowledge* (New York: Routledge and Kegan Paul, 1936 [1929]).

7. Congregation for the Doctrine of the Faith, *Donum veritatis* (*Instruction on Certain Aspects of the "Theology of Liberation"*), http://www.vatican.va/roman_curia/congregations/cfaith/documents/rc_con_cfaith_doc_19840806_theology-liberation_en.html.

8. Congregation for the Doctrine of the Faith, *Libertatis conscientia* (*Instruction on Christian Freedom and Liberation*), http://www.vatican.va/roman_curia/congregations/cfaith/documents/rc_con_cfaith_doc_19860322_freedom-liberation_en.html.

freedom and social development that underlie liberation theology, while alluding to the dangers of such thinking in a less stern manner.

It was reported by Vatican sources that it was John Paul II's idea to issue first a stern warning followed by a more moderate appraisal. The second document states clearly, "Between the two documents there exists an organic relationship. They are to be read in the light of each other" (*ICFL* 2). For this reason, it is possible to talk about an overall response of the Vatican to liberation theology.

The Vatican acknowledged the contemporary need to stress the importance of human freedom, beginning with freedom from sin through Christ, and including freedom from political and economic oppression. The struggle for justice, including change in social structures, is not an added extra to the gospel, but an essential part of it. The option for the poor, in which "poor" is understood as including all human afflictions and miseries, expresses an authentic dimension of the Christian message, especially as found in the spirit of the Beatitudes. The base ecclesial communities represent a source of hope for the future of the Catholic Church. Human solidarity, the interconnectedness of all people in a way that is prior to divisions into nations and classes, is an important Christian virtue that should motivate people to take seriously their obligations to share the goods of the earth with each other. By affirming these points, the Vatican has made room within official church teaching for some of the basic thrusts of liberation theology. Many of the concerns of the liberation theologians have deep intersections with the concerns expressed in the long tradition of CST.

At the same time, the Vatican's cautions about some aspects of liberation theology remain. Although the church must preach a message that ultimately has serious political implications, getting involved on the level of partisan politics remains the job of the laity, not the clergy or religious. Theologians are warned not to become too closely allied with systems of thought that are atheistic or that advocate systematic recourse to violent revolution. Recognizing the need to change unjust social structures should not lead to deemphasizing the basic truth that sin has its roots in the hearts and choices of individuals. In the end, though, these cautions do not erase the acknowledgment of the authenticity of several of liberation theology's main themes.

After the fall of world communism in 1989, liberation theology became even more distanced from Marxism. José Comblin, a liberation theologian who for many years had promoted radical economic change to address the plight of the poor, changed his mind. He reflected that, since Marxist and socialist ways of thinking had been discredited on the world stage, other means than socialist political action would have to be found to try to humanize, as much as possible, the global embrace of market-driven economies.[9]

---

9. José Comblin, *Called for Freedom: The Changing Context of Liberation Theology* (Maryknoll, NY: Orbis Books, 1998), xv–xvii; 138–70.

Summary

This chapter investigated some basic dimensions of liberation theology: base ecclesial communities, liberation in Scripture, social analysis, and the option for the poor. It then addressed some of the common criticisms of liberation theology such as the charges of Marxism and utopianism, as well as the official Vatican reactions and critiques.

Pope Francis's own assessment of liberation theology has gradually undergone many changes. He has increasingly come to believe that significant changes in national and international economic structures are needed to address the current plight of the poor. In response to an interview question concerning whether he is advocating a Marxist-type society, Pope Francis said,

> It has been said many times and my response has always been that, if anything, it is the communists who think like Christians. Christ spoke of a society where the poor, the weak and the marginalized have the right to decide. Not demagogues, not Barabbas, but the people, the poor, whether they have faith in a transcendent God or not. It is they who must help to achieve equality and freedom.

It would be unfair and inaccurate to deduce from one of Francis's many provocative statements that he is a Marxist as some people believe. It is more accurate to say that Pope Francis prefers not to cower before the accusations of those who promote economic exploitation. It is true, though, that Pope Francis is regarded as a strong supporter of liberation theology, even as he insists (as do most liberation theologians) on integrating personal religious conversion with work toward social transformation.

The next chapter will explore Pope Francis's own synthesis regarding evangelization, justice, and the importance of Christian community.

For Further Reflection

1. Does liberation theology tie religion too closely with politics?
2. How do you personally interpret the concept that God has a special concern for the poor?
3. Is liberation theology useful for the United States? If so, how might it be applied?
4. How might the collapse of Marxist economies influence the emphases of liberation theologians and their critics?
5. Which of the basic themes of liberation theology do you think is most important in a positive sense?

Suggested Readings

Amaladoss, Michael. *Life in Freedom: Liberation Theologies from Asia*. Maryknoll, NY: Orbis Books, 1997.

Boff, Leonardo. *Church: Charism and Power*. Translated by John W. Diercksmeier. New York: Crossroad, 1985 (1981).

Boff, Leonardo, and Clodovis Boff. *Introducing Liberation Theology*. Translated by Paul Burns. Maryknoll, NY: Orbis Books, 1987 (1986).

Comblin, José. *Called for Freedom: The Changing Context of Liberation Theology*. Maryknoll, NY: Orbis Books, 1998.

Gutiérrez, Gustavo, and Gerhard Ludwig Müller. *On the Side of the Poor: The Theology of Liberation*. Maryknoll, NY: Orbis Books, 2015.

Hayes, Diana L. *And Still We Rise: An Introduction to Black Liberation Theology*. New York: Paulist Press, 1996.

McGovern, Arthur F. *Liberation Theology and Its Critics: Toward an Assessment*. Maryknoll, NY: Orbis Books, 1989.

21

Pope Francis's Vision of the Church

Not long ago, I read a newspaper article reporting that officials in a government agency had been making decisions aimed at increasing their own power and wealth rather than serving the people the agency had been founded to serve. The story was sad but not unusual. What struck me about the article, though, was the tone. The journalist sounded shocked and outraged. Such feelings are ordinarily reserved for the editorial page. I wondered if maybe this reporter had been reading *Evangelii gaudium* (*The Joy of the Gospel*), in which Pope Francis laments that the majority of people accept, as usual, economic and social conditions that ought to evoke shock and outrage.

Evangelii gaudium is an apostolic exhortation, a document written by a pope in response to a synod of bishops.[1] This particular synod of bishops was held in Rome in 2012 on the topic of "the new evangelization." Evangelization is the sharing of the good news of the gospel. The new evangelization emphasizes the need for Catholics to be evangelized themselves before they go about spreading the news. In his book-length response, Pope Francis uses the theme of evangelization as a framework for expressing his vision of the Catholic Church and its mission in the world today.

Overview

The previous chapter was linked with chapter 6 of *Lumen gentium* because of its strong focus on base ecclesial communities. We discussed how Latin American liberation theology has been characterized by its insistence that working for social transformation in the face of abject poverty constitutes an integral imperative of the Christian gospel. This chapter will explore Pope Francis's vision of church community against the background of liberation theology. In the 1980s, the official Catholic response to liberation theology

---

1. Pope Francis, *Evangelii gaudium*, 2013, *https://w2.vatican.va/content/francesco/en/apost _exhortations/documents/papa-francesco_esortazione-ap_20131124_evangelii-gaudium.html.*

acknowledged this call for social transformation, but also called for more attention to an evangelization aimed at transforming the heart of each individual. Pope Francis's approach offers a full package that balances themes of personal conversion and social liberation.

The material in this chapter connects not only with *Lumen gentium* but also with another Vatican II document, *Gaudium et spes* (*Pastoral Constitution on the Church in the Modern World*).

Combining Evangelization and Liberation

Although some of the early liberation theologians in the 1960s may have placed political revolution above the gospel message, the most respected and internationally well-known liberation theologians, such as the Peruvian Gustavo Gutiérrez, the Salvadoran Jon Sobrino, the Brazilian Leonardo Boff, and many others, had balance at their core. Even in their cases, though, their sense of urgency and even outrage could, at times, obscure that balance in the eyes of other theologians and church leaders in more comfortable parts of the world.

Like Gutiérrez and Sobrino, Pope Francis hails from Latin America. In *Evangelii gaudium*, this Argentinian Pope Francis, without losing his balance, shares the urgency and outrage of the liberation theologians. He calls for Christians to say "thou shalt not" to an economy of exclusion and inequality. He asks, "How can it be that it is not a news item when an elderly homeless person dies of exposure, but it is news when the stock market loses two points?" (*EG* 53). He denounces what he calls "the globalization of indifference. . . . The culture of prosperity deadens us; we are thrilled if the market offers us something new to purchase; and in the meantime all those lives stunted for lack of opportunity seem a mere spectacle; they fail to move us" (*EG* 54). He declares that we are experiencing a profound human crisis in which the primacy of human dignity is being denied through the idolatry of money (*EG* 55). He dismisses trickle-down theories as expressing "a crude and naïve trust in the goodness of those wielding economic power and in the sacralized workings of the prevailing economic system" (*EG* 54). He declares that "the socio-economic system is unjust at its root" (*EG* 59) and that Christians should say no to the dictatorship of an impersonal economy (*EG* 55). He says these things without losing his simultaneous focus on the need for the personal interior transformation of each Christian.

Pope Francis's Synthesis

Pope Francis ties together themes of evangelization and liberation with the word *synthesis*. His use of *synthesis* carries with it three distinct yet overlapping layers of meaning connected with the heart, authentic expression, and the integration of traditional modes of thought with modern science and technology.

All three layers of meaning in Pope Francis's use of *synthesis* are connected with the task of evangelization in the modern world. Christians need to hold the treasure of the gospel in their hearts. They must be able to share it with others. They need to be able to understand and express their synthesis in ways that connect with modern cultures and forms of thought.

The First Layer: Personal Incorporation

The first layer of meaning of *synthesis* describes a personal incorporation of one's Christian faith within one's heart (*EG* 129, 143). The very title *Evangelii gaudium* (*The Joy of the Gospel*), names this personal synthesis, for it is what Christians should be prepared to share with others: gospel joy. Nor is this merely a textbook faith; rather, it is the faith of a converted heart. The kingdom of heaven lives and breathes within one. It is one's treasure, because "where your synthesis lies, there lies your heart" (*EG* 143).

Identifying one's synthesis with where one's heart lies, Pope Francis alludes to a passage from the Sermon on the Mount in which Jesus offers important and timeless advice:

> Do not store up for yourselves treasures on earth, where moth and rust consume and where thieves break in and steal; but store up for yourselves treasures in heaven, where neither moth nor rust consumes and where thieves do not break in and steal. For where your treasure is, there your heart will be also. (Mt 6:19–21)

Jesus is concerned about our hearts. Where do our hearts lie? Our hearts lie where we store up our treasure. In what do we place our deepest values? On what type of gains do we focus our energies and actions? What is it that we esteem as our treasure? Later in Matthew, Jesus compares our treasure with the kingdom of heaven itself: "The kingdom of heaven is like treasure hidden in a field, which someone found and hid; then in his joy he goes and sells all that he has and buys that field" (Mt 13:44).

The Second Layer: Authentic Expression

The second layer of meaning of *synthesis* describes the authentic expression of faith that is in one's heart as it is shared with others. This meaning connects with a well-known point made by Pope John XXIII in his opening speech at Vatican II. Pope John wanted the council not to issue new doctrines, but instead, to be pastoral. He said, "The substance of the ancient doctrine of the deposit of faith is one thing, and the way in which it is presented is another."[2] This distinction

---

2. "Pope John's Opening Speech to the Council," *Vatican II—Voice of the Church*, http://vatican2 voice.org/91docs/opening_speech.htm.

between the substance of doctrine and how doctrine and faith are presented echoes loudly in *Evangelii gaudium*. Pope Francis writes, "We should not think, however, that the Gospel message must always be communicated by fixed formulations learned by heart or by specific words which express an absolutely invariable content" (*EG* 129). He advises preachers, "The difference between enlightening people with a synthesis and doing so with detached ideas is like the difference between boredom and heartfelt fervor" (*EG* 143). Christians are called to communicate their synthesis not with cold formulas but genuinely and earnestly.

The Third Layer: Connecting Faith to the World

The third level of meaning of Pope Francis's use of *synthesis* is drawn from the Vatican II document, *Gaudium et spes* (*Pastoral Constitution on the Church in the Modern World*). *Gaudium et spes* called for "reading the signs of the times" and engaging in dialogue with people of different viewpoints. The word *synthesis* is used several times in *Gaudium et spes* to describe what is needed to address imbalances between (1) modern forms of science, technology, and culture and (2) more traditional forms of thought. The document calls for "artisans of a new humanity" who can interweave the fruits of the various academic disciplines with an integral view of the meaning of the human person and the needs of the human family. Rather than rejecting the modern world, Christians are called to achieve a synthesis of modern and traditional paths to knowledge in the light of Christian faith. Christians need to be able to connect their faith to the concrete realities of the world in which they live.

Spiritual Worldliness

In addition to affirming Christians who hold the joy of the gospel in their hearts, Pope Francis discusses the problem of Christians who seem to lack true conversion. There are Christians whose treasures are stored somewhere other than in heaven. Pope Francis labels this phenomenon, "spiritual worldliness," which he sees as a great danger to the Catholic Church (*EG* 93–97).[3] Religious people manifest a spiritual worldliness when they seek their own glory rather than the glory of God. It can be found in people in whom "we see an ostentatious preoccupation for the liturgy, for doctrine and for the Church's prestige, but without any concern that the Gospel have a real impact on God's faithful people and the concrete needs of the present time" (*EG* 95). Such people tend to be obsessed with appearances and judgmental toward others.

---

3. For the concept of "spiritual worldliness," Pope Francis cites Henri de Lubac, *Méditation sur l'Église* (Paris: Désclee de Brouwer, 1953), 321.

Pope Francis frequently expresses annoyance with those who legalistically stress doctrine or liturgy apart from other concerns. It is clear that both doctrine and liturgy are of utmost importance to Pope Francis insofar as they remain connected with faith as lived out in the world. When integrated together, Pope Francis values—simultaneously—Scripture, doctrine, liturgy, and social justice, each in the deepest and most serious ways. Even deeper than these elements, though, is the personal synthesis that lies in the heart of each Christian. When the moment arises, Christians should be able to share their faith, not simply by repeating formulas, but by speaking from their hearts. For Pope Francis, a spiritual worldliness is what characterizes a religious person who lacks such a personal synthesis.

Pope Francis's Distinct Agenda Expressed through Images of the Church

Pope Francis frequently reaffirms traditional church teachings, including those of all recent popes. He has a distinct agenda, however, when it comes to matters of tone and emphasis. Vatican II offered a fresh approach to understanding the church with a renewed emphasis on the local community and the role of the bishop in the diocese. Later, Popes John Paul II and Benedict XVI judged that the pace of change after the council had been too rapid and that pressures for more rapid and radical changes regarding authority, the role of women, and sexual morality should be resisted. They put a counterbalancing stress on centralization and uniformity within the church universal.

In *Evangelii gaudium*, Pope Francis explicitly expresses his preference for decentralization in matters of papal authority. When it comes to the organization of the Catholic Church in relation to evangelization, he stresses not only the diocese but even more so the parish. He describes the parish as "a community of communities, a sanctuary where the thirsty come to drink in the midst of their journey, and a centre of constant missionary outreach" (*EG* 28). He praises also "basic communities and small communities, movements, and forms of association," although he urges them "not to lose contact with the rich reality of the local parish" (*EG* 29). Pope Francis ultimately tries to find the proper balance between the local and global when it comes to centers of power within the Catholic Church (*EG* 234). He wants the basic structures of the church as well as church officials to be open to change in order to serve the needs of the people.

When it comes to images and phrases used to generalize about the church, Pope Francis displays his own ecclesial preferences. As discussed in chapter 6 of this book, *Lumen gentium* (*Dogmatic Constitution on the Church*) viewed the church as a mystery that could be best grasped through the use of images and symbols drawn from Scripture. After the council, two of the more popular images of the church, the Body of Christ and the People of God, emerged as banners for contrasting interpretations of the meaning of the council. The Body of Christ was embraced by conservatives; the People of God became the banner of the progressives. Popes John Paul II and Benedict XVI expressly favored the Body of Christ for its explicitly mystical and Christological focus. Progressive theologians, including liberation theologians, favored the People of God for its historical and inclusive connotations.

These "images" represent emphasis and direction; they are not matters of basic Catholic Church doctrine. Virtually every pope comes to office with a distinct agenda that differs, at least somewhat, from that of his predecessors. This was certainly the case when John Paul II came to office in 1978 sensing a need to slow down the pace of change experienced immediately after Vatican II. It is indicative of Pope Francis's theological direction that in *Evangelii gaudium* he uses some form of the phrase "People of God" to refer to the church about twenty-five times, whereas he only alludes to the church as the Body of Christ once. This is not to say that Pope Francis undervalues the Body of Christ image. If the document had been about the Eucharist rather than about evangelization, he likely would have used "Body of Christ" more frequently.

Ultimately, Pope Francis expresses what he wants from the Catholic Church in down-to-earth terms:

> I prefer a Church which is bruised, hurting and dirty because it has been out on the streets, rather than a Church which is unhealthy from being confined and from clinging to its own security. I do not want a Church concerned with being at the centre and which then ends by being caught up in a web of obsessions and procedures. If something should rightly disturb us and trouble our consciences, it is the fact that so many of our brothers and sisters are living without the strength, light and consolation born of friendship with Jesus Christ, without a community of faith to support them, without meaning and a goal in life. More than by fear of going astray, my hope is that we will be moved by the fear of remaining shut up within structures which give us a false sense of security, within rules which make us harsh judges, within habits which make us feel safe, while at our door people are starving and Jesus does not tire of saying to us: "Give them something to eat" (Mk 6:37). (*EG* 49)

Pope Francis wants the church, as the People of God, to be leaven in society. He connects the People of God with other ideas about the church, many drawn from Vatican II. The Catholic Church is to be active in cultivating its faith and in bringing in new members. It is not just to evangelize others, but to evangelize also itself on every level, including the level of the papacy. It is to be in constant mission, willing to transform itself in service to others. It is to be a place of mercy that does not judge but rather loves. It is to be a bride who is decorated with multiple cultural expressions. It is to be a mother who is open to everyone.

Evangelization and Inclusion

Pope Francis makes a connection between evangelization and the theme of inclusion. Christians need to share the joy of the gospel with everyone—and all need to have the joy of the gospel shared with them—including and sometimes especially, Christians. The gospel needs to be proclaimed anew to practicing Christians, those who have fallen away, and those who do not know of Christ—though Pope Francis is sensitive about respecting the existing faiths of others. Evangelization involves both the sharing of one's personal synthesis and listening to the personal synthesis of others.

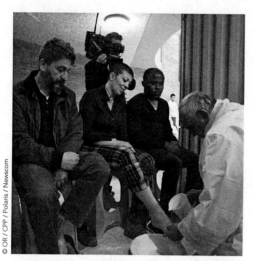

Pope Francis has often used the traditional foot-washing ceremony of Holy Thursday to make a statement about inclusivity and the social dimension of evangelization: he has washed the feet of Muslims, refugees, prison inmates, and women.

Inclusion, however, does not end with spoken words. Everyone who truly has a personal synthesis can connect the message of the gospel with the realities of the world in which we live. For Pope Francis, sharing the message of the gospel and working toward a more just society that is inclusive of everyone are not two separate things but part of the same process.

It is in this way that Pope Francis achieves his balance between evangelization and liberation theology. Sharing the gospel connects with living the gospel, and living the gospel connects with social and economic inclusion. There is no line to be drawn dividing faith from justice.

Christians need to evangelize. Christians need to be evangelized. Pope Francis calls for encounter and dialogue among people from all walks of life. Parishes must be open to the inclusion of everyone. Economies must be open to the inclusion of everyone. Pope Francis speaks not only of people who are in the lower ranks of society but also of those who are excluded. In other words, he distinguishes between people of the lower classes and those who are forgotten and urges that even, or rather especially, the latter also be included in society.

Summary

This chapter explored Pope Francis's vision of evangelization as a Christian's sharing of the joy of the gospel. Evangelization includes both one's personal synthesis of faith and working toward a more just and inclusive society.

I was positively impressed by the article mentioned at the beginning of this chapter, in which the journalist expressed shock and outrage about government officials who pursued their own power and wealth rather than serve the people their agency was founded to help. Could it be that in the future there will be more such articles as journalists recapture a sense of justified anger about abuses that should never be treated as normal? Perhaps there will be, as more and more Christians learn to share their personal synthesis. As Pope Francis says, the joy of the gospel encourages people to live in hope.

The next chapter will discuss the church as the Communion of Saints.

For Further Reflection

1. What have been your impressions of Pope Francis?
2. What does Pope Francis mean when he uses the word *synthesis*?
3. Can you relate with the notion of a "personal synthesis"?
4. What does Pope Francis mean by "spiritual worldliness"?
5. Can Pope Francis be called a "liberation theologian" without qualification?

Suggested Readings

Fernández, Victor Manuel, with Paolo Rodari. *The Francis Project: Where He Wants to Take the Church*. Mahwah, NJ: Paulist Press, 2016.

Francis, Pope. *The Church of Mercy: A Vision for the Church*. Chicago: Loyola Press, 2014.

Rausch, Thomas P., and Richard R. Gaillardetz, eds. *Go into the Streets! The Welcoming Church of Pope Francis*. Mahwah, NJ: Paulist Press, 2016.

Tornielli, Andrea, and Giacomo Galeazzi. *This Economy Kills: Pope Francis on Capitalism and Social Justice*. Collegeville, MN: Liturgical Press, 2015.

22

The Pilgrim Church

"Because we've always done it that way." The phrase reminds me of explanations I got in my childhood when I asked why we Catholics did certain things. Why do Catholics abstain from meat on Fridays? Why do Catholics pray the Stations of the Cross during Lent? Why are Catholics obliged to go to Mass on Sundays? The answer, and the great assumption, was that we had always done these things. We thought of the Catholic Church in the same way that we prayed to the three persons in one God: "Glory be to the Father, to the Son, and to the Holy Spirit. As it was in the beginning, is now, and ever shall be, world without end. Amen."

Many people today are critical of any notion of "tradition." Tradition is often presented as a storehouse of hang-ups that holds one back from growing as a person. Yet religious tradition is a wonderful and mysterious gift. It is something within which I dwell and upon which I draw as I live my life. It opens up to me the meaning of my life. Generally, this tradition does not hold me back in my human relationships but encourages me to forgive and love people.

I now know the origin of and the reason for many things in my faith, such as the obligation to attend Mass on Sunday. There remain parts of my faith that I accept but have not yet investigated historically, such as the origin of the Stations of the Cross.[1] The origins of many practices, such as priestly celibacy and the exclusion of women from the priesthood, are hotly debated topics today. But one thing I have definitely learned since I was a child is that my religious tradition has changed over time. Catholic belief and practice differ in striking ways from century to century.

Overview

Chapter 7 of *Lumen gentium* (*Dogmatic Constitution on the Church*) talks about a church that changes. It introduces the concept of the pilgrim church, one of the most important images of the church that emerged from

---

1. Having said this, I felt compelled to look it up. A discussion of the history of the Stations of the Cross can be found in Fred Krause, "A Humanizing Expression of the Faith: The Stations of the Cross," *Liturgy* 1 (1980): 49–54.

Vatican II. A pilgrim is a person who undertakes a journey. A pilgrim is someone who is on the way. Far from being a perfectly complete church, the church that is emerging from Vatican II is not finished yet.

This chapter will investigate the meaning and significance of the image of the pilgrim church in relation to the heavenly church. Together, the pilgrim church and heavenly church make up the Communion of Saints (see ch. 23). We will examine the relationship between continuity and change in the church, with a final consideration of the dark side of church history.

Perfection Only in Heaven

The comedian George Carlin once pointed out the very language of football tends to be rough: block, tackle, sack. Baseball, in contrast, sounds almost pastoral: walk, shag a fly, go home. The language expresses intangible differences in attitude and mood surrounding the games.

An early draft of what would become *Lumen gentium* spoke of the church militant and the church triumphant. The church triumphant was the church considered in its perfect, ideal state in heaven. The church militant was the church still fighting its battles in the course of this world. Although the terms have their own justifiable history, in the twentieth century, such language betrayed a mood of triumphalism, an attitude that overemphasized the achievement of the church to the neglect of the church's imperfections. A triumphal attitude lacks self-criticism, while disdaining anyone different from oneself. It is the attitude of one who has all the answers.

By the final draft of *Lumen gentium*, the language of the document had changed dramatically. The church triumphant became the heavenly church that exists eternally with God. The church militant became the pilgrim church. These two ideas of church were bonded together by the traditional concept of the Communion of Saints, which includes those who have died and are in glory, those who are being purified (in purgatory, though the word was not used), and those church members who are alive now, still on their journey. All of us are bonded in that we share the same grace and love of God.

The shift to speaking of the pilgrim church brings with it revolutionary connotations, attitudes, and moods. There is the exhilaration of a shared journey and a shared quest; the bond of a common past and an as-yet-to-happen future; the anticipation of the arrival at one's destiny. If before the Second Vatican Council the church could harmonize with battle marches, the postconciliar church is off to see the world. Life is more than a test and a battle; it is an exciting adventure.

Lumen gentium, chapter 7, puts an end to any pretensions the church might have to a current perfection:

> The church . . . will attain its full perfection only in the glory of heaven. . . . The church already on this earth is signed with a sanctity which is real although imperfect. . . . The pilgrim church, in her sacraments and institutions, which pertain to the present time, has the appearance of this world which is passing. . . . (*LG* 48)

Continuity Deeper than Change

Does my emphasis on change mean that I think the basic message of the gospel has changed? Wilfred Cantwell Smith (1916–2000), a scholar of world religions, argued that Christian tradition has differed so much through the centuries that we cannot claim that Christians have "believed" the same things. This is a striking, thought-provoking claim that is true in some respects, but false in other important ones. It is most likely true regarding the religious sensibility people develop in relating their faith to the modern world. But it is false when one considers how strong are the links that bind Christians today with Christians of the past. The faith in Jesus Christ and the transforming power of the gospel should not be underemphasized as points of continuity. Smith held that the way in which Christians today believe in these concepts is so different as to be further evidence of discontinuity:

> What all Christians have in common is that they have shared a common history. They have participated in a common process: namely, the Christian church in its ever-changing multiformity. They have in common also, no doubt . . . something transcendent. Yet to say what that transcendent reality is—the Real Presence, Christ, God; or to say that the church, in whose on-going life they variously participate, is itself the body of Christ; or however one conceptualises it—is to employ formulations that in turn are themselves not transcendent, and that historically are not stable.[2]

In contrast to Smith, I argue, admittedly on risky philosophical grounds, that it is ultimately the same Christ whom we encounter through our tradition. Part of my belief in the church is that it does not just help put me in touch with the transcendent in a general sense, but it puts me in touch with a particular relationship with God the Father through Jesus Christ who sends the Holy Spirit. This relationship with the triune God has deep commonalities with the relationship available to Christians throughout the history of the church.

Smith may have wanted to emphasize that throughout the ages we have understood Father, Son, and Spirit so differently that, in any particular sense, we

---

2. Wilfred Cantwell Smith, *Towards a World Theology* (Philadelphia: Westminster, 1981), 5–6.

are no longer talking about the same concepts or realities. Again, he would be making a challenging point that needs to be taken seriously. It is not enough to state simply that I believe otherwise. I need to study the Christian tradition in a critical manner that acknowledges changes and even aberrations. But again, my difference with Smith concerns what I believe the church to be. Is the church a fellowship of men and women who share the same resources but who understand them so differently as to have virtually unrelated beliefs from generation to generation? Or is the church, in a mystical sense, the continuation of the presence of Christ through the Holy Spirit in its journey through this world?

In this brief discussion, I have done more to raise this issue than to settle it. Like the church itself, the discussion is unfinished. I simply wanted, in this chapter on change, to mention a scholar who put a premium on change, and, without denying change, put in a personal word for continuity.

Change and Freedom

Many issues could be used to illustrate clear and profound change in the church. I focus on the way religious freedom is treated in official Catholic teaching in Pius IX's *Syllabus of Errors* (1864) and Vatican II's *Dignitatis humanae personae* (*Declaration on Religious Liberty*), 1965. These teachings illustrate a dramatic reversal on an important issue: whether people should be free to worship in whatever religion they choose.

In the nineteenth century, the official Catholic stand was consistent with a theology that stressed "no salvation outside the church," but inconsistent with a theology that stressed human freedom and dignity. The church insisted that Catholics in non-Catholic countries should be free to worship as they chose, but also held that in Catholic countries it was permissible to exclude other forms of worship. This position is expressed clearly in Pius IX's *Syllabus of Errors*, in which he condemns eighty propositions representing modern errors, among them:

> Every person is free to embrace and profess that religion which, led by the light of reason, that person may have thought true.
>
> In this our age it is no longer expedient that the Catholic religion should be treated as the only religion of the State, all other worships whatsoever being excluded.
>
> Hence it has been laudably provided by law in some Catholic countries, that people thither immigrating should be permitted the public exercise of their own several worships.[3]

---

3. A Latin and English text of *Syllabus of Errors* and the encyclical to which it was appended can be found in *Dublin Review* 4 (April 1865): 500–529. An English online version can be found at *http://www.papalencyclicals.net/Pius09/p9syll.htm.*

It is important to recognize that these statements were not being taught by Pius IX as truth; they were being condemned as falsehoods. In fairness to Pius IX it should be noted that he saw the church threatened by a rationalism, associated with the French Revolution, that was hostile to religion, and he thought he needed to do whatever he could to protect the church's mission. Few minds of the time could envisage a synthesis of church teaching with the concerns of the modern world. Yet the stands he took against freedom of religion clearly contradict the teaching that emerged at Vatican II.

Vatican II's *Dignatatis humanae* begins by affirming the basic dignity of human beings and the importance of human freedom. It argues that people must not be coerced to practice a particular religion; truth has its own power of gentle persuasion. The document supports a limited and humble secular state in which people have the right to worship as they choose:

> One of the key truths in Catholic teaching, a truth that is contained in the word of God and constantly preached by the Fathers, is that a person's response to God by faith ought to be free, and that therefore no one is to be forced to embrace the faith against one's will. The act of faith is by its very nature a free act. (*DH* 10)

The document points out that in taking this position it is "developing" the doctrine, although it stresses continuity with Scripture and Tradition and papal teaching concerning freedom and dignity without mentioning the reversal of the *Syllabus of Errors*.

This shift was not only significant for the issue of religious freedom but also for affirming that church teaching can indeed grow and change. John Courtney Murray, an American Jesuit whose theological works enabled him to champion the cause of religious freedom at Vatican II, wrote,

> The course of the development between *The Syllabus of Errors* (1864) and *Dignitatis Humanae Personae* (1965) still remains to be explained by theologians. But the Council formally sanctioned the validity of development itself; and this was a doctrinal event of high importance for theological thought in many other areas.[4]

Theologians today no longer argue about whether church teaching can change; rather, they argue about how to distinguish the essential from the nonessential and truth from the particular formulation. A document from the Vatican's International Theological Commission states, the basic truth of the gospel contained in church teaching remains always the same; the particular ways in

---

4. John Courtney Murray, "Religious Freedom," in *The Documents of Vatican II*, ed. Walter M. Abbott (New York: Guild, 1966), 673.

which this teaching is expressed will reflect the limitations and biases of various cultures and philosophical systems. Although interpretation is an intricate and often subtle affair, "What was once recognized as truth must . . . be acknowledged as true in an enduringly valid way."[5] That is, there is a fundamental insight in any church teaching that remains true even though it may have to be seriously reinterpreted within a new cultural context.

Does this mean there is something in Pius IX's condemnation of religious freedom that is to be sifted out of its cultural context and preserved as truth? Is it possible to argue that what Pius IX mistook religious freedom to be—a rebellious notion based on reason alone—deserved to be condemned until more nuanced concepts of religious freedom grounded in the dignity of the person could be developed? Perhaps there is something in that argument. I prefer to go a different route. I seek out what might have been legitimate in the document taken as a whole, but I feel no need to justify each statement on a line-by-line basis in the way some fundamentalists read the Bible. The *Syllabus of Errors* is ordinary papal teaching that reflects a mid-nineteenth-century reaction to modern developments. It is not an infallible proclamation, nor does it have the same status as a declaration of Vatican II. Pius IX was wrong on some points. This does nothing to change the enduring truth of the gospel. This shift in doctrine bolsters my confidence in church teaching; I trust leaders more if they sometimes admit they have been wrong. The traditional belief in the indefectibility of the Catholic Church does not mean the church will never make a mistake; it means the church will basically remain on the true path.

The Dark Side of Church History

In my early twenties, I took on a renewed interest in the Catholic Church. I wanted to find out as much as I could about my newfound love. I picked up a popular work on church history written by Philip Hughes.[6] I read it with deep hunger; unfortunately, much of it tasted bitter. I do not remember whether I really cried or not, but I remember that I wanted to. The church that I had thought was perfect had feet of clay. The spotless bride of Christ had been dragged through the mud. Rather than the story of glorious and civilizing love I had expected, I read of heresies and condemnations, disagreements and wars, corruption and reformation. Hughes's style lent itself to apologetic understatement, in this case, for example, of the Catholic Reformation:

5. International Theological Commission, "On the Interpretation of Dogmas," *Origins* 20 (May 17, 1990): 4. See also "Address of His Holiness Benedict XVI to the Roman Curia," Dec. 22, 2005, *http://w2.vatican.va/content/benedict-xvi/en/speeches/2005/december/documents/hf_ben_xvi _spe_20051222_roman-curia.html*, in which Pope Benedict describes a "hermeneutic of reform" that balances discontinuity with continuity.

6. Philip Hughes, *A Popular History of the Catholic Church* (New York: Macmillan, 1947).

> The popes continued to be, in many respects, the children of the age in which they fought to restore Catholic ideals, and they continued to make use of all the means open to them, the secular weapons of diplomacy and even war, and not merely the war of defence.[7]

In other words, Hughes is politely saying that popes started wars of aggression over matters of church doctrine and government. Hughes barely alludes to things that I was to learn later: the persecution of the Jews, the horrors of the Crusades, the corruption of the Renaissance popes, the tortures and executions of the Spanish Inquisition.

It seems as though the church has not always been a good pilgrim. How is a Catholic to come to terms with this dark side of the church's history? I have no final answers for this problem. Hans Küng suggests that, in the face of the centuries of Christian persecution of the Jews, "Shame and guilt must be our silent reply."[8] There are other suggestions, too.

First, it should be remembered that the dark episodes in church history are balanced by a long and glorious history of an institution that has accomplished immeasurable good throughout the centuries in areas such as education, health care, social work, art, and culture. Perhaps the truly balanced history of the church has yet to be written. Second, the history of the church is not to be assessed simply in terms of its institutional achievements, but also in terms of the lives of countless individuals for whom the church has opened tremendous potential for holiness. Of course, the lives of individual Christians also have their own dark side. Third, it is important to distinguish between what can be attributed to the Catholic Church and what can be attributed to individuals or groups who unfortunately may be acting in the name of the church. There have been times when even popes have not seemed to take the will of God into their deliberations. Fourth, we should not expect the human elements of the church to be perfect. This does not mean, however, that at certain points in history we should not have expected a lot better than what was delivered. There remains room for the shame and guilt of which Küng speaks.

Yet what is the purpose of shame and guilt other than to help us to grow beyond them in a way that incorporates their lessons? The Christian tradition calls us beyond our sins to a life of faith, hope, and love. The church is an important dimension of that tradition; like Christ, the church is a commingling of human and divine elements. The human side of the church, however, often messes things up, at times in a big way. We are a pilgrim people, not yet finished, journeying along with the treasure of our faith, which in the most important respects has remained the same throughout the ages.

---

7. Hughes, *A Popular History*, 162.

8. Hans Küng, *The Church*, trans. Ray and Rosaleen Ockenden (New York: Sheed and Ward, 1967), 137.

In the years leading up to the Jubilee Year of 2000, Pope John Paul II explicitly apologized for sins of Catholics against Jews, Eastern Orthodox, and Muslims. Although some claim that his words still do not go far enough, that he apologized has received almost universal approval.

Summary

This chapter discussed the pilgrim journey of the church. It focused on Vatican II's acknowledgment of imperfection, on change and continuity, on the specific case of religious liberty, and on the dark side of church history. Tradition remains crucially important to the Catholic Church, yet Catholics are more aware today that tradition does not cancel out change. Catholics can no longer simply buy the argument, "because we have always done it that way." In the words of theologian Monika Hellwig, "Tradition implies change in continuity with the past."[9]

The next chapter will discuss the meaning of life.

For Further Reflection

1. Why do you think there was a tendency in nineteenth- and early twentieth-century Catholicism to claim the church was perfect and unchanging?

2. Is the image of the "pilgrim church" too mundane to convey the majesty of the church? Is it going to the opposite extreme of the more triumphal images?

3. Amid the changes, what in Christianity stays the same? What do Christians of the twentieth century share with Christians of the first century?

4. How do you feel about the Catholic Church reversing itself on a position such as in the case of religious liberty? Does it weaken the credibility of the church to reverse itself?

5. How aware are you of the dark side of church history? How do you respond to it?

Suggested Readings

Accattoli, Luigi. *When a Pope Asks Forgiveness: The Mea Culpa's of John Paul II.* Translated by Jordan Aumann. Boston: Pauline Books and Media, 1998.

---

9. Monika K. Hellwig, *Tradition in the Catholic Church—Why It's Still Important* (Cincinnati: St. Anthony Messenger Press, 1981).

Congar, Yves. *Tradition and Traditions: A Historical and Theological Essay.* Translated by Michael Naseby and Thomas Rainborough. New York: Macmillan, 1966 (1960).

Congar, Yves. *True and False Reform in the Church.* Translated by Paul Philibert. Collegeville, MN: Liturgical Press, 2011 (1968).

Küng, Hans. *The Church Maintained in Truth: A Theological Meditation.* Translated by Edward Quinn. New York: Crossroad, 1980 (1979).

Murray, John Courtney. *We Hold These Truths: Catholic Reflections on the American Proposition.* New York: Sheed and Ward, 1960.

Thiel, John E. *Senses of Tradition: Continuity and Development in Catholic Faith.* Oxford: Oxford University Press, 2000.

Tilley, Terrence W. *Inventing Catholic Tradition.* Maryknoll, NY: Orbis Books, 2000.

The Meaning of Life

By the time I was in college, I had rejected my religion. I wanted to know the true meaning of life. I majored in English literature, thinking that perhaps the persons recognized as great authors would teach me something about this most important topic. I became interested in philosophy for the same reason. I learned a great deal in my studies, for which I will always be grateful. When it came to the meaning of life, however, I did not have much luck. Perhaps it was because I sought an "answer" to a question that doesn't have a clear, set one. Why do human beings exist? Why is there any reality? Does my life have a purpose?

I became especially interested in an area known as general semantics, where philosophy and linguistics intersect. To find out the meaning of life, I would first need to know the meaning of "meaning." If I could know what "meaning" itself means, I would be in a better position to know the meaning of life. What does it mean to "mean"? Why is there such a thing as "meaning"?

For various reasons, my college years were intense and depressing. I reached a breaking point in my early twenties. Through group support, I was led to reach out to God in prayer. Through continuing support, I grew in faith. After a time, I sought out the religion of my youth. Eventually, I made the academic study of religion, especially Catholicism, my main occupation.

Through faith and prayer I have come to trust that life does indeed have meaning. The academic study of religion is important to me, but it would mean much less to me if it were not related to my personal faith.

So what, after all of that, is the meaning of life? I still do not have an "answer." What I have found is that by striving to live a Christian life, by seeking the will of God, by struggling to live my life on a spiritual basis, I have come in contact with the meaning of life. I experience meaning within the context of my life journey. I do not "know" the meaning of life. It is not something that I could write out definitively in a paragraph or two. It is more something that I have an inkling of as meaning spills over into my daily activities. The less I anguish intellectually about the meaning of life, and the more I reach outside of myself to God and others, the more I experience the rich and deep meaning there is to be had in this great gift of life.

I have trouble relating with Albert Camus's claim that life is absurd, because the human heart cries out for meaning in a universe that gives no reply. Whether it is in the midst of the most wonderful things in my life or my deepest sufferings, I have become increasingly convinced that life has an ultimate meaning and purpose. I cannot quite see or hear this meaning and purpose, but I can taste, smell, and touch it. I know it is there, even if I cannot describe it in any final or definitive way.

Overview

Chapter 7 of *Lumen gentium* talks about the meaning of life in a way I can relate to. After proclaiming the ongoing activity of Christ in the world, through the church and through the Eucharist, it goes on to say,

> Therefore the promised restoration which we are awaiting has already begun in Christ, is carried forward in the mission of the Holy Spirit and through Him continues in the church in which we learn the meaning of our terrestrial life through our faith, while we perform with hope in the future the work committed to us in this world by the Father, and thus work out our salvation. (*LG* 48)

That is, by living a life in which one follows Christ, seeks the will of the Father, and listens to the promptings of the Spirit, one will learn the meaning of life, which allows one to carry on one's earthly work with hope for the future.

This chapter explores two themes from chapter 7 of *Lumen gentium* that help illuminate the meaning of life: eternal life and the Communion of Saints.

Eternal Life

If this life is all there is, then it seems to me to have little if any ultimate meaning. Does life end in death? Are we simply snuffed out of existence? Will the universe trudge on for all eternity, never to hear from us again?

Catholic teaching about the afterlife prior to Vatican II tended to be exceedingly clear. Heaven and hell were the two ultimate choices, with purgatory as a temporary but harsh middle ground and limbo as a neutral place for unbaptized infants and other innocent nonbelievers. Although it was always acknowledged that the actual nature of these places or states of being were far beyond our imaginations, the ways in which they were talked about was often quite detailed and concrete.

In *A Portrait of the Artist as a Young Man*,[1] James Joyce offers an exaggerated yet telling depiction of the kinds of things a Catholic retreat preacher might have said about hell in 1916. The preacher declares, "Hell is a straight and dark and foul smelling prison, an abode of demons and lost souls, filled with fire and smoke." He tells how the walls of hell are said to be four thousand miles thick; how horrible is the stench; how despicable the company of demons; how boundless and intense the fire; how painful to be deprived of divine light; how insufferably long is eternity. On each point, the preacher offers an extended, vivid description designed to drive home the fear of hell to his school-aged listeners. Although what is presented is much more extreme than ordinary Catholic preaching of the time, it is fair to say that Catholics operated with a fairly clear idea of what heaven and hell were like, and even of who was likely to go where.

Contemporary Catholic teaching about the afterlife has tended to focus on the mystery of it, with much less stress on the nature of heaven and hell and much more emphasis on the coming of the kingdom that Jesus preached. There is an attempt to balance any focus on individual souls with a focus on human relationships and social issues. Talk of afterlife is balanced with talk of the kingdom having its roots in this world—wherever the will of God breaks in to transform people and social structures. The kingdom is both individual and social; it is both here and yet to come; it is a reality we experience and a mystery we hope for.

Some theologians, writers, and artists have emphasized the experience of the eternal dimension of reality as we encounter it now. They stress the "already present" aspect of the kingdom. William Blake wrote of experiencing "a world in a grain of sand."[2] In *Our Town*, Thornton Wilder depicts a world whose present moments go by largely unappreciated unless it is by a poet or someone who has returned from the dead.[3] T. S. Eliot writes in *Four Quartets* of "a lifetime burning in every moment."[4] In *Total Presence*, T. J. J. Altizer speaks of the contemporary experience of an immediacy that signifies the death of interior consciousness and the end of history. He claims, "The only regained paradise is the final loss of paradise itself."[5] These authors challenge us not to simply put heaven off to the day when we die but to appreciate the depth dimension of our lives as we live them.

---

1. James Joyce, *A Portrait of the Artist as a Young Man* (New York: Viking, 1964 [1916]). The sermon on hell is found interspersed between 110 and 133.

2. William Blake, "Auguries of Innocence," Poetry Foundation, *https://www.poetryfoundation .org/poems/43650/auguries-of-innocence*.

3. Thornton Wilder, *Our Town* (New York: Coward-McCann, 1938).

4. T. S. Eliot, *Four Quartets* (New York: Harcourt, Brace and World, 1943), 17.

5. Thomas J. J. Altizer, *Total Presence* (New York: Seabury, 1980), 108.

This mosaic, in Guernica, in Basque country, pays homage to Picasso's painting of that name. The painting vividly conveys the horrors of war suffered by that village during the Spanish Civil War.

Other theologians and artists remind us of the not-yet aspect of the kingdom. Picasso's oil painting *Guernica* stands as a symbol of the terrible reality of modern warfare. Elie Wiesel's book *Night* helps us to keep in mind the horrors of the Holocaust and of human hatred.[6] Gustavo Gutiérrez's classic *A Theology of Liberation* tells of a world that has too much human suffering to simply lend itself to acceptance and appreciation.[7] These thinkers remind us that the fullness of the kingdom is still a long way off.

As was the case with the mystery of the church itself, *Lumen gentium* speaks about the afterlife in images and symbols drawn from the Scriptures. There is no attempt at an overly clear definition or description. The reader is told,

> Since however we know not the day nor the hour, on Our Lord's advice we must be constantly vigilant so that, having finished the course of our earthly life, we may merit to enter into the marriage feast with Him and to be numbered among the blessed, and that we may not be ordered to go into eternal fire like the wicked and slothful servant, into the exterior darkness where "there will be the weeping and the gnashing of teeth." (*LG* 48)

---

6. Elie Wiesel, *Night* (New York: Hill and Wang, 1960 [1958]).

7. Gustavo Gutiérrez, *A Theology of Liberation: History, Politics, Salvation*, trans. Sister Caridad Inda and John Eagleson, Spanish and English ed. (Maryknoll, NY: Orbis Books, 1988 [1971]).

In the original text, this single sentence contains five footnotes to scriptural passages, drawing heavily from Matthew 25, but referring also to Matthew 22 and Hebrews 9. It is surrounded by other heavily footnoted sentences that borrow liberally from the letters of Paul and John. In other words, when it comes time to discuss the afterlife, the document relies exclusively on highly symbolic images from the New Testament.

Such a reliance on Scripture does two things. First, it helps reestablish the afterlife as a mystery of the faith rather than as some piece of information that we know all about. Gone are the days when a retreat master might be tempted to speak of heaven and hell as literally as if describing the house down the street. Catholics still believe firmly in the reality of heaven, but are inclined more to remember the symbolic and analogous nature of the language that is used to talk about it.

Second, though, the reliance on scriptural texts reinforces the importance of this mystery in the total scheme of Catholic belief. The church echoes Scripture as it calls believers to remain vigilant as they live in confident hope for eternal life. As church teaching has evolved, that hope, at least, has not changed.

Communion of Saints

My father died some years ago. Where has he gone? Will I ever meet him again?

When I was a child I did not think of the Communion of Saints as having to do with ordinary people I had known. I thought of the saints as amazingly holy people to whom one would pray, because they had the power to grant special favors. For example, if I lost something, I prayed to St. Anthony. If I found it, I would pay St. Anthony by putting a dollar in the poor box at church. (Today, if I am really desperate, I may still resort to doing this.)

Lumen gentium, drawing upon the depths of the Catholic tradition, includes in the Communion of Saints not only those addressed as "Saint," but those who have died and are now with God. It also includes those who are struggling to live lives of holiness now. That is, the Communion of Saints includes not only those extraordinarily holy people who have been canonized, but also people like my father and me. The point of the belief in the Communion of Saints is that all are joined with one another in the shared grace of a loving God. We remain related to each other in a community. My father and I are still both part of the mystical body of Christ; that he has died and that I remain alive has not erased our continuing relationship. Only death separates us; we are united through our love of God. I know nothing concrete of what eternal life is like, but I know that I believe in it and that I hope to meet my father again.

Lumen gentium still talks about the saints as those who, through their merits, can intercede for us with God; this belief, however, is complemented by an even greater emphasis on the role of the saints as inspiring examples and companions in a fellowship of love. Vatican II did not tell me to stop praying to St. Anthony when I lose something; what I hear the document saying, however, is that my prayers for intercession should be complemented by a knowledge of the life of the particular saint and an openness, on my part, to become a more open and loving person through that saint's example. In other words, for me to receive the grace of God through the intercession of a saint is connected with my knowledge of that saint and my openness to being inspired. In this light, the document calls for growth in the way one relates with saints:

> We urge all concerned, if any abuses, excesses or defects have crept in here or there, to do what is in their power to remove or correct them, and to restore all things to a fuller praise of Christ and of God. Let them therefore teach the faithful that the authentic cult of the saints consists not so much in the multiplying of external acts, but rather in the greater intensity of our love, whereby, for our own greater good and that of the whole church, we seek from the saints "example in their way of life, fellowship in their communion, and aid by their intercession." (*LG* 51)

This passage suggests that Christians avoid superstitious petitioning of saints through repetitive prayers. The Catholic Church advocates saints as a help in relating with God, not a substitute. Individuals are encouraged to study the life of any saint to whom they might pray, sense their connectedness with him or her, and be open to be inspired.

The Catholic Church still holds a special place for those saints who have been canonized. It is hoped that many, many people, both those alive and those who have gone before us in death, can qualify for the generic title, "Saint," but there have been some people who have led such recognizably holy lives that they stand out as shining lights for the rest of us. These people are canonized by the church much in the way that baseball players are inducted into the Hall of Fame. They are proposed to a committee, investigated and reviewed, and finally voted and decided upon. The pope has the final say. To be canonized a saint is to receive an official endorsement by the Catholic Church that you are a fit model for veneration and inspiration. Unlike the Hall of Fame, people are not eligible for canonization until after they have died.

Pope John Paul II, during his long reign (1978–2005), canonized 482 saints, which represents a pace more rapid than his recent predecessors.[8] Part of his motivation for doing so has been to expand the types of saints the faithful have available to them, for one of the functions of saints is to show how the Christian

---

8. A table listing all of the saints canonized by John Paul II can be found at *http://www.vatican.va/news_services/liturgy/saints/index_saints_en.html#*.

life can be lived faithfully in a variety of life situations and circumstances. He included more women, more non-Europeans, more middle-class, and more married people. Some liberation theologians have argued that the Catholic Church should give more emphasis to reformers and political activists who work for systemic change than to "saints of the system" who do not challenge the status quo.[9] It is important to remember, however, that the number of saints in the Catholic Church (and, I would add, beyond) is far greater than the number of those who have been canonized.

Summary

In this chapter, the meaning of life was discussed in relation to Catholic belief concerning eternal life and the Communion of Saints.

I am fairly certain that my father will never be officially canonized; I live in hope, though, that he is now with God as sure as is St. Peter, and that someday we will meet again. The next chapter will examine different styles of theology that have emerged in the Catholic Church since Vatican II.

For Further Reflection

1. What do you think of when you hear the phrase, "the meaning of life"?
2. The journey theme is popular in contemporary spirituality. What are its limitations? Does it need to be balanced by other images?
3. Some art and literature stress the need to appreciate life now. Other works stress the horrors of the realities we face. How might these contrasting emphases fit together?
4. Do you know anyone you consider a "saint"? What is that person like?
5. Do you believe in eternal life?

Suggested Readings

Cunningham, Lawrence. *The Meaning of Saints.* San Francisco: Harper and Row, 1980.

DeLorenzo, Leonard J. *Work of Love: A Theological Reconstruction of the Communion of Saints.* Notre Dame, IN: University of Notre Dame Press, 2017.

---

9. Leonardo Boff, *Church: Charism and Power: Liberation Theology and the Institutional Church,* trans. John W. Diercksmeier (New York: Crossroad, 1985 [1981]), 123. See also Boff's *St. Francis: A Model for Human Liberation* (New York: Crossroad, 1984 [1982]).

Johnson, Elizabeth A. *Friends of God and Prophets: A Feminist Theological Reading of the Communion of Saints.* New York: Continuum, 1998.

Küng, Hans. *Eternal Life? Life after Death as a Medical, Philosophical, and Theological Problem.* Translated by Edward Quinn. Garden City, NY: Doubleday, 1984 (1982).

Levering, Matthew. *Jesus and the Demise of Death: Resurrection, Afterlife, and the Fate of the Christian.* Waco, TX: Baylor University Press, 2012.

Thompson, William M. *Fire and Light: The Saints and Theology.* New York: Paulist Press, 1987.

Pilgrims and Saints

onflicts sometimes arise between people in the Catholic Church who represent different points of view. It was reported that church representatives at an international conference on AIDS held at the Vatican objected to a slogan carried on many posters: "The Body of Christ Has AIDS." Their objection was that when the church is referred to as the mystical Body of Christ, it is understood as being without sin, stain, or blemish.

The Body of Christ image has functioned in a way similar to the image of the church as the "spotless bride of the spotless lamb"—it is the church understood in an ideal, mystical sense. The church, in this sense, is a great gift from God, something more than a human invention. It is Christ's continuing presence, the way of salvation, the fountain of grace, the light of the peoples that remains ever untarnished. Church officials, understanding the Body of Christ in this manner, were offended at the suggestion that the Body of Christ has AIDS.

© LE PICTORIUM / Alamy Stock Photo

Sister Mary of Maryknoll Sisters speaks with a Burmese woman about her medication for HIV. Sister Mary runs the Hope Center in northern Burma, a social and medical center supported by the Catholic Church.

The people who carried the signs at the AIDS conference were most likely operating out of a contrasting set of images of the church. These people would tend to think more of the unfinished and changing pilgrim church than of the spotless bride of the spotless lamb. They would resonate more with the church as the People of God ever in need of reform and renewal than with the church as an untarnished ideal. They would be more inclined to focus on the Body of Christ as broken and bloody than as risen and glorified. They might recall the words of Paul about the Body of Christ:

> God has so arranged the body, giving the greater honor to the inferior member, that there may be no dissension within the body, but the members may have the same care for one another. If one member suffers, all suffer together with it; if one member is honored, all rejoice together with it. (1 Cor 12:24–26)

Seen in this perspective, to say that the Body of Christ has AIDS is another way of saying we share in each other's suffering. Both perspectives, it seems, can find much support in Scripture and Catholic Church Tradition.

Overview

This chapter will explore more deeply some of the differences between contrasting schools of thought in the Catholic Church today. For the sake of simplicity, two such schools are identified, although in reality there exists a wide spectrum of approaches. The main point of difference focused on here is the manner in which each group interprets Vatican II. The chapter will close with a consideration of the "Extraordinary Synod" of 1985, a Vatican meeting that tried to create harmony among the often cacophonous voices.

This material relates to chapter 7 of *Lumen gentium* insofar as that chapter introduces and harmonizes two images of the church that tend to be favored, respectively, by the two schools of thought: the pilgrim church and the Communion of Saints. This chapter will label the groups "Pilgrims" and "Saints." Most Pilgrims would be among those supporting the slogan, "The Body of Christ Has AIDS"; most Saints would be among those strongly objecting.

Pilgrims

Theologians who tend to favor images such as the "pilgrim church" and the "People of God" identify the major gains of Vatican II as a set of progressive changes: the ecumenical openness, the more positive attitude toward other world religions, the focus on the laity, the emphasis on religious freedom, and the special concern for matters of peace and economic justice. Writing in the early decades after Vatican II, these theologians, such as the Dutch Dominican Edward Schillebeeckx and the Brazilian liberation theologian Leonardo Boff, applauded what they saw as a major shift at Vatican II—from a church too concerned about itself as an institution to a church trying to reform itself and engage in constructive interaction with the world. The church was no longer a fortress against the world but a force within the world working toward social change.

For Pilgrims, the basic theological shift that underlies the changes at Vatican II is twofold:

- *From* the Catholic faith considered as a systematic and complete "package" that was delivered intact from Jesus and passed down through the apostles
- *To* an understanding of the Christ-event in more historical and social terms

The focus is on human experience. Thus Schillebeeckx began his theology not with a Jesus who "comes down" from heaven but with the man Jesus who has a unique experience of transformation through his encounter with his "Abba" or Father. Jesus' "Abba experience" becomes the experiential basis for his ministry and mission. After Jesus' death, the experience that the disciples have of Jesus as Lord transforms them and becomes the basis of the Christian community. Today, the continued experience of Jesus as Lord brings people together in communities based on a love that leads them to engage in transforming society.[1]

Pilgrims stress the ability of the church to change and adapt as it faces new situations. For this reason, both Schillebeeckx and Boff focused on the role of the Holy Spirit in the founding of the church. Rather than emphasizing the church as established by Jesus and, therefore, not subject to change, they emphasize that the disciples founded the church by addressing new situations with the aid of the Holy Spirit. Therefore, as new situations arise today, church leaders should feel capable of making necessary changes. Both Schillebeeckx and Boff, for example, favored allowing married priests and the ordination of women.

Pilgrims are people who strike out for new territories. Like Schillebeeckx and Boff, Pilgrims sense an urgent need for change in church and society. It is not surprising that they should focus on those elements of Vatican II that represent what they see as social progress.

Saints

Theologians who tend to favor less historical, more mystical images of the church, such as the "Communion of Saints," the "bride of Christ," and the "Mystical Body of Christ," identify two distinct sets of progressive changes at Vatican II, and then

---

1. Schillebeeckx's theology can be found in his trilogy, *Jesus: An Experiment in Christology; Christ: The Experience of Jesus as Lord;* and *Church: The Human Story of God* (New York: Crossroad, 1981, 1981, 1990 [1974, 1977, 1989]).

subordinate one set to the other. For these scholars, such as the Swiss Hans Urs von Balthasar and the German Joseph Ratzinger (later Pope Benedict XVI), the shift from an overemphasis on the hierarchy to a concept of church as including the whole People of God was a useful but relatively minor change. The major shift at Vatican II was from a church too concerned with the juridical and official to a church aware of itself as a mystery that expresses the love of God for humankind. These theologians neither ignore nor reject the progressive teachings of Vatican II about ecumenism, the laity, religious freedom, or peace and justice, but they interpret these teachings within a framework that emphasizes the church as the mystical Body of Christ with a hierarchical structure.

For Saints, the basic theological shift that underlies the changes of Vatican II involves the church becoming newly aware of its mission to evangelize the world with its message of the love of the three persons in God made known through Jesus, the Incarnate Word of God. It is a matter of the same church, which has been in existence since Christ, being awakened to its pastoral charge. The shift in understanding the church is not a shift away from an institutional model toward some other type of model, but rather, a shift from an overly juridical institutional model to a model still significantly institutional but set afire by the love of Christ. A church that does not emphasize the importance of Jesus becomes simply another social service organization.

Saints stress the ability of the church to face new situations in ways that remain faithful to the tradition that has been handed down intact throughout the ages. For this reason, von Balthasar and Ratzinger emphasized that it is Christ who founded the church and that the human beings running it should be extremely hesitant to change it. Ratzinger's emphasis led him to a position in contrast with that of Boff:

> My impression is that the authentically Catholic meaning of the reality "church" is tacitly disappearing, without being expressly rejected. Many no longer believe that what is at issue is a reality willed by the Lord himself. Even with some theologians, the church appears to be a human construction, an instrument created by us and one which we ourselves can freely reorganize according to the requirements of the moment.[2]

Ratzinger saw this view as undermining the Catholic faith itself:

> The church is indeed composed of men who organize her external visage. But behind this, the fundamental structures are willed by God himself, and therefore they are inviolable. Behind the human exterior stands the mystery of a more than human reality, in which reformers, sociologists, organizers have no authority whatsoever. If the church,

---

2. Joseph Ratzinger, with Vittorio Messori, *The Ratzinger Report* (San Francisco: Ignatius, 1985), 45.

instead, is viewed as a human construction, the product of our own efforts, even the contents of the faith end up assuming an arbitrary character: the faith, in fact, no longer has an authentic, guaranteed instrument through which to express itself. Thus, without a view of the mystery of the church that is also supernatural and not only sociological, Christology loses its reference to the divine in favor of a purely human structure, and ultimately it amounts to a purely human project: the Gospel becomes the Jesus-project, the social-liberation project or other merely historical, immanent projects that can still seem religious in appearance, but which are atheistic in substance.[3]

Ratzinger thus held that the church, including its most fundamental structures, is, in an important sense, a mystery beyond this world that remains untouchable by merely worldly criticisms.

Communion Ecclesiology

The theological differences between Pilgrims and Saints have resulted in many practical differences. Pilgrims are often perceived as liberals who want the church to keep changing in dialogue with the world. Saints are often perceived as conservatives who wish to maintain a distinctively Catholic identity in the face of a world that is overly chaotic. Pilgrims tend to see Saints as backward and repressive theologians who are trying to reestablish the Catholic faith as an ideology that is unresponsive to changing human experience. Saints tend to see Pilgrims as loose, dangerous villains who would water the faith down to nothing in hope that the world would find them acceptable. These tensions among theologians are often reflected in similar liberal-conservative tensions throughout the church.

The beginning of this chapter referred to a problem of putting everyone in two groups and thus painting an overly polarized picture that does not capture the complexity of the situation. The world of Catholic theologians cannot really be divided into the Pilgrims and the Saints; these are simply explanatory categories that may distort as much as they reveal. In reality, Catholic theologians are spread out along a wide spectrum of positions. Most are somewhere in the middle. This is true also of the church as a whole. The liberal-conservative polarizations fade when they are placed against the background of the reality of a wide spectrum of positions, again with most people falling somewhere in the middle.[4]

---

3. Ratzinger, *The Ratzinger Report*, 46.

4. For a study of liberal-moderate-conservative positions among Catholic theologians and parishioners, see Dennis Doyle, Michael Barnes, and Byron Johnson, "Pluralism or Polarization: The Results of a CTS Survey," in *Raising the Torch of Good News*, ed. Bernard Prusak (Lanham, MD: University Press of America, 1988), 275–96.

In 1985, a meeting of bishops, known as the Extraordinary Synod, was held in Rome. What technically made it "extraordinary" was that it was held as a special event in addition to the now "ordinary" synods that convene once every three years. The main purpose of this meeting was to review and assess the progress that the church has made since Vatican II. Some Pilgrim theologians at the time were afraid that the Saints were going to march in and try to take back the progress that Vatican II had achieved. Most commentators after the fact believed that this did not happen at all. The Extraordinary Synod resoundingly reaffirmed Vatican II, while issuing some cautions and suggestions concerning its implementation.

A major theme put forth by the synod was called "communion ecclesiology." This concept is presented as the key to interpreting Vatican II: "The ecclesiology of communion is the central and fundamental idea of the council's documents."[5]

Communion ecclesiology is an understanding of the church that has roots in the early Christian centuries. It sees community first of all in the love of the three persons of the Trinity for each other; the church is a community that reflects this love. Through the Eucharist, "holy communion," people are brought together in Christ's love.

Communion ecclesiology also emphasizes that the church is a communion of local churches. It has some elements that Saints find satisfactory, such as a stress on unity through Christ and the hierarchy, and other elements that Pilgrims find satisfactory, such as a stress on the legitimate diversity and pluriformity of local churches.

The Extraordinary Synod promoted communion ecclesiology as a bridge between differing theological approaches. It called for an end to approaches that ideologically prefer some Vatican II statements over others; in their place, it called for approaches that respect each document as a whole, the interrelationship among the documents, and the intentions of those who wrote and affirmed them:

> The theological interpretation of the conciliar doctrine must show attention to all the documents, in themselves and in their close interrelationship, in such a way that the integral meaning of the council's affirmations—often very complex—might be understood and expressed.[6]

The synod, thus, called for a higher vision that moves beyond partisan theological concerns to an attentive listening to the multidimensional teaching of Vatican II.

Critics on either extreme interpreted the Extraordinary Synod as reinforcing their views. Some Saints declared victory through the synod insofar as it

---

5. "The Final Report: Synod of Bishops," *Origins* 15 (December 19, 1985): 448.

6. "The Final Report," 445.

warned against overly optimistic views of the world and overly loose interpretations of the council. Some Pilgrims announced, against the background of their own sometimes irrational fears, their relief that the synod affirmed rather than withdrew Vatican II.

My own optimistic view is that the synod did call for a higher vision and provided at least a start in the direction of achieving one. One particular sign of hope is a movement, known as the Catholic Common Ground Initiative, promoted by the late Cardinal Joseph Bernardin of Chicago. This effort, which still exists today, brings together Catholics from all points of the theological spectrum to dialogue, reach mutual understanding, and bring all concerned to a fuller living of the gospel message in contemporary culture.

It is possible to read Popes John Paul II and Benedict XVI as Saints and Pope Francis as a Pilgrim. In chapter 21, I argued that deep differences in emphasis should not be read as canceling out the much deeper continuities. I am glad that we have some people in the church who carry signs that read: "The Body of Christ Has AIDS." At the same time, I am glad that we have other people who object to such views. Both groups have much of value to share; neither has a corner on the market in truth or theological appropriateness. This is not to say that I am a relativist. I believe that the Christian message is true. I also believe that some theological approaches are better than others. On so many issues, though, there is plenty of room for a legitimate spectrum of positions. I embrace both Pilgrims and Saints in our church, a few who are even more extreme, and the many who stand somewhere in the middle.

Summary

This chapter has examined two contrasting schools of thought that have emerged since Vatican II. The Pilgrims tend to think the Catholic Church has not changed enough, and much more needs to be done regarding issues of justice, gender, and internal church reform. The Saints tend to think the church has changed enough already, and it is now time to put a lid on the madness and concentrate on the basics. Somewhere in the tension between these two visions, the future of the church is being worked out.

The next chapter will discuss the place accorded to Mary in the Catholic vision.

For Further Reflection

1. In what ways have you been aware of theological tensions within the Catholic Church?
2. How do you react to the slogan "The Body of Christ Has AIDS"?

3. Do you favor the position of Pilgrim or Saint? Why?

4. If two statements in a Vatican II document seem to be in conflict, what might be a good way to arrive at an interpretation?

5. What dangers are there in categorizing people into two polarized groupings?

Suggested Readings

Alberigo, Giuseppe, Jean Pierre Jossua, and Joseph A. Komonchak. *The Reception of Vatican II.* Washington, DC: Catholic University of America Press, 1987.

Bernardin, Joseph Cardinal, and Oscar H. Lipscomb. *Catholic Common Ground Initiative: Foundational Documents.* New York: Crossroad, 1997.

Doyle, Dennis M. *Communion Ecclesiology: Vision and Versions.* Maryknoll, NY: Orbis Books, 2000.

Faggioli, Massimo. *Vatican II: The Battle for Meaning.* Mahwah, NJ: Paulist Press, 2012.

Gaillardetz, Richard R. *An Unfinished Council: Vatican II, Pope Francis, and the Renewal of Catholicism.* Collegeville, MN: Michael Glazier, 2015.

Gaillardetz, Richard R., and Catherine Clifford. *Keys to the Council: Unlocking the Teaching of Vatican II.* Collegeville, MN: Liturgical Press, 2012.

Hebblethwaite, Peter. *Synod Extraordinary: The Inside Story of the Rome Synod.* Garden City, NY: Doubleday, 1986.

O'Malley, John W. *What Happened at Vatican II?* Cambridge, MA: Belknap Press of Harvard University Press, 2008.

Rynne, Xavier. *John Paul's Extraordinary Synod: A Collegial Achievement.* Wilmington, DE: Michael Glazier, 1986.

Mary as Symbol of the Church

often go jogging with a friend of mine. When I jog alone, however, I pray the rosary. The rosary is a series of prayers, most of which are addressed to Mary. Traditionally, these prayers have been said while counting on prayer beads. I do not carry rosary beads. I use my fingers, of which there are, conveniently, ten. I begin with the Apostle's Creed, followed by the Lord's Prayer (Our Father) and then repeat three times a prayer to Mary, the Mother of God, that begins "Hail Mary." Then for each of the five decades (units of ten prayers) in the rosary, I say an Our Father, ten Hail Marys, and a brief prayer to the Trinity that begins, "Glory Be to the Father." While I say (silently) the prayers, I meditate on the mysteries of the rosary. There are four different sets: the Joyful Mysteries, the Mysteries of Light, the Sorrowful Mysteries, and the Glorious Mysteries. I meditate on only one set each time I jog. I close with a prayer that begins, "Hail, Holy Queen."

I learned to pray the rosary as a child. I rejected the rosary with the rest of my faith somewhere in my teenage years. I tried the rosary again when I re-embraced my faith in my early twenties. I had ambivalent feelings about it. I started out saying the prayers by concentrating on asking Mary for help and favors. I treated the rosary as if it were a magic formula prayed over magic beads. At times, it embarrassed me (although I always said it silently as I jogged). I remember on one occasion angrily throwing my beads in the back of a drawer and slamming it.

The prayer itself is something else. It has become less and less a magical incantation and more and more a deep meditation on my life in relation to Mary and the church. The rosary comforts me as it connects me with my past. It challenges me as it connects me with a long tradition of prayer that I share with others. When I say the opening prayers, I concentrate on consciously intending the words. Once I move into the five decades, though, I am meditating. The words of the prayers resound quietly in my consciousness like a mantra. I think about the scriptural and traditional events of each mystery, but at the same time, I think about my everyday life in relation to these events. I review my human relationships, work life, personal goals, feelings, and upcoming decisions as I explore what I have come to think of as the "dynamics" of each story.

Take, for example, the story of finding Jesus in the Temple. This "joyful mystery" refers to the story from Luke 3:41–52 in which Jesus' parents search for him for three days and finally find him teaching in the Temple. I tend to agree with those biblical critics who doubt the historical nature of this particular event. What is relevant for me is the dynamics of the story. Drawing upon those issues that are currently important in my life, I can put myself in the place of Jesus, who says he must be about his Father's business. I know I am called to do what I have to do, even if at times it causes pain to others. (If one of my own boys did what Jesus did in that story, he would have a lot to answer for.)

I can also put myself in the place of Mary and Joseph. What must it be like to lose a child for three days? I once lost one of my boys in a mall for about twenty minutes. I was utterly heartsick and panic-stricken. I think of how many things in life are beyond my control. I think of how there are many things, often painful, that I have to accept in this life. I think of the joy of finding my lost child. I think of the objects, situations, and relationships in my life that I have lost and found, the many things about which I need to grieve and rejoice.

What I have written here barely begins to scratch the surface of what the rosary means to me. Yet I can say many of the same things about Mary herself that I have said about the rosary. Mary was an important part of my faith as a child. When I re-embraced my faith, I turned to Mary. At first, I related to Mary in an immature way. For example, I once said a set of prayers that a pamphlet told me would guarantee my salvation through a special visit from Jesus and Mary fifteen days before I would die. The pamphlet is now way in the back of my drawer, far beneath my rosary beads (which really do not deserve such treatment). Through the years, I have grown to appreciate Mary both as an inspiring historical person to whom the Scriptures testify and as a symbol of the church.

The Catholic Church has been on a journey in relation to Mary, one that is similar to my own experience. It would be difficult to underestimate the importance of Mary in the church prior to Vatican II. Sometimes, Catholics paid more attention to Mary than to God. There was not only the rosary, but also processions, medals, hymns, and various prayers and devotions honoring Mary.

Yet, after the council, Catholics seemed to put Mary in the back of a drawer for a while. Devotion to Mary seemed to be superstitious and nonecumenical to many. In recent years, however, the church has brought out devotion to Mary as a newly polished treasure. The approach to Mary has been more scriptural and Christ-centered, with increasing attention to her symbolic and potentially ecumenical aspects.

Overview

This chapter will examine the treatment of Mary in *Lumen gentium* (*Dogmatic Constitution on the Church*), with comments on how Mary has functioned in relation to God and church. This material is related to chapter 8 of *Lumen gentium*.

The Culminating Chapter of *Lumen Gentium*

At Vatican II, it was debated whether the chapter on Mary should be part of *Lumen gentium* or made into its own document. Some favored turning the chapter into its own document, because they felt it would highlight Mary's importance. Others wanted the chapter removed from *Lumen gentium*, because they felt that focusing on Mary distracted from the document's ecumenical flavor. The majority thinking, which obviously won out, was that the chapter on Mary should be included, because it is appropriate to highlight Mary's role as an essential part of the church. John Paul II, who was a bishop at the council, had argued that the chapter on Mary should come much earlier in the document to emphasize the significance of her role in the church. The compromise was that Mary became the culminating chapter.

The brief chapter on Mary is divided into five sections. Section 1 emphasizes that Mary is truly the Mother of God, and as such, although she is at one with all other creatures, holds a privileged place both in heaven and on earth. She is honored "with filial affection and piety as a most beloved mother" (*LG* 53). She plays an integral part in the mystery of salvation that is continued in the church.

Section 2 outlines the specific nature of Mary's role in the history of salvation. Like other sections of *Lumen gentium*, it relies on references to Scripture and the use of carefully phrased symbolic language. The section tells of the following:

- How Mary is foreshadowed in the Old Testament
- Her immaculate conception
- Her faithful acceptance of God's will
- Her virginal conception of Jesus
- Her pilgrimage of faith
- Her role in the public life of her son
- Her sorrow at the cross
- Her presence at the birth of the church at Pentecost
- Her assumption into heaven
- Her final exaltation

Throughout this section, Mary's relationship with Jesus is highlighted.

Significant emphasis in section 2 is given to Mary's *fiat* (let it be), her response to the angel of the Annunciation. Mary's freely chosen acceptance of the will of God is contrasted with the disobedience of Eve.[1] As a woman was connected with the Fall, so a woman is also at the heart of the process of redemption. Like Jesus in the Garden of Gethsemane when he accepts God's will rather than his own, Mary allows God's will to be done. Her faithful, courageous decision stands at the core of the Christian faith.

Section 3 directly examines the connection between Mary and the church. Before it does so, however, it spends time addressing the relative ranking of Christ and Mary. For ecumenical purposes, the section greatly stresses that Christ is the one Mediator and that Mary is subordinate to Christ. Within this context, it is appropriate to honor Mary as the creature above all other creatures, with traditional titles such as "Advocate, Auxiliatrix, Adjutrix, and Mediatrix" (*LG* 62).

Although the motivations for dealing with the issue of ranking are understandable, one wonders what Jesus might think about the stress on his mother's subordination to himself, even when limited to the realm of salvation and divinity. This is less an issue of technically acknowledging the problem of the worship of Mary in place of God than it is an issue of good taste.

The main images that the section uses to connect Mary with the church are mother and virgin. The church is a mother in that it brings forth sons and daughters to a new immortal life through baptism and the Holy Spirit. In other words, as Mary gave life to Jesus, so each of us is born anew through the church, our mother. As Jesus lived a totally graced life, so the church opens up to us the life of grace and the way of salvation. The church is a virgin in that it remains faithful to Christ, its spouse. The church "keeps with virginal purity an entire faith, a firm hope and a sincere charity" (*LG* 64).

Calling Mary the "Type" (symbol) of the church, the document connects Mary's *fiat*, her virginal faithfulness, with the calling of all Christians: seeking after the glory of Christ, the church becomes more like her exalted Type, and continually progresses in faith, hope, and charity, seeking and doing the will of God in all things (*LG* 65). In other words, when Christians seek and do the will of God in their lives, they imitate Mary. The document then explicitly calls Christians to be, symbolically speaking, mothers: "The Virgin in her own life lived an example of that maternal love, by which it behooves that all should be animated who cooperate in the apostolic mission of the Church for the regeneration of men and women" (*LG* 65).

I find it meaningful that the Catholic Church calls me, a man, to be animated by maternal love. There is a strong feminine dimension to the love that guides one in Christian activities.

---

1. Some biblical scholars strongly challenge traditional interpretations that blame Eve for the Fall. See also Elaine Pagels, *Adam, Eve, and the Serpent* (New York: Random House, 1988).

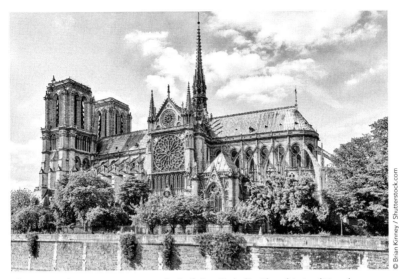

© Brian Kinney / Shutterstock.com

There is perhaps no greater symbol of the Catholic Church's traditional venera-tion of the Virgin Mary than the magnificent Cathedral of Notre Dame de Paris, viewed here from the River Seine.

Section 4 of *Lumen gentium*'s treatment of Mary deals with the tradition of prayers and devotions to her. As in the previous section, Mary's subordinate ranking to Christ is stressed. Given this qualification, the document encourages devotion to Mary, especially through liturgy. At the same time, the document warns against abuses: "the magisterium of the Church . . . exhorts theologians and preachers of the divine word to abstain zealously both from all gross exag-gerations as well as from petty narrow-mindedness in considering the singular dignity of the Mother of God" (*LG* 67).

In other words, Christians are encouraged neither to overdo nor to unrea-sonably object to Marian devotions. As with other saints, Christians are exhorted to ground their prayers in a true relationship that leads one to imitate Mary's virtues. One needs to grow in knowledge of Mary in order to imitate her.

Although abuses should be acknowledged, the Catholic emphasis on Mary rests on the strong ground that she truly is the Mother of God, who is remem-bered in the Catholic community above all for who she is and the life she lived. The Catholic imagination throughout history has discerned a richness associ-ated with Mary, which is beautifully expressed in prayers, teachings, and art. As David Macaulay put it in his video program, *Cathedral*:

> Most of the prominent cathedrals of [the medieval] period were ded-icated to Notre Dame, Our Lady. In an age of chivalry and exalted womanhood, it is as if an entire society had fallen in love. Mary is per-ceived as the Mother of God and as the human vessel through which

God became flesh. She is therefore both of heaven and of earth, just like the cathedrals that bear her name.[2]

The Middle Ages had a love affair with Mary. This love affair continues in Catholic Tradition, although it takes different forms as it develops. Any study of Marian art from a historical and international perspective reveals the depth of affection and cultural embrace offered by Christians throughout the world.

Section 5 closes the chapter with a final comparison between Mary and the church as figures of hope, and with a prayer for Mary's intercession that all families of people may be gathered in the one People of God.

The chapter on Mary in *Lumen gentium* leaves the overall impression that the church cannot be given a justified treatment without consideration of Mary, and that the role of Mary cannot be appreciated apart from the context of the church.

What Is Said about Mary Is Said about the Church

Mary has been so closely associated with the church throughout the history of Christianity that many scriptural sayings and traditional teachings about her can also be understood as sayings and teachings about the church. Many regard Mary as "the first Christian." She gave birth to Jesus and raised him. She was with him during his public ministry, and she was there at the foot of the cross. Mary was with the apostles on Pentecost when the Holy Spirit descended. Mary played an important role in each moment of the church's birth.

The Catholic Marian scholar and feminist theologian Elizabeth Johnson has investigated the symbolic nature of speech about Mary.[3] She begins with the premise that Marian statements refer to both Mary and the church. Throughout the Christian tradition, Mary has served as a vehicle for the church to express its ideal self-realization. This is appropriate because of who Mary is as the mother of Jesus and because of how Mary is remembered for her role in the earliest of Christian communities. Thus, in the Christian tradition, memories of Mary and beliefs about the ideal Christian community are mixed; this is not a bad thing, however, because what can be said about one can also be said about the other.

Many Scripture passages about Mary are interpreted as being about the church as well. For example, I have heard Luke 2:51, "his mother treasured all these things in her heart," interpreted as foreshadowing the way the church has developed and enlarged its body of teachings throughout the centuries. The

---

2. David Macaulay, *Cathedral: The Story of Its Construction* ([Arlington, VA]: PBS Home Video, 2006), quoted words spoken by Caroline Berg, *https://www.youtube.com/watch?v=MZpOd2pHiI0*.

3. Elizabeth A. Johnson, "The Symbolic Character of Theological Statements about Mary," *Journal of Ecumenical Studies* 22 (1985): 312–35.

church is pondering what it already knows in its heart. Mary's order to the servants at Cana in John 2:5, "Do whatever he tells you," has been interpreted also as the advice of the church to each individual Christian. Jesus' words from the cross to Mary and John in John 19:26–27—"'Woman, here is your son.' Then he said to the disciple, 'Here is your mother'"—have been interpreted as referring to the relationship between the church and each Christian disciple. Mary's Immaculate Conception, that she herself was conceived without sin, has been interpreted as referring not only to Mary but also in an ideal sense to the graced life that is offered to every person. Mary's Assumption, her being taken bodily into heaven at the completion of her life, has likewise been interpreted as signaling in some way the fate that awaits all redeemed persons.

In the Catholic tradition, the belief in Mary's Immaculate Conception and Assumption refers to her "privileges" that recognize her unique role in the plan of salvation as the Mother of God. At the same time, however, Mary's privileges are not intended to isolate her by cutting her off from the body of Christians; rather, these privileges signify things for which Christians and people of good will have reason to hope. Elizabeth Johnson has argued that in a church community that acknowledges the fundamental equality in spiritual dignity of all Christians, Mary and the saints ought to be understood as companions in hope, from whom all can learn valuable lessons about Christian discipleship.[4]

Summary

This chapter examined the treatment of Mary in chapter 8 of *Lumen gentium*. It also discussed how things said about Mary and things said about the church often can be applied interchangeably. I am glad Mary has been making a comeback in Catholic spirituality. Getting back in touch with Mary parallels the Catholic journey in articulating what we believe the church—and we ourselves—should be.

The next chapter will discuss feminist views of contemporary issues in the Catholic Church.

For Further Reflection

1. Why do you think Mary has traditionally played such an important role for Catholics? Do you feel comfortable with this importance?

2. Are you more inclined to think of the rosary as a meditative prayer or as a superstitious prayer?

---

4. Elizabeth A. Johnson, *Truly Our Sister: A Theology of Mary in the Communion of Saints* (New York: Continuum, 2003).

3. Why is Mary's *fiat* (let it be) so important for understanding her role in Christian history? How does this *fiat* apply to all Christians?

4. In what way are questions about Mary ecumenical issues?

5. Why is it important to understand some of the things said about Mary as "symbolic"?

Suggested Readings

Brown, Raymond E., et al., eds. *Mary in the New Testament: A Collaborative Assessment by Protestant and Roman Catholic Scholars.* Philadelphia: Fortress, 1978.

Buby, Bertrand, SM. *Mary: The Faithful Disciple.* New York: Paulist Press, 1985.

Buby, Bertrand, SM. *Mary of Galilee.* 3 vols. New York: Alba House, 1994, 1995, 1997.

Eberthäuser, Caroline H., et al. *Mary: Art, Culture, and Religion through the Ages.* Translated by Peter Heinegg. New York: Crossroad, 1998.

Johnson, Elizabeth A. *Truly Our Sister: A Theology of Mary in the Communion of Saints.* New York: Continuum, 2003.

Pelikan, Jaroslav. *Mary through the Centuries: Her Place in the History of Culture.* New Haven, CT: Yale University Press, 1998.

Women and the Catholic Church

lizabeth Johnson argues that, within history, Christian sources and practices have been tainted by the patriarchal cultures in which they took
form.[1] I have used Johnson's Catholic feminist book, *She Who Is*, in graduate classes many times throughout the years. Johnson finds this patriarchal bias
especially evident in the almost exclusive use of male language to refer to God.
In her writing, Johnson draws upon the contemporary experience of women to
uncover such patriarchal influences on the Bible and Christian tradition and to
retrieve those aspects of the sources that can help to reshape our current discourse about the divine.

For example, in both the Old Testament and the New Testament, Johnson also finds God sometimes referred to using female metaphors. In Isaiah,
God says, "As a mother comforts her child, so I will comfort you" (66:13). In
the Old Testament, *Sophia* (Greek for "wisdom") is personified as a woman
(Prov 8:1–9:12). As Divine Wisdom, *Sophia* can be linked with God's Spirit.
In the New Testament, Jesus, who is infused with the Holy Spirit, is thereby
associated with Divine Wisdom. In the Gospels of Matthew and Luke, Jesus
says, "Jerusalem, Jerusalem, the city that kills the prophets and stones those who
are sent to it! How often have I desired to gather your children together as a
hen gathers her brood under her wings, and you were not willing!" (Mt 23:37;
Lk 13:34). Johnson builds upon these references and many others to explore the
persons of the Trinity as Spirit-Sophia, Jesus-Sophia, and Mother-Sophia. She
recommends that, over time, a balance of female and male language and images
be used in Christian discourse about the absolute mystery we call God.

Johnson has become a controversial figure in recent years. She is regarded
with the highest esteem by most academic theologians but has been deeply criticized by some conservatives as well as by the Committee on Doctrine of the
US Conference of Catholic Bishops.[2] One of the reasons I have used Johnson's

---

1. Elizabeth A. Johnson, *She Who Is: The Mystery of God in Feminist Theological Discourse* (New York: Crossroad, 1992).

2. Among the criticisms of Johnson are that she replaces the classical concept of the impassability of God with a God who suffers and she conflates the ideas of metaphor and analogy in speech about the divine. See Richard A. Gaillardetz, ed., *When the Magisterium Intervenes: The Magisterium and*

book so frequently is that I greatly admire it as an academic text. Johnson is clear about her theological methods and is consistent and creative in the way she applies them.

Overview

Matters concerning gender in the Catholic Church are important, debated, and at times confusing. This chapter begins by considering the topic of patriarchy, examines basic positions expressed by Catholic feminist theologians in the decades immediately following the Second Vatican Council, and then looks at more recent discussions of women's issues. Questions concerning women and ministry are reserved for the following chapter.

Patriarchy

A central theme of the feminist movement as it has affected Catholic theology is the recognition that Western civilization—and indeed most cultures throughout history—has been patriarchal, and patriarchy is a highly limiting, repressive system of human organization. This realization should lead not only to a massive reinterpretation of history, but to a challenging of contemporary institutions and social roles. Feminist social change looks to a future that is egalitarian and liberating for both women and men.

Feminist scholar Gerda Lerner defined *patriarchy* as

> the manifestation and institutionalization of male dominance over women and children in the family and the extension of male dominance in society in general. It implies that men hold power in all the important institutions of society and that women are deprived of access to such power. It does not imply that women are either totally powerless or totally deprived of rights, influences, and resources.[3]

An egalitarian society would thus be one in which women and men are equal partners in the family and in which they share equal access to power in society at large.

More than power or justice is at stake, however. Many feminists claim that patriarchal beliefs and patriarchal thinking determine the reality in which we dwell. A society transformed by feminism would not, therefore, simply be the

---

Theologians in Today's Church (Collegeville, MN: Liturgical Press, 2012). This book contains all of the official correspondence between the Committee on Doctrine of the USCCB and Johnson as well as scholarly articles by a number of theologians. The controversy centers on a more recent book by Johnson, *Quest for the Living God: Mapping Frontiers in the Theology of God* (New York: Continuum, 2007).

3. Gerda Lerner, *The Creation of Patriarchy* (Oxford: Oxford University Press, 1986), 8–9.

world as we now know it with a dash more justice sprinkled on top. Feminist social change demands a radical overhaul of our culture. Feminists claim that whether we are female or male, because of our culture, we tend to be patriarchal in our ways of feeling, thinking, imagining, and behaving. Achieving a gender-equal society requires fundamental changes in the ways we feel, think, imagine, and behave.

Patriarchy in Christian Tradition

Feminist scholars have little difficulty finding evidence of patriarchal cultures reflected in the Scriptures as well as in the history of the church. But is the gospel message itself patriarchal? Does the basic Christian message need to be critiqued and revised according to feminist standards?

The late radical feminist theologian Mary Daly, whose early work *The Church and the Second Sex*[4] called for equality within the church, came to reject her own early approach as not radical enough. In a later work, *Beyond God the Father*,[5] Daly found sexism at the heart of the Judeo-Christian tradition, starting with Eve and ending with a male God and a male redeemer. She called for women to begin anew with a fresh naming of the forces of the cosmos. In later works, *Gyn/Ecology*[6] and *Pure Lust*,[7] Daly undertook this task by practically inventing a new language for articulating a feminist ethic.

Somewhat in contrast with Daly's approach is that of the feminist biblical scholar Elisabeth Schüssler Fiorenza. Fiorenza argues the original gospel message was radically egalitarian.[8] She points to what has come to be known as the "women's passage" from Galatians 3:28: "There is no longer Jew nor Greek, there is no longer slave or free, there is no longer male and female; for all of you are one in Christ Jesus." With this passage and others from the New Testament, Fiorenza constructs a picture of some of the earliest Christian communities as preaching and living out a gospel that calls for inclusion of women on all levels of discipleship and leadership. In particular, in Mark and in John, women are portrayed as inspiring role models. Fiorenza speculates it is likely women also presided at the Eucharist, although this speculation is hotly debated.

---

4. Mary Daly, *The Church and the Second Sex* (San Francisco: Harper and Row, 1968). This work was reissued in 1975 with a new introduction by the author.

5. Mary Daly, *Beyond God the Father: Toward a Philosophy of Women's Liberation* (Boston: Beacon, 1973).

6. Mary Daly, *Gyn/Ecology: The Metaethics of Radical Feminism* (Boston: Beacon, 1978).

7. Mary Daly, *Pure Lust: Elemental Feminist Philosophy* (Boston: Beacon, 1984).

8. Elisabeth Schüssler Fiorenza, *In Memory of Her: A Feminist Theological Reconstruction of Christian Origins* (New York: Crossroad, 1984).

What happened to the original gospel message that included the equality of the sexes? Fiorenza argues it struggled against a patriarchal culture and the culture won. Through the New Testament and other early Christian documents, she traces how submission and patriarchy triumphed over altruistic love and service. In other words, Fiorenza argues the last two thousand years of Christian tradition were skewed by the submergence of the authentic egalitarianism of the basic gospel message.

Is this a less radical position than that of Daly? Yes, it is, insofar as it finds the grounds for an ultimate hope in the gospel. Yet in some ways, it is not so different, because it also calls for a rethinking and reinvestigation of ways Christian symbols and power structures have been used and abused throughout Christianity.

Vatican II and Women

The historical emergence of feminism is often spoken of in terms of "waves." First-wave feminism is mainly associated with the suffrage movements in the nineteenth and early twentieth centuries. Second-wave feminism focused on a wider range of women's rights. This second wave began roughly in the early 1960s, paralleling the years of the Second Vatican Council (1962–65). There were sixteen women observers during the third session (1964), and nine more attended the final session, for a total of twenty-three (1965).[9] However, there is little mention of women's issues in the council documents. As observers, these women had neither voice nor vote.

Still, the major teachings of Vatican II on the laity have had a significant impact on the role of women in the Catholic Church. The council taught that the church is to be thought of as the People of God, an image that includes all of the church's members. All members of the People of God share in the threefold ministry of Christ as priest, prophet, and king. All members of the church share a basic equality in spiritual dignity. All members of the church are called to holiness. Christians of today are to read the "signs" of the times and appreciate those cultural developments that can be discerned as positive. Few cultural shifts have been as significant as the growing appreciation for the dignity and role of women in society.

Women-Church

In the years following Vatican II, a movement emerged called "women-church," which involves women gathering to pray and celebrate, analyze the issues they face together, and support each other in their struggles. Fiorenza forcefully expresses the purpose of women-church (which she calls the "*ekklēsia of women*"):

---

9. Carmel Elizabeth McEnroy, *Guests in Their Own House: The Women of Vatican II* (New York: Crossroad, 1996), 46.

A feminist Christian spirituality, therefore, calls us to gather together the *ekklēsia of women* who, in the angry power of the Spirit, are sent forth to feed, heal, and liberate our own people who are women. It unmasks and sets us free from the structural sin and alienation of sexism and propels us to become children and spokeswomen of God. It rejects the idolatrous worship of maleness and articulates the divine image in female human existence and language. It sets us free from the internalization of false altruism and self-sacrifice that is concerned with the welfare and work of men first to the detriment of our own and other women's welfare and calling. It enables us to live "for one another" and to experience the presence of God in the *ekklēsia* as the gathering of women. Those of us who have heard this calling respond by committing ourselves to the liberation struggle of women and all peoples, by being accountable to women and their future, and by nurturing solidarity within the *ekklēsia* of women. Commitment, accountability, and solidarity in community are the hallmarks of our calling and struggle.[10]

Fiorenza is calling women to gather in worship communities in a way similar to the base ecclesial communities of Latin America. In this regard, feminist theology can be read as a form of liberation theology.

Theologian Anne Carr describes "women-church" in a way that captures this similarity to the base ecclesial communities:

Their gatherings sometimes include men who share the hunger for more inclusive, relational, and communitarian expressions of Christian life. Activities take the form of new kinds of structure, decision making, social action, and liturgy that can eventually be incorporated in ordinary parish communities. But at present, the existence of women-church simply allows for the time and space in which experimentation can occur and discoveries be refined. The very existence of women-church signals the determination of women, as the symbol of all the other groups who have been excluded from the life of the church, to find a Christian life that is concretely expressive in today's world of the message of the gospel.[11]

In other words, such groups of women (and some men) are experimenting with what church and spirituality might be like if fully informed by a feminist perspective. These groups tend to be ecumenical. Some consider themselves "catholic" while cutting off ties to official Roman Catholicism. Others remain within official boundaries while pushing hard for changes. They draw upon the

---

10. Fiorenza, *In Memory*, 346.

11. Anne E. Carr, *Transforming Grace: Christian Tradition and Women's Experience* (San Francisco: Harper and Row, 1988), 200.

Christian tradition and other sources to devise their own forms of prayer, support, and liturgy. Women and all others are included as coequal partners. Many of those in the women-church movement look forward to a time when the church will change sufficiently as to no longer make such a movement necessary.

Theological Anthropology

Some Catholic feminists argue that a serious rethinking of concepts of gender, on the level of theological anthropology, is needed if other important changes are to be carried out in attitude as well as in more practical issues of leadership and authority. The Vatican's overall approach to matters of gender, a position commonly labeled "complementarity," holds that women and men, though equal as human beings, are different in important ways that complement each other. Jane Kopas, drawing upon a range of feminist authors, suggests the "complementarity" approach to gender has serious limitations.[12] It tends to be essentialist and ahistorical; in other words, it imposes abstract categories that might not always fit the people who actually live in history. Kopas prefers a relational anthropology that is more open to transformation. She wants more attention paid to how gender identity is linked with particular cultures. Moreover, she wants to link theological anthropology with ethics: what is the real impact of various understandings of gender on the lives of women and men? Do our suppositions about gender identity lead to social repression or to liberation?

Most Catholic feminists do not dismiss the notion that women and men share a common human nature and that sexuality is a deep aspect of human differentiation. Their main argument is that matters of gender are more complex and a simplistic overemphasis on differentiation has been intertwined historically with discrimination and oppression. Elizabeth Johnson argues it is time "to re-order the two-term and one-term systems into a multiple term schema, one which allows connection in difference rather than constantly guaranteeing identity through opposition or uniformity."[13]

More Recent Directions

Since the 1990s, second-wave feminism, associated with equal rights for women, has passed into further waves. On the one hand, some claim that, at least theoretically, the quest for equality for women has achieved notable milestones in attitudes, law, and social practices. I have at times heard older women complain

---

12. Jane Kopas, "Beyond Mere Gender: Transforming Theological Anthropology," in *Women and Theology*, ed. Mary Ann Hinsdale and Phyllis H. Kaminski (Maryknoll, NY: Orbis Books, 1995), 220–22, 229–30.

13. Johnson, *She Who Is*, 156.

that the younger generation of women has no idea of what it used to be like and little appreciation for what their forebears went through to achieve the current gains. On the other hand, others claim sexual discrimination in many forms is alive and well and true equality is a long way off. It strikes me that each of these views pose valid claims.

Catholic feminism has developed in several ways throughout the past few decades. First, it has become important not to focus on gender in a way that separates it from other social and cultural matters; rather, gender needs to be appreciated as one issue within the context of many other interrelated social issues, such as class, ethnicity, and race, including LGBTQ+ issues. In the 1990s, womanist theology, written with a special focus on poor black women, arose as an alternative to what was seen as affluent white feminism.[14] Since that time, mainstream feminism has embraced a wider range of concerns.

Second, Catholic women have worked toward addressing a wide range of theological issues from a feminist perspective. They hope in the long run Catholic feminism will become not a separate subcategory, but rather, an integral dimension of all Catholic theology. Elizabeth Johnson, for example, in *Friends of God and Prophets*, undertakes a study of the traditional doctrine of the Communion of Saints.[15] This is not simply a book about women directed only toward women. Written from a feminist perspective, it breathes new life into a traditional teaching and brings out its relevance for contemporary spirituality.

Third, Catholic feminism has claimed a wider range of witnesses, including more conservative voices. Conservative Catholic feminists offer appreciation for the special gifts of women, for some aspects of traditional family roles, for the protection of the unborn, and for the need for all Christians, including women, to submit to the will of God. Although some progressive women dismiss these conservative women as not being truly feminist, others have entered into fruitful dialogue with them.[16] Both groups appear to agree that the basic dignity and equality of women is immensely important.

Summary

This chapter first examined the topic of patriarchy, then considered basic positions expressed by Catholic feminist theologians in the decades immediately following the Second Vatican Council, and finally considered more recent

14. Diana Hayes, *Standing in the Shoes My Mother Made: A Womanist Theology* (Minneapolis: Fortress, 2010).

15. Elizabeth A. Johnson, *Friends of God and Prophets: A Feminist Theological Reading of the Communion of Saints* (New York: Continuum, 1998).

16. Elizabeth A. Johnson, *The Church Women Want: Catholic Women in Dialogue* (New York: Crossroad, 2002). See also *Catholic Women Speak: Bringing Our Gifts to the Table*, ed. by Catholic Women Speak Network (Mahwah, NJ: Paulist Press, 2015).

discussions of women's issues. The power of the contemporary #MeToo movement's protests against sexual harassment and assault arose from many decades of hard work. Feminist thinkers continue to deepen their understandings as they work for positive social change for women and for all who suffer discrimination and exclusion.

In the next chapter, we will focus on official Catholic teaching about women in the church.

For Further Reflection

1. Do you think that the current range of opinions about feminism reflect generational differences? How so?
2. Do you buy the argument that certain characteristics are "male" and others "female"?
3. Do you agree that Western civilization as well as most cultures throughout history have been tarnished by patriarchy?
4. Does the women-church movement sound attractive to you?
5. Is exposure to feminist ideas ultimately liberating for men?

Suggested Readings

Catholic Women Speak Network, ed. *Catholic Women Speak: Bringing Our Gifts to the Table.* Mahwah, NJ: Paulist Press, 2015.

Clifford, Anne M. *Introducing Feminist Theology.* Maryknoll, NY: Orbis Books, 2000.

Johnson, Elizabeth A. *The Church Women Want: Catholic Women in Dialogue.* New York: Crossroad, 2002.

McEnroy, Carmel Elizabeth. *Guests in Their Own House: The Women of Vatican II.* New York: Crossroad, 1996.

Pui-lan, Kwok. *Postcolonial Imagination and Feminist Theology.* Louisville: Westminister John Knox, 2005.

Ruether, Rosemary Radford. *Women and Redemption: A Theological History.* Minneapolis: Fortress, 1998.

Schüssler Fiorenza, Elisabeth. *In Memory of Her: A Feminist Reconstruction of Christian Origins.* New York: Crossroad, 1984.

Wexler, Celia Viggo. *Catholic Women Confront Their Church: Stories of Hope and Hurt.* Lanham, MD: Rowman and Littlefield, 2016.

Women and Official Catholic Teaching

At a Vatican-sponsored academic conference in Rome in September 2000, I met an Italian woman in her early twenties, Angela. A graduate student in theology, Angela was participating in a conservative Catholic movement called "Communion and Liberation." We had both been attending sessions in which scholars supportive of John Paul II's views expressed traditional-sounding positions concerning gender and the role of women in church and society. One speaker, Reverend Angelo Scola of Rome, had argued that stressing the differences that exist between men and women does not take away from a fundamental human equality. The true danger lies in the promotion of an androgynous society in which sexuality becomes a mere choice or option rather than a revelatory gift from God.[1]

Another speaker, Professor Jutta Burggraf of Pamplona, expressed the position that men and women complement each other. They experience the world in different ways. The roles of father and mother cannot be reduced to the biological. Men and women need each other for their fulfillment. Burggraf applauded the many social gains made by women in modern times, and she spoke forcefully of the difficulties that often accompany married life. She acknowledged, moreover, that not everyone fits easily into clear-cut categories. However, she saw the great challenge of today as the need to appreciate the gift of sexuality, the nuptial mystery. Minimizing the sexual differentiation of male and female, in her judgment, will lead to inestimable losses. At our present cultural moment, valuing such differentiation will go hand in hand with valuing our common humanity.[2]

Several of the presentations struck similar themes. In the hallway between sessions, I remarked to Angela, the young woman from "Communion and Liberation," that some of my American women friends who are theologians would

---

1. Reverend Angelo Scola, "Opening Address," in congress "Man: The Way of the Church," World Meeting of University Professors, Rome, September 6, 2000.

2. Professor Jutta Burggraf, "Communion Appreciates Difference: Anthropological Dimensions of Marriage Ministry," in congress "Man: The Way of the Church," World Meeting of University Professors, Rome, September 7, 2000.

be upset and even angry at these talks. The look on her face was somewhere between horrified disbelief and sad confirmation of what she already knew. She asked me in an almost pleading tone to explain to her why these American women do not see that the pope's view (as supported by the speakers) is both true and liberating for women, and not at all oppressive. Some women, I said, would interpret the language of complementarity as an instrument of power to keep women out of positions of authority, especially in the church.

I did not argue fine points with Angela (for example, that there is a wide spectrum of positions taken by American women). Nor did I argue the major point that gross misunderstandings may lie on both sides of the divide. Her English was so-so. My Italian was virtually nonexistent. What struck me most was how sincere Angela was, and how convinced she was that women in America would be eager to change their positions once she could get them to see they are making a big mistake.

Overview

This chapter examines official Catholic teaching about women, focusing especially on Pope John Paul II's view as expressed in his apostolic letter *Mulieris dignitatem* (*On the Dignity and Vocation of Women*), 1988. This material continues the discussion of women's issues linked with chapter 8 of *Lumen gentium*.

Unity in Difference

Are women and men more the same or more different? John Paul II's basic approach to understanding the relationship between women and men represents the stance we have labeled "complementarity." In contrast with those who tend to downplay differences, John Paul II highlighted sexual differentiation as part of the plan of creation and as a wonderful gift from God. In contrast with those who find the two gender categories of "male" and "female" limiting, and who argue in favor of a larger number of genders, John Paul II stressed that each of us is created not simply as human but as male or female.[3]

John Paul II did not deny that women and men share a common humanity. In fact, he emphasized that they do. He stressed, "Both man and woman are human beings to an equal degree" (*MD* 6). Like Jutta Burggraf, John Paul II

---

3. In his 2016 post-synodal exhortation *Amoris laetitia* (*The Joy of Love*) (no. 56), Pope Francis expresses a somewhat more nuanced approach. He rejects ideologies that radically separate biological sex and gender identity, asserting themselves "as absolute and unquestionable, even dictating how children should be raised." Yet he also acknowledges that such ideologies "seek to respond to what are at times understandable aspirations."

believed that a stress on a common humanity and a stress on sexual differentiation can go hand in hand.

So too, in John Paul II's vision, women and men are called to go hand in hand. Through a reading of the creation stories in Genesis, John Paul II found that, from the beginning, women and men are called to live in communion with each other. This reading is echoed in Vatican II's *Gaudium et spes* (*Pastoral Constitution on the Church in the Modern World*): "This partnership of man and woman constitutes the first form of communion between people" (*GS* 12). As John Paul II expressed it, "Man and woman, created as a 'unity of the two' in their common humanity, are called to live in a communion of love, and in this way to mirror in the world the communion of love that is in God, through which the Three Persons love each other in the intimate mystery of the one divine life" (*MD* 7).

In John Paul II's view, as women and men, we are different from each other, yet we share a common humanity. All human beings are called to interpersonal communion and to give themselves to another. The differentiation between women and men goes to the core of what makes the giving of one's self to another possible.

Progressive Positions

John Paul II supported many progressive positions on matters of faith and gender. For example, he argued in no uncertain terms that God is not a "man." He spoke of God's creativity:

> This "generating" has neither "masculine" nor "feminine" qualities. It is by nature totally divine. It is spiritual in the most perfect way, since "God is spirit" (John 4:24) and possesses no property typical of the body, neither "feminine" nor "masculine." Thus even *"fatherhood" in God is completely divine* and free of the "masculine" bodily characteristics proper to human fatherhood. (*MD* 8)

John Paul II also distanced himself from several traditional theological opinions that have been unfavorable to women. He found, for example, in Genesis that the first sin cannot simply be attributed to Eve as the sin of a woman, but is instead the sin of human beings. He argued that inequalities that result from the Fall do not represent God's intentions, but rather are the result of sin. He quoted approvingly Galatians 3:28, that "there is neither male nor female . . . in Christ Jesus." He emphasized the important roles women played in the ministry of Jesus and how women were the first witnesses of the Resurrection. He praised the contributions of Christian women through the centuries, noting, especially, that these women have often had to overcome social discrimination. He held that marriage is in no way intended to be a union in which the man should dominate the woman, but rather, that husband and wife are called to mutual respect and self-giving.

Stress on Otherness

Some people conclude that there is a contradiction between John Paul II's progressive positions and his teaching that priestly ordination is not open to women. How could he fight against social discrimination against women, and then shut them out from the priesthood? For John Paul II had not simply ruled out ordaining women as priests for the present moment, but had declared, in *Ordinatio sacerdotalis* (*Priestly Ordination*), 1994, that the church does not have the authority to ordain women and that this matter is not to be considered open to debate. *Ordinatio sacerdotalis* is a brief statement that does not develop its arguments. John Paul II addressed this matter more fully in *Mulieris dignitatem*, and in that document he relied in the background on a document from the Congregation for the Doctrine of the Faith (CDF), *Inter insignores* (*Declaration on the Question of Admission of Women to the Ministerial Priesthood*), 1976.

Before exploring the reasoning behind John Paul II's decision, however, it is important to consider the point made earlier—that he saw no contradiction in stressing simultaneously the shared common humanity and the important differences between women and men. John Paul II had been especially influenced on this point by Swiss theologian Hans Urs von Balthasar. Women have a distinctive calling, a special role to play in the drama of salvation, von Balthasar argued. The existence of the feminine and the masculine are part of God's plan.

According to John Paul II, a woman receives love in order to give love. This is true both biologically and spiritually. A man can deposit seed and go on his merry way. But a woman receives seed and gestates within herself a new life.

In the spiritual realm, in relation to God, a human being is one who must first receive love in order to be able to give it. In this sense, the way of loving most appropriate to women takes on a certain priority for all human beings. As John Paul II expressed it, "In God's eternal plan, woman is the one in whom the order of love in the created world of persons takes first root" (*MD* 29).

It is significant to John Paul II that, at the center of the Christian salvific event, one finds a woman, Mary. Mary is the archetype of the human race. Yet she plays out her role in salvation in a way that could only be done by a woman. She receives God's offer of love and then gives love back. By carrying the son of God within her womb, she achieves union with God in a way that is not accessible to men. Still, through her fiat, through her saying "yes" to God's offer of love, she becomes a model for all human beings, both female and male. John Paul II phrased this emphatically: "The dignity of every human being and the vocation corresponding to that dignity find their definitive measure *in union with God.*

Mary, the woman of the Bible, is the most complete expression of this dignity and vocation" (*MD* 5).

Christian love, as John Paul II saw it, is more directly related to feminine love than to masculine love. He went so far as to say,

> The moral and spiritual strength of a woman is joined to her awareness that *God entrusts the human being to her in a special way*. Of course, God entrusts every human being to each and every other human being. But this entrusting concerns women in a special way—precisely by reason of their femininity—and this in a particular way determines their vocation. (*MD* 30)

John Paul II connected this distinctive vocation of women with the royal priesthood of all the faithful. He said that women are not called to the ministerial priesthood of the church. But in the temporal sphere (the world that the laity is called to transform through Christian service and love), women have a greater role to play. When it comes to the common priesthood of the faithful, it is women who need to teach men how to be Christian.

Reasons for Not Ordaining Women as Priests

It is important, I believe, not to read this section without having read the previous section of this chapter. Whether one agrees with the teaching of John Paul II, one cannot sufficiently understand his teaching about the ordination of women without understanding what he thought about the relationship between the feminine and the masculine in the realm of Christian love. John Paul II did not think he was implying anything negative about the dignity of women by excluding them from ordained priesthood. He believed that Mary, who was not an ordained minister, holds the highest dignity among humans. He stressed that the highest honors in heaven go to the saints, not to ordained ministers. And he thought that, in the world in which the Christian mission is carried out as importantly as it is in the church, women have a greater role.

In what follows, I blend positions expressed by John Paul II in *Mulieris dignitatem* with related points made in the CDF's *Inter insignores*. The most central point in the Vatican argument is that it is possible that Jesus himself intended that only men preside at the Eucharist. This seems to be indicated by the New Testament stories of the Last Supper that depict Jesus as having present only the twelve apostles, who were all men. Jesus broke through other social barriers regarding gender. He may have had something important in mind by including only men when he instituted the Eucharist. The early tradition of the church developed a male-only priesthood, often in tension with heretical groups in which women had strong roles of ministerial leadership. The Vatican admits that the supporting data is debatable, but it believes the burden of proof is on those who want to change this long-standing tradition.

But why would Jesus have wanted to exclude women from those who preside at Eucharist? All other indications are that Jesus was radically inclusive regarding women. The Vatican, admitting that it is speculating, believes Jesus had in mind the ritual symbolization of the coming together of Christ the Bridegroom with the Church, his bride. Catholics have long held that the Eucharist is both a meal and a sacrifice. The Vatican draws upon certain select dimensions of the Catholic tradition to proclaim that the Eucharist is, in addition, a nuptial event, and that Jesus may have foreseen and intended this dimension to be expressed.[4]

Christ Is the Bridegroom and the Church Is the Bride

The mystery of the church, understood as the coming together of Christ the Bridegroom with the Church, his bride, draws upon various traditional sources. The Old Testament book, Song of Songs, was originally a wedding hymn celebrating the relationship of the bride and the groom in sensual terms. Christians have traditionally interpreted this biblical hymn as foreshadowing the relationship between Christ and the Church. In the Gospels, there are several sayings and parables in which Jesus refers to himself, either directly or symbolically, as a bridegroom.[5] Similar references can be found in the letters of Paul and in Revelation.[6] Various figures in Christian tradition, especially Bernard of Clairvaux, Teresa of Avila, and John of the Cross, expressed mystical visions connecting sexual imagery with the Eucharist. On the altar, through the union of Christ, the bridegroom, with the church, his bride, the new life of grace is generated.

In *Mulieris dignatatem*, John Paul II emphasized that Catholics, both female and male, are called to love as a bride loves, to receive love in order to give love back, to take in the love that is offered, and to gestate new life. So it is appropriate in this ritual drama that the congregation be made up of both women and men. But it is also appropriate, says the Vatican, that the one who acts in the person of Christ be a man. According to the CDF document *Inter insignores*, this may be what Jesus intended. This is (debatably) the unbroken two-thousand-year-old tradition of the church.

---

4. This connection between the Church as the bride of Christ and the Eucharist as a nuptial event is explored in Angelo Scola, "The Theological Foundation of the Petrine Dimension of the Church: A Working Hypothesis," *Ecclesiology* 4 (2007): 12–37. Scola draws much upon the work of Hans Urs von Balthasar.

5. See Mt 25:1–18; Mk 2:18–22; Jn 3:29; 14:1–3. See also Phillip J. Long, *Jesus the Bridegroom: The Origin of the Eschatological Feast as a Wedding Banquet in the Synoptic Gospels* (Eugene, OR: Wipf and Stock, 2013).

6. See 2 Cor 11:2; Eph 5:25–27; Rev 19:9–11; 21:2, 9–11.

Maarten de Vos's engraving (c. 1590), in keeping with traditional Christian interpretation, depicts the Song of Songs as an allegory for Christ's love for the church.

As already mentioned, Vatican documents claim the burden of proof is on those who want to make the change. John Paul II believed he did not have the authority to reverse such a long-standing tradition that may have been willed by Christ. And, though not stated explicitly in official documents, a point implied by the Vatican is that retaining a gender-based distinction in the church's most sacred ritual may speak against tendencies in the contemporary world to do entirely away with gender-based distinctions. Jutta Burggraf, cited earlier in this chapter, fears that the loss of all gender distinctions would bring with it an incalculable cultural loss.

Alternative Voices

As mentioned previously, in 1994, John Paul II declared that the ordination of women as priests is to be considered a closed question, not open to debate.[7] Not everyone, however, has been satisfied with that stance.

---

7. Pope John Paul II, *Ordinatio sacerdotalis*, 1994, *http://w2.vatican.va/content/john-paul-ii/en/apost _letters/1994/documents/hf_jp-ii_apl_19940522_ordinatio-sacerdotalis.html.*

As was discussed in chapter 26, the majority of feminists reject the vision of gender complementarity put forth by von Balthasar and John Paul II as being simplistic and two-dimensional. The historical reality of gender has been more multifaceted. The main arguments given by those who favor the ordination of women as priests are as follows:

- Jesus' selection of the Twelve probably reflects more the sociohistorical situation of a patriarchal culture than some explicit intention of Jesus.
- Ordaining women would be in continuity with the main thrust of Jesus' ministry to include women in contrast with the cultural expectations.
- Women had leadership roles in the early church that were suppressed as church structures gradually conformed to the patriarchal culture.
- The church has the power to make structural changes to address new cultural situations as they arise.
- The new recognition of the equality and dignity of women calls upon the church to practice what it preaches and to be an institutional role model rather than a regressive force in society.

Some also argue that, if both women and men can participate in the congregation as symbols of the bride, why cannot our symbolic consciousness permit both women and men to play the role of Christ? Added to these arguments are some practical concerns—for example, that ordaining women would help in addressing the shortage of priests; some women feel strongly that they are called to be priests; women would bring dimensions to the priesthood that it now lacks; and ordaining women would be a good move in the direction of ecumenical unity.

In the late 1980s and early 1990s, the bishops of the United States wrote several drafts of a pastoral letter on the concerns of women in relation to church and society. After receiving strident criticism from all sides after each draft, the bishops finally shelved the project. They issued, instead, a relatively brief pastoral reflection on the topic in 1994, "Strengthening the Bonds of Peace." One of the document's main themes was the need to promote the service of women in leadership roles in the Catholic Church. This point is important, because in Catholic history, the ordained have been not only those who preside at the Eucharist but also those who govern the Church and proclaim the gospel. It is one thing to rule women out of the priest's role at Mass; it is another to rule women out of the halls of power and authority in the Catholic Church.

In 1998, the Bishops' Committee on Women in Society and in the Church issued a follow-up document intended to build upon and implement the 1994 reflection. They put forth three goals:

1. To appreciate and incorporate the gifts of women in the church
2. To appoint women to church leadership positions
3. To promote collaboration between women and men in the church

The committee's specific suggestions for implementing the second point included various means of training women, employing women, and monitoring the situation. The US bishops, while accepting the Vatican ban on the ordination of women as priests, began developing practical strategies that challenge traditional structures reserving positions of leadership for ordained men. In more recent years, however, the culture wars have opened up new divides on these issues in various dioceses.

Women and Pope Francis

Pope Francis operates with his own form of complementarity:

> When women are not there, harmony is missing. We might say: But this is a society with a strong masculine attitude, and this is the case, no? The woman is missing. "Yes, yes: the woman is there to wash the dishes, to do things. . . ." No, no, no! The woman is there to bring harmony. Without the woman there is no harmony. They are not equal; one is not superior to the other: no. It's just that the man does not bring harmony. It's her. It is she who brings that harmony that teaches us to caress, to love with tenderness; and who makes the world a beautiful place.[8]

Most US Catholics not only support Pope Francis, but they find in him a breath of fresh air. When it comes to his position on women, however, some progressive Catholics find disappointing his strong emphasis on the complementary differences between men and women, which they believe historically has supported discrimination.[9] Still, Francis has announced his intention to "increase the number of women in decision-making positions in the church" and has set up a commission to study the possibility of ordaining women as deacons.[10] Women were ordained as deacons in the early church, though it is debated by scholars what actual roles they played.

Summary

This chapter examined some official positions concerning the role of women in the Catholic Church, with a strong focus on the teachings of John Paul II.

---

8. Vatican Radio, "Pope: Women Bring Harmony That Makes the World Beautiful," February 2, 2017, *http://en.radiovaticana.va/news/2017/02/09/pope_women_bring_harmony_that_makes_the _world_beautiful/1291436.*

9. See, for example, Jamie Manson, "It's Time to Be Honest about Pope Francis and Women," *National Catholic Reporter*, May 19, 2016, *https://www.ncronline.org/blogs/grace-margins/its-time -be-honest-about-pope-francis-and-women.*

10. Elisabetta Povoledo and Laurie Goodstein, "Pope Francis Says Panel Will Study Whether Women May Serve as Deacons," *New York Times*, May 12, 2016.

A colleague of mine once said it is the Vatican's deeply entrenched fear of women that holds them back from ordaining women as priests. Another colleague thinks the Vatican sincerely believes it has a two-thousand-year-old tradition to safeguard and thereby does not feel it can change according to the cultural winds without knowing clearly that such is the will of God. In any case, it is difficult to make judgments concerning the inner disposition of Vatican officials.

My Italian friend, Angela, is aghast at US opposition to Vatican positions on gender. Some of my students in the United States are aghast at Angela's being aghast. Yet among my students, both women and men, I find a notable diversity of views on these complex and difficult issues.

The next chapter will examine how, at Vatican II, the Catholic Church emphasized its role as a servant within the world.

For Further Reflection

1. Why do you think John Paul II found it is important to preserve some degree of distinction between the sexes?

2. Which arguments concerning the ordination of women do you find most convincing? Which arguments do you find least convincing?

3. What is your reaction to John Paul II's claim that women play a crucial leadership role in the common priesthood of the faithful?

4. Does the possibility of ordaining women as deacons seem to you like a bad idea, a good compromise, or a small step in the right direction?

5. What would you like to say to my Italian friend, Angela?

Suggested Readings

Helman, Ivy A. *Women and the Vatican: An Exploration of Official Documents.* Maryknoll, NY: Orbis Books, 2012.

Leadership Conference of Women Religious (LCWR). *Creating a Home: Benchmarks for Church Leadership Roles for Women.* Edited by Jeanean D. Merkel. Silver Spring, MD: LCWR, 1996.

Macy, Gary, William T. Ditewig, and Phyllis Zagano. *Women Deacons: Past, Present, Future.* Mahwah, NJ: Paulist Press, 2011.

Zagano, Phyllis. *Women Deacons? Essays with Answers.* Collegeville, MN: Liturgical Press, 2016.

Zagano, Phyllis, ed. *Holy Saturday: An Argument for the Restoration of the Female Diaconate in the Catholic Church.* New York: Crossroad, 2000.

3
PART

GAUDIUM ET SPES: THE CHURCH ENGAGING THE WORLD

28

CHAPTER

The Servant Church

The legend of St. Christopher, as I have heard it told,[1] goes something like this:

St. Christopher was a very large and strong man. When he was young, he decided he should serve only the greatest of kings. The king in his area claimed that he was the greatest of kings, and so for some time, Christopher served him.

One day, Christopher discovered his king was frightened of the emperor. He therefore set off in search of this emperor who did, indeed, claim to be the greatest ruler.

After serving the emperor for many years, Christopher learned the emperor was frightened of Satan. So Christopher set out in search of Satan. He found Satan riding at the head of a large army and claiming to be the most powerful ruler. So Christopher entered his service.

One day, when the army was marching through the desert, Satan altered their course to avoid going near a small cross that was planted in the sand. When Christopher asked why, he learned Satan was terribly afraid of Christ. So Christopher went in search of Christ and inquired after Christ's whereabouts from a ferryman. Although the ferryman did not know where to find Christ, he suggested that if Christopher relieved him as ferryman he might find out, since in time, nearly everyone in the world would cross that river.

Christopher served many years as a ferryman who took people across the river. He met none who could tell him of the whereabouts of Christ. Then one night, as a storm arose, a small boy asked for passage across the river.

Christopher took the boy upon his back and began to cross. He found the boy to be surprisingly heavy. By the time he was halfway to the shore, the storm raged mercilessly and the boy felt exceedingly heavy. Nevertheless, Christopher continued to struggle until he had reached the other side. By the time he put the boy down, he felt as though the weight of the world had been lifted off his shoulders.

---

1. For this version of the story, I am indebted to a children's book by John Ryan, *One Dark and Stormy Night: The Legend of St. Christopher* (London: Bodley Head, 1986).

The boy thanked him and then proclaimed that he himself was the Christ whom Christopher had been seeking. Christopher asked to accompany Christ on his journey and serve him. Christ replied that Christopher had been serving him all along, whenever he helped people cross the river. Christopher asked again if he might serve Christ more directly by going with him. Christ responded that the best help Christopher could give to him would be to continue helping people cross the river.

In the legend of St. Christopher, Christ insists that Christopher has been serving Christ simply by doing his work, helping others. *Gaudium et spes* similarly emphasizes that work in the world can be a means of serving Christ.

Christopher continued his work. To this day he is popularly known as the patron saint of travelers.

Overview

The legend of St. Christopher expresses a deep Christian belief that Christ can be served through one's work in the world. At Vatican II, this belief burst to the surface to become one of the major themes of *Gaudium et spes* (*Pastoral Constitution on the Church in the Modern World*). The issue was addressed in terms of the relationship between the church and the world. This chapter will comment briefly about the church-world relationship in the history of Christianity, examine the shift at Vatican II, and then discuss the assessment of the Extraordinary Synod of 1985.

The first twenty-seven chapters of this book took their basic organization and inspiration from *Lumen gentium* (*Dogmatic Constitution on the Church*). The remaining nine chapters follow roughly the organization of *Gaudium et spes*. This chapter addresses an underlying theme that runs throughout the document.

Historical Background

The relationship between the Catholic Church and the "world" has undergone complex developments throughout Christian history. Strong strains that are world-affirming and strong strains that are world-denying can both be traced within the large Catholic-Christian tradition. New Testament communities often saw themselves as bastions of salvation from an evil world. Particularly in the Gospel of John, the world is a horrible place of lies and temptations. Yet that very Gospel also says, "For God so loved the world that he gave his only Son, so that everyone who believes in him may not perish but may have eternal life" (3:16). Acts of the Apostles presents frequent evidence of a God who calls the apostles to be increasingly world-embracing as the Christian mission spreads. Also evidenced is a "natural theology" that identifies the God of Christians as the one anticipated in the pagan nature religions (Acts 17:22–29). The scriptural testimony concerning the goodness of the world therefore has its own tensions and ambiguities.

Christianity entered the fourth century as an underground, sometimes persecuted religion. This position profoundly affected the church's attitude toward the world. In 313 CE, with the issuing of the Edict of Milan, Christianity was officially tolerated. In 380 CE, Christianity became the official religion of the Roman Empire. Within the space of one century, Christianity was well on the way to becoming, in many ways, a "worldly" religion, insofar as it related to the state and cared for the temporal well-being of people. Over the years, the offices in the church came to resemble offices in the state.

Also in the fourth century, however, desert monasteries that were home to solitary monks who sought God by escaping city life became increasingly popular. These monks developed ascetical practices, believing that worldly concerns would stand between them and God.

The tension between the worldly and the otherworldly in Christianity can also be seen in church attitudes toward art. In the early Greek church, those who favored the use of icons in worship clashed with "iconoclasts" (literally, smashers of symbols), who believed that the injunction in the first commandment to "make no graven images" was as true for Christians as it was for the Jews who made the golden calf. Iconoclasts attempted to throw art out of the churches, seeing attempts to represent the divine as offensive to God.

The church of the Middle Ages tended to choose the worldly option in regard to art and architecture but the otherworldly in regard to lifestyle. The church of the Renaissance favored the worldly option. The great Protestant Reformers, Luther and Calvin, perceived the Roman Catholic Church to be worldly in a way that opposed the gospel.

Luther and Calvin, each in his own way, advocated an otherworldly approach to religion, although with some complexity. Both stressed that humankind's Fall into sin had disastrous consequences, such as complete helplessness apart from the special intervention of God. Luther emphasized the salvation of the individual through faith alone rather than through works performed in this world. Still, he emphasized that a saved Christian is deeply motivated to perform good works, and he emphasized the Christian's call to holiness within the family and the workplace. Calvin taught the predestination of the saved and the damned, which ironically led to a concern for one's status in this world as a sign of one's eternal destiny. The rise of Protestantism paralleled the emergence of a secular world in which religious faith would come to be seen as marginal to the spheres of politics and business.

The Council of Trent, reacting to Luther and Calvin, asserted a more positive understanding of the human person. The council agreed that original sin was serious and that human beings had thereby lost their holiness and righteousness; but the Fall was not total, for human beings still retained a free will and were made in the image and likeness of God. In other words, the Fall was seriously distorting but not absolute. From the Catholic point of view, the issue was whether people could be said to be responsible for their eternal destiny, while at the same time acknowledging the necessity of grace. Trent's position classically articulates the Catholic emphasis that human beings and the world remain always God's creation and are basically good.

For the Reformers, what they perceived as the Catholic overemphasis on sacraments and art was tied in with its worldliness. Many Protestants themselves have historically preferred crosses to crucifixes, sermons to sacraments, music to sculpture, and the Bible to great cathedrals. The Catholic emphasis has been on a sacramental sensibility: that God can be encountered in and through the things of this world.[2] The Protestant emphasis has been on the saving power of the Word proclaimed to sinners in this fallen world.

The parallel and often overlapping histories of Catholicism and Protestantism show wide variety and complex shifts taking place within all denominations and local churches in regard to the status or value accorded the "world." If Catholic anthropology and art appreciation of recent centuries have been world-affirming, Catholic attitudes and policies often have not. Perhaps somewhat ironically, Protestantism was seen from the Catholic perspective to be "worldly" in that it took political and spiritual power away from the church and put it in the hands of nation-states. The separation of church and state, which often took the form of the subordination of the church to the state, was strongly resisted by the Catholic Church. From the Catholic standpoint, a balance of power could only be preserved by a relationship between nation-states and a universal church, not between nation-states and national churches.

As discussed in chapter 2, for several centuries prior to Vatican II the Catholic Church saw movement after movement arise that challenged its authority and its place in the world. From the Enlightenment with its emphasis on science and hostility to religion, to the French Revolution with its persecution of the church, to the rise of industrialization with its new forms of poverty and philosophies of atheistic materialism, the Catholic Church felt threatened. Thus, while retaining, in relation to Protestantism, a relatively positive theological view of humankind and the world, the Catholic Church of the last few centuries saw the world in practical terms as an evil and ugly place. During the first half of

---

2. An interesting discussion of biblical themes in art history can be found in Richard Mühlberger, *The Bible in Art: The Old Testament* (New York: Portland House, 1991), and *The Bible in Art: The New Testament* (New York: Portland House, 1990).

the twentieth century, the Catholic Church had developed what many commentators call a "fortress mentality" or a "ghetto mentality." It was the Catholic
Church over and against the world, presenting itself as the way to salvation for
those who would escape the world's clutches.

Dialogue with the World

Vatican II attempted to bring the church beyond the fortress mentality. The
openness of Vatican II represented a virtual about-face—from a suspicious scru-
tiny of a world seen as hostile to a sensitive reaching out to a world seen as
bursting with potential. Some commentators view this as the single most significant development of the council.[3]

Pope John XXIII helped to usher in this shift with his calls for *aggiornamento* (updating) leading up to Vatican II. The most important achievement of
Vatican II, in regard to dialogue with the world, was *Gaudium et spes*. *Lumen
gentium* states its purpose as expressing the "nature and mission" of the church;
Gaudium et spes states its purpose as explaining "the presence and activity of the
church in the world today" (*GS* 2). The "world" in *Gaudium et spes* is seen as
a basically good though ambiguous place. It is full of potential but also dangers: "The modern world shows itself at once powerful and weak, capable of
the noblest deeds or the foulest; before it lies the path to freedom or to slavery,
to progress or retreat, to brotherhood or hatred" (*GS* 9). The document further
explains that the "religious" is not opposed to the "human": "Christians are convinced that the triumphs of the human race are a sign of God's grace and the
flowering of God's own mysterious design" (*GS* 34).

Gaudium et spes several times expresses the desire of the Catholic Church to
enter into conversation with the modern world: "This Council can provide no
more eloquent proof of its solidarity with, as well as its respect and love for the
entire human family with which it is bound up, than by engaging it in conversation about these various problems" (*GS* 3).

The gospel message needs to be reformulated in accordance with the "signs
of the times" (*GS* 4). Among the signs of the times is that the world has entered
into a new stage of history characterized by rapid social change and tremendous
potential for good and for ill. These times lead people to ask deep questions
about why life is the way that it is. Are there grounds for hope? Is there ultimate
meaning? What is any of this struggle for?

The role of the church is to address these questions by offering, to the
world, its teaching about the saving mystery of Christ. This, in itself, is nothing
new. What is most new in the document is the emphatic manner in which the

---

3. Karl Rahner, "Toward a Fundamental Theological Interpretation of Vatican II," *Theological
Studies* 40 (December 1979): 716–27.

church acknowledges that God can be served either through explicit witness or through service. People can do the will of God in many ways:

> Now, the gifts of the Spirit are diverse; while the Spirit calls some to give clear witness to the desire for a heavenly home and to keep that desire fresh among the human family, the Spirit summons others to dedicate themselves to the earthly service of human beings and to make ready the material of the celestial realm by this ministry of theirs. (*GS* 38)

The world is good. Human beings possess the fundamental dignity of being made in the image and likeness of God. Yet individuals are not isolated; human beings are social by nature. Human efforts are not in vain; despite the dangers, God is on the side of those who work for human advancement. Human progress helps lay a groundwork in preparation for the coming of God's kingdom. In Christ, we find the assurance that life, which does not end in death, contains these meanings. Such is the message *Gaudium et spes* holds out to the world.

Church as Leaven in the World

Gaudium et spes goes deeper than seeing the world as a good place and engaging in conversation with it; it also recognizes the world as the main arena of human activity, and the church as a servant to the world. One way the church expresses its message is to say, "To those, therefore, who believe in divine love, God gives assurance that the way of love lies open to human beings and that the effort to establish a universal brotherhood is not a hopeless one" (*GS* 38).

In the centuries prior to Vatican II, the Catholic Church pictured itself mainly as a refuge from the world of vanity and temptation. In *Gaudium et spes*, the church portrayed itself "as a leaven and as a kind of soul for human society as it is to be renewed in Christ and transformed into God's family" (*GS* 40). In other words, the church approves of many elements of contemporary social movements and sees itself as wishing to collaborate and make a contribution to that which is already good.

To put it yet another way: prior to Vatican II, the leadership of the Catholic Church tended to perceive its role as being servants to Christ and spiritual rulers of those who had converted to the church from the world. In *Gaudium et spes*, the church is presented as the servant to what is good in the world, whether or not the world has explicitly converted to Christ. The sinful nature of human beings and the insufficiency of merely earthly progress are noted; however, working for peace and economic justice ceased being optional extras and are seen instead as integral to the gospel message. The opening lines of the document capture its overall stress on the importance of human solidarity: "The joys and hopes, the griefs and the anxieties of the people of this age, especially those who are poor or in any way afflicted, these are the joys and hopes, the griefs and anxieties of the followers of Christ."

Message from the Sixties?

Gaudium et spes was issued at the close of Vatican II in 1965. In the United States, the following years found hippies, Vietnam War protests, Woodstock, and widespread social change often expressed through sex, drugs, and hard rock. It was the days of the early peace movement, Martin Luther King Jr., and landing on the moon. Electric bards told us to tear down the walls, give peace a chance, get together and try to love one another right now. Many youth expected that it would not be so difficult to overthrow the corrupt world of their parents and build a new peaceful society based on justice and universal love.

Gaudium et spes itself is not quite so optimistic. It discusses the sinful nature of human beings in three different passages (*GS* 10, 13, 25). It never discusses the goodness of the world without mentioning also its ambiguities. It does not believe that total human emancipation can be achieved through human effort alone. It stresses the importance of human progress but, in several passages, it is clear that the world can also take quite a different turn if human beings do not take proper responsibility.

Yet, when measured against former church documents, *Gaudium et spes* is extremely optimistic in its hope for human progress on a global scale. Some church leaders have felt that it was too optimistic. The following passage from the final document of the Extraordinary Synod of 1985 cautiously affirms *Gaudium et spes* while reasserting the important role played by church authority:

> The church as communion is a sacrament for the salvation of the world. Therefore the authorities in the church have been placed there by Christ for the salvation of the world. In this context we affirm the great importance and timeliness of the pastoral constitution, *Gaudium et spes*. At the same time, however, we perceive that the signs of our time are in part different from those of the time of the council, with greater problems and anguish. Today, in fact, everywhere in the world we witness an increase in hunger, oppression, injustice and war, sufferings, terrorism, and other forms of violence of every sort. This requires a new and more profound theological reflection in order to interpret these signs in the light of the Gospel.[4]

---

4. Sacred Congregation for the Doctrine of the Faith, "The Final Report," *Origins* 15 (1985): 449.

In the English version, this subsection of the document is ironically entitled, "Importance of the Constitution, *Gaudium et spes*." As I read it, it says *Gaudium et spes* is too optimistic, that it needs to be read in a context that highlights the importance of church authority, that the world has not gotten better but indeed is much worse, and that we are in need of a more profound theology if we are to carry out our mission in the world.

The synod document suggests that a theology stressing the goodness of creation needs to be more fully balanced by a theology stressing the importance of the cross, and that regeneration of the world needs to take place through an encounter with the proclamation of the good news. The document seems to present itself as more realistic than *Gaudium et spes*: "When we Christians speak of the cross, we do not deserve to be labeled pessimists, but we rather found ourselves upon the realism of Christian hope" (II D 2). The overall message of the Extraordinary Synod was a resounding affirmation of Vatican II; its reservations and qualifications, however, make for a strong undercurrent.

Popes John Paul II and Benedict XVI continued to emphasize the need for a counterbalance regarding overly optimistic views. Pope Francis, though careful not to contradict his predecessors, brings a new sense of urgency for Christians to work for the transformation of the world in the streets. For those who are old enough, Francis's message is reminiscent of the original vision of *Gaudum et spes*.

Summary

This chapter examined the complex history of Catholics and Protestants and the ways they have viewed the relationship between the church and the world. Against that background, this chapter discussed how Vatican II set a new, optimistic tone for Catholic attitudes toward dialogue with the world, as well as how a 1985 Catholic synod took a more pessimistic outlook toward the current state of world affairs. Today, the example of Pope Francis indicates that the pendulum of particular emphases continues to swing.

The dream of a world united in peace and love seems farther off now than it did in the 1960s. I cannot help but think, however, that *Gaudium et spes* is a deep reflection of the message of the gospel for our times. Christians can still hear the lesson of St. Christopher even as they listen seriously to the cautions of the Extraordinary Synod.

The next chapter will discuss the relationship of Christianity with other world religions.

For Further Reflection

1. Does the story of St. Christopher speak to you? If so, in what ways?
2. Is it possible for religion to be too "worldly"? Is it possible for religion not to be "worldly" enough?
3. Have today's youth lost their idealism in contrast with students of the 1960s?
4. Can one serve God just as well by working within the world as through explicitly religious ways?
5. If you had to choose, would you be more supportive of *Gaudium et spes* or of the Extraordinary Synod of 1985 on points where they seem to be in contrast?

Suggested Readings

Eggemeier, Matthew T. *A Sacramental-Prophetic Vision: Christian Spirituality in a Suffering World.* Collegeville, MN: Liturgical Press, 2014.

Grebe, Anja. *Vatican: All the Paintings; The Complete Collection of Old Masters, Plus More Than 300 Sculptures, Maps, Tapestries, and Other Artifacts.* New York: Black Dog and Leventhal Publishers, 2013.

Greeley, Andrew. *The Catholic Imagination.* Berkeley: University of California Press, 2000.

Himes, Michael J., and Kenneth R. Himes, OFM. *Fullness of Faith: The Public Significance of Theology.* New York: Paulist Press, 1993.

Reiser, William, SJ. *To Hear God's Word, Listen to the World: The Liberation of Spirituality.* New York: Paulist Press, 1997.

29

CHAPTER

Religious Pluralism

When I had completed most of my doctoral work in religious studies, I took a trip to Egypt. While there, I visited several mosques. Most of the mosques I entered were large ones accustomed to receiving tourists. There were designated places to leave one's shoes outside.

One afternoon, I was walking a narrow backstreet in Cairo when I came upon a small, neighborhood mosque. Curious, I took off my shoes and went in. Several people were sitting on the ground praying. I put my shoes down and did the same.

While I was in prayer, a young man of about twenty approached and asked me if I was a Muslim. I said, "No, I am a Christian." He shooed me out of the mosque by motioning with his hands, saying, "Muslims only. Muslims only." I apologized and was out the door before I knew it.

Moments later, as I was tying my shoes, the young man and a companion came out to talk with me. The companion asked what I had been doing in the mosque. When I told him I was praying, he invited me back in.

Again I removed my shoes, and the three of us went inside and sat down together. We were quickly joined by three more young men. The man who had chased me out explained that when I place my shoes down the soles must be facing each other; when he had seen my shoes sole-side down, he knew something was wrong, because such was an insult to God.

These young men were all of college age. One was studying to be a veterinarian, another to be an aeronautical engineer. All knew some English, and a few were fluent in it.

They asked what I thought about their holy book, the Qur'an. Because I had recently been studying academic perspectives on world religions (from a somewhat sociological point of view), I felt comfortable saying, "The Qur'an is the word of God." In saying this, I was not intending to give personal testimony, but to acknowledge that I recognize how the Qur'an authentically functions as the word of God for hundreds of millions of people.

The young men were getting excited. They wanted to know what I thought of Muhammad. From the same perspective that I had affirmed the Qur'an, I repeated another of their formulas: "Muhammad is God's prophet."

After a brief consultation in Arabic, one of them ran out and came back a couple of minutes later with three books, each of which had Arabic on one side and English on the other. They made a present to me of these books, and asked me to read aloud some basic professions of faith from one of them.

It was at this point I realized they did not think, as I did, that we were simply engaging in interreligious dialogue. They thought they had a convert on their hands and were formally welcoming me into their religion by having me make a public profession of faith. For a moment, I was scared. Ancient images of Muslims using large saber swords to lop off the heads of infidels flashed through my mind. But I summoned the courage to say, "No, no, you misunderstand. I respect and revere your religion, but I wish to remain Christian."

It was as though a sigh of disappointed relief swept through the mosque. Without uttering a word, the looks on their faces read, "But why didn't you say so in the first place?" I had gotten them all excited, but their making of a new Muslim was not to be.

Our conversation soon recovered from this low point, however. We had an interesting discussion about religious beliefs. They brought up the ridiculousness of the Christian belief in the Trinity. I assured them that Christians profess ultimately to believe in one God. I explained to them that Jesus functions in our religion something like the Qur'an functions in theirs; that is, just as they believe God's word has come to them most fully in the Qur'an, Christians believe God's word has come to them most fully in the person of Jesus. Most Christians do not place the Bible on as high a level as Muslims place the Qur'an. No Muslim places Muhammad on the same level that Christians place Jesus. From my point of view, I explained, the doctrine of the Trinity is not ridiculous; it is a formal way for Christians to express their experience of Jesus as Lord and their belief that the Spirit is at work within them.

My new friends were surprised to hear that Christians believe in hell. In retrospect, I think their surprise stemmed from a combination of thinking their own most basic beliefs are unique and that the Western world is too corrupt to be populated by any large number of people who are aware that hell is a possibility.

I corresponded with one of these young men for a couple of years afterward. I look back on the incident fondly as a wonderful religious interchange and as a reminder that what begins in misunderstanding can end in fruitful conversation.

Overview

This chapter investigates how the official attitude of the Catholic Church toward other religions shifted at the Second Vatican Council. After a brief look at prior attitudes, the chapter examines the position taken at Vatican II, and finally, discusses various stances Christians take concerning this issue.

This chapter is related to *Gaudium et spes* insofar as that document calls for dialogue with the world; it is more directly related, however, to the council's *Nostra aetate* (*Declaration on the Relation of the Church to Non-Christian Religions*).

The One True Faith

Throughout the history of Christianity, the majority of Christians have held that Christianity is the one true faith and that Jesus is the savior of the world in a cosmic sense. The quantity and seriousness of this testimony is something no Christian can afford to take lightly. There are many lines in the New Testament that have been interpreted as buttressing this view:

- "Very truly, I tell you, no one can enter the kingdom of God without being born of water and Spirit." (Jn 3:5)
- "Those who believe in him are not condemned; but those who do not believe are condemned already, because they have not believed in the name of the only Son of God." (Jn 3:18)
- Jesus said to [Thomas], "I am the way, and the truth, and the life. No one comes to the Father except through me." (Jn 14:6)
- "There is salvation in no one else, for there is no other name under heaven given among mortals by which we must be saved." (Acts 4:12)

Some Christians have believed that only Christians can be saved at the end of the world. Many others have maintained that whereas Christ is the only real savior, many non-Christians can be saved because the grace of God that comes through Christ is somehow made available to all. That is, many people are saved by embracing the grace that is available to them, even though they may not know the name of Christ or have, perhaps, rejected an inadequate presentation of Christianity.

Both of these positions are based in the belief that salvation ultimately comes through Christ. Although these positions may have their drawbacks, their clear strength is their fidelity to the long-standing Christian claim that Jesus came not just to save a few but to effect the salvation of the human race from the original sin that continues to distort it. Jesus did not just teach a good path but is, in himself, the incarnation of God, who set right the relationship between God and the human race. Christians who are quick to embrace other religions as equal may have trouble reconciling their stance with traditional claims within their own tradition.

I do not in any way mean to imply here that the explanations offered by theologians who argue for the salvific potential of other religions are not often good ones. Christian sayings that seem to imply other religions are false can often be interpreted as encouragements to insiders not to abandon their faith in the face of pagan cults; they were not originally intended to be universal condemnations of other world religions. Also, such language can be interpreted as being like love language; to say to a lover, "you are the only one," or "you are the most wonderful person in the world," is to express something real without pretending it to be a fully objective statement. Another explanation of such statements is that they reflect the intensity of the experience of early Christians; one can embrace the Christian experience today without embracing exaggerated implications of the ways in which it was expressed.

Those who say Christianity is the only real path to salvation have had their own set of problems that need explaining. How can one account for the goodness and wisdom of the long and often venerable religious traditions of the world? Catholic textbooks written prior to Vatican II, at times, reflected more prejudice than accuracy when describing other world religions.

Although the following example is a bit extreme, it represents the kind of attitude that can develop. In a 1939 Irish textbook for a first-year college theology course, Bishop Michael Sheehan gives an unflattering description of the origin and teaching of Buddhism, and then offers the following as one of the main reasons for Buddhism's popularity: "its toleration of sin, for it taught that those who indulged their passions did not lose, but merely delayed, their final happiness."[1] After a likewise unflattering description of Islam, Sheehan accounts for its popularity by "its pandering to base passions; but above all to the might of the sword." Sheehan goes on to say that, unlike Christianity, neither Buddhism nor Islam has ever "received the divine testimony of manifest and well authenticated miracles."[2] Sheehan's presuppositions about the inadequacies of other religions prevent him from giving a fair or accurate assessment.

Vatican II on Other Religions

Vatican II's *Nostra aetate* differs greatly in approach and tone from Sheehan's textbook.[3] The document begins with an affirmation that human beings form one community and that we share a common destiny in God. It then gives a sympathetic description of various world religions, especially highlighting Hinduism and Buddhism:

> Thus, in Hinduism people explore the divine mystery and express it both in the limitless riches of myth and the accurately defined insights of philosophy. They ask release from the trials of present life by ascetical practices, profound meditation, and recourse to God in confidence and love.

---

1. Michael Sheehan, *Apologetics and Catholic Doctrine* (Dublin: M. H. Gill and Son, 1939), 1:67.

2. Sheehan, *Apologetics and Catholic Doctrine*, 1:169.

3. *Nostra aetate*, 1965, http://www.vatican.va/archive/hist_councils/ii_vatican_council/documents/vat-ii_decl_19651028_nostra-aetate_en.html.

Buddhism in its various forms testifies to the essential inadequacy of this changing world. It proposes a way of life by which people can, with confidence and trust, attain a state of perfect liberation and reach supreme illumination either through their own efforts or by the aid of divine help. (*NA* 2)

The document then expresses the new openness in attitude of the Catholic Church:

The Catholic Church rejects nothing of what is true and holy in these religions. The church has a high regard for the manner of life and conduct, the precepts and doctrines which, although differing in many ways from its own teaching, nevertheless often reflects a ray of that truth which enlightens all people. (*NA* 2)

Now, read closely, the above passage is not an overwhelming endorsement of these religions. Taken out of historical context, it might be read as "damning with faint praise." After all, it merely says these religions reflect "a ray" of the truth to which all people have access. The paragraph goes on to remind Christians that it remains the duty of the church to proclaim Christ, who is the way, the truth, and the life.

Read within its historical context, however, the passage represents a major shift in the Catholic position in the direction of openness and dialogue. Indeed, the document urges Christians to engage in discussion and collaboration with people of other faiths.

Muslims and Jews

The declaration has a separate section for Islam and another for Judaism. This is because of the special ties between Christianity and these other Western, monotheistic religions. In regard to Islam, the document notes its many links with the faith of Christians and expresses regrets for past quarrels and dissentions.

Of all the religions, Judaism is engaged most deeply by *Nostra aetate*. In the wake of the Holocaust during World War II, Jewish-Christian relations needed sorely to be addressed. In fact, the initial draft of *Nostra aetate* had been limited to this topic and then later expanded to include a wide range of religions. The document discusses, at length, the deep ties formed within a shared religious heritage. It mentions that the initiating figures of Christianity were all of Jewish descent; that although the Jews did not accept Jesus, they remain dear to the God who has not taken back his promise of the covenant; that it is inappropriate to speak of the Jews as rejected or accursed; that although some Jewish authorities pressed for the death of Jesus, Jews cannot be indiscriminately charged with this crime today; and that the church reproves all religious persecution, particularly any that has been leveled from any source against the Jews.

Nostra aetate closes with a rejection of discrimination against anyone on the basis of race, color, condition in life, or religion. Overall, its outlook toward other religions is positive, looking forward to dialogue and collaboration.

Contemporary Positions

The position represented by Michael Sheehan and others who reject other religions as false and misleading is known as *exclusivism*. The position that one's own religion is the highest religion but that other religions are basically good insofar as they reflect truth in a partial way is known as *inclusivism*. That is, one's own religion is extended in a broad way as including all people of good will.

The Jesuit theologian Karl Rahner proposed a well-known form of inclusivism by claiming that people of other faiths who live a good life are actually Christian although they do not know it. Rahner believed the Christ event is the highest and unsurpassable expression of the drama that underlies every life story. Anyone who affirmatively answers the call to embrace the mystery of life has thereby accepted Christ. At first, Rahner referred to such a person as an "anonymous Christian." He later dropped the term because some people found it offensive, although he still defended the concept. (Those who found the term offensive thought it showed disrespect for other religions in and of themselves.)

Nostra aeatate represented a theological shift from an exclusivist to an inclusivist position. Christianity is still presented as the final, cosmic truth about the meaning of life. On a political level, however, the document recognized that the freedom of religion of people of all faiths must be respected. There is no justification whatsoever for discrimination on the basis of religion. Human beings are to be treated as brothers and sisters and their basic dignity and rights must be respected.

Many theologians and scholars of religion do not believe an inclusivist position goes far enough. Few scholars would hold a position traditionally known as *indifferentism*, which is the belief that all religions are basically the same. Many scholars today operate out of what can be called a *mutuality* model.[4] This position acknowledges great differences among religions, but also presumes no one religion can claim a corner on the market of ultimate truth. All major religions are fundamentally good but also incomplete.

This is the position I associate most with Raimon Panikkar, whose mother was Catholic and whose father was Hindu. In his work *The Intra-Religious Dialogue*,[5] Panikkar gives several images that try to illustrate analogously how the various religions are related: they are like bands of color in the rainbow;

---

4. I draw some of my ideas and terminology from a work by Paul F. Knitter, *Introducing Theologies of Religion* (Maryknoll, NY: Orbis Books, 2002).

5. Raimon Panikkar, *The Intra-Religious Dialogue* (Mahwah, NJ: Paulist Press, 1978).

they are like different types of maps for the same territory; they are like different languages. Panikkar encourages dialogues in which people try, in a sense, to trade faiths for a while and to speak to each other from within the other's faith.

Wilfred Cantwell Smith offers another version of the mutual model. A well-known Christian scholar of Islam, Smith spent a good portion of his academic career wrestling with the question of how faiths that are so different can express ultimate truth in such a personal way to various peoples.[6]

Some theologians, however, do not find it satisfactory to put on the shelf the matter of the ultimacy of their own faith. Yet some, too, want to move beyond an inclusivism that presumes superiority. Such is the position of Dutch theologian Edward Schillebeeckx,[7] who takes what I label a stance of *coexistence*. This is the position that one testifies to the belief or experience of ultimacy within one's own tradition, but remains willing to engage in dialogue with people of other faiths without assuming their inferiority. Schillebeeckx says, "I believe in Jesus of Nazareth." He is then ready to engage in interreligious discussion without presupposing that another religion could not also in some way be authentically experienced as ultimate.

A stance of coexistence is a delicately balanced position that can easily collapse back into an inclusivism or a mutuality model. There are thus various versions of this model, some relatively conservative and others more progressive. Schillebeeckx, for example, after laying out a coexistence approach, seems to arrive at the advantages of Christianity when he does, in fact, engage in comparative discussions.

CONTEMPORARY POSITIONS ON OTHER RELIGIONS	
Position	**Viewpoint**
exclusivist	other religions are false and misleading
inclusivist	my religion is the highest; others are good
mutuality	religions are different; study them open-mindedly
coexistence	my religion has ultimacy; I am radically open to dialogue with other religions without presupposing either superiority or inferiority

---

6. A good place to begin reading Wilfred Cantwell Smith is his *Religious Diversity* (New York: Harper and Row, 1976). See also *Towards a World Theology* (Philadelphia: Westminster, 1981).

7. Edward Schillebeeckx can be observed in dialogue with other religious traditions in *Christ: The Experience of Jesus as Lord* (New York: Crossroad, 1981 [1977]), 672–723; his statement of belief in Jesus can be found in *Interim Report on the Books "Jesus" and "Christ"* (New York: Crossroad, 1981 [1977]), 125–43.

Recent Vatican Positions

Recent popes have tried to express the inclusivist position of Vatican II in positive and welcoming tones. In September 2000, however, the Congregation for the Doctrine of the Faith issued a controversial document, *Dominus Iesus*. The main theme of the document was not new. Its tone, however, was a bit cautious or even defensive as it expressed an inclusivist position in line with Vatican II. It emphasized strongly the universal significance of salvation through Christ and the unique importance of the Catholic Church. The document attacked a "relativistic mentality" concerning Christian truth, stating,

> It would be contrary to the faith to consider the church as one way of salvation alongside those constituted by the other religions, seen as complementary to the church or substantially equivalent to her, even if they are said to be converging with the church toward the eschatological kingdom of God. (*DI* 21)

The blunt phrasing of some of the document's positions, however, lacked the nuance and sensitivity of other Catholic statements on these subjects. For example, although acknowledging that elements of world religions may come from God and serve as preparations for the gospel, *Dominus Iesus* cautioned, "It cannot be overlooked that other rituals, insofar as they depend on superstitions or other errors (cf. 1 Cor 10:20–21), constitute an obstacle to salvation." It adds, "If it is true that the followers of other religions can receive divine grace, it is also certain that objectively speaking they are in a gravely deficient situation in comparison with those who, in the Church, have the fullness of the means of salvation" (*DI* 22).

Negative reactions to *Dominus Iesus* were swift, numerous, and loud. Many Catholics working in ecumenical and interreligious circles felt embarrassed by it. Much of the criticism focused on the document's one-sidedness and insensitivity of expression. Other criticisms, however, revealed the relativism that *Dominus Iesus* was attacking.

The reactions of my own students were mixed. Some found the document appalling. Others argued the problem of religious relativism runs so deep among people of their generation that a little pounding on the other side of the issue might not be so bad.

Summary

This chapter discussed the shift at Vatican II from an exclusivist position concerning other religions toward an inclusivist position. It also discussed the range of positions that are reflected in theology today.

Interreligious dialogue raises great questions about truth and the meaning of life. After my interreligious dialogue with the Muslim students in Cairo, I am convinced of one thing: I do not know the final answers to these questions; probably only God does.

The next chapter will discuss Vatican II's response to atheism and the question of God.

For Further Reflection

1. If Christians believe Jesus Christ is God incarnate, does it necessarily follow that other religions cannot be quite as good?
2. What do you think is the best way to interpret the exclusivist language often used within the history of the Christian tradition?
3. Do all religions boil down to basically the same principles?
4. What is your position concerning the relationship among the major religions of the world?
5. Is religious relativism a problem in today's world?

Suggested Readings

Cornille, Catherine, and Stephanie Corigliano, eds. *Interreligious Dialogue and Cultural Change*. Eugene, OR: Cascade, 2012.

DiNoia, J. A. *The Diversity of Religions: A Christian Perspective*. Washington, DC: Catholic University of America Press, 1992.

Dupuis, Jacques. *Christianity and the Religions: From Confrontation to Dialogue*. Maryknoll, NY: Orbis Books, 2002 (2001).

Heft, James L., SM. *Catholicism and Interreligious Dialogue*. Oxford: Oxford University Press, 2012.

Knitter, Paul F. *Introducing Theologies of Religion*. Maryknoll, NY: Orbis Books, 2002.

Nostra aetate (Declaration of the Relation of the Church to Non-Christian Religions). 1965. *http://www.vatican.va/archive/hist_councils/ii_vatican_council/documents/vat-ii_decl_19651028_nostra-aetate_en.html*.

Ratzinger, Joseph Cardinal (later Pope Benedict XVI). *Truth and Tolerance: Christian Belief and World Religions*. San Francisco: Ignatius, 2004 (2003).

Thinking about God in Relation to Atheists and Nonreligious People

n today's world, many people distinguish sharply between "spirituality" and "religion." Spirituality is connected with values, purpose, and meaning. Religion is connected with rituals, rules, and doctrines. As a Catholic, I experience a deep interconnectedness between spirituality and religion. I am often impressed, however, by the spiritual insight and moral integrity of people who label themselves "nonreligious."[1] Some nonreligious people reject the label "atheist," although there are others who embrace it. Some nonreligious people are hostile to religion, but by no means all.[2] Many nonreligious people say they are spiritual but not religious. Some lack an interest in religion or a compelling rationale to join one. Others find that in a pluralistic world it is difficult to choose one religion over another without appearing to be exclusive or superior-minded.

Overview

This chapter examines the challenge of Marxism and other atheistic philosophies that lurk in the background of *Gaudium et spes*, investigates the approach to the question of God offered by the great theologian Karl Rahner, and then considers how Rahner's approach influenced Vatican II's interpretation of atheism.

This material is related to the discussion of atheism in chapter 1 of *Gaudium et spes*.

---

1. Lois Lee, "Talking about a Revolution: Terminology for the New Field of Non-Religion Studies," *Journal of Contemporary Religion* 27 (January 2012): 129–39. *Nonreligious* is a relatively recent term that was not in use until long after Vatican II.

2. Some books hostile to religion have made the bestsellers lists. See Richard Dawkins, *The God Delusion* (London: Bantam, 2006), and Christopher Hitchens, *God Is Not Great: How Religion Poisons Everything* (New York: Twelve Books, 2007). These learned authors engage many sources, but they tend to ignore the works of trained theologians.

The Systematic Expression of Atheism

Atheism can refer to any system of thought that includes the claim that there is no God. *Gaudium et spes*, without mentioning names of persons, singles out two types of atheism. The first resembles most closely the existentialism associated with mid-twentieth-century writers such as Jean-Paul Sartre and Albert Camus. Existentialism is a philosophy that strongly emphasizes the freedom of human beings to shape reality without being hampered by preset categories. *Gaudium et spes* says,

> Those who profess atheism of this sort maintain that it gives human beings freedom to be an end unto themselves, the sole artisans and creators of their own history. They claim that this freedom cannot be reconciled with the affirmation of a Lord Who is author and purpose of all things, or at least that this freedom makes such an affirmation altogether superfluous. (*GS* 20)

The document's response to existentialism can be found in an earlier passage that links true freedom with God:

> Human dignity demands that people act according to a knowing and free choice that is personally motivated and prompted from within, not under blind internal impulse nor by mere external pressure. People achieve such dignity when, emancipating themselves from all captivity to passion, they pursue their goal in a spontaneous choice of what is good and procure for themselves, through effective and skilful action, aids to that end. Since human freedom has been damaged by sin, only by the aid of God's grace can people bring such a relationship with God into full flower. (*GS* 17)

Such a general discussion was not intended to be either a full presentation of existentialism or a full response to it. It was simply an allusion to existentialist philosophy and a statement that the key to disagreements lies in the meaning of freedom and in the relationship of freedom to God.

Gaudium et spes gives a somewhat fuller (but by no means complete) treatment of a second type of atheism, Marxism:

> Not to be overlooked among the forms of modern atheism is that which anticipates the liberation of humankind especially through economic and social emancipation. This form argues that by its nature religion thwarts this liberation by arousing hope for a deceptive future life, thereby diverting people from the constructing of the earthly city. Consequently when the proponents of this doctrine gain governmental power they vigorously fight against religion, and promote atheism

by using, especially in the education of youth, those means of pressure which public power has at its disposal. (*GS* 20)

As is the case with existentialism, neither Marxism nor Marx is mentioned explicitly by name.

Gaudium et spes takes seriously the Marxist charge that the church's teaching about afterlife encourages people not to take this life seriously. It reaffirms that "the church has been taught by divine revelation and firmly teaches that human beings have been created by God for a blissful purpose beyond the reach of earthly misery" (*GS* 18). Yet in several passages it makes the point that a belief in eternal life should help rather than hurt one's motivation to work for the betterment of this world. The document states, "While we are warned that it profits a man nothing if he gain the whole world and lose himself, the expectation of a new earth must not weaken but rather stimulate our concern for cultivating this one." (*GS* 39) An injunction often repeated in the document is that "a hope related to the end of time does not diminish the importance of intervening duties but rather undergirds the acquittal of them with fresh incentives" (*GS* 21). The salvation of the human race clearly remains the mission of the church; however, "salvation" is considered not simply as something that happens on the last day but as a multidimensional process with its roots in this life. We are to begin working toward the kingdom right here and right now.[3]

Although it is not a simple issue, it could at least be argued that Marxism has been one positive factor in motivating the Catholic Church to emphasize the this-worldly dimension of the gospel message.

The Endpoint of Our Self-Transcendence

To understand the response of *Gaudium et spes* to atheism, it is helpful to examine the approach to the question of God taken by Karl Rahner, an influential figure at Vatican II as well as one of the most important Catholic theologians of the twentieth century.[4] Rahner is not so much interested in giving a classical "proof" for the existence of God as he is in demonstrating what believers appropriately mean when they speak of "God."

Rahner argues that, to talk about who God is, it is useful to begin by talking about who human beings are. The most important consideration is that human beings are *self-transcendent*; that is, they are not purely self-contained within limited boundaries but have the capacity to move beyond themselves.

---

3. This is true not only throughout *Gaudium et spes* but also in *Lumen gentium*, chapter 4, which discusses how the laity in their work in the world participate in the salvific mission of the church.

4. Karl Rahner's best summary of his position on God can be found in *Foundations of Christian Faith* (New York: Seabury, 1978 [1976]), especially the first four chapters.

Karl Rahner, on the left in this 1974 photo, discussed the ramifications of accepting God on both a transcendent level and on a categorical level, or one but not the other. Echoes of Rahner's thinking can be discerned in *Gaudium et spes*.

Our self-transcendence can be seen in our experience of knowing, willing, and loving. When we seek to know something, we are aware not only of our personal limitations but also of our awareness of an ultimate context within which some things are true. We want to know not just things that seem true; we want to know what is really true in the highest possible context outside of ourselves. Within each of us, if we dig deeply enough, we can get in touch with this inner drive toward self-transcendence, the desire to know what is true, no matter what we might otherwise wish to be true for our own convenience.

Similarly, when we seek to do what is good, we seek a goodness that is beyond our immediate desires and satisfactions. Within each of us is a desire to do what is good, even if this, at times, requires personal suffering. Likewise, when we truly love another person, we move beyond ourselves to a concern for that person as he or she is, not just for what that person can do for us.

None of us is, at all times, in complete touch with our inner drives toward self-transcendence. Some may rarely or never consciously experience such drives. Yet Rahner believes it is part of the nature of the human being to have this potential to transcend oneself. Human growth in general can be characterized as the experience of growing beyond one's narrow and limited concerns to a personal identification with higher perspectives that take the well-being of others into account.

Having established that human beings are self-transcendent, Rahner is ready to give an account of what we should mean by "God." I have constructed the following "definition" to try to represent what Rahner means: God is the endpoint of our transcendence—when we are moving beyond ourselves toward truth, goodness, and love. I use the word "endpoint" to translate the German word *woraufhin*, which also has been translated as "whither," "term," and "orientation." The definition is saying that when we transcend ourselves by moving in the direction of truth, goodness, and love, the One toward whom we are ultimately moving is God. God is the endpoint of our inner drive toward self-transcendence.

Rahner emphasizes that each of us must come to grips with our relationship with God in our own way. The following passage, though long and difficult, illustrates this point:

> The individual person, of course, experiences this [awareness of relation to God] best in that basic situation of his own existence which occurs with special intensity for him as an individual. If, therefore, he is really to understand this reflection on "proofs" for God's existence, the individual person must reflect precisely upon whatever is the clearest experience for him: on the luminous and incomprehensible light of his spirit; on the capacity for absolute questioning which a person directs against himself and which seemingly reduces him to nothing, but in which he reaches radically beyond himself; on annihilating anxiety, which is something quite different from fear of a definite object and is prior to the latter as the condition of its possibility; on that joy which surpasses all understanding; on an absolute moral obligation in which a person really goes beyond himself; on the experience of death in which he faces himself in his absolute powerlessness. Man reflects upon these and many other modes of the basic and transcendental experience of human existence. Because he experiences himself as finite in his self-questioning, he is not able to identify himself with the ground which discloses itself in this experience as what is innermost and at the same time what is absolutely different. The explicit proofs for God's existence only make thematic this fundamental structure and its term.[5]

In other words, each of us needs to find a way to come to grips with our own self-transcendence. When we do this, we can recognize what it means to say that in our experience of self-transcendence we become aware of a mysterious ground beyond ourselves that makes self-transcendence possible. This infinite mystery that grounds our ultimate questioning, striving, suffering, and loving, is what we mean by "God."

Rahner believes this God of infinite mystery has been unsurpassably revealed in the person of Jesus Christ and that it is most appropriate to relate to

---

5. Rahner, *Foundations of Christian Faith*, 69–70.

God as "personal." However, on the basis of the structure of our own experience, we encounter God first as the infinite mystery that calls us forth toward truth, goodness, and love.

Anonymous Theists?

Have you ever known something to be so, but in a way you could not yet put into words? Though I had never heard about it before, the first time I heard a lecture on family systems analysis, it spoke to my own experience of family so much that I realized, in a way, I had known these things all along. The inklings I had of this prior knowledge through my own experience are what Karl Rahner calls *prereflective* knowledge. The clear concepts and tools of analysis discussed in the lecture represent what Rahner calls *categorical* knowledge.

Rahner uses a similar distinction to talk about two different levels on which we "know" God. We do not simply deduce logically that God is the term of our transcendence; on a deep level of consciousness, we actually experience God in this way as the one toward whom we are drawn. According to Rahner, *transcendental* knowledge of God refers to this basic experience of God prior to any reflection or conceptualization. It is a prereflective experience of God. *Categorical* knowledge of God refers to ideas and concepts of God we can clearly think about and communicate with others.

Rahner's distinction can be helpful for understanding what he means by God. To accept God on a transcendental level is to embrace the call to respond to life's challenges in an open, willing, and loving manner. It is to be disposed to choose truth, goodness, and love over self-deceit, narrowness, and selfishness. To reject God on a transcendental level is to refuse to affirm life or to accept life's challenges for growth. It is to be closed inward upon one's own narrow world, being disposed to act most often simply in one's own selfish interests without regard for others.

To accept God on a categorical level is to have some notion or idea of God and to say, "I believe in God." To reject God on a categorical level is to say, "I do not believe in God. I am an atheist."

Here is where I find Rahner's analysis especially interesting. It is possible, as with many people, to accept God on both a transcendental and a categorical level. A good theist does this. It is also possible to reject God on both a transcendental and a categorical level. A stereotypical atheist does this.

It is also possible, however, as Rahner argues, to accept God on a transcendental level through one's commitment to truth, goodness, and love, while at the same time, rejecting one's concept of God on a categorical level. This person says, "I am an atheist." At the same time, though, this person lives life in an ongoing affirmation of the transcendent mystery that Christians call "God." In a sense, according to Rahner, such a person accepts God but without knowing it. Rahner labels such a person an "anonymous theist."

How does it happen that a person becomes an anonymous theist? Usually, it is because that person rejects the more common concepts of God that are available in their milieu. In other words, the more often inadequate concepts of God are preached and lived out by Christians, the more likely it is that basically good people will become "atheists." Anonymous theists reject not the one who God is, but their own inadequate concepts of God.

Yet Rahner's analysis does not end here. Rahner also takes the position that on a categorical level most Christians believe not in the true God of infinite mystery but in an inadequate concept of God, something of an idol. That is, most Christians have tended to settle for a nice old man or a fearsome judge rather than the infinite One who calls them forth in their deepest being. Yet Rahner also believes the majority of such people do accept God on a transcendental level; that is, they are basically good people who could do with a few major adjustments in how they think about God.

SUMMARY OF RAHNER'S ANALYSIS OF ACCEPTANCE OF GOD		
Stance	Accepts God on the transcendental level?	Accepts God on the categorical level?
Christian believer	yes	yes (God as mystery)
Stereotypical atheist	no	no
Anonymous theist	yes	no
Christians with an inadequate concept of God	yes	yes (God as idol)

A Catholic Response to Atheism

Gaudium et spes shows the influence of Karl Rahner in its approach to God and atheism. On the one hand, it presents a clear rejection of atheism:

> The church has already repudiated and cannot cease repudiating, sorrowfully but as firmly as possible, those poisonous doctrines and actions which contradict reason and the common experience of humanity, and dethrone human beings from their native excellence. (*GS* 21)

On the other hand, however, it reaches out to atheists, in an explicit acknowledgment of the profound issues raised by atheism, and an attempt to explore sympathetically the causes of atheism.

The document mentions several causes of atheism:

1. The use of philosophical methods that are locked into their own skeptical presuppositions
2. The belief that science can explain everything
3. An extravagant affirmation of human beings without leaving room for God
4. The absence of religious stirrings
5. The rejection of inadequate and false ideas about God
6. A violent protest against the existence of evil and suffering
7. Putting certain human values (e.g., nationalism, social status) in the place of God
8. Willfully shutting out God from one's heart
9. A critical reaction to certain religious beliefs and practices, sometimes against the Christian religion in particular[6]

The influence of Rahner can be seen throughout these reasons, particularly in reasons 4 and 5. In Rahnerian terms, reason 4 says many people are out of touch with their inner drives toward self-transcendence. Reason 5 says some people reject, on a categorical level, the ideas and concepts of God to which they have been exposed.

An even more important influence of Rahner can be detected in the document's discussion of reasons 8 and 9. As I read the document, it is saying that although some people who are atheists may truly know what they are doing when they reject God, it is also likely that many atheists are basically good people who have been presented with an inadequate picture of religion, particularly Christianity. The document says, "Believers themselves frequently bear some responsibility for this situation" (GS 19).

In other words, following Rahner, the document is critical of believers whose categorical concepts of God and whose lifestyles may contribute to the existence of atheism. Thus it says, "The remedy which must be applied to atheism, however, is to be sought in a proper presentation of the church's teaching as well as in the integral life of the church and her members" (GS 21).

Although it rejects atheism, "root and branch," *Gaudium et spes* says all human beings, "believers and unbelievers alike, ought to work for the rightful betterment of this world in which all alike live; such an ideal cannot be realized, however, apart from sincere and prudent dialogue" (GS 21). The comments on atheists conclude with an expressed hope for their salvation: "since Christ died for all human beings, and since the ultimate vocation of human beings is in fact one, and divine, we ought to believe that the Holy Spirit in a manner known

---

6. Adapted from *Gaudium et spes* 19.

only to God offers to every person the possibility of being associated with this paschal mystery" (*GS* 22).

Summary

This chapter investigated Vatican II's response to atheism, with special emphasis on the theology of Karl Rahner and his influence on *Gaudium et spes*.

Rahner's explanations concerning God and atheism are intriguing. His ideas on these issues have influenced me more than those of any other theologian. But his positions also have significant limitations. His focus on the experience of God through our self-transcendence can too easily be used to overlook the political realities of the concrete world. In a different vein, some critics of Rahner, such as Hans Urs von Balthasar, fear that linking God too closely with human self-transcendence obscures the unique way in which God's actual revelation through Christ shatters all prior expectations.

Yet another criticism has become especially relevant today. Rahner's position that good atheists are unwittingly good Christians does not seem to do justice to what atheists and other nonreligious people think about themselves. Throughout the past fifty years, there has emerged a new urgency to appreciate people as "other," and not simply as how they can be interpreted within one's own perspective.

Rahner himself readily admitted his approach needed to be complemented by other approaches. I am certain Rahner would find, in my dissatisfactions and in my hope for an even better explanation, a sign of my self-transcendent questioning, which will ultimately bring me face to face with the experience of infinite mystery we call "God."

The next chapter will examine the underlying principles of Catholic social teaching.

For Further Reflection

1. Have you ever been struck by how some people whose worldview radically differs from your own can appear to be especially good and moral?
2. Have you ever encountered someone who talked a lot about God or who quoted the Bible frequently but who did not seem to be a good person?
3. Do you agree with Karl Rahner that on a categorical level many people worship an "idol"?
4. Did Vatican II go too far in suggesting that some atheism may be caused by the failings of Christian believers?
5. In what ways have you grown in your life concerning how you think about God?

Suggested Readings

Craigo-Snell, Shannon. *Silence, Love, and Death: Saying "Yes" to God in the Theology of Karl Rahner.* Milwaukee: Marquette University Press, 2008.

Haught, John F. *God and the New Atheism: A Critical Response to Dawkins, Harris, and Hitchens.* Louisville: Westminster John Knox, 2008.

Lane, Dermot A. *The Experience of God: An Invitation to Do Theology.* Dublin: Veritas, 2003.

Rahner, Karl. *Foundations of Christian Faith.* Translated by William V. Dych. New York: Seabury, 1978 (1976).

Wuthnow, Robert. *The God Problem: Expressing Faith and Being Reasonable.* Berkeley and Los Angeles: University of California Press, 2012.

Underlying Principles of Catholic Social Teaching

I n her short story "Revelation,"[1] Flannery O'Connor tells of Ruby Turpin, a Southern white woman of the 1950s who has the world divided into neat rankings of people:

> Mrs. Turpin occupied herself at night naming the classes of people. On the bottom of the heap were most colored people, not the kind that she would have been if she had been one, but most of them; then next to them—not above, just away from—were the white trash; then above them were the home owners, and above them the home-and-land owners, to which she and Claud belonged. Above she and Claud were people with a lot of money and much bigger houses and much more land. But here the complexity of it would begin to bear in on her, for some of the people with a lot of money were common and ought to be below she and Claud and some of the people who had good blood had lost their money and had to rent and then there were colored people who owned their own homes and land as well.

Mrs. Turpin uses this mental diagram to convince herself of what a good person she is. O'Connor gives us this further peek into her mind:

> To help anybody out who needed it was her philosophy of life. She never spared herself when she found somebody in need, whether they were white or black, trash or decent. And of all she had to be thankful for, she was most thankful that this was so. If Jesus had said, "You can be high society and have all the money you want and be thin and svelte-like, but you can't be a good woman with it," she would have had to say, "Well don't make me that then. Make me a good woman and it don't matter what else, how fat or how ugly or how poor!" Her heart

---

1. Flannery O'Connor, *The Complete Stories* (New York: Farrar, Straus and Giroux, 1971), 488–509.

rose. He had not made her a nigger or white trash or ugly! He had made her herself and given her a little of everything. Jesus, thank you! she said.

Mrs. Turpin's rationalizations make her blissfully unaware of her own deep prejudices.

In the course of the story, Mrs. Turpin has a soul-shaking encounter with a young woman who calls her a "warthog from hell." The superstitious Mrs. Turpin takes this to be a revelation from God. At the end of the story, Mrs. Turpin has a vision of many people marching through the sky toward heaven. At the front of the line are black people and white trash. Bringing up the rear are the people like Ruby Turpin.

The story brings to mind several passages from the New Testament, such as, "The last will be first, and the first will be last" (Mt 20:16). The ranking of those who have the most dignity in the eyes of God is not likely to match the rankings most commonly assigned to and by people in our society.

Most people operate with categories of social ranking that place some types of people above others. Perhaps a few people in history, like St. Francis of Assisi, escape carrying such prejudices, but the great majority of people do not. Ruby Turpin may be less sophisticated than many of us, but for that very reason her rankings may be less insidious than our own rationalizations that assign social rankings to people.

Overview

Who ranks as an important person? What is the source of human dignity? What is it about any person that might make him or her worthy of respect? Am I worthwhile? If so, why? How do I rank in relation to other people? Am I a valuable creature in the eyes of God?

Gaudium et spes (*Pastoral Constitution on the Church in the Modern World*) addresses these questions. The responses it gives form the underlying basis of Catholic social teaching, whether in regard to family, race relations, peace, or social justice. This chapter examines the teaching of Vatican II concerning the dignity of the human person, the social nature of the human person, and the existence of one human family.

These themes are drawn from the first four chapters of *Gaudium et spes*, which make up part 1 of the two major parts of the document. These principles lay the foundation upon which the more specific teachings in part 2 are based.

The Dignity of the Human Person

My wife and I had a conversation about mutual acquaintances who were having marital difficulties. My wife mentioned that the woman, whom we will call
Sylvia, said she had no respect for her husband, because he was still making
the same amount of money he did ten years ago. When I heard that, I had
trouble maintaining respect for Sylvia. I knew that her husband, who makes
about three times as much as I do, was in a profession that was experiencing
shifts and transitions. He is an honest, intelligent, hard-working man. As I
perceived it, his wife was too interested in material trifles and in keeping up
with her rich neighbors. I wondered aloud what kind of respect Sylvia must
have for *me*.

At that point, however, I caught myself using my own categories to rank
Sylvia in a way similar to how she ranks me and her husband. In my personal
"Ruby Turpin diagram," people like her are way at the bottom, while people like
her husband and myself are near the top. Is my system of ranking morally higher
than hers? Somehow, I suspect it is not.

Gaudium et spes draws upon Genesis to teach that human beings are made
in the image and likeness of God. It quotes Psalm 8 to the effect that human
beings are made little less than the angels, crowned with glory and honor. This
teaching applies to all human beings. Our being made in the image and likeness
of God is the source of the basic dignity of each of us.

Thus the most basic source of our dignity is something that we share with
other human beings, not something that divides us or makes some of us better than others. Among our most precious qualities are our intellects, emotions,
consciences, and freedom, yet even those human beings who lack one or more of
these are recognized as being of inestimable value. Although the presence of sin
is pervasive, each human being is called to share in the divine life.

Does this mean I need to respect Sylvia and all that she says and thinks? No.
Traditionally, Christians have distinguished the sinner from the sin. I need to
respect Sylvia, but not all that she says and thinks. It means, too, that I need to
love myself, but I have to examine critically the things I say, think, and do.

This is particularly true when I catch myself losing respect for Sylvia and
ranking myself above her. What makes me worthwhile is the same thing that
makes Sylvia worthwhile. If I deny her basic dignity, I implicitly deny my own.
When I do that, I falsely value myself solely for my personal achievements and
accomplishments and attitudes, and I lose touch with the true source of my dignity through my relationship with God. When that happens, I am in the grip
of a subtle self-rejection that will continually try to cover itself with personal
achievements and glory. The great paradox here is that my ability to love and
accept myself as worthwhile is directly related to my willingness to love and
accept others.

Does this mean that I can draw none of my own dignity from personal achievements or status? I do not think so. Rather, it means the personal worth I draw from such things must remain grounded in grateful awareness of being a creature made in the image and likeness of my Creator. What is good in me ultimately comes from God. What socially recognizable "success" I may have in life does not make me fundamentally better than others. The more I am able to recognize that Sylvia is to be treasured beyond measure as one of God's creatures and that she herself is trapped by her materialistic values, the more I am able to treasure myself and realize the prejudices and traps set within my own value system.

The Social Nature of the Human Person

In Catholic social teaching, the dignity of the human person cannot be considered apart from the social nature of the human person. Catholic tradition avoids both the extreme of an individualism that denies the fundamental interconnectedness of humankind and the extreme of a collectivism that denies the importance of individual freedom.

Gaudium et spes finds the initial basis for interpersonal communion in the existence of men and women. In other words, the complementarity between two beings who are fundamentally the same and yet different provides a root meaning for human social relationships. The document names a growing interdependence as one of the characteristics of modern times; as society becomes increasingly complex, people need each other more.

As human goodness is manifested both individually and socially, so too is human sinfulness. In *Gaudium et spes* is found the beginnings of Catholic teaching about what is now termed sin embedded in social structures:

> To be sure the disturbances which so frequently occur in the social order result in part from the natural tensions of economic, political, and social forms. But at a deeper level they flow from human pride and selfishness, which contaminate even the social sphere. When the structure of affairs is flawed by the consequences of sin, human beings, already born with a bent toward evil, find there new inducements to sin, which cannot be overcome without strenuous efforts and the assistance of grace. (*GS* 25)

Catholic documents consistently teach that sin takes root in the individual human heart. Yet having acknowledged this, Catholic teaching also recognizes that the results of individual sins pervade our institutions in such a way that the institutions themselves are, in an analogous sense, "sinful" and help lead individuals to sin.

One could exemplify this point with virtually any large institution or class structure. Take, for example, the private and public educational systems in the United States. Although the United States strives to be the land of equal opportunity, the country is full of cities that have struggling inner-city schools surrounded by affluent suburbs with highly superior schools. In many cases, opportunities are not only unequal; they are not even comparable. Yet the great discrepancies in opportunity in this country are buttressed by the myth that everyone is given a fair chance and, if they do not make it, it is simply their own fault.

Of course, the issue of equal opportunity is much more complex than a brief mention of what one system or institution will allow. Catholic teaching on the social nature of the individual attempts to spell out the proper balance between social obligation and individual freedom: human persons take first place; people should acknowledge their many interdependencies and their responsibilities for each other; institutions must remain always at the service of human beings. Philosophies that place too much stress either on the need to look out for "Number 1" or on the need for individuals to be controlled by the state do not fit easily within a traditional Catholic outlook.

One Human Family

There is a real difference between the material concept of blood/legal ties and the ideal concept of one human family. And yet an important question to pose to Christians concerns the size and quality of the gap between the two. Jesus is portrayed several times in the New Testament as calling people beyond established boundaries of blood, nationality, and religion to take their place as part of the larger human family. At one point when he is teaching, he is told that his mother and brothers are outside. Jesus says, "Who are my mother and my brothers?" And looking around at those seated around him, he says, "Here are my mother and my brothers! Whoever does the will of God is my brother and sister and mother" (Mk 3:33–35).

The famous parable of the Good Samaritan (Lk 10:29–37) illustrates a similar point in regard to nationality and religion. Since the Jews and the Samaritans tended to despise each other, it would have been shocking to Jewish ears to hear Jesus speak approvingly of the Samaritan who helped his neighbor in need.

Vatican II taught clearly that human beings are members of one family, with God as their creator: "God, who has fatherly concern for everyone, has willed that all human beings should constitute one family and treat one another in a spirit of brotherhood [and sisterhood]" (GS 24). In former documents, such as Humani generis (On Human Origins), the oneness of the human family had been taught mainly as a way to illustrate the universality of original sin and the universal need for redemption in Christ. Vatican II, however, emphasized human interconnectedness and personal responsibilities toward each other.

Gaudium et spes referred to this interconnectedness of human beings as "solidarity." This term was picked up not only by the famous Polish labor union of that name, but also by a famous Pole, Pope John Paul II. John Paul explained solidarity as a recognition of interdependence, a readiness to serve others, a readiness to lose oneself, and a recognition of each other as persons. Traditionally, the highest Christian virtue has been called "charity" or "love." John Paul connected solidarity with love: "Solidarity is undoubtedly a Christian virtue. In what has been said so far it has been possible to identify many points of contact between solidarity and charity, which is the distinguishing mark of Christ's disciples."[2] For the pope to link solidarity with love and to suggest that it is an essential part of being a Christian is no small matter.

Gaudium et spes links solidarity with the concept of one human family and the belief that God saves us not just as individuals but as members of a community: "This solidarity must be constantly increased until that day on which it will be brought to perfection. Then, saved by grace, human beings will offer flawless glory to God as a family beloved of God and of Christ their Brother" (*GS* 32). This is one of several passages that suggest a link between the progress of the human family and the coming of the kingdom of God. It is balanced by other passages that emphasize the two are not the same: "Hence, while earthly progress must be carefully distinguished from the growth of Christ's Kingdom, to the extent that the former can contribute to the better ordering of human society, it is of vital concern to the Kingdom of God" (*GS* 39).

Thus, at Vatican II, the mission of the church is spelled out both as the need to proclaim the gospel of Christ and the need to work for the betterment of human society. The underlying principles are that each human being is of tremendous worth and that we are all interconnected with each other in a growing solidarity.

Students React

Once during a class discussion about how everyone is in some deep sense equal in dignity, I acknowledged that something about the concept bothered me. I wondered aloud if my hesitations have something to do with the corruptions of my own soul. I recounted how, in my early twenties, I was struck by the tremendous insight that I am not better than anybody else. That was soon followed, however, by a further insight that, as one of the few people who truly understood that I am not better than anybody else, I am just slightly better than most people.

Of course, the class laughed. Then one student said she did not think we should classify Mother Teresa as having the same degree of dignity as Adolf

---

2. Pope John Paul II, *Sollicitudo rei socialis*, 1987, 40, *http://w2.vatican.va/content/john-paul-ii/en/encyclicals/documents/hf_jp-ii_enc_30121987_sollicitudo-rei-socialis.html.*

Hitler. But another student said what made Mother Teresa so good is that she was aware of the immense dignity of every human person. I indicated that my previous point was being reinforced—because Mother Teresa realized the inherent dignity of every person, she was better than most other people.

Perhaps it would not be too hard for a philosophically minded person to make a simple distinction between "dignity" in one sense or frame of reference and "dignity" in another sense or frame of reference. But that day in class, we enjoyed the paradox without attempting to resolve it.

Idealistic Fluff?

Some people think these underlying principles are idealistic fluff. They are nice to think about, but how do they apply in the real world? Catholic social teaching rarely, if ever, gets concrete and specific. By its nature, it refers to basic attitudes and general orientations. Many documents, as well as the concluding chapters of *Gaudium et spes*, attempt to apply these principles to particular issues, but even there the air stays pretty rarified.

Pope Francis has managed to be somewhat more specific in his teachings. In *Evangelii gaudium* (*The Joy of the Gospel*), he writes,

> Just as the commandment "Thou shalt not kill" sets a clear limit in order to safeguard the value of human life, today we also have to say "thou shalt not" to an economy of exclusion and inequality. Such an economy kills. How can it be that it is not a news item when an elderly homeless person dies of exposure, but it is news when the stock market loses two points? This is a case of exclusion. Can we continue to stand by when food is thrown away while people are starving? This is a case of inequality. Today everything comes under the laws of competition and the survival of the fittest, where the powerful feed upon the powerless. As a consequence, masses of people find themselves excluded and marginalized: without work, without possibilities, without any means of escape. (no. 53)

Even this passage, however, speaks more to attitudes and orientations than to concrete solutions.

Still, attitudes and orientations are crucial, much more crucial than most people would care to admit. Within each of us lies a Ruby Turpin diagram by which we judge others and ourselves. To be asked to give it up is frightening. To accept from the start that other people, even those whom we tend to rank low, share a basic dignity equal to our own, threatens our fragile sense of self-worth. The great paradox is that when we do accept the basic dignity of all members of the human family, we find ourselves promoted to a new sense of our true worth that is not threatened by the goodness of others. When we can love others

despite their terrible sins and rationalizations, we will find it easier to love ourselves despite our own.

Summary

This chapter examined the basic principles that underlie Catholic social teaching: the dignity of the human person, the human person's social nature, and the
ideal existence of one human family.

The next chapter will discuss the first of a series of specific social/cultural
issues raised in *Gaudium et spes*: marriage and the family.

For Further Reflection

1. What various types of standards do people today use to rank each other?
2. What is it that ultimately makes a person valuable and worthwhile?
3. Can the idea of "one human family" be taken too far? Are you at one with
   the scruffy people who panhandle on the city streets?
4. What objection can be raised to focusing too much on the sinfulness of
   social systems? What objection can be raised to not focusing on such
   systems?
5. Is "solidarity" idealistic, or might it work to bring about social improvements?

Suggested Readings

Bellah, Robert, et al. *Habits of the Heart: Individualism and Commitment in American Life*. Berkeley: University of California Press, 1996 (1985).

Clark, Meghan J. *The Vision of Catholic Social Thought: The Virtue of Solidarity
and the Praxis of Human Rights*. Minneapolis: Fortress, 2014.

Massingale, Bryan N. *Racial Justice and the Catholic Church*. Maryknoll, NY:
Orbis Books, 2014.

Moltmann, Jürgen. *On Human Dignity: Political Theology and Ethics*. Translated
by M. Douglas Meeks. Minneapolis: Fortress, 2007

O'Connor, Flannery. "Revelation." In *The Complete Stories*. New York: Farrar,
Straus and Giroux, 1971.

Sobrino, Jon, and Juan Hernandez Pico. *Theology of Christian Solidarity*. Translated by Phillip Berryman. Maryknoll, NY: Orbis Books, 1985 (1983).

32

CHAPTER

Marriage and the Family

My wife and I are friends with a married couple, George and Susan, who have two daughters. George and Susan are devout Catholics. One daughter, Beth, whose wedding we attended, was married in a local parish church. She and her husband now have two small children, the elder of whom attends kindergarten in a Catholic school. George and Susan's other daughter, Ruth, will be married at a local courthouse, with her "destination" reception to be held in Mexico, where only close relatives are invited.

We had dinner recently with George and Susan. Ruth is marrying a nonreligious person. Ruth says that she is not sure what she believes when it comes to religion, but she knows she wants to marry this man, and a nonreligious ceremony is part of the deal. George told us he expressed just the slightest disappointment to Ruth but acknowledged that religious freedom was an important consideration. In this day and age, people must be free to make their own decisions. Susan, in contrast, communicated to Ruth her deep disappointment with a touch of anger. Now, after their initial reactions, George and Susan are ready to move on and offer their full support. They are helping to pay for the reception and look forward, with joy, to the event. What else, they asked, could they do? After all, it is her life.

The subject came up briefly again during dessert, although in an oblique way. George and Susan had a few things to say about how important their shared faith has been to their own marriage. Perhaps, I thought, they are not as reconciled to their daughter's nonreligious wedding as they think.

Overview

In contemporary society, the meaning of marriage and family is caught up in the culture wars. Those who oppose gay marriage are often staunch defenders of conservative ideals regarding the traditional family.[1] Some avid

---

1. See, for example, an article on the website of Focus on the Family, "SCOTUS and Gay Marriage: No Court Can Change the Truth," *http://jimdaly.focusonthefamily.com/scotus-and-gay-marriage-no-court-can-change-the-truth/*.

supporters of alternative lifestyles favor the use of "parent" versus what they consider the gender-exclusive terms of "father" and "mother," not just in government documents but in everyday speech.[2]

This chapter explores Catholic teaching on marriage and the family with an eye toward contemporary culture. The first part draws a few points from chapter 1 of part 2 of *Gaudium et spes*. The focus then shifts to Pope Francis's apostolic exhortation, *Amoris laetitia* (*The Joy of Love*).[3]

The Importance of Marriage and Family in *Gaudium et Spes*

For many theologians, the most dramatic characteristic of contemporary theology is its awareness of how deeply human culture influences religious experience and expression. Theology involves a true dialogue between religious tradition and culture. If this is the case, then why does the chapter on marriage and the family come before the chapter on culture in *Gaudium et spes*? Would it not have been more logical to begin with the deeper issue of culture and include family as one of the specific applications of how religion and culture interact?

The arrangement of chapters is no mistake, however. In the eyes of the authors of *Gaudium et spes*, marriage and family are deeper and more foundational matters than particular cultural variations. True, every culture and society has its legitimate customs and variations; the basic unit of the family, however, provides the underlying structure for healthy societies. The creation story in Genesis is interpreted as showing that the most fundamental form of companionship among human beings is that between a man and a woman who, "by their compact of conjugal love, 'are no longer two but one flesh'" (*GS* 48; Gen 2:24; Mt 19:5–6). *Gaudium et spes* adds that marriage offers the appropriate context for the raising of children as well as for the spouses to aid each other in spiritual growth.

In the novel *Brave New World* (1932), Aldous Huxley describes a future when children are conceived in test tubes and sex becomes a recreational expression of temporary intimacy.[4] Catholic social teaching is diametrically opposed to such a future. In this perspective, sexual morality is not only about personal choices that may help or hurt other individuals, it is also about what kind of world one wants to live in.

---

2. See Andrew Solomon, "Families Have Evolved. Now Language Must Too," *Guardian*, April 24, 2017, *https://www.theguardian.com/commentisfree/2017/apr/24/families-evolved-language -words-relatedness-traditional*.

3. Pope Francis, *Amoris laetitia*, 2016, *https://w2.vatican.va/content/dam/francesco/pdf/apost _exhortations/documents/papa-francesco_esortazione-ap_20160319_amoris-laetitia_en.pdf*.

4. Aldous Huxley, *Brave New World* (New York: Harper, 2006 [1932]).

Why, however, is the society described in *Brave New World* a bad idea? Could not a healthy society be structured such that institutions other than the family could care for children? Is the world necessarily a better place if most children are born to two parents who are already married to each other?

Questions like these touch on values so deep they cannot be definitively answered by rational arguments. How important to us are the concepts of mother, father, daughter, son, sister, brother? How much are we willing to shape our behaviors and commitments to support a world that is based on these relationships? It is the collective judgment of Catholic Church leaders interpreting the Christian tradition that "Christians, redeeming the present time and distinguishing eternal realities from their changing expressions, should actively promote the values of marriage and the family, both by the example of their own lives, and by cooperation with other people of good will" (*GS* 52). For such crucial judgments of values, each of us must reach into the deepest part of our beings to say why we agree or why we do not.

Marriage Is a Sacrament

The *Gaudium et spes* chapter on family contains inspiring passages on the meaning of love and sex within marriage.[5] Far from seeing sex as negative, the document says, "The actions within marriage by which the couple are united intimately and chastely are noble and worthy ones." Yet it is recognized that the love between spouses "far excels mere erotic inclination, which, selfishly pursued, soon enough fades wretchedly away" (*GS* 49).

In contrast, the love between spouses, "merging the human with the divine, leads the spouses to a free and mutual gift of themselves, a gift proving itself by gentle affection and by deed; such love pervades the whole of their lives: indeed, by its active generosity it grows better and grows greater" (*GS* 49). A great stress is placed upon the interrelationship between married love and divine love. Marriage is a sacrament because it is one of the primary means by which Christ comes to dwell in the lives of the spouses. Married love is enriched with Christ's redeeming power to act as an aid in the partners' mutual quest to live lives of holiness. Married couples "should realize that they are thereby cooperators with the love of God the Creator, and are, so to speak, the interpreters of that love" (*GS* 50).

---

5. This chapter also contains passages regarding Catholic teaching about abortion and birth control. Abortion and infanticide are called "unspeakable crimes" (*GS* 51). Catholics are told to follow present regulations concerning birth control, but that the question is under study. Paul VI reasserted the traditional Catholic ban on artificial contraception in the 1968 encyclical *Humane vitae, http://w2.vatican.va/content/paul-vi/en/encyclicals/documents/hf_p-vi_enc_25071968_humanae-vitae.html.*

Why Aren't All Families Like This?

Church documents tend to speak in the language of ideals. One problem contributing to the large number of failed marriages is that people sometimes enter into them with unrealistic expectations. Although it mentions the sacrifices that accompany married life, *Gaudium et spes* does not dwell on the difficulties that people often experience.

Few married couples spend every waking moment feeling deeply in love. Indeed, many, many married couples experience serious problems in communication. Most marriages have their ups and downs, and the downs can be pretty low.

Can the sometimes harsh realities of married life be seen as compatible with the lofty ideals of *Gaudium et spes*? I think they can. Couples who grow together in their marriages can recognize their own relationships being described through the analogies with divine love. High ideals can challenge and sustain people who grapple with the less than perfect realities of everyday life. Saint Paul said, "Now we see in a mirror, dimly, but then we will see face to face" (1 Cor 13:12)." *Gaudium et spes* tries to reveal to us the true nature of married love, even though we sometimes experience it through our dark glasses.

This isn't to overemphasize the struggles of married life; I simply want to make up somewhat for *Gaudium et spes*'s neglect of them. I also like to encourage married people to be open to marriage counseling or other therapeutic opportunities at the first signs of trouble in communicating and relating. Many families develop patterns that are today labeled "dysfunctional"; various counseling techniques and self-help groups exist for dealing with these issues. I also like to encourage married people to consider involvement with groups such as Marriage Encounter, which is designed not for "problem" marriages, but for making good marriages better. Love is bigger than all of us, but we still have to work at it.

Pope Francis and Marriage in the World of Today

In *Amoris laetitia*, Pope Francis affirms traditional Catholic teachings about marriage and the family as he struggles to address contemporary challenges and opportunities. This document stirred controversy because some bishops believe it violates traditional church teachings, particularly about the indissolubility of marriage. Francis writes as someone who clearly wants to move beyond the culture wars. That is, Francis wants to emphasize the special importance of traditional marriage between one man and one woman while at the same time expressing a welcoming and joyous attitude to families of various types. He is by no means a relativist who thinks all arrangements are objectively equal in a moral sense. He does, however, wish to lead a church that is willing to accompany, compassionately and mercifully, all people in their life journeys.

Does Francis's approach involve a contradiction in terms? I think not, but the matter is hotly debated. On the one hand, Francis explicitly privileges "the exclusive and indissoluble union between a man and a woman" as the ideal of marriage (*AL* 52). He says that Christian marriage is fully realized in the union between a man and a woman who do the following:

- Give themselves to each other in a free, faithful, and exclusive love
- Belong to each other unto death
- Are open to the transmission of life
- Are consecrated by the sacrament, which gives them the grace to become a domestic church and a leaven of new life for society

Francis uses additional theological concepts to explore the meaning of marriage. Marriage is a spousal covenant, that is, a contractual relationship of love that includes not only the couple but also God. The family is the icon of the Trinity, a unity of persons who are most intimately connected with each other.

On the other hand, Francis tries to come to terms with many of the challenges facing Christian marriage in our times. He speaks of the "need to acknowledge the great variety of family situations that can offer a certain stability" (*AL* 52). He gives special mention to single parents and the divorced and wants church communities to fully include people who find themselves in various life situations.

Francis also thinks it important to recognize the constructive elements in unions that may realize the ideal of marriage in a partial or analogous way, such as in civil marriage and even cohabitation. Francis sees these phenomena as a source of concern but tries empathetically to think through some of the social reasons or pressures inclining people in these directions. He urges that pastors engage these couples in dialogue and that respect be shown for "those signs of love which in some way reflect God's own love" (*AL* 294). He hopes, eventually, such couples might be led to embrace "the Gospel of marriage in its fullness" (*AL* 293).

Drawing upon a concept first expressed by Pope John Paul II, Francis explores the "law of gradualness" (*FC* 295),[6] a principle that recognizes different stages in a person's moral growth. John Paul II applied this principle to Catholics who were using artificial birth control methods. Rather than condemning them, he emphasized the possibility that they might gradually come to appreciate and accept the church's teaching in this area. Francis, however, is taking a step beyond John Paul II by applying the principle of gradualness to couples living in irregular situations in regard to marriage.

In no way does Pope Francis want to weaken the church's teachings, but he does think those living in irregular situations should be included in the care and accompaniment of the church. Francis thinks it is possible to respect traditional teachings while, at the same time, reaching out mercifully to those whose lives, for whatever reasons, do not conform to those rules.

---

6. Pope John Paul II, *Familiaris consortio*, 1981, 134, *http://w2.vatican.va/content/john-paul-ii/en/apost_exhortations/documents/hf_jp-ii_exh_19811122_familiaris-consortio.html.*

Those Divorced and Remarried

A controversial segment of *Amoris laetitia* addresses Catholics who have divorced and then remarried without an annulment. Traditional Catholic teaching considers such couples to be sacramentally still married to their original spouses and thus living in mortal sin.

Pope Francis takes a different approach. He thinks, in most cases, it is better to include people than to reject them. He stresses that Catholics who have remarried without annulment are not excommunicated, but rather, they remain part of the ecclesial community. To include such people should not be considered a weakening of the church's teaching on the indissolubility of marriage, but rather, a merciful expression of the church's charity.

Francis calls for the annulment process to be more accessible and streamlined. There are still cases, though, in which people may not be able to prove to a church tribunal that their first marriage was not valid at the time it took place. Francis calls upon pastors to accompany such couples in what he refers to as an "internal forum"—a process of guiding a couple in discerning the reality of their situation in the light of church teaching.

Stressing that not all cases are the same, Francis explains there are often mitigating factors that can diminish moral culpability in irregular situations. Also, people may find themselves in a situation that cannot be altered without further sin. Take, for example, a case where a remarried couple has been caring, together, for children for a length of time. Separating this couple from each other may do more harm than good. In addition, Francis argues that people's individual consciences need to be more fully incorporated into situations in which there are many concrete factors that do not easily correspond with a general rule or law. Such discernment must be done humbly, with respect for church teaching and a sincere search for the will of God. Francis teaches, "It can no longer be said that all those in any 'irregular' situation are living in a state of mortal sin and are deprived of sanctifying grace."

Francis has thereby empowered pastors to admit to the Eucharist Catholics who have divorced and remarried without an annulment but who can discern in an internal forum that they are doing their best under the circumstances to live in accordance with the will of God. Still, he emphasizes, "In order to avoid all misunderstandings, I would point out that in no way must the Church desist from proposing the full ideal of marriage" (*AL* 307). Francis thinks he is changing, not church teaching about the indissolubility of marriage, but rather pastoral practices concerning people whose complex life choices may have fallen short of the ideal but who still need to be fully included in a community that manifests the merciful love of God. Francis often points out that everyone, including himself, in some ways falls short of the ideal and stands in need of God's mercy.[7]

---

7. Pope Francis, *The Name of God Is Mercy*, trans. Oonagh Stansky (New York: Random House), 2016.

LGBTQ+ Relationships

It can be difficult to address LGBTQ+ unions or marriages in today's world, because the issue is culturally divisive. Plenty of people are absolutely and passionately convinced of their position and have disdain for the other side.

Yet there are few people today who do not have close relatives and friends who are openly gay. The broad consensus of medical science is that sexual orientation is simply a fact, not a disease. In many modern countries, including the United States, gay and lesbian marriages have become acceptable and legal. Many consider this development to be a matter of basic human rights.

Young people might today find it hard to grasp or imagine how rapid has been the cultural revolution that, in a few decades, has resulted in an about-face for most people on LGBTQ+ rights. At the time of Vatican II, only a small minority would have had anything positive to say on the matter. Outlooks and language that had been widespread then would today be considered rank prejudice by most. Scientific data and popular media have helped radically change attitudes and opinions. According to the Pew Research Institute, even as late as 2001, 57 percent of US adults opposed gay marriage. By 2017, 62 percent approved, with positive responses being much higher among younger adults.[8]

Official Catholic teaching holds homosexual activity to be sinful. Deep in Catholic tradition is the assumption that marriage and sex are integrally connected with the natural generation of children. Sexual activity without openness to children is thought to lack essential elements of meaning. A marriage between a man and a woman who are infertile is considered legitimate, because they do not intentionally obstruct conception and otherwise their sexual activity is analogous to that of fertile couples. Marriages in which one of the people is sexually impotent are not considered legitimate. Traditionally, a marriage has not been legally binding until it has been sexually consummated through heterosexual intercourse.

Still, Catholic pastoral approaches to homosexuality have undergone some significant shifts throughout the years. In a 1985 document, the Congregation for the Doctrine of the Faith recognized a distinction between homosexual orientation and homosexual activity, saying that the former in itself is not sinful.[9] The overall approach of that document suggested that even if homosexual activity is sinful, Catholics still need to love their brothers and sisters no matter what their orientation. More recent documents from the US bishops have reordered

8. Pew Research Center, "Changing Attitudes on Gay Marriage," June 26, 2017, *http://www .pewforum.org/fact-sheet/changing-attitudes-on-gay-marriage/*.

9. Congregation for the Doctrine of the Faith, "Letter to the Bishops of the Catholic Church on the Pastoral Care of Homosexual Persons," October 1, 1986, *http://www.vatican.va/roman_curia /congregations/cfaith/documents/rc_con_cfaith_doc_19861001_homosexual-persons_en.html*.

the emphasis: we all need to love each other; some of those among us have a homosexual orientation.[10]

In *Amoris laetitia*, Pope Francis says that same-sex unions may not be equated with marriage, because they are closed to the transmission of life. He also says, though, that the boundless love of Christ must be offered to all people without exception. When once asked about gay priests, he famously responded, "Who am I to judge?" During his 2015 trip to the United States, Pope Francis met with Kim Davis, a Kentucky state clerk who had violated the law by refusing to issue state marriage licenses to gay couples. Later, however, the Vatican qualified that the meeting had been set up by the office of the Vatican's ambassador to the United States, not by the Vatican itself, and that the pope had no intention of endorsing her position in all of its complexities and particularities. Not long before that, Francis had a scheduled audience with a former student of his, along with the student's gay partner. His student said, "I don't think he was trying to say anything in particular. He was just meeting with his ex-student and a very close friend of his."[11]

A rainbow flag at this parish in San Diego indicates a welcoming attitude toward LGBTQ+ persons. Conservative Catholics fear that such openness detracts from the Catholic Church's traditional emphasis on heterosexual marriage and the family.

A student in my class recently asked about church teaching in regard to attending LGBTQ+ weddings and other events. The Catholic Church does not

10. US Conference of Catholic Bishops, "Ministry to Persons with a Homosexual Inclination: Guidelines for Pastoral Care," 2006, *http://www.usccb.org/about/doctrine/publications/homosexual -inclination-guidelines-page-set.cfm*, and "Always Our Children: A Pastoral Message to Parents of Homosexual Children and Suggestions for Pastoral Ministers," 1997, *http://www.usccb.org/issues -and-action/human-life-and-dignity/homosexuality/always-our-children.cfm*.

11. Jim Yardley and Laurie Goodstein, "Before Pope Francis Met Kim Davis, He Met with Gay Ex-Student," *New York Times*, October 2, 2015, *https://www.nytimes.com/2015/10/03/world/europe /pope-francis-kim-davis-meeting.html?rref=collection%2Fnewseventcollection%2Fpope-francis-us-vis it&action=click&contentCollection=us&region=stream&module=stream_unit&version=latest&content Placement=1&pgtype=collection&_r=0.*

have an explicit teaching on this subject, but leaves the decision to the prudential judgment of each Catholic. Some Catholic bishops forbid their priests and deacons to attend such ceremonies and otherwise urge lay Catholics to choose not to do so.[12] In 2017, US Cardinal Joseph Tobin made news by officially welcoming lesbian, gay, bisexual, and transgender Catholics to Mass at his cathedral in Newark, New Jersey. He said, "I am Joseph, your brother. I am your brother, as a disciple of Jesus. I am your brother, as a sinner who finds mercy with the Lord."[13]

Cardinal Tobin is known as a "Francis bishop," an informal term for a bishop appointed by Francis who appears to operate with a similar style. I am not exactly sure what Pope Francis would advise about gay weddings, but I am inclined to think he might encourage attendance—while being clear that Catholics should support the full ideal of marriage—and then add that you should invite the couple to dinner soon.

Summary

This chapter discussed the importance of marriage and the family in *Gaudium et spes* as well as Pope Francis's attempts to move beyond the culture wars. Remember my friends, George and Susan; I believe Francis would share the concerns they had about their daughter's nonreligious wedding. Still, he would urge them to continue trying to understand and support them.

The next chapter will examine the church's position on the relationship between faith and culture.

For Further Reflection

1. Is it possible to emphasize the importance of traditional marriage as between one man and one woman open to having children and, at the same time, be radically open to accepting various types of families? Must one of these concepts die if the other is to live?

2. Are marriage and the family worth saving? Would the society of *Brave New World*, which lacks these institutions, be just as good as the society that has them?

---

12. "A Comprehensive Look at Catholic Bishops' Reactions to Gay 'Marriage' Ruling," *LifeSiteNews*, July 15, 2014, *https://www.lifesitenews.com/news/a-comprehensive-look-at-catholic-bishops-reactions-to-gay-marriage-ruling*.

13. Sharon Otterman, "As Church Shifts, a Cardinal Welcomes Gays; They Embrace a 'Miracle,'" *New York Times*, June 13, 2017, *https://www.nytimes.com/2017/06/13/nyregion/catholic-church-gays-mass-newark-cathedral.html?_r=0*.

3. Should one's vision of the ideal society influence one's personal sexual morality, or should sexual behavior be a matter of individual choice?

4. Is Pope Francis right in opening up the possibility that, in some cases, Catholics who have remarried without an annulment might be admitted back to receive the Eucharist?

5. Are there positions concerning traditional marriage and gay marriage that move beyond the polar opposition of the culture wars?

Suggested Readings

Cahill, Lisa Sowle. *Family: A Christian Social Perspective.* Minneapolis: Fortress, 2000.

Farley, Margaret A. *Just Love: A Framework for Christian Sexual Ethics.* New York: Continuum, 2006.

Francis, Pope. *Amoris laetitia (The Joy of Love).* 2016. *https://w2.vatican.va/content/dam/francesco/pdf/apost_exhortations/documents/papa-francesco_esortazione-ap_20160319_amoris-laetitia_en.pdf.*

Gaillardetz, Richard R. *A Daring Promise: A Spirituality of Christian Marriage.* Liguori, MO: Liguori/Triumph, 2007.

Martin, James. *Building a Bridge: How the Catholic Church and the LGBT Community Can Enter into a Relationship of Respect, Compassion, and Sensitivity.* San Francisco: HarperCollins, 2017.

Rubio, Julie Hanlon. *Hope for Common Ground: Mediating the Personal and the Political in a Divided Church.* Washington, DC: Georgetown University Press, 2016.

Culture

E mily was a student of mine in a course that addressed issues of faith and culture. She wrote a paper about a Catholic religious sister from Africa who was raised in a polygynous family. In such a family, there is one husband who has many wives. *Polygyny* is a descriptive term from cultural anthropology. Emily uses the somewhat negative word, *polygamy*, a legal term which refers to either a man or a woman having many spouses. Emily said of the sister,

> She came from a very large polygamous family and was grateful for it. Her biological mother did actually live with her father and the nun was very close to her. She explained that her family relationship was like the sun. Her natural mother was like the sun who shone on all her children just like our sun shines on all the earth. Although her mother, the sun, loved all the children and shone over all of them, the nun's relationship to her mother was special, like the sun shining at a strong angle. In a sense, this is like our relationship with God. We are all special and unique in his eyes.

Emily had strong but ambiguous feelings about this arrangement:

> At first I was shocked at this nun for being Catholic and advocating this lifestyle. But, I do realize that no matter how much she was influenced by being in the United States, she was still rooted in her culture. Where she comes from, polygyny, strange as it may seem, does have value. I would not know how to draw the line on the church's position on culture.

Overview

Emily's ambivalence reflects a personal wrestling with what has been one of the most important issues in theology during the past one hundred years: the relationship between faith and culture. This is not only an issue in Africa; it is an issue everywhere, including in the United States. How can the gospel interact with the various social systems, beliefs, values, and behaviors ingrained within any particular cultural setting?

The relationship between Christian tradition and US culture has arisen in several places in this text. This chapter focuses on Christianity in Africa to highlight some of the points of tension between the Christianity of missionaries from European cultures and the cultures of the people in Africa whom they evangelized. It then examines the treatment of faith and culture at Vatican II and in contemporary discussion. This material is related to chapter 2 in part 2 of *Gaudium et spes*.

Polygyny in Africa

Emily makes an important point when she indicates that polygyny has meaning and value within African culture. It is, however, not simply a matter of a meaningful relationship between a particular daughter and her mother; polygyny is part of the fabric of the social structure in many traditional societies.

A priest who once visited my parish, Father John, a Nigerian of the Igbo tribe, shared with me personal insights on the topic of polygyny. Father John was born to Christian, monogamous parents. His father, however, was the first son of his grandfather's fifth wife. Father John has many relatives within his extended family. He says that, at times, he does not know whether to call them cousins or half-brothers; there are often no strict English equivalents to describe the relationships.

Father John told me that soon after he was ordained, he received a visit from one of his "cousins." The cousin told Father John that he now wanted to become a Christian. Father John said, "You know that you cannot do that. You have two wives." The cousin said, "Yes, but now that you are a priest you can fix things up." Father John explained to him that although he was now a priest he did not control the rules of the Catholic Church. It was different from their traditional arrangements, where the holy man had the power to "fix things."

I asked Father John if he wished he could change the rules and baptize his cousin. He laughed at first and evaded the question. Upon being pressed, however, Father John insisted I realize that, as a Catholic priest, he supports the policies of the church on this matter. He would not advocate among his people that polygyny be recognized as acceptable among Christians. He said, though, since we were two scholars talking with each other, he would share his personal opinion. He emphasized that he does not consider his personal opinion to be on the same level as the official teaching of the church.

Father John distinguished between two levels of culture: Capital "C" Culture, which includes things that are universally human and thus apply to all people, and small "c" culture, which refers to things that are specific to particular peoples. He thinks monogamous marriage is ultimately better and should be acknowledged as belonging to Culture. Ideally, he believes, societies should at least move in the direction of recognizing monogamy has worthwhile advantages, especially regarding the dignity of the woman. Problems of jealousy and domination often arise among the wives in a polygynous marriage, although he was quick to add such is not always the case.

Concerning polygynous marriage, though, Father John expressed his personal opinion with great passion. He referred to Jesus' teaching against divorce and suggested Jesus would not approve of wives being cast aside. He spoke of the many wives of Abraham and of Solomon, and declared, "God spoke to them! God did not turn away because they had many wives!" Father John said the Lord would not reject people on account of such a small thing as being rooted in a polygynous culture, nor would he force a man to divorce his wives, or wives to leave their husband.

In other words, Father John's opinion (which is similar to that of several other African Christian theologians), is that whereas those who are already baptized should remain monogamous, those who are already polygynous should be allowed to remain so and still be baptized.

Throughout Africa, many African traditional religions as well as independent Christian sects accept the customary ways of life, including polygyny. In recent years, some Christian denominations, such as the Anglican and some Lutheran churches, adopted the policy Father John recommended—of baptizing those who are already in polygynous marriages, while rejecting future polygynous marriages for those already baptized. The Catholic Church will not officially baptize those involved in polygynous marriages, but the cultural tensions remain. For example, Catholic theologian Stephen Annan, a priest of Ghana, writes of the urgent need for the Catholic Church to make changes to overcome the harsh social and ecclesial effects of sacramental exclusion.[1]

Aspects of African Culture

Although Christian missionaries in Africa in the nineteenth and early twentieth centuries came from various countries and represented many denominations, most shared a common belief concerning how Christianity should relate to African culture. They thought the European culture in which Christianity was rooted should replace African culture, which they perceived to be primitive and often barbarous. This is not to say there were not some exceptional missionaries more sensitive to African culture; as a rule, however, Christian preaching and education were directed toward replacing traditional beliefs and customs.

Christian missionaries in Africa were not without reasons for wanting to make serious changes in traditional African practices. Although the tremendous variety of tribes and customs makes generalization difficult, some practices

---

1. Stephen Annan, "Rethinking the Sacrament of Reconciliation/Healing in the Light of Post-Modern Thought," In *Ecclesiology and Exclusion: Boundaries of Being and Belonging in Postmodern Times*, ed. Dennis M. Doyle et al. (Maryknoll, NY: Orbis Books, 2012), 279–91.

common to many peoples were repulsive to those with European values. For example, in many African tribes, twins were considered an abomination and were killed at birth. This practice has virtually vanished from Africa today. Another custom found repulsive was female genital mutilation, which is still practiced in some places in Africa.

The belief in spirits and magic is another dimension of traditional African life. This style of religion, known as *animism*, finds the presence of spirits throughout nature and the cosmos. These spirits must be appeased and sometimes manipulated for protection or to bring about desired results. Especially important are the spirits of ancestors who bring blessings when pleased but who cause famine, illness, and death when angered. Some tribes believe death is always the result of punishment by an ancestor. Also common is a belief in reincarnation. Children are told, at an early age, of whose spirit they are a reincarnation; they then develop their talents in accordance with what was known of that ancestor. Of course, the process of discerning whose spirit they contain involves an assessment of the child's talents and temperament.

These elements of African societies were unacceptable to Christian missionaries. A problem arose, however, in that the missionaries often tried to do away with elements of the culture, both positive and negative. They did not tend to think of European culture as just one culture among others; they thought of it as the high point of human civilization, as something that could be imposed on others without guilt or apology. At the same time, however, missionaries often failed to condemn European practices of war, exploitation, and slavery on the African continent.

Another View of African Culture

The early twenty-first century is marked by a heightened awareness of cultural pluralism. Educated people are no longer likely to consider their own culture as offering a "one-size-fits-all" manner of living. It is almost universally recognized that various constellations of meanings and values can constitute humanly acceptable ways for people to live their lives.

With these new attitudes come significant attempts to appreciate the positive dimensions of African cultures. Africans are deeply spiritual people. Long before the coming of Christian missionaries, their lives were filled with stories, rituals, art, songs, and proverbs. Their traditions regarding the extended family were and remain full of meaning and warm affection. Africans speak of the church as the "family of God."[2] African practices regarding ancestors lay the

---

2. John Paul II used this African phrase eight times in his apostolic exhortation, *Ecclesia in Africa*, 1995, http://w2.vatican.va/content/john-paul-ii/en/apost_exhortations/documents/hf_jp-ii_exh_14091995_ecclesia-in-africa.html.

Missionaries to Africa in the nineteenth and early twentieth centuries tended to conflate European culture with the gospel. In contrast, this depiction of Jesus, from Kalacha, Kenya, places Christianity in an African cultural setting.

groundwork for deep experiential connections with the Christian belief in the Communion of Saints.[3]

The Shift at Vatican II

The chapter on culture in *Gaudium et spes* represents a shift in official Catholic thinking to an embrace of cultural pluralism. The gospel is still given priority over any particular culture, but unlike in the past, the meaning of the gospel can be distinguished from the particular cultures with which it has been associated historically. In other words, the Christian faith can and must be distinguished from European culture and Western civilization. Various cultures are recognized as legitimate and necessary dialogue partners.

The document distinguishes between a general sense of "culture" that refers to basic human capacities for producing social ways of living, and a more specific sense of "culture" that refers to diverse lifestyles, values, and customs. This is the same distinction Father John referred to as capital "C" culture and small "c" culture. It is in this second sense of "culture" that the document speaks of a "plurality of cultures" (*GS* 53). This distinction is important in the context of traditional Catholic theology, because it recognizes a level of being human in which all people share and to which the gospel must speak. That is, there are certain things common to all human beings; any presentation of the gospel should keep this in mind.

---

3. Agbonkhianmeghe E. Orobator, *Theology Brewed in an African Pot* (Maryknoll, NY: Orbis Books, 2008). See also Thomas Ochieng Otanga, *Luo Ancestor Veneration and the Christian Doctrine of the Communion of Saints: Toward the Development of an African Christian Theology of Ancestors* (PhD diss., Catholic University of America, 2013).

The distinction between different meanings of "culture" is also crucial to contemporary Catholic theology, however, because of the clear way in which it recognizes cultural pluralism as legitimate. Catholic theology expresses explicit concern for the preservation of the heritage of various peoples: *Gaudium et spes* thus wishes to protect particular cultures from being swallowed up as the new global community emerges. The document speaks hopefully of "a new age of human history" in which human beings have opportunities for building a more just world on a global scale (*GS* 54). It attests to "the birth of a new humanism, one in which human beings are defined first of all by their responsibilities to their brothers [and sisters] and to history" (*GS* 55).

Gaudium et spes also cites the tremendous potential of science and technology in contributing to human progress. At the same time, however, while acknowledging the positive values of contemporary culture, the document points to the danger of taking either human science or human beings as self-sufficient and thereby "no longer seek the higher things" (*GS* 57). The positive values of culture, while accepted as good in themselves, are also seen as providing "some preparation for the acceptance of the message of the gospel" (*GS* 57). Although it is recognized that the Word of God is, to some extent, already present in the culture, the church is put forth as making a crucial contribution.

Some scholars argue that although Vatican II's approach to faith and culture represents welcome growth, it does not go far enough. British missionary theologian Aylward Shorter contends that rather than simply planting the seeds of the gospel in foreign soil, more attention should be given to the seeds of the gospel that already exist within a given culture. It is better to begin with a culture and then integrate Christianity within it rather than vice versa.[4] US scholar Robert Schreiter has developed an elaborate flow chart to capture the complexities of relating faith to culture.[5] He calls his theory the "contextual model," because it looks first to the cultural context within which Christianity must be integrated. Both of these scholars are more radically accepting of established traditional customs than is the current policy of the church.

Globalization and US Culture[6]

The spiritual openness to transcendent meaning on the part of African cultures (and traditional cultures throughout the world) contrasts with a relative lack of openness in the modern, technocratic culture of the United States and many European countries. Commentators are divided in their assessments of the dominant culture of the United States. Many routinely speak of consumerism,

---

4. See Aylward Shorter, *Toward a Theology of Inculturation* (Maryknoll, NY: Orbis Books, 1988).

5. Robert J. Schreiter, *Constructing Local Theologies* (Maryknoll, NY: Orbis Books, 1985), 25.

6. This subsection builds upon Dennis M. Doyle, "The Concept of Inculturation in US Catholicism: A Theological Consideration," *US Catholic Historian* (2012): 1–13.

materialism, rationalism, and extreme individualism, whereas others extol glories with few criticisms. There is general agreement, though, that US culture plays a dominant role on the world scene.

Hispanic theologian Roberto Goizueta analyzes the dominant culture of the United States in terms of an individualism he breaks down into three categories: economic, political, and religious. In contrast, US Hispanic culture fosters an experience of the human person as more basically relational and inter-connected. Hispanics in the United States find themselves living "in-between" the dominant culture and their more traditional one.[7]

Various peoples throughout the world are influenced by American culture but manage to live, as Goizueta calls it, "in-between." Schreiter speaks of the phenomenon of "glocalization" by which local peoples, strongly affected by US culture, nevertheless forge a distinctively local way of life that remains, in many ways, connected with their traditions.[8] A phenomenon emerges that cannot be understood adequately by focusing on either its global or local elements alone.

Globalization and the proliferation of social media raise the question as to how long there will be distinct traditional cultures into which the gospel can be incar-nated, or even whether such cultures still exist. Though cultural diversity remains, there are more and more varieties of "glocalized" or hybrid communities rather than traditional cultures. Some of these communities, such as virtual societies existing only on the internet, transcend geographical space. Yet almost all contemporary communities are deeply influenced by a dominant world culture, even if only by their opposition to it. If the dominant world culture is commercial and technocratic, tending toward a marginalization of cultural elements open to the transcendent, then evangelization and inculturation face huge challenges in the time to come.

Summary

This chapter explored the shift in attitude toward culture at Vatican II, viewed against the background of the relationship between Christianity and African traditions, as well as the phenomenon of globalization.

Relating gospel and culture remains challenging. On the one hand, many elements of US culture, from widespread addiction to out-of-wedlock pregnancy to the high divorce rate to pervasive materialism and consumerism, could stand some correction by the message of the gospel. On the other hand, some ele-ments, such as our stress on tolerance, freedom, innovation, and participation, might contribute in a positive way to the ongoing struggle to live out the mes-sage of the gospel today.

---

7. Roberto A. Goizueta, *Caminemos con Jesús: Toward a Hispanic/Latino Theology of Accompani-ment* (Maryknoll, NY: Orbis Books, 1995).

8. Robert J. Schreiter, *The New Catholicity: Theology between the Global and the Local* (Maryknoll, NY: Orbis Books, 1997), 12.

The next chapter will discuss the teaching of Vatican II concerning economic justice.

For Further Reflection

1. Do you think Father John's polygynous "cousin" should be permitted to be baptized?
2. Does the teaching of Vatican II go far enough in promoting respect for various cultures? If not, how should the Catholic Church strengthen its approach?
3. Can concerns for "cultural pluralism" be taken too far?
4. What negative elements of US culture need to be addressed by the gospel message? What elements of US culture could make a positive contribution to the Catholic Church?
5. Are the overall effects of globalization more positive or more negative in today's world?

Suggested Readings

Burke, Joan F. *These Catholic Sisters Are All Mamas! Towards the Inculturation of the Sisterhood in Africa: An Ethnographic Study*. Leiden: Brill, 2001.

Gaillardetz, Richard R. *Ecclesiology for a Global Church: A People Called and Sent*. Maryknoll, NY: Orbis Books, 2008.

Irarrázaval, Diego. *Inculturation: New Dawn of the Church in Latin America*. Translated by Phillip Berryman. Maryknoll, NY: Orbis Books, 2000.

Matovino, Timothy. *Latino Catholicism: Transformation in America's Largest Church*. Princeton: Princeton University Press, 2012.

Miller, Vincent J. *Consuming Religion: Christian Faith and Practice in a Consumer Culture*. New York: Bloomsbury, 2013 (2003).

Orji, Cyril. *Ethnic and Religious Conflict in Africa: An Analysis of Bias, Decline, and Conversion Based on the Works of Bernard Lonergan*. Milwaukee: Marquette University Press, 2008.

Schreiter, Robert J. *The New Catholicity: Theology between the Global and the Local*. Maryknoll, NY: Orbis Books, 1997.

Shorter, Aylward. *Toward a Theology of Inculturation*. Eugene, OR: Wipf and Stock, 2006 (1988).

Economics

We live in divided times.

I have an acquaintance, Joe, who rolls his eyes when he hears the phrase "economic justice." He thinks of it as a misleading label for a plot to take wealth away from hard-working citizens and give it to the lazy. He associates the word *taxes* with stealing. He calls all forms of social support "entitlements." He backs politicians who say they want to blow up the government (metaphorically, I hope).

I have another acquaintance, Sam, who assures me virtually all people want to work if you can offer them a job with a decent salary and benefits. He feels the real problem is the system is rigged to favor those at the top. What we really need is higher taxes on big corporations and the wealthy along with a major expansion of social, medical, and educational benefits.

Joe tells anecdotes about the people who cheat the system. Sam tells anecdotes about corporate corruption. As far as I see it, Joe and Sam have two things in common. First, they both tend to ramble on without pausing much for responses. Second, both would be challenged by Catholic social teaching (CST), if they cared to learn about it.

Overview

CST does not offer a clear program between capitalism and socialism. It does, though, criticize extreme positions on either side. More importantly, it offers basic principles that can guide Christians as they work for an ever more just structuring of society.

Chapter 3 in part 2 of *Gaudium et spes* (*Pastoral Constitution on the Church in the Modern World*) deals with economic and social issues. This chapter of this text examines nine basic principles for economic justice and then discusses the meaning of success and the place of material goods in the Christian lifestyle.

Principles for Economic Justice

Gaudium et spes articulates many principles that lie at the heart of Catholic teaching concerning economic justice. What follows is my summary of these principles.

1. *Neither pure socialism nor pure capitalism is a morally acceptable alternative.* In line with the larger tradition of CST, *Gaudium et spes* rejects both the extreme that says government control will create justice and the extreme that claims the free market will create justice. CST calls for government to play a significant role in forming a just society, and yet to be only one factor among others: "Growth is not to be left solely to a kind of mechanical course of economic activity of individuals, nor to the authority of government" (*GS* 65). Either system, taken to an extreme, will necessarily lead to gross injustices, according to CST. Although CST does not propose an alternative system, a workable solution should land somewhere between the two extremes. Contemporary Catholic teaching has found market systems to be acceptable starting points if implemented within a higher social vision.

2. *Human beings are the end of social and economic life.* Labor is not just another factor for figuring out spreadsheet calculations. Labor is performed by people, and people are ultimately served by institutions, not vice versa. People are not to be treated like numbers or cogs in a machine. Profit is important, but human beings must also be taken into account when making economic decisions. Investments should be directed toward providing employment and other social goods. Economic development is good insofar as it serves human beings.

3. *Current gaps between rich classes and poor classes and between rich countries and poor countries are too great.* CST does not oppose the existence of classes whatsoever; rather, it calls for harmony and cooperation among them. Increasing inequality, however, is a matter for concern. The document points out that although economic growth could potentially mitigate social inequalities, instead "extravagance and wretchedness exist side by side" (*GS* 63). It calls for "strenuous efforts . . . to remove as quickly as possible the immense economic inequalities, which now exist and in many cases are growing and which are connected with individual and social discrimination" (*GS* 66).

4. *Economic development should follow the principle of subsidiarity.* Subsidiarity recognizes there are various layers and types of social groupings and stands as a challenge to Western social contract theories that imagine society strictly in terms of the relationship between individuals and a larger society. In CST, there exists before society not only individuals but also social

Healthy foods such as fresh fruits and vegetables are readily available in affluent neighborhoods but nowhere to be found in many poor neighborhoods. Such "food deserts" are emblematic of the growing gap between rich and poor in the United States.

groups such as families, clans, tribes, neighborhoods, and various forms of community. Individuals have rights, but so also do families.

Laws and policies that automatically favor individual rights over community rights stand in tension with Catholic tradition. A community can have the right, for example, to ban so-called adult entertainment facilities or at least to limit them to select areas. Decision-making should be done on the most local level possible and include participation of the people most directly involved. International decisions should include all nations involved. National decisions should include all localities involved. Community problems should be addressed at the level of the community. Neighborhood problems are often best solved within the neighborhood. One should not make a federal case out of local issues. Workers, too, should participate as much as possible in the administration and profit-sharing of the enterprises where they are employed.

5. *Employment is the most important factor in considerations of economic justice.* Work is the means by which people support themselves and their families, contribute to society, and express their identities. Through work, people "unfold their own abilities and personality" (*GS* 71). Workers have the right to form unions; at the same time, workers have a duty to contribute to the best of their ability. Jobs should provide sufficient wages, as well as time for rest and leisure.

6. *Ownership is a legitimate right but not an absolute right.* The goods of the earth are intended for the use of all. Goods should be available in an equitable manner. People should regard their possessions not only as their own but also "as common in the sense that they should be able to benefit not only the owner but also others as well" (*GS* 69). People who have more than they need have a duty to provide for the relief of the poor, "and to do so not merely out of their superfluous goods" (*GS* 69). All are called to share their earthly goods.

7. *Christians should grow beyond materialism and consumerism to embrace lifestyles of creative simplicity. Gaudium et spes* laments that "many people, especially in economically advanced areas, seem, as it were, to be ruled by economics, so that almost their entire personal life is permeated with a certain economic way of thinking" (*GS* 63). Simultaneously, "the greater part of the world is still suffering from so much poverty that it is as if Christ Himself were crying out in these poor to beg the charity of the disciples."

   In the encyclical *Sollicitudo rei socialis* (*On Social Concern*), 1987, John Paul II asked Christians to distinguish between "being" and "having." Who we are is prior to and more important than what we own. John Paul writes, "This then is the picture: There are some people—the few who possess much—who do not really succeed in 'being' because, through a reversal of the hierarchy of values, they are hindered by the cult of 'having'; and there are others—the many who have little or nothing—who do not succeed in realizing their basic human vocation because they are deprived of essential goods" (*SRS* 28). Christians are called to value people more than things by loving their neighbors as themselves and being willing to alter their lifestyles accordingly.

   Gaudium et spes does not use the precise phrase "preferential option for the poor," but this concept, which runs throughout CST, is strongly present in the document. Christians should strive to see reality through the eyes of the poor, accompany the poor, and make economic and political decisions with the poor in mind. The option for the poor is not to be understood as choosing poor people as more worthy than rich people but rather as recognizing that the poor are fully members of the human family, and it is in everyone's interest to have a special concern for their needs.

8. *Attempts to transform social structures should be rooted in conversion of heart.* *Gaudium et spes* calls Christians to live the spirit of the Beatitudes, particularly the spirit of poverty. If we first seek the kingdom of God, we will be moved to perform "the work of justice under the inspiration of charity" (*GS* 72). Working for justice purely out of a sense of outrage and self-righteousness is a dead end. We all have our own poverties and shortcomings; we are always to retain our humility and the awareness of our own need for God as we work to bring about needed change.

9. *Christians must be convinced they can make a contribution to the improvement of economic and social conditions.* Catholics are not utopian dreamers who think the kingdom of God will necessarily be here in its fullness overnight. Yet Catholics are called to maintain a realistic hope that true progress can be made when human beings work together in divine hope. No one is asked to do it alone or carry the weight of the world on one's shoulders. We are asked simply to strive to do what we can in accordance with our station and capacities in life.

Centesimus Annus

In his encyclical *Centesimus annus* (*On the Hundredth Anniversary of Rerum novarum*), published in 1991, just two years after the fall of the Soviet bloc, John Paul II continued to reject "capitalism" when understood as an extreme form of laissez-faire economics. He goes on to say, however, that capitalism is an appropriate model for developing countries to follow today, "if by 'capitalism' is meant an economic system which recognizes the fundamental and positive role of business, the market, private property and the resulting responsibility for the means of production, as well as free human creativity in the economic sector" (*CA* 42). In addition to a market, John Paul II emphasizes the need for three critically important things: First, government must play a significant role. Second, various forms of community, such as families, unions, and various social and political groups, must contribute. Finally, any approach to economics can work only if it is implemented within a culture of solidarity, also called a culture of love.

It is important to understand that John Paul II is not offering a blanket endorsement of capitalist ideology. In fact, he explicitly warns against interpreting his words in that way. Many claim John Paul II played a significant role in bringing down the Soviet bloc. Yet he himself warns against the temptation to say that everything associated with socialism is bad and everything associated with capitalism is good. He writes,

> The Marxist solution has failed, but the realities of marginalization and exploitation remain in the world, especially the Third World, as does the reality of human alienation, especially in the more advanced countries. Against these phenomena the Church strongly raises her voice. Vast multitudes are still living in conditions of great material and moral poverty. The collapse of the Communist system in so many countries certainly removes an obstacle to facing these problems in an appropriate and realistic way, but it is not enough to bring about their solution. Indeed, there is a risk in that a radical capitalist ideology could spread which refuses even to consider these problems, in the *a priori* belief that any attempt to solve them is doomed to failure, and which blindly entrusts their solution to the free development of market forces. (*CA* 42)

The Successful Life

Most of my students find Catholic teaching on economic justice to be inspiring and refreshing. A few students in most classes, however, are put off by this teaching. Some are disturbed because their core values have been challenged. They have placed material concerns at the forefront of their lives, and are either not ready or not willing to consider major changes. I can only hope that someday they will realize that materialistic values give them no real advantages but simply hold them back from living their lives to the fullest.

Note that I say "materialistic values" and not "material values." There is nothing wrong with valuing material things as long as such values are placed below one's relationships with other human beings. There is nothing wrong with making a living, even a very good living. One should remain aware, however, of injustices in a social system that often denies interdependencies by promoting the myth that "successful" people make it all on their own and owe nothing to anyone.

For what is the meaning of "success"? If we could travel ahead to the moment of our death and look back at the life we lived, what would constitute a "successful" life?

The Russian novelist Leo Tolstoy tells the story of Ivan Illich, a judge who lived a selfish and corrupt life. Throughout his life, his only real concerns were for his personal wealth and social status. He would even make decisions as a judge based on his own political advantage. When Ivan Illich is on his deathbed, however, he is able to look back at his life and realize that the wealth and status he valued were worth nothing. He then sees that things he had considered trivial, such as kindness and mercy to other human beings, were what he should have valued all along.

Gaudium et spes makes a point similar to that of Tolstoy by recalling a scriptural injunction: "Not everyone who cries, 'Lord, Lord,' will enter into the kingdom of heaven, but those who do the Father's will by taking a strong grip on the work at hand. Now the Father wills that in all human beings we recognize Christ our brother and love Him effectively, in word and in deed" (*GS* 93).

In other words, without discounting the value of material goods and the need for people to make a living, *Gaudium et spes* claims the truly successful life is lived by one who seeks the will of God above all. One who seeks the will of God will, in some sense, be called to a life of service to others, whether in the context of the business world, family life, religious life, science and technology, education, manual labor, or to whatever combinations of options one is drawn.

A Specific Question

Most of my students are amenable to these suggestions, but they are left with many questions. One question that is often asked (with infinite variations, of course) is "Is it okay to own a BMW?"

I do not know the answer. I suspect the answer varies from case to case. I myself would feel uncomfortable owning any luxury car in the face of widespread poverty in our country. Owning a luxury car would not be in harmony with my commitment to live a life of creative simplicity.

However, I would feel even more uncomfortable declaring that no one should own a BMW or that BMWs should not exist. There is sometimes a fine line between garish luxury and excellent quality. I am not, in principle, opposed to excellent quality.

At times, I think our society will be heading in the right direction when more and more people get sick to their stomachs in the face of garish luxury. Again, I do not know the answer to this question. I only know that within this question there is a real issue with which people need to wrestle.

Traditionally, CST has distinguished between what a person needs to maintain one's station in life and what constitutes superfluous goods. It is not reasonable that a prince be forced to live like a pauper. If, like Francis of Assisi, a rich person embraces a life of poverty, that person likely is answering a higher call, not what is expected of everyone. Today, I suppose it could be argued that it is not reasonable to say a business executive should not own a BMW, yet a business executive who embraces a life of great simplicity might favor an economy vehicle instead.

Yet Catholic teaching also has stressed that those with means have a duty to come to the aid of the poor, and that one should dig deeper than one's superfluous goods. Of particular concern is the widening gap between the rich and the poor. This is a structural issue. It is a matter of seeking changes in the system. Yet changes in the system must be accompanied by changes in the hearts of people. If enough individuals act out of the attitudes and principles articulated in CST, positive changes can be accomplished.

Liberation theologians such as the Peruvian Gustavo Gutiérrez and Salvadoran Jon Sobrino go so far as to say that if your relationship with God is not directing you to be concerned about the poor, then the God you worship is an idol, not the true God revealed in Christ.

Summary

This chapter examined basic principles of Catholic teaching on economic matters and discussed some practical implications.

What have I said in this chapter, other than things within our system need to be changed? We knew that already. Has CST offered any concrete solutions? By its nature, CST cannot be too concrete. The gospel is not full of specific advice for structuring economic systems. Yet it is easy to underestimate the effects of general principles if people truly set about practicing them.

Remember the acquaintances I described at the beginning of this chapter? Frankly, I think that Joe's world would be rocked more deeply than Sam's if he were to take CST to heart. It seems to me that Joe needs a new attitude. Current gaps between the rich and poor are much too great. The market by itself cannot be trusted to create the most just conditions possible. Ownership is a legitimate right, but not an absolute right.

Still, if Joe got a change of heart and toned down some of his extremes, he might be able to convince Sam of a few things. Government by itself cannot be trusted to create the most just possible conditions. The government needs to value the advantages of a market economy and work as a corrective, not as a replacement. Most people do need to be motivated to work.

The next chapter examines Catholic teaching concerning peace and politics.

For Further Reflection

1. Of the nine principles from *Gaudium et spes*'s chapter on economics listed in this chapter, which do you find to be the most important?
2. Which of *Gaudium et spes*'s principles do you find the most disturbing?
3. Can we distinguish between excellent quality and garish luxury?
4. Do you believe progress is possible in the realm of economic justice?
5. What, in your opinion, would constitute a life of creative simplicity?

Suggested Readings

Clark, Meghan J. *The Vision of Catholic Social Thought: The Virtue of Solidarity and the Praxis of Human Rights.* Minneapolis: Fortress, 2014.

Himes, Kenneth, ed. *Modern Catholic Social Teaching: Commentaries and Interpretations.* Washington, DC: Georgetown University Press, 2005.

Massaro, Thomas, SJ. *Living Justice: Catholic Social Teaching in Action.* Lanham, MD: Rowman and Littlefield, 2016.

Massingale, Bryan N. *Racial Justice and the Catholic Church.* Maryknoll, NY: Orbis Books, 2014.

O'Brien, David J., and Thomas A. Shannon, eds. *Catholic Social Thought: The Documentary Heritage.* Maryknoll, NY: Orbis Books, 2010.

Pontifical Council for Justice and Peace. *Compendium of the Social Doctrine of the Church.* English translation. Washington, DC: US Conference of Catholic Bishops, 2005.

35

Peace and Politics

n the mid-1980s, I was seated at a dinner next to a physician who had been a bomber pilot during World War II. He told me that he had flown five bombing missions over Germany.

When this doctor, a Catholic, found out I was a Catholic religion teacher, he expressed how furious he was at the letter on peace issued by the US Catholic bishops, *The Challenge of Peace*.[1] He was especially outraged by the bishops' teaching that the people of the United States need to develop a spirit of repentance regarding the bombings of Hiroshima and Nagasaki at the end of World War II:

> After the passage of nearly four decades and a concomitant growth in our understanding of the ever growing horror of nuclear war, we must shape the climate of opinion which will make it possible for our country to express profound sorrow over the atomic bombing in 1945. Without that sorrow, there is no possibility of finding a way to repudiate future use of nuclear weapons. (*The Challenge of Peace* 302)

The doctor believed these bombings were morally justified because they brought the war to an end quickly and efficiently. "The bishops shouldn't poke their noses into areas where they have no qualifications," he said. "They just don't know what they're talking about when it comes to war. In war, it's you against them. They're trying to kill you, and you're trying to kill them back. When you're in that situation, you do whatever you can to win. It's a matter of life and death. It's easy to sit back and make high moral pronouncements when it's somebody else's life on the line. The bishops are just too far away from what war is really about to have anything worthwhile to say on the subject."

My immediate reaction to the doctor was somewhat defensive. I said there are two ways to not see a situation clearly. One way is to be too far away. The other is to be too close.

---

1. *The Challenge of Peace: God's Promise and Our Response*, 1983, *http://www.usccb.org/upload /challenge-peace-gods-promise-our-response-1983.pdf*.

The doctor turned away and did not speak to me or in my direction the rest of the evening. I suppose he did not want to get into a debate with someone who probably understood even less than the bishops. A little later, when he left the table, his wife mentioned she was worried about him because he seemed obsessed with the topic of World War II. His main hobby was watching film clips of World War II combat and reading books about military strategy. He spent hours absorbed in this hobby.

That helped me to convince myself that he was the one who owned the problem, but when I left the dinner party, I felt uneasy about my part in the conversation. After all, the doctor had a point. Things do look different when one is engaged in combat; if combat is to exist at all, the perspective of the combatants is not to be ignored. From that point of view, the position of the bishops is perhaps difficult to appreciate. These are indeed complex issues.

Overview

The position of the Catholic Church, however, cannot be that "all is fair in love and war." It is the business of the church to interpret the gospel in response to the major issues of our times. This chapter examines the basic teaching of the Catholic Church on matters of peace and politics. This material corresponds with chapters 4 and 5 in part 2 of *Gaudium et spes*.

A Just War?

Gaudium et spes presents the traditional Catholic teaching of the just war theory, which provides conditions that must be fulfilled if the presumption for peace is to be overridden. The US bishops document, *The Challenge of Peace*, summed up these conditions in seven points (listed here in in abbreviated form):

1. *Just Cause.* War is permissible only to confront a real and certain danger, that is, to protect innocent life, preserve conditions necessary for decent human existence, and secure basic human rights.
2. *Competent Authority.* War must be declared by those with responsibility for public order, not by private groups or individuals.
3. *Comparative Justice.* Which side is sufficiently "right" in a dispute, and are the values at stake critical enough to override the presumption against war? Do the rights and values involved justify killing?
4. *Right Intention.* Right intention is related to just cause—war can be legitimately intended only for the reasons set forth above as a just cause. During the conflict, right intention means pursuit of peace and reconciliation, including avoiding unnecessarily destructive acts or imposing unreasonable conditions.

5. *Last Resort.* For resort to war to be justified, all peaceful alternatives must have been exhausted.

6. *Probability of Success.* This is a difficult criterion to apply, but its purpose is to prevent irrational resort to force or hopeless resistance when the outcome of either clearly will be disproportionate or futile.

7. *Proportionality.* The costs incurred by war must be proportionate to the good expected by taking up arms.

The bishops taught not only these principles concerning whether to enter into a war, but also added two traditional principles concerning how to conduct matters when engaged in warfare. These principles become especially important in an age when human beings have the power to wipe out entire populations and even destroy the earth. The first principle applies *proportionality*, #7 above, by stating, "Response to aggression must not exceed the nature of the aggression." It is wrong to wage "total war" that risks the destruction of civilization as we know it. The second principle is *discrimination*, that aggression must be directed against unjust aggressors and that "the lives of innocent people may never be taken directly" (*Challenge* 104).

Pacifism, Military Service, and International Progress

Many people pay no attention to the just war theory. On the one hand are those who can be described as "militarists," persons who see military action not as a moral issue but simply as a means of defending oneself or even procuring one's goals. On the other hand are people who reject the just war theory and are called "pacifists," persons who reject violence and killing under any circumstances.

Contemporary Catholic teaching rejects all forms of militarism. Pacifism, however, is recognized as a way individuals may legitimately interpret the Christian tradition: "We cannot fail to praise those who renounce the use of violence in the vindication of their rights" (*GS* 78). In other words, official Catholic teaching holds that individuals may decide for themselves whether they interpret pacifism or just war theory as the more authentic path of following Christ. Governments, however, "cannot be denied the right to legitimate defense once every means of peaceful settlement has been exhausted" (*GS* 79). Pacifists, of course, contend that no war can be justified. In recent years, a number of Catholics, though not a large percentage, have become pacifists.[2]

How does the Catholic Church officially address the question of military service? The US bishops quote from *Gaudium et spes*:

---

2. Anne Klejment and Nancy L. Roberts, eds., *American Catholic Pacifism: The Influence of Dorothy Day and the Catholic Worker Movement* (Westport, CT: Praeger, 1996).

Millions of you are Catholics serving in the armed forces. We recognize that you carry certain responsibilities for the issues that we have considered in this letter. Our perspective on your profession is that of Vatican II: "All those who enter the military service in loyalty to their country should look upon themselves as the custodians of the security and freedom of their fellow-countrymen; and where they carry out their duty properly, they are contributing to the maintenance of peace." (*Challenge* 309; *GS* 79)

The bishops urge military professionals to understand their vocation as the defense of peace and to carry out their duties in that light. The bishops do not imply in any way that one cannot be a good Catholic and a good soldier too.

Issues of individual choices and commitments find their larger context within the Catholic vision of a global community, within which disputes can be mediated peacefully. *Gaudium et spes* relates peace to "an international order that includes a genuine respect for all freedoms and amicable brotherhood between all" (*GS* 88). To this end, the document supports the establishment of a universal public authority, although it does not specifically mention the name of the United Nations. The document links peace with justice, arguing the two go hand in hand. The arms race is denounced as "an utterly treacherous trap for humanity, and one which ensnares the poor to an intolerable degree" (*GS* 81).

Just Peacemaking?

In the 1990s, much discussion of just war theory focused on the morality of military intervention to prevent human atrocities. Two cases in particular, both involving US-led actions, brought these issues to the fore.

One case concerned a 1992 famine in Somalia. A huge amount of relief aid was prevented from getting through to starving people because of political and military interference on the part of Somalian military forces. Is it just to take military action to allow the aid to reach those in desperate need? The United States, with the United Nations's approval, judged that it was and sent in troops.

Another case concerned Bosnia, part of the former Yugoslavia. In 1995, the North Atlantic Treaty Organization (NATO) was concerned not only that a vicious war was taking place between Serbs and other ethnic groups but that actual genocide, the wiping out of entire ethnic groups, was being carried out. Is it just to take military action to prevent genocide? NATO allies judged that it was, and military action was taken. The war officially ended with the 1995 Dayton Peace Agreement, although there have been many military flare-ups, some war-size, since then.

These cases are not as clear and simple as they may appear. One does not have to search far for writings that condemn these actions as politically motivated. The uncertainties that accompany any prudential judgment remain. The issue that presses with a new force is: by what principles can one justify military aggression in a situation in which one's own citizens or territory are not threatened?

Characteristics of Acceptable Governments

Several characteristics of acceptable forms and practices of government can be identified in *Gaudium et spes*. Although these principles are general, it should be kept in mind that many governments do not value them and many more do not live up to them:

1. Recognize the rights of citizens, such as freedom of association, speech, and religion.
2. Foster participation in government decision-making and in the economic and social life of the nation. Recognize the rights of minorities.
3. Seek the common good; it is the only purpose for which the political community exists.
4. Be pluralistic; recognize that different people have the right to prefer different solutions to common problems.
5. Appoint political leaders through the free will of the citizens.

Church and State

Catholic teaching upholds the basic principle of the separation of church and state, though not the absolute version of that principle. *Gaudium et spes* recognizes a legitimate autonomy to governments: "The church and the political community in their own fields are autonomous and independent from each other" (*GS* 76). *Gaudium et spes* also teaches, however, that the church has a word to speak on political matters. This is because "the political community and public authority are founded on human nature and hence belong to the order designed by God" (*GS* 74). Political institutions are not somehow exempt from judgment according to moral and religious principles.

When Catholic Church leaders express particular opinions on political matters, they consider themselves to be adding their own voice to the public debate.[3] In principle, they do not intend take positons so specific that they become entangled in party politics. At times, however, the line between gospel principles and party politics is not so clear.

For example, the US bishops have taken a firm public stand on immigration policy. In 2003, they issued a joint statement with the bishops of Mexico,

---

3. See, for example, the US bishops' *Economic Justice for All*, no. 27: "We want to add our voice to the public debate about the directions in which the US economy should be moving."

Strangers No Longer: Together on the Journey of Hope, in which they called for a "globalization of solidarity."[4] Changes the bishops called for included the following:

* Broad-based legalization (permanent residency) of the undocumented of all nationalities
* Reform of our family-based immigration system to allow family members to reunite with loved ones in the United States
* Reform of the employment-based immigration system to provide legal pathways for migrants to come and work in a safe, humane, and orderly manner
* Abandonment of the border "blockade" enforcement strategy
* Restoration of due process protections for immigrants[5]

Since 2003, the US bishops have consistently and vociferously opposed policies that focus solely on law enforcement and have supported comprehensive immigration reform as well as "sanctuary cities" that place limits on the enforcement of federal immigration laws.[6] This stance comes into conflict with expressed positions of some politicians.

Particular bishops have at times supported or opposed political candidates because of their stand on abortion. Often this is done in a slightly indirect manner by naming the issue without naming the candidates. But the sensitivity of such actions and the outcry they raise demonstrates that most Catholics today expect church leaders to articulate basic guidelines but not in any way tell them how to vote. Many Catholics protest against what they label "one-issue politics" that support antiabortion candidates no matter what their positions on other issues. Some Catholics argue that other issues are indeed important, but that abortion is so important it rightfully takes a certain priority. Thus the basic principle of religious influence without undue interference gets played out in real life under circumstances that are often less than clear-cut.

Clear Distinctions

Sometimes students ask why, if the Catholic Church is so interested in politics, does it not allow priests and religious to run for and hold political office? Wouldn't that be a good way for the church to help to bring about a better world?

---

4. Catholic bishops' conferences of Mexico and the United States, *Strangers No Longer: Together on the Journey of Hope*, no. 57, *http://www.usccb.org/issues-and-action/human-life-and-dignity /immigration/strangers-no-longer-together-on-the-journey-of-hope.cfm.*

5. US Conference of Catholic Bishops, "Justice for Immigrants," *http://www.usccb.org/about /migration-policy/justice-for-immigrants.cfm.*

6. Brian Fraga, "Trump vs. Sanctuary Cities: Catholic Leaders Push Back," *National Catholic Register*, May 11, 2017, *http://www.ncregister.com/daily-news/trump-vs.-sanctuary-cities-catholic -leaders-push-back.*

The primary reason for the ban on priests and religious in politics is so that the church, through its official representatives, does not become overly involved with any particular government, political party, or social movement. Put simply, it is acceptable for a Catholic to be a Republican, Democrat, or member of any number of political parties. It would, I believe, be contradictory to Catholicism to be a Nazi or a Ku Klux Klan member. But beyond these anti-Catholic extremes, one is called only to follow one's conscience. Which party or platform holds the most promise for the common good? It is a difficult matter to move from the gospel to such a determination; such a decision must be left up to the individual Christian. Church teaching that restricts clergy from political office reflects the belief that such a degree of entanglement overcommits the church on a too-specific political level.

Liberation theologian Leonardo Boff of Brazil expressed this distinction as one between capital "P" Politics and small "p" politics. Capital "P" Politics addresses the ideals to which governments must aspire; small "p" politics involves the level of partisan platforms and particular interests. The official church should operate only on the level of Politics; lay members should find specific ways of living out the Christian life in the world of politics. At times, Christians will diametrically oppose each other on political matters, while at the same time, do the best they can to live out the same Politics of the Christian tradition. *Gaudium et spes* calls for yet another distinction: "between the tasks which Christians undertake, individually or as a group, on their own responsibility as citizens guided by the dictates of a Christian conscience, and the activities which, in union with their pastors, they carry out in the name of the church" (*GS* 76).

Pope Benedict XVI elaborated upon these distinctions in his 2005 encyclical, *Deus caritas est* (*God Is Love*). The church forms consciences; it is not to replace the state. It is the task of the state, not the church, to work toward the most just society possible. Particular political policies are to be determined by reason, not directly by faith. The task of the church is "to contribute to the purification of reason and to the reawakening of those moral forces without which just structures are neither established nor prove effective in the long run" (*DCE* 29).

Many charitable organizations, such as Caritas International and the St. Vincent de Paul Society, provide services in the name of the Catholic Church. These organizations are to address immediate needs as they remain independent of political parties and ideologies.

In contrast to the official Catholic Church and its charitable organizations, Benedict explains that laypeople (those who are not officials in the church) have "the direct duty to work for the just ordering of society" (*DCE* 29). Lay church members are encouraged not only to act individually but also to band together to work for political, economic, and social improvements. In other words, they are to work on the level that includes partisan politics. When lay church members do so, however, they are acting in their own name. Although they may be doing so out of the motivation of their Christian consciences, their group is not an official representation of the Catholic Church.

Summary

This chapter examined official Catholic teaching on matters of peace and politics. It discussed the just war theory, pacifism, military service, and many aspects of the relationship between the church and political matters.

To carry out its mission to the world, the church must avoid two extremes: not getting involved in political matters and getting too involved by taking sides on what are legitimately partisan concerns. The doctor in the opening story of this chapter, I believe, only grasped one side of this complex matter. However, he is a man who faced mortal danger in a way that I never have; I need to listen to and respect his opinion, even as I disagree.

In the next chapter, Pope Francis's teaching on ecology in his encyclical *Laudato si': On Care for Our Common Home* will be explored.

For Further Reflection

1. Does the bomber pilot/doctor have a point?
2. Can the just war theory be a useful tool for deciding whether particular military actions are just?
3. Are you personally more inclined to be a pacifist or to accept some form of the just war theory?
4. To what extent should one's religious beliefs influence one's choice of a political party (or stance)?
5. Can religious faith be helpful in moving people beyond political polarization? Or is religious faith just another element in the mix?

Suggested Readings

Catholic Church. *Forming Consciences for Faithful Citizenship: A Call to Political Responsibility.* Washington, DC: US Conference of Catholic Bishops, 2015.

Collier, Elizabeth W., and Charles R. Strain. *Global Migration: What's Happening, Why, and a Just Response.* Winona, MN: Anselm Academic, 2017.

Dionne, E. J. *Our Divided Political Heart: The Battle for the American Idea in an Age of Discontent.* New York: Bloomsbury, 2012.

Egan, Eileen. *Peace Be with You: Justified Warfare or the Way of Nonviolence.* Maryknoll, NY: Orbis, 1999.

Groody, Daniel G. *Globalization, Spirituality, and Justice: Navigating the Path to Peace.* Maryknoll, NY: Orbis, 2015.

Heyer, Kristen E. *Kinship across Borders: A Christian Ethic of Immigration.* Washington, DC: Georgetown University Press, 2012.

Hollenbach, David. *The Global Face of Public Faith: Politics, Human Rights, and Christian Ethics.* Washington, DC: Georgetown University Press, 2003.

Kidder, Tracy. *Mountains beyond Mountains: The Quest of Dr. Paul Farmer, a Man Who Would Cure the World.* New York: Random House, 2003.

Klejment, Anne, and Nancy L. Roberts, eds. *American Catholic Pacifism: The Influence of Dorothy Day and the Catholic Worker Movement.* Westport, CT: Praeger, 1996.

Merton, Thomas. *Thomas Merton on Peace.* New York: McCall, 1971.

Wills, Garry. *Under God: Religion and American Politics.* New York: Simon and Schuster, 1990.

36

Ecology

n his encyclical *Laudato si': On Care for Our Common Home*, Pope Francis describes an "integral ecology" that appreciates the interrelatedness among all members of God's creation, whether animate or inanimate. He calls for an "ecological conversion" on the part of everyone—both as individuals and communities (*LS* 211, 217). He wants us to change the way we believe, think, feel, and behave in response to the ecological crisis. He includes a "summons to solidarity and a preferential option for the poorest of our brothers and sisters" (*LS* 158).

This encyclical has had an impact far beyond Catholic circles, having been discussed favorably in serious scientific journals.[1] At least ten world leaders referred to the encyclical during the two-week summit that produced the 2015 Paris Climate Agreement.[2] President Donald Trump pulled the United States out of the agreement on June 1, 2017, eight days after his visit to Rome when Pope Francis handed him a copy of *Laudato si'* and personally asked him to read it.

Throughout the letter, Francis emphasizes the connection between abuse of the environment and the cry of the poor. It is the poor who are most immediately and deeply affected by climate change, and yet it is the overconsumption of the richer nations and their disproportionate use of natural resources that drives the devastation. Developed countries even go so far as to export solid waste and toxic liquids to developing countries. Multinationals produce pollution in poor countries in ways they would not dream of doing in richer nations, often leaving behind "great human and environmental liabilities such as unemployment, abandoned towns, the depletion of natural reserves, deforestation, the impoverishment of agriculture and local stock breeding, open pits, riven hills, polluted rivers, and a handful of social works which are no longer sustainable" (*LS* 51).

Francis's linking of environmental devastation and poverty sent me in search of my file from a course I taught in 2001 on liberation theology, an approach that focuses on the gospel demand for economic and social transformation in

---

1. Martin Maier, SJ, "Global Response to *Laudato si'*," *Europeinfos* 187 (November 2015), *http://www.europe-infos.eu/dl/nnNLJMOJKOOlJqx4KJK/187NovemberEN.pdf?ts=1446589133.*

2. Joe Ware, "COP21: *Laudato Si'* a Major Talking Point at Climate Change Talks in Paris," *The Tablet*, December 6, 2015, *http://www.thetablet.co.uk/news/2885/0/cop21-laudato-si-a-major-talking-point-at-climate-change-talks-in-paris.*

response to the plight of the poor and marginalized. One of the key concepts associated with liberation theology is the "preferential option for the poor." That is not to say it is an option against the rich; rather, it recognizes that it is in the interests of the entire community to see reality through the eyes of the poor and to give priority to their needs.

To explore this concept, on a small yellow pad, I had made a whimsical list of a few concrete things one might do to take the option for the poor. I brought the pad to every class, and the students and I added to it occasionally throughout the semester. This approach was unsystematic, "serious fun," and we ended up with fifteen points:

- Include the option for the poor in our prayers
- Write an article or a book on this theme
- Turn off the TV
- Avoid food after dinner
- Avoid a big coffee cup
- Maintain relations with poor people
- Eat beans
- Take the bus sometimes
- Learn Spanish
- Work with the St. Vincent de Paul Society in my parish
- Cultivate economically modest tastes and sensibilities
- Live in the city
- Dress like the Tibetan monks
- Give clothes away to the poor
- Work to change unjust social and economic structures

What strikes me now, years later, is how closely my old list about taking the option for the poor corresponds with the changes that Pope Francis recommends when calling for an ecological conversion. Francis speaks of changing not only the ways we produce and consume but also how we think and feel. He recommends resurgence in saying grace before meals, because these prayers remind us of the earth that produces our goods and of the workers who gather and prepare them. He calls for rest on the Sabbath as a way of valuing receptive and gratuitous dimensions of life that are sometimes dismissed as unproductive, such as relaxation and festivity. He desires that cities be designed with quality of life in mind. He asks for improvements in public transportation. He makes appeals for education in aesthetics, a way of thinking in which appreciating beauty and being ecologically sensitive are deeply related. He advocates that ecological sensitivity be translated into new habits and lifestyles.

If Francis is correct in his assessment that the ecological crisis is much more than just a technological problem, then it follows that it would be hard if not impossible to have an ecological conversion without also taking the option for the poor. These are just different names for the same path.

Overview

In 1965, few people thought there was an ecological crisis, and so *Gaudium et spes* did not deal directly with ecological concerns. If the document were written today, I have little doubt it would contain a separate chapter on ecology. Pope Francis himself traces the development of Catholic teaching on the environment starting with the postconciliar writings of Pope Paul VI in 1971 and then as expanded by Pope John Paul II and Pope Benedict XVI.

In this chapter, we first address two ecologically relevant statements, one from Genesis, that human beings were given dominion over all the earth, and another from *Gaudium et spes*, that all things on earth should be related to human beings as their center and crown. We then focus our attention on Pope Francis's teaching in *Laudato si'*.

Dominion over All the Earth?

Much debate concerning Christian attitudes toward the environment has revolved around the following passage from Genesis:

> Then God said, "Let us make humankind in our image, according to our likeness; and let them have dominion over the fish of the sea, and over the birds of the air, and over the cattle, and over all the wild animals of the earth, and over every creeping thing that creeps upon the earth." . . . God said, "See, I have given you every plant yielding seed that is upon the face of all the earth, and every tree with seed in its fruit; you shall have them for food. And to every beast of the earth, and to every bird of the air, and to everything that creeps on the earth, everything that has the breath of life, I have given every green plant for food." (Gen 1:26, 29–30)

This passage confirms the cosmic hierarchy established by the order of creation. God creates human beings last, as the final masterpiece to which all of creation was leading.

Gaudium et spes reinforces this hierarchy within creation: "According to the almost unanimous opinion of believers and unbelievers alike, all things on earth should be related to man as their center and crown" (*GS* 12). In 1965, the authors of *Gaudium et spes* were in dialogue with secular humanists who would agree about the central role of human beings in the universe. Today, however, thinking that humans have the highest place in the created universe and that everything else is subordinate is widely criticized as being *anthropocentric*. Anthropocentrism includes the belief that nature exists not so much for its own sake but for the use and service of human beings.

In a well-known essay published in 1967, historian Lynn White said, "Christianity bears a huge burden of guilt" in regard to the ecology crisis.[3] White held that the environmentally exploitative nature of contemporary science and technology finds its roots within the anthropocentrism of the Christian tradition. The belief that human beings have mastery over nature led human beings to justify abusing the environment without any regard for the environment itself. White, himself a Christian, called for the liberation of nature from the destructive domination of human beings. In this sense, the ecological movement is a liberation movement not unlike feminism or liberation theology.

In a 1985 article, theologian H. Paul Santmire revisited and evaluated White's seminal essay.[4] He reviewed some of the vehement criticisms White's essay has received. Although in the end Santmire was sympathetic to White's major concerns, he offered the following points:

1. Religion has not been the only factor shaping Western attitudes toward technology and the environment. Underlying economic forces have also been especially important.

2. The anthropocentric strain in Christianity is complemented by other strains that lead to concern for the environment. This is especially true of the theocentrism, or God-centeredness, that runs deeper than the human-centeredness. It also applies to the basic goodness of creation and the cosmic dimensions of the redemption.

Santmire, therefore, gave Christianity's role in shaping ecological attitudes a more mixed review than did White. Although Santmire was critical of White, he also took to task other critics of White who had failed to appreciate the important challenge underlying White's thesis. Are Christians called to overthrow their attitudes of human dominance that have helped justify the rape of the earth?

Santmire concluded with an openness toward White's idea that St. Francis of Assisi, because of his solidarity with creation, is a most appropriate model for Christians today. Santmire simply disagreed with White's implication that St. Francis necessarily contradicts the mainstream Christian tradition rather than representing an important strain within it.

---

3. Lynn White Jr., "The Historical Roots of Our Ecologic Crisis," *Science*, March 10, 1967, 1203–7.

4. H. Paul Santmire, "The Liberation of Nature: Lynn White's Challenge Anew," *Christian Century*, May 22, 1985, 530–33.

Pope Francis and Saint Francis

Pope Francis chose his name in honor of St. Francis of Assisi, mentioning especially concern for the poor.[5] He begins *Laudato si'* with words from St. Francis's *Canticle of the Creatures*: "Praise be to you, my Lord, through our Sister, Mother Earth, who sustains and governs us, and who produces various fruit with coloured flowers and herbs" (*LS* 1).[6] The pope mentions the saint several more times throughout the encyclical. He devotes an early subsection to drawing poetic inspiration from St. Francis's openness, awe, and wonder, particularly in his ability to "speak the language of fraternity and beauty" in his relationship with the world. All of God's creatures are as brothers and sisters to St. Francis. For the saint, "rather than a problem to be solved, the world is a joyful mystery to be contemplated with gladness and praise" (*LS* 11, 12).

As one who blends interior conversion with commitment to the poor, peace, and the environment, St. Francis models an "integral ecology." He is a mystic whose cosmic vision of the interconnectedness of all things enabled him "to feel intimately united with all that exists" (*LS* 11). Pope Francis calls St. Francis "the patron saint of all who study and work in the area of ecology" (*LS* 10).

Christian Understanding of the Human Person

Anthropocentrism has been at the heart of the academic debate concerning Christianity's historic role in environmental destruction. Many contemporary commentators condemn anthropocentrism and argue that human beings must humbly accept they are but one type of creature in this vast universe. For example, Arne Naess, the founder of the deep ecology movement, held a position known as "biocentric egalitarianism," a philosophical refusal to value human beings over other life forms.[7]

Pope Francis rejects both "modern" anthropocentrism and biocentric egalitarianism. In *Laudato si'*, he labels this modern form of anthropocentrism "tyrannical," "distorted," "excessive," and "misguided." He associates it with human

---

5. David Gibson and Allessandro Speciale, "Pope Francis Explains Why He Chose His Name, Urges a 'Church of the Poor,'" *Religion News Service*, March 16, 2013, *http://religionnews .com/2013/03/16/pope-francis-explains-why-he-chose-his-name-urges-a-church-of-the-poor/.*

6. The encyclical cites *Canticle of the Creatures*, in *Francis of Assisi—The Saint: Early Documents* (New York: New City, 1999), 1:113–14.

7. David R. Keller, "Deep Ecology," *Encyclopedia of Environmental Ethics and Philosophy*, 2 vols. (New York: Macmillan Reference USA, 2008), 1:206–11.

arrogance and domination. He acknowledges that the teaching in Genesis concerning the "dominion" given to humankind has, at times, been misinterpreted, but he rejects the charge that such misinterpretation represents the deeper tradition of the church:

> We are not God. The earth was here before us and it has been given to us. This allows us to respond to the charge that Judaeo-Christian thinking, on the basis of the Genesis account which grants man "dominion" over the earth (cf. Gen 1:28), has encouraged the unbridled exploitation of nature by painting him as domineering and destructive by nature. This is not a correct interpretation of the Bible as understood by the Church. Although it is true that we Christians have at times incorrectly interpreted the Scriptures, nowadays we must forcefully reject the notion that our being created in God's image and given dominion over the earth justifies absolute domination over other creatures. The biblical texts are to be read in their context, with an appropriate hermeneutic, recognizing that they tell us to "till and keep" the garden of the world (cf. Gen 2:15). "Tilling" refers to cultivating, ploughing or working, while "keeping" means caring, protecting, overseeing and preserving. This implies a relationship of mutual responsibility between human beings and nature. (*LS* 67)

Several recurring key themes of the encyclical are contained in this passage. Francis believes that the misinterpretation of "dominion," whether by religious believers or atheists, results from a forgetfulness of God. It is one of the effects of original sin by which human relations with God, each other, and creation are broken. Ultimately, all things belong to God. Human ownership cannot be absolute. Creation is given to human beings for sustenance and enjoyment, not for abuse. All of God's creatures have an intrinsic value. "Dominion," understood in its biblical context, includes the responsibility to care for the earth and respect the balance among all created things.

Pope Francis embraces the teaching of Genesis when interpreted in what he considers to be a correct manner. Human beings are made in the image and likeness of God. He quotes the *Catechism of the Catholic Church* concerning the immense dignity of each person, "who is not just something, but someone. He is capable of self-knowledge, self-possession and freely giving himself and entering into communion with other persons" (*LS* 65).[8] Francis thus rejects biocentric egalitarianism in favor of the unique dignity of human persons. He sums up his position:

> A spirituality which forgets God as all-powerful and Creator is not acceptable. That is how we end up worshipping earthly powers, or

---

8. *Catechism of the Catholic Church*, 357, *http://www.vatican.va/archive/ENG0015/_INDEX.HTM*.

ourselves usurping the place of God, even to the point of claiming an unlimited right to trample his creation underfoot. The best way to restore men and women to their rightful place, putting an end to their claim to absolute dominion over the earth, is to speak once more of the figure of a Father who creates and who alone owns the world. Otherwise, human beings will always try to impose their own laws and interests on reality. (*LS* 75)

Everything Is Connected

Laudato si' explores the ecological crisis as a multidimensional problem requiring multidimensional solutions. The crisis is at once technological, scientific, philosophical, cultural, anthropological, social, economic, personal, and theological. Pope Francis accepts the "very solid scientific consensus" that the current ecological crisis is linked with global warming, the main cause of which is greenhouse gases produced by human activity. He pleads with world leaders to join together in making the big decisions that can disrupt the damage being done to the atmosphere through these gases and to reverse the loss of forests and biodiversity.

For Francis, however, these decisions on the macro-level are, by themselves, not enough. He thinks that we live in a throwaway culture and a cultural revolution is called for. He believes the tiniest things are important and refers to St. Therese of Lisieux, who "invites us to practice the little way of love, not to miss out on a kind word, a smile or any small gesture which sows peace and friendship" (*LS* 230). Changes need to be made in all dimensions of life. We need to overcome, on a cultural level, the one-dimensional overemphasis on technological progress by which so-called advances are pursued apart from philosophy and social ethics. Echoing *Gaudium et spes*, Francis muses, "An authentic humanity, calling for a new synthesis, seems to dwell in the midst of our technological culture, almost unnoticed, like a mist seeping gently beneath a closed door. Will the promise last, in spite of everything, with all that is authentic rising up in stubborn resistance?" (*LS* 112; *GS* 30, 43, 56).

Overcome Denial to Live in Hope

Making the environment a matter of special concern is not simply a benevolent concession. It is a matter of survival for the human race and for the planet. What will be left for future generations after present society is done pillaging the earth?

Psychologists talk about the problem of "denial." Denial involves the conscious repression of things that we are aware of unconsciously. An alcoholic who will not admit to having a problem is in denial. But there are other, more subtle ways of being in denial. A person who says, "I admit that I am an alcoholic," but who goes right on drinking or only slightly alters some peripheral habits is still enmeshed in a web of denial. That person is denying the seriousness of the problem and is failing to take appropriate measures.

Pope Francis calls upon the modern world to wake up from its denial:

> As often occurs in periods of deep crisis which require bold decisions, we are tempted to think that what is happening is not entirely clear. Superficially, apart from a few obvious signs of pollution and deterioration, things do not look that serious, and the planet could continue as it is for some time. Such evasiveness serves as a licence to carrying on with our present lifestyles and models of production and consumption. This is the way human beings contrive to feed their self-destructive vices: trying not to see them, trying not to acknowledge them, delaying the important decisions and pretending that nothing will happen. (*LS* 59)

Yet Francis also recognizes that significant advances have been made in the ecological movement. His message is not one of gloom and despair, but of joy and hope: "there is reason to hope that humanity at the dawn of the twenty-first century will be remembered for having generously shouldered its grave responsibilities" (*LS* 165).

Summary

This chapter reflected on the ecological crisis in relation to Christianity, focusing mainly on Pope Francis's encyclical *Laudato si'*.

Francis's encyclical demonstrates that ecological concerns represent not simply an addendum to the matters of special urgency addressed in the second half of *Gaudium et spes*, but rather, offer a context within which the most important issues concerning God, creation, and humankind can be woven together into a coherent whole. After all, everything is connected.

For Further Reflection

1. Do you agree more with Pope Francis or the biocentric egalitarians when it comes to the dignity and value of human beings relative to other creatures? Why?

2. Do you think that talk of the ecological crisis is either understated or overblown?

3. Describe in your own words an individual who is "ecologically converted."

4. Is our society in denial about the ecological crisis?

5. Do you agree that underlying the ecological crisis is a moral and religious crisis?

Suggested Readings

Berry, Thomas. *The Christian Future and the Fate of the Earth*. Edited by Mary Evelyn Tucker and John Grim. Maryknoll, NY: Orbis Books, 2009.

Cloutier, David. *Walking God's Earth: The Environment and Catholic Faith*. Collegeville, MN: Liturgical Press, 2014.

Johnson, Elizabeth A. *Ask the Beasts: Darwin and the God of Love*. London: Bloomsbury, 2014.

Levering, Matthew. *Engaging the Doctrine of Creation: Cosmos, Creatures, and the Wise and Good Creator*. Grand Rapids: Baker Academic, 2017.

Miller, Vincent J., ed. *The Theological and Ecological Vision of* Laudato si': *Everything Is Connected*. New York: Bloomsbury T&T Clark, 2017.

Peppard, Christiana Z. *Just Water: Theology, Ethics, and the Global Water Crisis*. Maryknoll, NY: Orbis Books, 2014.

Index

Note: The abbreviations *c, i, s, t,* or *n* that follow page numbers indicate charts, illustrations, sidebars, tables, or notes, respectively.

utopianism, 191–92
Ut Unum sint (*That They May Be One*) (John Paul II), 94

V

Vatican I (First Vatican Council), 26–27, 35, 100
Vatican II (Second Vatican Council). *See also related topics*
 council authenticity affirmation, 26
 documents of, 31–39
 historical context of, 24–25, 44, 260–61
 Holy Spirit guidance, 168, 175
 legacy of, 31
 modern issues addressed by, 27–28, 28–29
 overview, 17n1, 27
 participants at, 20n4
 process descriptions, 20
 purpose, 20, 28–29, 261–62
 reception of, 168, 222
 on religious orders, 182
 reviews of, 226–27
 women observers at, 240
venial sins, 151
Veritatis splendor (*The Splendor of Truth*) (John Paul II), 124
virgin (symbolic image), 232
Voltaire, 191
volunteers, 139
Vos, Maarten de: *Solomon's Song*, 251i
vows, 176, 177–80

W

Waldensianism, 26, 82
Walsh, James Edward, 182
war, 210, 216, 216i, 320–24
WCC (World Council of Churches), 89, 95–96
wealth. *See also* poverty
 and church power, 188
 disparity of, 21, 190, 312, 314, 318
 Jesus's warnings on, 162–63, 189

weddings, 250–51, 251i, 300–301
White, Lynn, 332
white martyrdom, 177
Wiesel, Elie, 216
Wilder, Thornton, 215
wisdom, 171, 237
women and women's issues. *See also* ordination of women
 abortion, 56, 101, 123, 124, 295n5, 325
 birth control, 56, 101, 123, 295n5, 297
 conservative *vs.* progressive views on, 243
 feminism, 238–39, 240, 242–43
 foot washing rituals and inclusion of, 18
 gender relationship descriptions, 242, 246–58, 252, 288
 liberation theology and activism, 172
 patriarchy and sexism, 238–40
 religious communities of, 182–83, 184
 religious movements for, 240–42
 roles of, 232, 239, 240, 243, 247–49, 252–53
 theological anthropology, 242
women-church movement, 240–42
Wood, Susan, 112
work
 dignity of, 145–47
 economic justice and, 147, 312, 314
 as lay activity sphere, 131, 131t, 132
 and leisure, 148–49
 main purposes of, 143, 144–45
 as personal relationship with God, 144, 148
 spirituality of, 143–49
workers' rights, 147, 312, 314
world. *See* society
World Council of Churches (WCC), 89, 95–96
World Day of Prayer, 95, 96i
World War II, 320–21
Wyclif, John, 26

Z

Zacchaeus (biblical character), 162
Zizioulas, John, 112